John Ruskin's Continental Tour 1835
The Written Records and Drawings

LEGENDA

LEGENDA is the Modern Humanities Research Association's book imprint for new research in the Humanities. Founded in 1995 by Malcolm Bowie and others within the University of Oxford, Legenda has always been a collaborative publishing enterprise, directly governed by scholars. The Modern Humanities Research Association (MHRA) joined this collaboration in 1998, became half-owner in 2004, in partnership with Maney Publishing and then Routledge, and has since 2016 been sole owner. Titles range from medieval texts to contemporary cinema and form a widely comparative view of the modern humanities, including works on Arabic, Catalan, English, French, German, Greek, Italian, Portuguese, Russian, Spanish, and Yiddish literature. Editorial boards and committees of more than 60 leading academic specialists work in collaboration with bodies such as the Society for French Studies, the British Comparative Literature Association and the Association of Hispanists of Great Britain & Ireland.

The MHRA encourages and promotes advanced study and research in the field of the modern humanities, especially modern European languages and literature, including English, and also cinema. It aims to break down the barriers between scholars working in different disciplines and to maintain the unity of humanistic scholarship. The Association fulfils this purpose through the publication of journals, bibliographies, monographs, critical editions, and the MHRA Style Guide, and by making grants in support of research. Membership is open to all who work in the Humanities, whether independent or in a University post, and the participation of younger colleagues entering the field is especially welcomed.

ALSO PUBLISHED BY THE ASSOCIATION

Critical Texts
Tudor and Stuart Translations • *New Translations* • *European Translations*
MHRA Library of Medieval Welsh Literature

MHRA Bibliographies
Publications of the Modern Humanities Research Association

The Annual Bibliography of English Language & Literature
Austrian Studies
Modern Language Review
Portuguese Studies
The Slavonic and East European Review
Working Papers in the Humanities
The Yearbook of English Studies

www.mhra.org.uk
www.legendabooks.com

John Ruskin's Continental Tour 1835

The Written Records and Drawings

Edited by
Keith Hanley and Caroline S. Hull

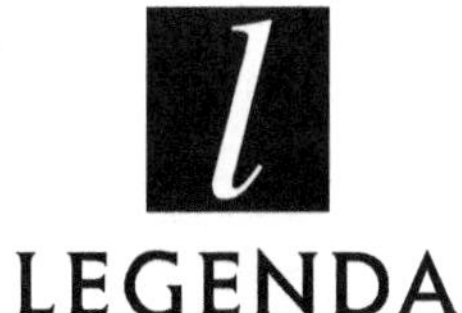

LEGENDA
Modern Humanities Research Association
2016

Published by Legenda
an imprint of the Modern Humanities Research Association
Salisbury House, Station Road, Cambridge CB1 2LA

ISBN 978-1-906540-85-2 (HB)
ISBN 978-1-781883-00-6 (PB)

First published 2016

Printed in Great Britain

Copy-Editor: Richard Correll

CONTENTS

Acknowledgements ix
Introduction 1
Ruskin's Early Travels 1
Background to Cultural Tourism 6
Mode of Travel 9
Media of Representation 14
The Interdisciplinary Gaze 21
1835: The Written Records and Drawings 26
Bibliography 32
The 1835 Itinerary 36

THE TEXTS

Textual Note 38
1 *The 1835 Diary* 41
2 Verse Journal: *A Tour Through France to Chamouni* 117
3 Two Rhyming letters:
'A Letter from France' 151
'Letter to Willoughby Jones' 160

THE DRAWINGS

The Drawings 167
Catalogue 213

APPENDIX

1 Poems
'[Verona]' 233
'Venice' 234
'[The Invasion of the Alps]' 235
2 Other Literary Outcomes
The Ascent of the St. Bernard: A Dramatic Sketch 238
Chronicles of St. Bernard 255
3 John James Ruskin's Diary, 1835 286

ACKNOWLEDGEMENTS

John Batchelor was an early encourager of this project, for which Caroline S. Hull became an MHRA-funded Research Associate. The Drawings Catalogue has been meticulously revised by Stephen Wildman, Director of the Ruskin Library and Research Centre, Lancaster University, and we are indebted for many details to his catalogued exhibition, '"This Mountain Paradise": Ruskin on the Continent, 1835', in the Ruskin Library, Lancaster University, 12 May–19 September 2014. David C. Hanson of Southeastern Louisiana University has very generously shared his knowledge and advice as he has been progressing his edition of *The Early Ruskin Manuscripts, 1826–1842*. Diane Tyler, Assistant Curator, and Jen Shepherd, Secretary, of the Ruskin Library, have been unfailingly helpful in answering queries and making material available.

The following have kindly helped with our enquiries regarding the drawings: Suzannah Brown, Documentation Assistant, Lakeland Arts, Blackwell; Catherine Casley, Ashmolean Museum, Oxford; Robin Darwall-Smith, Archivist, Magdalen College, Oxford; Laure Decomble, Musée Alpin, Chamonix; Aprile Gallant, Curator of Prints, Drawings, and Photographs, Smith College Museum of Art, Northampton, MA; Lauren Karazija, Santa Barbara Museum of Art, Santa Barbara, CA; Josh Mckeon, Librarian, Berg Collection, New York Public Library; Louise Pullen, Ruskin Curator at Museums Sheffield; Andrea Reithmayr, University Library, University of Rochester, NY; Maria Isabel Molestina, Reader Services Librarian, Morgan Library and Museum, New York; Andrea Rosen, Curatorial Assistant and Manager of Student Programs, Bowdoin College Museum of Art, Brunswick, ME; Grant Scanlan, Senior Curator, Kirklees Museums & Galleries, Huddersfield; A. J. Slowe, Curator, The Ruskin Museum, Yewdale Road, Coniston.

We are grateful to the Trustees of the Ruskin Foundation (Ruskin Library, Lancaster University) for permission to reproduce the drawings from this tour and our edited versions of the MSS of Ruskin's 1835 *Diary* and *John James Ruskin's Diary, 1835*. The Ruskin Foundation, which owns the materials used in this edition, has sought to establish the copyright for John Ruskin's unpublished literary manuscripts, but has been unable to do so on the basis of all the information currently known to it. The MS of the rhyming letter, *To Willoughby Jones*, held in the Beinecke Rare Book and Manuscript Library, Yale University, has been edited here in accordance with the Beinecke's Public Domain and Fair Use Policy for broad access. Danielle Dye researched the background to the MS for a dissertation unit on her MA in English Literary Studies at Lancaster University and she and Christopher Jotischky helped with deciphering that letter. The copies of the printed books from which

Figures 1, 3, 4, 5, 6, 7 and 8 in the introduction are taken belong to Keith Hanley. Tim Aspden drew the map. Our editor at Legenda, Graham Nelson, has been extremely patient while this project unfolded. All faults and deficiencies are finally the responsibility of Keith Hanley.

K.H. & C.S.H., Lancaster, December 2015

INTRODUCTION

Keith Hanley

Ruskin's Early Travels

Ruskin was a lifelong traveller. From early childhood, accompanied by his nurse, family tours took him to carefully selected destinations throughout Britain. Their expeditions were primarily commercial travels round Britain as his father, John James, a constant and enthusiastic traveller, built up trade for the wine-importing firm of Ruskin, Telford and Domecq in which he was head-partner, but they were also organised to provide therapeutic recreation and instruction. The Ruskins borrowed a chariot or hired a post-chaise usually around the middle of May, just after his father's birthday. While toiling alone in London, John James had never taken a holiday, but from the early 1820s, driven partly by a serious personal enthusiasm for aesthetic and cultural attractions, specialising in the Romantic fringes to take in places of historical, literary and picturesque interest, he arranged matters so that his wife, Margaret, could superintend the health and moral benefits of well-planned and hard-earned vacations. An added motive was to become increasingly the improvement of their gifted and adored son's mind.

The first journey of the family, who lived on Herne Hill in the southern London suburbs, was a sea voyage to Scotland in Ruskin's third year, 1822. They travelled inland to the south and south-west of England in 1823 and to the English Lakes in 1824,[1] proceeding on a family visit to Perth, returning there in the summer of 1826 and again in 1827, when they also visited the West Country. An important addition to their company in 1828 was Ruskin's cousin, the fourteen-year old Mary Richardson, who on the death of her mother came to live with the family until 1848. Four years older than Ruskin, she became his childhood companion, a responsible playmate who, like Ruskin, was privately tutored from her arrival, sharing and spurring some of his fields of interest. The first to take drawing lessons, she produced works which were copied by Ruskin who requested similar instruction in 1831. In 1829 the family visited Derbyshire, which the whole household, including Mary and Ruskin's nurse, Anne Strachan, passed through once more on their 'great tour through the Lakes and North',[2] when Ruskin was eleven, in 1830. In the summer of 1832 it was the West Country and North Wales. The culmination of their early domestic travelling, during which Ruskin reckoned that he 'saw all of the high-roads, and most of the cross ones of England and Wales; and great part of lowland Scotland' (35.16),[3] came in the summers of 1837 and 1838, when the Lakes

1 See W. G. Collingwood, *The Life and Work of John Ruskin*, 2 vols (London: Methuen, 1893), I, 20.

2 Ibid, p. 38.

3 This and all other quotations from Ruskin's works, unless otherwise indicated, are taken from

and Scotland were the principal destinations respectively,[4] and though he was to make infrequent holiday and recuperative visits throughout the subsequent decades, especially to Scotland, North Yorkshire, the Lakes, and English coastal resorts, his most serious touring was definitively reorientated towards the Continent after the family's formative early journeys there from 1833 and 1835.

His maiden continental tour to Paris and some principal Belgian cities (Brussels, Ghent and Bruges) and to the battlefield of Waterloo took place in 1825, when he was six, and he was to cross the channel repeatedly until 1888, in his seventieth year. That first expedition lasted a month, and John James announces the significant new departure in his diary as 'Our very first Continental journey' (1.xxv). For all the future importance that travel was to assume in his life, Ruskin's early journeys began as happy family holidays. In a letter to his American friend, Charles Norton, in 1872 he records reading 'one of my Father's diaries for my solace, giving account of all our continental journeys, from the time I was six years old, when he and my mother, and I, and a cat, whom I made a friend at Paris, and an old French man-chambermaid, were all very happy (yet not so much in degree as completeness) at Paris — my Father some twelve years younger than I am now [...]' (37.52). But it was not until Ruskin's thirteenth birthday, in 1832, when he was presented with a copy of Samuel Rogers's *Italy*, that his imagination and eye were first captivated by continental scenes.[5] That volume was a poetical journal evoking history and travel interspersed with meditative passages in both prose and verse, and, most impressively, it was illustrated with engraved vignettes by J. M. W. Turner. Subsequently, he and his father became fascinated by the lithographed streets and buildings in Samuel Prout's *Sketches in Flanders and Germany*, which John James subscribed to and acquired when it appeared in 1833, having been delighted by the specimen plates. Momentously, his mother suggested a determined alternative to their desultory domestic tours in visiting the original places: 'Why should we not go and see some of them in reality? My father hesitated a little, then with glittering eyes said — why not? And there were two or three weeks of entirely rapturous and amazed preparation' (35.79).

The decision led to their embarking on their second continental tour, from May to September 1833, when Ruskin was fourteen, carefully planned according to Prout's itinerary and also taking in Turner sites. As E. T. Cook notes of the rhyming letters which Ruskin wrote to his father, 'often [...] we seem, as it were, to be catching father and son in the act of devising confidential schemes for sentimental tours on the Continent' (2.xxxiv). Untouched by Sterne's amorous titillations, they were rather boyish collaborations which shared a sense of novelty and amateur enthusiasm. Cook notes that the itinerary Ruskin gives in his autobiography, *Praeterita* (1885–89), is inaccurate: they actually travelled 'by Calais (May 11), Cassel,

The Library Edition of the Works of John Ruskin, ed. by Edward Tyas Cook and Alexander Wedderburn, 39 vols (London: George Allen, 1903–12). As here, references in the text are to volume and page numbers.

4 See a full account in Keith Hanley, *John Ruskin's Romantic Tours, 1837–1838: Travelling North* (Lewiston, NY, Queenston, and Lampeter: The Edwin Mellen Press, 2007).

5 This was most probably the occasion of his first acquaintance with Rogers's *Italy*, though in his autobiography, *Praeterita*, Ruskin suggests it could have been a year later: the inscription by his father commemorating the presentation is undated.

Lille, Tournay and Brussels, Namur, Liege, Spa, and Aix-la-Chapell to Cologne. Then, up the Rhine, to Heidelberg and on to Strassburg. Thence through the Black Forest to Schaffhaussen; by Constance to Coire: across the Splugen to Como, Milan, Lago Maggiore, Geneva, Turin, Great St Bernard, Vevey, Interlaken, Chamouni; returning via Paris, they reached Herne Hill on September 21' (2.340). They had intended to reach Rome but were deterred by the heat at Genoa.

What struck Ruskin most forcibly, as recorded in the first of the verse descriptions, were the differences between Britain and continental Europe: 'Sudden and marked the change you find, — / Religion, language, even mind' (2.341). He is recurrently affected by empowering visual expansiveness: as in the view from Cassel: 'I love a view like this, for it looks as if you were looking over the wide, wide world and were ruling over it' (2.344). He especially responded to rock scenery and Gothic architectural features, venting his then characteristic religious prejudice ('Rome's religion' hides 'the poison mantling in the bowl', 2.343), moralising on Rubens's 'unholiness, a cast of bacchanalian revelry' (2.352), and responding to occasional historical associations along the Rhine: 'I love to look upon the crags that Caesar has scaled, and upon the towers that his legions have founded' (2.355). It is with great excitement that he describes his first, momentous, sight of the Alps (35.115).[6] His various attempts to draw architecture and landscape reflect the works of Prout and Turner which had prompted the whole project. In the evenings, he worked up the sketches made inside the travelling carriage to produce 'some thirty sheets or so of small pen and Indian ink drawings' (35.80), with a rudimentary technique derived from copying George Cruikshank's vignettes. He intended a characteristically over-ambitious plan of 'about 150 pieces of prose and poetry, and at least as many drawings', but he only got as far as the Rhine in his fair copy of writings and drawings. He did, however, continue to produce his records following his return, and he writes that 'It had excited all the poor little faculties that were in me, to their utmost strain [...] The winter of '33, and what time I could steal to amuse myself in, out of '34, were spent in composing, writing fair, and drawing vignettes for the decoration of the [...] poetical account of our tour' (2.340). He also began to publish the fruits. Poems in the style of Rogers included 'Salzburg', which was published in *Friendship's Offering*, and his already significant interest in geology resulted in two of the articles published in *Loudon's Magazine of Natural History* (1834), on the colour of the water of the Rhine and the geological strata of Mont Blanc and the Swiss Alps, illustrated with engravings after his own sketches.

The longer and more fully fledged tour of 1835, when Ruskin was sixteen, was crucially formative. Tim Hilton notes that 'For Ruskin it was an extended period of pure delight, perhaps the most important of the early family tours and a model for those long sojourns on the Continent which produced so much of his writing.'[7] It was planned and eagerly anticipated throughout the year, as Ruskin and his cousin Mary improved their French, and Salvador, their courier on the Continental tours of 1833, 1835 and 1841, prepared the routes for their journey.[8] In a rhyming letter to

6 See below, p. 5.

7 Tim Hilton, *John Ruskin: The Early Years* (New Haven, CT, and London: Yale University Press, 1985), p. 33.

8 See Ruskin's verse letters to John James, 18 February and 10 May 1835, and Mary Richardson's

his father, on 18 February, Ruskin had already begun to sketch out his own ideas:

> The way over Jura
> By Dijon, et cetera,
> I think is better far
> Than to toil through the sand of the Netherland routes
> With their Dutchmen (their cheeses) and Germans (the brutes)
> What care we for Germany? Leave her, oh leave her!
> We will dash down to Paris, and jump on Geneva,
> By the road that shines white on the Jura so bare,
> When you look from the house that remembers Voltaire,
> And which sees from its height all the clouds that do wheel on
> The mountains of Berne, and the crest of Mont Velan.[9]

John James had acquired the original French edition of Johan Gottfried Ebel's *Manuel du Voyageur en Suisse*, which was acknowledged to be the best guidebook to Switzerland.[10] His journey lasted six months, from 2 June to 10 December, taking him through France, Switzerland (principally, from 2 July to September, travelling through Geneva to Chamonix, Courmayeur, Vevay, Basel, Zurich, St Gotthard, Thun, Lausanne), and Italy. It inaugurated what was to become the Ruskins' favoured and recurrent route through France and Switzerland to Italy, with prolonged stays at Chamonix and Venice. The journey brought him his first encounters with Rouen and Venice, as well as impressing on him the 'meek simplicity and healthy purity' (35.164) of the Swiss natural culture. He kept a diary of the Swiss part of the journey, and in a rhyming letter written to Willoughby Jones, a school-friend from Venice he described his jumbled studies:

> Then through the whole of Switzerland as merrily we went,
> I took my pencil in my hand, my Horace on my knee,
> And now I sketched a mountain scene, or anything that did me please,
> And then I puzzled out a sentence of the cramp Thucydides.[11]

His aesthetic and literary interests were complemented by further serious studies in geology which contributed to the highly fertile combination he described as 'science mixed with feeling' (35.116). The *Voyages dans les Alpes* (1779–96), by the botanist and geologist, Horace Bénédict de Saussure, a fifteenth-birthday present, was now as much a guide as Prout's and Turner's drawings and Byron's poetry, which replaced Rogers as the object of his imitation. Throughout his life an absorbed love of rocks was fundamental to his religious and artistic engagements with landscape.

letter to her uncle, 23 February 1835, *Ruskin Family Letters: The Correspondence of John James Ruskin, his Wife, and their Son John, 1801–1843*, ed. by Van Aikin Burd, 2 vols (Ithaca, NY: Cornell University Press, 1973), I, 297, 315, and 305.

9 *The Ruskin Family Letters*, I, 297.

10 James S. Dearden notes that John James annotated and signed his copy now held in the Ruskin Library, Lancaster University, inscribed on the flyleaf 'Herne Hill near London 1835' and drew a map of Zermatt on the front paste-down. Ruskin possessed another copy of this book and the English translation of an earlier version, 1820. See Dearden's *The Library of John Ruskin* (Oxford: The Oxford Bibliographical Society, 2012), items 802–04, p. 104.

11 See below, p. 162.

Yet there is also evidence of some humorous detachment. Ruskin was also self-conscious of his pretensions as a teenage prodigy. The dramatic sketch he produced of the family's *Ascent of the St. Bernard* gives a portrait of a youth whose head is poetically in the clouds, occasionally to his father's irritation. The same piece depicts the superciliousness and uninformed arrogance of some English travellers as well as pointing to the responses of different national types.[12]

A core cultural geography was becoming mapped as he describes in 'The Col de la Faucille' chapter in *Praeterita*. At Abbeville he now discovered 'the preface and interpretation of Rouen' where 'art (of its local kind), religion, and present human life, were yet in perfect harmony' (35.156). The sight of Rouen and its cathedral, together with 'the following journey up the Seine to Paris, then to Soissons and Rheims , determined [...] the first centre and circle of [his] future life' (35.158). He savoured in memory the details of the journey from Paris to Geneva, describing the changing landscapes en route, evoking the cumulative recollections of what became a familiar direction in the years to come. After leaving La Cloche at Dijon for Genlis in the early morning a routine had formed: 'Genlis, Auxonne, Dole, Mont-sous-Vaudrey — three stages of 12 or 14 kilometres each, two of eighteen; in all about 70 kilometers = 42 miles, from Dijon gate to Jura foot — we went straight for the hills always, lunching on French plums and bread' (35.159). His observations on the landscape were to find expression in the series of essays entitled *The Poetry of Architecture* (1837–38).

His re-encounter with Switzerland focused a new sense of commitment. His emotional response to first glimpsing the Alps 'high above the Rhine' at Schaffhausen in 1833 was to the sacred sublime, a displacement of Biblical topography: 'They were clear as crystal, sharp on the pure horizon sky, and already tinged with rose by the sinking sun. Infinitely beyond all that we had ever thought or dreamed, — the seen walls of lost Eden could not have been more beautiful to us; not more awful, round heaven, the walls of sacred Death' (35.115). In 1835, though, they marked his dedication to a newly emergent agenda, summoning him to 'the Holy Land of my future work and true home in this world' (35.167). His calling as an art critic, communicating that Edenic construction of landscape beauty was soon to find its focus in his early celebration of Turner in an unpublished essay of 1836, and was in time to become the theme of volume one of *Modern Painters* (1843).

The Italian leg had been intended to stretch as far as Rome, but they were deterred by the news of an outbreak of cholera in Italy. 1833 and 1835 turned out to have been rehearsals for what over the years was to become the paradigmatic format of following 'The Old Road', from Calais to Geneva, the Alps and Northern Italy, taking Ruskin to those landscapes and towns situated in Northern France, Western Switzerland and Savoy, and the Northern Italian States to which he repeatedly returned. In the early days they were guided partly by religious prejudice when the Ruskins avoided the Catholic cantons in Switzerland whenever possible, while the changing political situations in revolutionary Europe also affected their movements. Like his domestic tours through the Romantic margins of Britain, their continental atlas featured alternative topographies of nineteenth-century Europe. Ruskin's

12 See below, the *table-d'hôte* in Scene 4, pp. 246–50.

France is provincial, deliberately skirting mushrooming conurbations. His Venice is distinctly *not* on the Path to Rome. Switzerland and Savoy are prized precisely for being off the beaten track, at that time relatively unfrequented and unspoilt by modern incursions. Ruskin seldom travelled beyond these core itineraries, visiting Germany very occasionally, and refusing the opportunity of visiting Greece in 1852 due to his parents' fear of his risking the sea voyage.[13] 1843 was the only year in that decade he did not travel on the Continent, extending his range to the Low Countries in 1842. He remained in England for only two years in each of the subsequent two decades, before his foreign travel became progressively reduced in the '70s and '80s, travelling the Old Road for the final time in 1888.

Background to Cultural Tourism

The Ruskins' tours were middle-class emulations of the aristocratic 'Grand Tour', which 'had first appeared in the early seventeenth century with reference to a tour of the French provinces', but which towards the end of that century 'had become associated with a more extensive European tour focused on Italy',[14] and with an explicitly educational and cultural emphasis. Imaginatively, aesthetic experience and authority was located chiefly in Italy and according to Enlightenment thinking was to be acquired with 'the truth of one's eyes'.[15] A sense of deference to Italian culture had been conventionalised by the time of the Restoration. William Aglionby's translation of Vasari's *Lives of the Artists* in his *Painting Illustrated in Three Dialogues* (1685), attributed a national cultural deficit to the effects of the English revolution,[16] and the countering rite of cultural passage through extensive and well guided continental travel became increasingly *de rigueur* for the heirs of leading British families. In 1734 the Society of Dilettanti was formed for the study of antiquities by noblemen who had been on the Grand Tour, and as many associated publications fostered the fashion for collecting classical antiquities, it was laying the foundations of future institutions and scholarly specialisms. Given the pre-Christian focus and Protestant and anti-Catholic undercurrents, the aesthetic was regularly under suspicion of becoming separated from a moral educational agenda, but it could also represent the acquisition of an elevating liberal culture, as in Jonathan Richardson's *A Discourse on [...] The Science of the Connoisseur* (1719): 'If gentlemen were Lovers of Painting, and Connoisseurs, this would help Reform Them, as their Example, and Influence would have the like Effect upon the Common People.'[17] Thomas Nugent's *The Grand Tour* argued that travel made 'the complete gentleman', by exposing him to a different order of experiences, including the removal of

13 See J. A. Hilton, '"Sailing to Byzantium": Ruskin's Imaginary Travel to Greece', in *Ruskin, Venice and Nineteenth-Century Cultural Travel*, ed. by Keith Hanley and Emma Sdegno (Venice: Le Bricole, 2010), pp. 361–79.

14 Nicholas T. Parsons, *Worth the Detour: A History of the Guidebook* (Stroud: Sutton Publishing, 2007), p. 148.

15 Peter D. Osborne, *Travelling Light: Photography, Travel and Visual Culture* (Manchester: Manchester University Press, 2000), p. 9. Osborne is summarising the argument made in Judith Adler, 'Origins of Sightseeing', *Annals of Tourism Research*, 16.1 (1989), 17–29.

16 See Parsons, p. 161.

17 Ibid.

prejudices, as the educative Renaissance programme shaded into an increasingly confident patriotism. John Chetwode Eustace's book, *A Classical Tour Through Italy* (1813; the seventh edition came out in 1841), was to be the last significant guide for the Grand Tourist addressed 'solely to persons of a liberal education' with the explicit aim of 'moral improvement'.[18]

The Grand Tour remained a minority interest throughout the eighteenth century, though the English travelled abroad more than other Europeans, due to their relative prosperity and island location. Italy remained the chief destination, but with the rise of French literature and polished manners, it became increasingly fashionable to prolong the stay in France on the way to Italy in order to sample a different taste, represented by public and communal buildings and art collections. The paths through the Swiss Alps and Savoy, however, emerged by the second half of the eighteenth century as themselves offering curious detours from the major route, and, as the educational benefits of nature were coming to the fore, a diversion, even an alternative destination, became established in order to accommodate the new vogue for mountains and glaciers, communing with which bore overtones of Protestant spirituality.

Humanist and neoclassical cultural tourism mutated into what John Urry describes as 'the nineteenth-century "romantic Grand Tour" which saw the emergence of "scenic tourism" and a much more private and passionate experience of beauty and the sublime'.[19] English Grand Tourists had approached their travels with an increasing sense of their superiority as Citizens of the World, confident of their trade-based prosperity and political reputation for 'liberty', though they were drawn to the prestige of arts and letters abroad. But during the Napoleonic period this pattern was revolutionised by the military occupations of the French. Cut off from the Continent, cultural travel turned inward to explore the native beauty and history of mainland Britain, and domestic tourism, more immediately accessible to the rising middle classes, increased substantially.

The aesthetic and literary representation of Britain responded and contributed to the construction of nationalism, which was culturally as well as economically colonising the Continent. After British victory, Byron's poetic travelogue, *Childe Harold's Pilgrimage* (1812 and 1816–17), epitomised the age's collective desire for fantasy travel — he coined the word 'guidebook' in *Don Juan* (1823). Samuel Rogers's own sub-Byronic poem, still in touch with the attitudes of the Grand Tour as it had been practised by the cognoscenti of the eighteenth century, was an important early model for Ruskin's travel verse. From 1803, Rogers's seven rooms at 22 St James's Place became a considerable private museum with antique casts, curious collections, paintings, and engravings. A connoisseur banker and patron of all the arts, he was able to fund handsomely illustrated gift books featuring state-of-the-art steel engravings, particularly after Turner's drawings, which enabled a new delicacy and precision of representation. His own unlively verses in *Italy* confirmed the sense of place by Romantic association and historical allusion which fed into Ruskin's emergent notion of the 'poetry of architecture'.

18 Parsons, p. 171.
19 John Urry, *The Tourist Gaze*, 2nd edn (London: Sage Publications, 2002), p. 4.

The proliferation of print culture disseminated images and descriptions and boosted the prestige of British art and letters themselves through prints, which featured the paintings of a succession of Picturesque artists, and through the works of picaresque novelists and the Romantic writers. Following the Napoleonic Wars, the new almost exclusively middle-class clientele required the kind of detailed information and practical advice which featured in 'the prototype of the "bourgeois" guidebook',[20] Mariana Starke's *Letters from Italy* (1800). The cultivated middle classes also desired aesthetic direction, and expert opinions were provided. Her *Travels on the Continent*, expanding the coverage of useful travel information, went through eight editions, and a composite of her earlier books entitled *Information and Direction for Travellers on the Continent* (1824), published by Galignani, prefigured the great standard guides to come. Though Ruskin's touring began before the first *Murray's Hand-book for Travellers in Holland, Belgium and North Germany* appeared in 1836, it prefigured the coming agenda, based on newly acquired economic resources, and it presaged the habits and approaches which would emerge, partly to be influenced by Ruskin's own subsequent writings, as the pattern of '[h]olidays with a serious purpose', made by the kind of comfortably-off middle-class Victorians bent on self-improvement who were to become, for example, Thomas Cook's continental tourists, 'with a Murray's guide or Baedeker in hand'.[21]

At this moment, travelling became a profound metaphor for individual development. Over his career, Ruskin was to conduct himself and his readers on a journey to a wider apprehension of European Christian civilisation. He was slow to surrender his insular prejudices to a full encounter with continental art and culture — it took until 1845, when he travelled without his parents for the first time, to become 'swept away' by the 'mare maggiore' (35.372) of Venetian art in his response to Tintoretto in the magnificent rooms of the Scuola di San Rocco.[22] But he was open to what was to become an increasingly tremendous attraction from the start. As soon as he crossed the channel, he felt its power: 'I cannot find words to express the intense pleasure I have always in first finding myself, after some prolonged stay in England, at the foot of the old tower of Calais church' (6.11). Such resilient and living monuments admitted him to a continuing communal tradition which he felt the British compulsion for novelty tended to obscure:

> Abroad, a building of the eighth or tenth century stands ruinous in the open street; the children play round it, the peasants heap their corn in it [...] we feel the ancient world to be a real thing, and one with the new: antiquity is no dream; it is rather the children playing about the old stones that are the dream. But all is continuous; and the words, 'from generation to generation,' understandable there. (6.13)

20 Parsons, p. 139,

21 F. M. L. Thompson, *The Rise of Respectable Society: A Social History of Victorian Britain, 1830–1900* (London: Fontana Press, 1988), p. 263.

22 See Keith Hanley, Introduction, *Ruskin, Venice and Nineteenth-Century Cultural Travel*, pp. xxiii–xxvi.

Mode of Travel

Ruskin comments at the start of his 'Verse Journal, A Tour Through France to Chamouni' that in 1835 the family were advised, on health grounds, not to over-exert themselves. Ruskin had suffered from an attack of pleurisy in the spring, and the recommendation helped to set the slow pace of their travelling:

'Now, as you need not ride with whip and spur, I
   Beg very seriously to advise
That you should never travel in a hurry.'
   Thus slowly spoke the doctor, looking wise.[23]

Choosing the most suitable conveyance was a chief delight in their preparations before and during the journey, and Ruskin was something of an expert on the whole animating business of horse-drawn traffic, evoking '[t]he city coach, that vehicle historical', 'the darting gig or curricle', '[t]he mail coach [...] When "Troo, taroo, turuw!" comes on the wind!', and 'a chariot [...] On softest springs for luxury designed'.[24] He was familiar with the sturdy and secure service of the char-à-banc with its rows of bench seats:

   Up to the door with rattling rumble daundered
Those very strange compounds of wood and leather: —
   Oh, *char-a-banc*, thou vehicle most honoured
Of all the vehicles e'er put together!
   What though thy cushions be to sit on hard,
And though they scarce can hold their well-squeezed three,
   And though thou lookest ancient, worn and brown,
[...]
The river, and the precipice I've past
   Safely and most delightfully in thee![25]

In *Praeterita* he describes the whole business of settling their continental transport:

> For a family carriage of this solid construction, with its luggage, and load of six or more persons, four horses were of course necessary to get any sufficient way on it; and half-a-dozen such teams were kept at every post-house [...] The French horses, and more or less those on all the great lines of European travelling, were properly stout trotting cart-horses [...] As a rule there were four steady horses and a good driver, rarely drunk, often very young, the men of stronger build being more useful for other work [...] [The avant-courier's] primary office it was to ride in advance at a steady gallop, and order the horses at each post-house to be harnessed and ready waiting, so that no time might be lost between stages. His higher function was to make all bargains and pay all bills, so as to save the family unbecoming cares and mean anxieties, besides the trouble and disgrace of trying to speak French or any other foreign language [...] Murray [...] did not exist in those days; the courier was a private Murray, who knew [...] not the things to be seen only, but those you would yourself best like to see, and gave instructions to your valet-de-place accordingly [...] He invariably attended the ladies in their shopping expeditions. (35.107–10)

23 See below, p. 117.
24 See below, p. 145.
25 Ibid.

The 1830s marked the highpoint of the age of coaching which was on the verge of becoming old-fashioned in England in the later 1830s. Though it was only to become apparent towards the end of the decade, the Ruskins were enjoying the end of the horse-drawn era of transport from the time the railway began to take over, in 1838. They had found that the large, comfortable, old English travelling chariot, which they borrowed from John James's business partner for their domestic journeys before acquiring their own carriages, wonderfully matched their purposes. It signalled their social achievement, and it provided a miniature study on wheels. Of great importance was the leisurely pace itself which enabled a constantly protracted visual intake: Ruskin later wrote that he was unsure whether one should use the expression to 'do' or 'see' a carriage-drive (see 16.336). He especially bemoaned the effect of mechanical transport in destroying the quality of sensory perceptions which the 'jog-trot pace' of the hired post-chaise and pair provided, and the stable picture-like prospects available 'through the panoramic opening of the four windows [...] ' (35.16). Indeed, he thought the most 'profitable travelling' was on foot, and he described his own experience of trains to one correspondent in 1846 as the negation of travel as he had understood it:

> [...] the general effect of them is to render all the time that we pass in locomotion the same, except in feverishness, as that passed at home, and to enable us to get over ground which formerly conveyed to us a thousand various ideas, and the examination of which was fertile in lessons of the most interesting kind, while we read a page of the morning paper. (36.62)

Ruskin saw the revolution as subverting the exercise of individual agency and control: 'Going by railroad I do not consider as travelling at all; it is merely "being sent" to a place, and very little different from becoming a parcel' (5.370). With the introduction of rail travel, the calculation of speed and distance preoccupied the traveller's attention, and Ruskin feared that the motive of simply getting there had become primary.

The mode of unhurried travel formerly adopted, following the family's personal tempo and chosen direction, was integral to the total experience. Ruskin's father never employed couriers, and he relished making all the arrangements before and during their journeys.[26] He controlled and arranged the times and places on their itinerary and determined every detail of convenience, as is described in the *Praeterita* account of the family's later visits to Mr Hopkinson's of Long Acre, from where they obtained their horse-drawn vehicles. Carriages which had attained a new level of sophistication in design were hired for more ambitious expeditions on the Continent:

> The poor modern slaves and simpletons who let themselves be dragged like cattle, or felled timber, through the countries they imagine themselves visiting, can have no conception whatever of the complex joys, and ingenious hopes, connected with the choice and arrangement of the travelling carriage in old times. The mechanical questions first, of strength — easy rolling — steady and safe poise of persons and luggage; the general stateliness of effect to be obtained

26 See Richard Mullen and James Munson, *'The Smell of the Continent': The British Discover Europe* (London: Pan Macmillan, 2009), p. 232.

> for the abashing of plebeian beholders; the cunning design and distribution of store-cellars under the seats, secret drawers under front windows, invisible pockets under padded lining, safe from dust, and accessible only by insidious slits, or necromantic valves like Aladdin's trap-door; the fitting of cushions where they would not slip, the rounding of corners for more delicate repose; the prudent attachments and springs of blinds; the perfect fitting of windows, on which one half the comfort of a travelling carriage really depends; and the adaptation of all these concentrated luxuries to the probabilities of who would sit where, in the little apartment which was to be virtually one's home for five or six months; — all this was an imaginary journey in itself, with every pleasure, and none of the discomfort, of practical travelling. (35.106–07)

Parallel to fitting out everything in accordance with the foreseen experience of travelling is the imaginative selection of, and planned itineraries for the scenes to be visited, so as ideally to present the travellers with confirmation of the images they had already mentally formed in their reading of books and viewing of paintings, prints and engravings. The magical sleight ('necromantic valves like Aladdin's trap-door'), which in the boy's mind turns the vehicle into the journey itself — the medium of imaginative travel — is an allusion to the Arabian Night's 'Tale of Aladdin', a text later to become the cue for the lecture, 'Of King's Treasuries', in his most popular work, *Sesame and Lilies* (1865), where he speaks of the imaginative potential embedded in cultural institutions, especially libraries, when they are put to proper use: '[...] bread made of that old enchanted Arabian grain, the Sesame, which opens doors; doors, not of robbers', but of King's Treasuries' (18.105).

The dramatic sketch of the 1835 tour, *The Ascent of the St. Bernard*, satirically evokes all the fussing about convenience and critical selection of vehicles the family demanded. But most importantly, the nurturing of a special vision, highly regulated though leisurely, had helped to produce his exceptional 'thirst for visible fact', and develop 'that patience in looking, and precision in feeling, which afterwards, with due industry, formed [his] analytic power' (35.51).

His personal nostalgia for pre-railway travel is bound up with his pervasive lament for a kind of seeing that was about to disappear from general experience at the time of his earliest travels. His appeal to his age to look — at what there was in creation, and at what was happening to it — was largely one to slow down, as he insisted in the third volume of *Modern Painters*: 'There was always more in the world than men could see, walked they ever so slowly; they will see it no better for going fast [...] A fool always wants to shorten space and time; a wise man wants to lengthen both' (5.381). Entirely symptomatic for him was what was to become the Murray's guidebook approach, represented by the *Handbook to Northern Italy* (1876), which described 'how to see all the remarkable objects in Venice in a single day' (11.360).[27] The cultural travelling which Ruskin enjoyed in childhood and later both in Britain and on the Continent, and about which he reminisced at the beginning of the second volume of *The Stones of Venice*, offers a sensation of touring, of moving on from place to place, with serial and localised impressions of approach and arrival in a rhythm of anticipation and realisation:

27 The Library Edition notes: 'So also in the current edition; but the less hurried visitor is given a week. Baedeker's plan allows him "3–4 days"' (11.360).

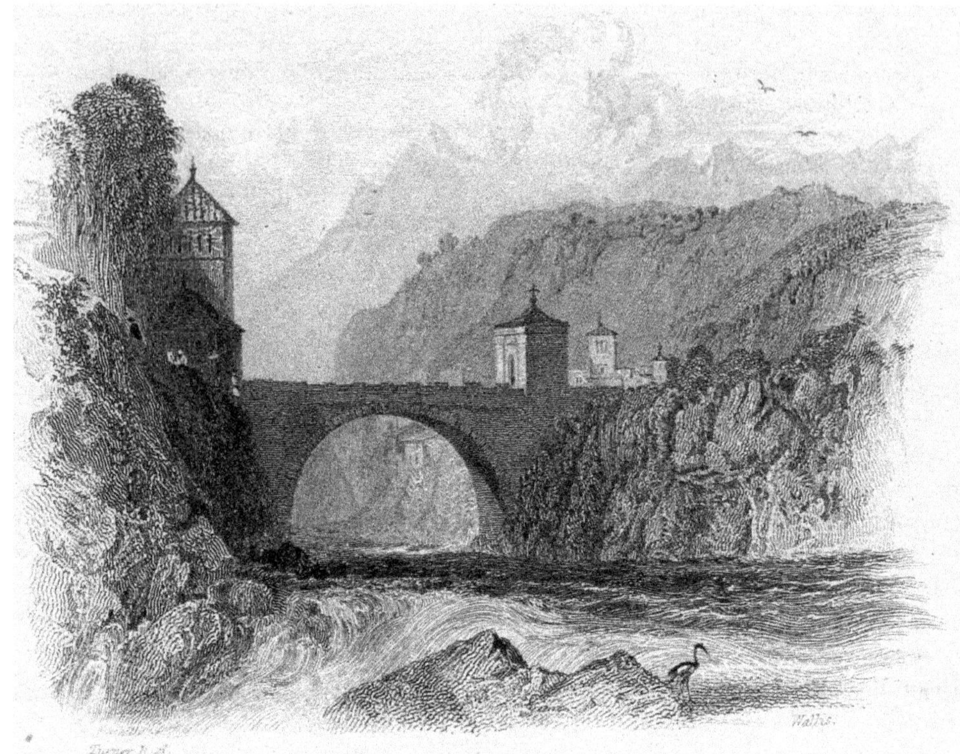

Fig. 1. J. M. W. Turner, *St Maurice.* Engraved by Robert Wallis. From Samuel Rogers, *Italy*, (London: Printed for T. Cadell and E. Moxon, 1830), p. 29. Private copy.

> In the olden days of travelling, now to return no more, in which distance could not be vanquished without toil, but in which that toil was rewarded, partly by the power of deliberate survey of the countries through which the journey lay, and partly by the happiness of the evening hours, when from the top of the last hill he had surmounted, the traveller beheld the quiet village where he was to rest, scattered among the meadow beside its valley stream; or, from the long-hoped-for turn in the dusty perspective of the causeway, saw, for the first time, the towers of some famed city, faint in the rays of sunset-hours of peaceful and thoughtful pleasure, for which the rush of the arrival in the railway station is perhaps not always, or to all men, an equivalent, — in those days, I say, when there was something more to be anticipated and remembered in the first aspect of each successive halting-place, than a new arrangement of glass roofing and iron girder, there were few moments more fondly cherished by the traveller, than that which [...] brought him within sight of Venice [...] (10.3)

In this way, the drawn-out procedures of the travelling process act out the sensations of the imaginative processes he was over time to formulate as 'Turnerian Topgraphy' in Book Four of *Modern Painters* (1856). Ruskin's favourite Turner vignette from Rogers's *Italy*, *St Maurice* (Fig. 1), for example, shows the Rhone running in the wrong direction, yet it succeeds in giving a truthful 'mental impression he had himself received' of 'the rapidity of the massy river', and Ruskin comments that 'It might indeed have been long before this audacity — for it is not an error — had been detected; for the railroad passes the scene in a tunnel, and not one traveller in a thousand ever sees either the bridge or the river' (21.212). The upshot of a continuously various shift of perspectives, the travelling eye, most memorably co-ordinated in Ruskin's painstaking reconstruction of Turner's *The Pass of St. Gothard, near Faido*, would be the representation of 'a perfect summary of Alpine truth' (6.380), an overall fidelity to the cumulative visual experience rather than reproducing a single snapshot.[28]

Ruskin recounts a travelling regime which sometimes started at six, covering twenty miles before breakfast, but more typically at eight or nine, accomplishing forty to fifty miles a day, and then he 'sate down to dinner at four, — and [he] had done two hours of delicious exploring by [himself] in the evening; ordered in punctually at seven for tea, and finishing [his] sketches till half-past nine — bed-time' (35.111). The family never travelled on Sundays, nor did Ruskin climb or sketch on that day until late in life. The punishing daily schedule was to some extent a deliberate choice, born of an awareness of their economically privileged situation, which Ruskin was later to consider in relation to his encouragement of workers' education and his purpose to impart the fruits of his own special opportunities to an intelligent working class. In Letter 56 of *Fors Clavigera* (1875), for which the discarded title was 'Horses out!' (the cry in the yards of posting inns), Ruskin addresses an audience of aspirant workmen, and wonders how representative his particular childhood experience could ever be — 'how far education, and felicities, of the same kind, may be attainable for young people in general' (28.391), asking: 'How far [...] supposing my education to be in any wise exemplary, can all these advantages be supplied by the modern school board, to every little boy born in the prosperous England of this day?' (392). Ruskin then considers the diverse kinds of labour which had gone into the production of a 'peaceful day of mental development' (391) for the seemingly spoiled child figure which he now draws of himself. He did arrive in later life at a sense of his unusual indulgence, and in particular he later wrote remorsefully about the different status within the household of his cousin and travelling companion, Mary, and their divergent tastes, as she took up a position on an outside seat of the carriage. Here, however, he is anxious to situate his travelling in the network of awarenesses to which it had led him to become an active social and cultural critic. He includes in his calculations all the labourers in the Spanish vineyards, the packagers and sailors involved in the export of the wine, his own father's paperwork together with the contributions of all his staff, the tailors and carriage-makers, as well as all those historical figures who had built and peopled the architectural remains, the great painters, the monks, abbots, stonemasons, and so on. He then contrasts his appreciation of the hidden social and economic implications of his childhood travels in a private carriage — 'my triumphal progress; and [...] my nurse behind in the dickey' (393) — and the version of cultural tourism it represented with the insouciant consumption of the aristocratic Grand Tourist:

> For the impression on the aristocratic mind of the day was always (especially supposing I had been a squire's or a lord's son, instead of a merchant's) that

28 See Keith Hanley, *John Ruskin's Romantic Tours, 1837–1838*, pp. 258–67.

> such a little jaunty figure, trotting in its easy chariot, was, as it were, a living diamond, without which the watch of the world could not possibly go; or even, that the diminutive darling was a kind of Almighty Providence in its first breeches [...] And it never once entered the head of any aristocratic person [...] that a great part of the world had been literally put behind me as a dickey [...] (393–94)

Media of Representation

Ruskin recorded his tours contemporaneously in a variety of media including diary-journals, verse-letters, drawings, poems and other literary genres, and in letters to family and friends. He incorporated features of his experience of landscape, art and architecture throughout his works and described his past travels in his late autobiography. Starting out by seeing his routes and destinations with the eyes of a geologist, the Romantic poets and Picturesque painters, his application of them was deepened and complicated by his growing historical studies and the economic and scientific analyses which came to the centre of his critical and creative purposes.

We can see the makings of an experimental apprenticeship in his critical methods from his earliest records. They exemplified familiar '[r]ecurring genres within childhood writings [...] — for instance the diary, the homemade family journal, and the letter home',[29] provided for domestic consumption. Ruskin worked together with Mary on summarising sermons, and she was his leading collaborator on their journal of the 1830 tour to the Lakes from which Ruskin himself fashioned his poem of over two thousand lines of rhymed anapaestics, *Iteriad; or Three Weeks Among the Lakes*, with topographical notes, composed between 28 November 1830 and 11 January 1832.[30] Though Ruskin was an only child, he and Mary followed a typical pattern of 'the collaborative literary games played among siblings', as aspiring child writers in imitation of adult publications.[31] But he also took up extra interests which he characteristically pursued with unusual application, especially what were then called the earth sciences of mineralogy and geology. He read Joyce's *Scientific Dialogues* (1807), when he was seven and continued to read works of scientific interest so that by the age of ten his fascination with minerals had formed 'in the sparry walks at Matlock' and he had started studying silicas there by acquiring 'a piece of iron oxide with Bright Bristol diamonds' (35.94). That and 'some dog-tooth spar', costing about 'three half-crowns', he suggested, gave him more delight than all his subsequent collections, though he did not know the exact names of the stones and could note even spell them (see 27.62). He commenced a mineralogical dictionary at the age of twelve, following the enlargement of his collection during the Lakes tour of 1830, in order to prepare 'articles' which he worked on up to spring 1835, and compiled other notes from a range of reference texts between 1835 and 1836.

29 Introduction, *The Child Writer from Austen to Woolf*, ed. by Christine Alexander and Juliet McMaster (Cambridge: Cambridge University Press, 2005), p. 3.

30 The invented title 'Iteriad' means 'The story of a journey'. A full presentation of this poem, based on a transcript of a 'fair copy' made by Cook and Wedderburn and now at the Ruskin Library, Lancaster University, is printed in *Iteriad; or Three Weeks Among the Lakes*, ed. by James S. Dearden (Newcastle upon Tyne: Frank Graham, 1969).

31 *The Child Writer*, p. 3.

It was on an ascent of Snowdon, in the summer of 1832, that he celebrated 'the finding for the first time in my life a real "mineral" for myself, a piece of copper pyrites!' (35.96). Guided by Robert Jameson's three-volume *A System of Mineralogy* (1821), which his father bought him that year and against which he compared the minerals in the British Museum, he compiled an impressive catalogue of his collection of specimens. Among the Alps, especially at Chamouni, on the 1833 tour he was able to do the field work behind his earliest prose publications, further stimulated by his chosen fifteenth-birthday gift in 1834, Saussure's *Voyages dans les Alpes* (1779). The author avoided putting his theories first and 'had gone to the Alps, as I desired to go myself, only to look at them, and describe them as they were, loving them heartily [...] ', producing 'clear and trustworthy' (6.476) descriptions which remained a constant reference throughout Ruskin's working life. His own first efforts, written for *Loudon's Magazine of Natural History*, were 'Enquiries on the Causes of the Colour of the Water of the Rhine' (September 1834), and 'Facts and Considerations on the strata of Mont Blanc, and on some instances of twisted strata observable in Switzerland' (December 1834). He compiled further mineralogical notes from 1835 probably into the following year, and two further articles on meteorological subjects were to follow in the same publication in 1836. The diary-journal of 1835, which covers the Swiss part of the tour, is filled with exact geological observations, introducing the stream of research findings devoted to that science which found chief expression in the fourth volume of *Modern Painters* (1856), *The Ethics of the Dust* (1866), and, the major work, *Deucalion* (1875–83).

As David Hanson has demonstrated, Ruskin's formative readers were his parents, who occasionally added 'improvements' to his writings, and his writings were aimed to placate their wishes: his father's proud encouragement (soon after his eighth birthday he referred to his son as 'surely the most intellectual creature of his age that ever appeared in any age'[32]) was counterbalanced by 'the domestic ideology that [his mother] invoked to quell his prolific invention'.[33] While his father, whose first aspiration was for Ruskin to become a poet, and who was accordingly presented with a series of rhyming verse letters on his birthdays and at New Year, was ambiguously impressed with his outpourings, Margaret was unambiguously opposed to his unnatural and excessive productivity. At twelve Ruskin writes: 'Mamma is continually [...] saying that prolific writing will "weary out my brain or brains"'.[34] She objected to his incontinent habit of never bringing his efforts to completion, writing apprehensively in 1831: 'I do not think it will be easy to stop his rhyming.'[35] A less problematic demonstration of his seeking to please his mother's wishes were his sermons on the Pentateuch, written between 1832 and 1834.[36] John James, on the other hand, provided the encounter with Romantic literature whose

32 See David C. Hanson, 'Precocity and the economy of the evangelical self', in *The Child Writer*, ed. by Alexander and McMaster, pp. 200–21 (p. 200).

33 Ibid, p. 201.

34 *The Ruskin Family Letters*, I, 233.

35 Ibid, p. 224.

36 See Van Aikin Burd, 'Ruskin's Testament of his Boyhood Faith: Sermons on the Pentateuch', in *New Approaches to Ruskin: Thirteen Essays*, ed. by Robert Hewison (London: Routledge and Kegan Paul, 1981), pp. 1–16. Also Hanson, 'Precocity and the Economy of the Evangelical Self', n. 55, p. 220.

associations infused their touring geography. In evenings at home his father read aloud from his preferred canonical authors as well as from contemporary writers, particularly Byron and Scott. By 1829, having made three visits to Perth, Ruskin versified Scott's *The Monastery* in a fragment of around four hundred lines. Ruskin was seven when he started to pen his first extant poems, six in all and 'printed in imitation of book-print' (2.254). The first group includes 'Glen of Glenfarg', reflecting the Scottish scenery he had seen on a recent summer journey and touched with a peremptory moralism which is undoubtedly an internalisation of his mother's puritan indoctrination.

His multimedia approach was formed from the start. John James encouraged his son's first attempts to record their travels in his first work of the kind at the age of seven. *HARRY AND LUCY CONCLUDED [...] PRINTED and composed by a little boy and also drawn* (1826–28) was part of a story in three volumes (he originally planned four) based on several popular books of scientific instruction for children: Maria Edgeworth's *Harry and Lucy Concluded* (1825), and earlier volumes in the same series, as well as Jeremiah Joyce's *Scientific Dialogues* and works by Anna Letitia Barbauld. Various inland journeys provided material for these experiments, and it is easy to see the seeds of Ruskin's characteristic methods of composition and illustration in this creatively mixed educational genre. Ruskin attempted to emulate engravings, including one copied directly from a diagram in Joyce, in what he termed his own 'copper plates'. Joyce's habit of including verse quotations influenced some of Ruskin's own attempts in one of the manuscripts of *Harry and Lucy*. It added to the eclecticism of what Ruskin describes as 'the interwoven temper of my mind, at the beginning of days just as much as at their end' and the 'dipartite writings' (35.56) so produced. Behind them all was a great deal of homework. Ruskin described his extraordinarily driven activities in a letter to his father, who taught him Latin and Greek when he was twelve: 'I find time now still more scarce than ever; for what with Livy and Lucian, Homer, French, drawings, arithmetic, globe work and mineralogical dictionary, I positively am all flurry and hurry' (2.xxxii).

His concurrent projects became so ambitious and creatively diverse that, like *Harry and Lucy*, which foundered at this time, they inaugurated a recurrent pattern of non-completion. As well as starting to turn *The Monastery* into verse, he barely commenced an epic, 'Eudosia; Or A poem On the Universe' (the title refers to the 'good gifts' of creation), and began to construct a Punch and Judy theatre, with pasteboard figures described in the third volume of *Harry and Lucy*, for which he supplied a manuscript notebook, *The Puppet Show; or, Amusing Characters for Children*, with twenty-nine characters in all, as well as composing a two-act verse play on 'The Battle of Waterloo'. Yet nearly all these enterprises launched continuing preoccupations which informed future works and came to various kinds of resolution over time. In *Praeterita*, Ruskin quotes lines from 'Eudosia' 'as the real beginning at once of *Deucalion* and *Proserpina*' (35.59), his ruminations on geology and botany which appeared in parts stretching between 1875 and 1886.

Early on, his intentions began to exceed the limited family context as his works were submitted to and commissioned by the editors of journals and popular literary albums. In his poems of 1828 fresh influences appear: as well as imitating Byron's and Southey's use of anapaestics they allude to Pope's translations from Homer and to Milton. His eye scans the scene for scientific evidence and other kinds of information, moving from close natural observation to historical and mythic presences. A combination of the real and the imagined informs his evocation of places: for example, Book Two of 'Eudosia' starts with a description of Swiss topography which he had not yet seen in actuality, while his references to the field of Waterloo in a song and ballad on that theme were inspired by his having been taken there three years before. A poem, which was composed initially for his father's birthday in 1829 and which looked back to the Lakes visit of 1826 combined with his later imaginings of the summer's cancelled trip of 1828, is memorable as constituting his first publication, before anything in prose, when it was split into two pieces, 'Lines Written at the Lakes in Cumberland' and 'On Skiddaw and Derwent Water', written when he was nine and printed in the August 1829 and February 1830 issues of *The Spiritual Times* when he was eleven.[37] 'Salzburg' and 'Fragments from a Metrical Journal' (including 'Andernacht' and 'St Goar') came out in *Friendship's Offering* for 1835, published the previous autumn by John James's friend, Thomas Pringle. This was one of the popular literary annuals which flourished from the 1820s to the 1840s with leading literary contributors, and Ruskin supplied verses for similar publications including *The Amaranth*, *The Keepsake* and *The Book of Beauty*. They often included expertly engraved plates, and Ruskin was later to supply three of his own illustrations to *Friendship's Offering*. Though they include love and 'Herodotean' subject matter derived from academic study, these earliest pieces are travel verses.

Ruskin's childhood drawings up to the age of thirteen started with pencil sketches to illustrate his own little books, created after those of Maria Edgeworth around 1826–27. They progressed to imitations of engraved works and maps in pen and ink washed with watercolour, emulating George Cruikshank's illustrations for Grimm's fairy-tales, *German Popular Stories*, in 1828. Pen and ink was his father's favourite medium, and his amateur interest and efforts were the original influence on Ruskin's art. After the Lakes tour of 1830, Mary received instruction in drawing, and Ruskin's keen interest in copying her work led to an arrangement being made for his own regular drawing lessons in the spring of 1831, when he was twelve. However schooled his draughtsmanship was to become, there was always a spontaneous drive behind the activity. He was an obsessive drawer all his life, as he wrote to his father: '[...] there is the strong instinct in me which I cannot analyse to draw and describe the things I love — not for reputation, nor for the good of others, nor for my own advantage, but a sort of instinct like that for eating or drinking' (10. xxvi). His first drawing master, Charles Runciman, discontinued the pen-and-ink drawing and taught him how to use pencil and watercolour sketching, giving him exercises in perspective and encouraging 'a swiftness and facility of hand' (35.77), though Ruskin occasionally resumed the use of the pen. Some reworking of actual topography was integral to the practices of the Picturesque employed by Runciman

37 The history of this poem was first discovered by James Dearden, in 'John Ruskin's First Published Work', *Book Collector*, 42 (Summer 1994), 299–300.

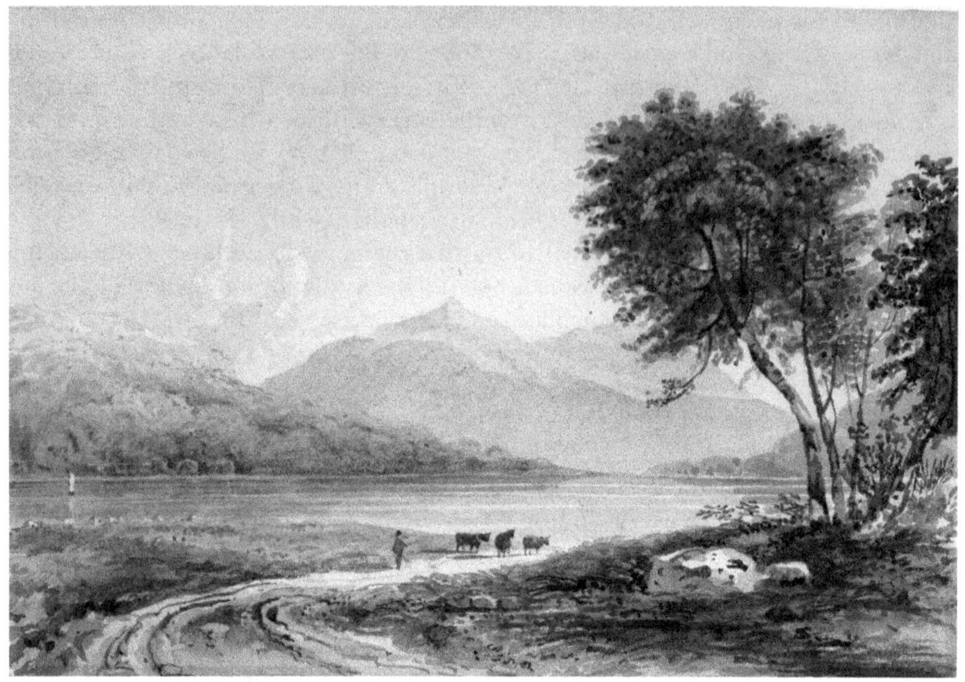

FIG. 2. John Ruskin, *Loch Achray and Ben Venue*, 1834–35. Watercolour.
By permission of the Ruskin Foundation (Ruskin Library, Lancaster University).

and subsequent drawing masters working in that dominant vogue, which had been introduced by French drawing masters working in England from the 1760s and thereafter became popularised by William Gilpin's manuals. His own fundamental penchant, however, was to remain for the reproduction of what he actually saw: 'I never saw any boy's work in my life showing such little original facility, or grasp of memory. I could literally draw nothing, not a cat, not a mouse, not a boat, not a bush, "out of my head" [...]' (35.75).

Next of Ruskin's formal masters, from 1834 to 1835, was Anthony Vandyke Copley Fielding, the inaugural President of the Old Water-colour Society. Ruskin's father had himself imitated Fielding in a painting of Conway Castle, and he had begun his private collection with the purchase of Fielding's *Between King's House and Inveroran, Argyllshire* in 1832, followed by a sea piece in 1833. Ruskin honours him as 'the simplest of painters, without a vestige of romance, but the purest love of sunshine and the constant hills' (35.213). His '[f]aithful and simple rendering of nature' (3.196), however, were based on the ready-made conventions of picturesque watercolour painting which in a series of lessons he first imparted to the fifteen-year-old, as Ruskin recalls:

> And thus the proposed six lessons in Newman Street ran on into perhaps eight or nine, during which Copley Fielding taught me to wash colour smoothly in successive tints, to shade cobalt through pink madder into yellow ochre for skies, to use a broken scraggy touch for the tops of mountains, to represent calm lakes by broad strips of shade with lines of light between them [...] to

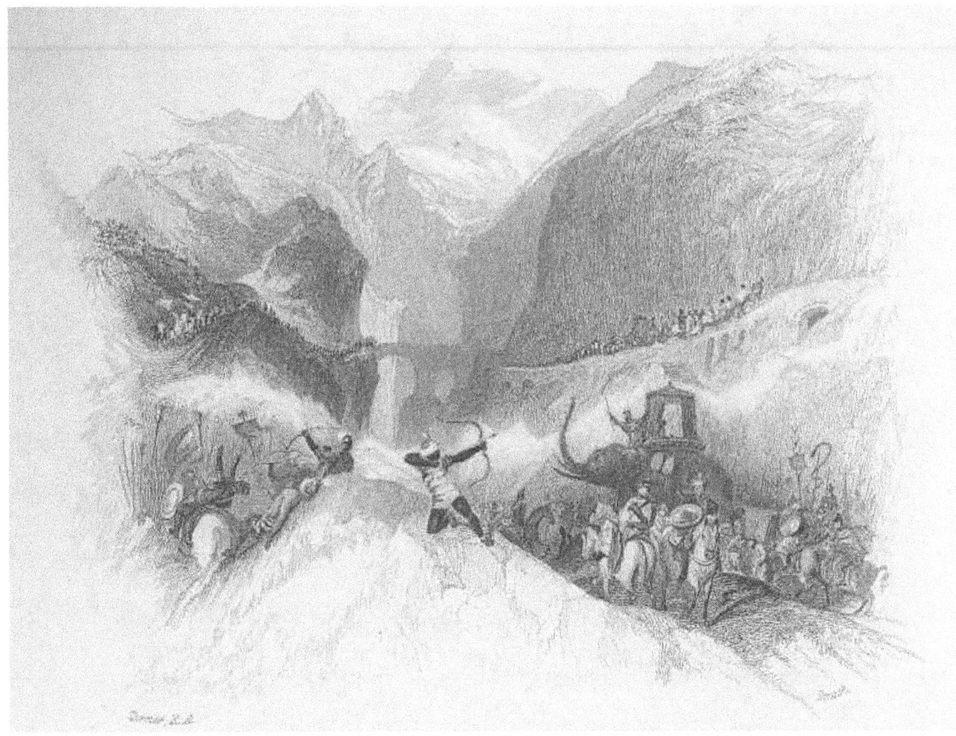

FIG. 3. J. M. W. Turner, *Hannibal Crossing the Alps*. Engraved by W. R. Smith. From Samuel Rogers, *Italy* (London: Printed for T. Cadell and E. Moxon, 1830), p. 29. Private copy.

> produce dark clouds and rain with twelve or twenty successive washes, and to crumble burnt umber with a dry brush for foliage and foreground. With these instructions, I succeeded in copying a drawing which Fielding made before me, some twelve inches by nine, of Ben Venue and the Trossachs, with brown cows standing in Loch Achray [...] (215–16). (Fig. 2)

Though he welcomed the new facility of these studio-based formulas, he gradually came to appreciate the limitations of what he later regarded as mechanical methods, and the point came when his frustrated attempts to imitate his master seemed anyway misplaced:

> I saw that my washes, however careful and multitudinous, did not in the end look as smooth as Fielding's, and that my crumblings of burnt umber became uninteresting after a certain number of repetitions. With still greater discouragement, I perceived the Fielding processes to be inapplicable to the Alps. My scraggy touches did not to my satisfaction represent the aiguilles, nor my ruled lines of shade, the Lake of Geneva. (35.216)

At the same time he was making more particularised geological and architectural sketches from the age of fourteen, some of which turned into woodcut illustrations for scientific articles and for *The Poetry of Architecture* (1837–38).

More inspiring for Ruskin was the effect of his first exposure to '[h]is real masters

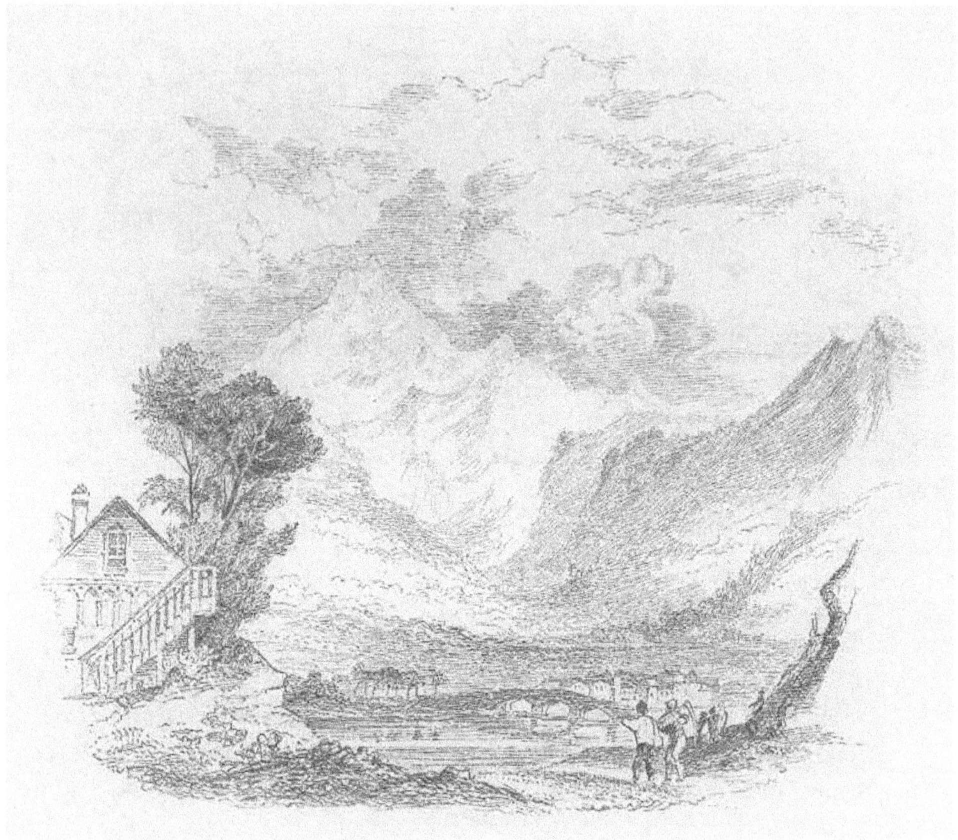

FIG. 4. John Ruskin, *The Jungfrau from Interlaken* (1833). Photogravure of pen drawing. From *The Poems of John Ruskin*, ed. by W. G. Collingwood, 2 vols (Orpington and London: George Allen, 1891), vol. 1, facing p. 140. Private copy.

[...] Turner and Prout and Roberts',[38] especially in copying their engraved and lithographed works. Ruskin seems to have seen watercolours displayed by Turner's publisher, Charles Heath, in the Egyptian Hall, Piccadilly, in 1829,[39] and he may have seen a Turner oil in a private collection on the Isle of Wight in the early 1830s, but the original major impact came from Turner's watercolour drawings for half the steel engraved illustrations for Rogers's *Italy*, when Ruskin was thirteen in 1832, which Ruskin imitated meticulously in pencil (see Figures 3 and 4).

He confirmed his continuing masters during these years in *Praeterita*: '[...] still, for a year or two longer, I persevered in the study of Turner engravings only, and the use of Copley Fielding's method for such efforts at colour as I made on the vac-

38 W. G. Collingwood, *The Art Teaching of John Ruskin* (London: Percival and Co., 1891), p. 6.

39 See the handlist in the Ruskin Library, Lancaster University. These drawings were intended for the *England and Wales* series, the first three parts of which were engraved and published in 1827 and 1829. Sixty engravings were published in 1832, and another exhibition was held in 1833. Turner had produced over one hundred drawings when Longman collected ninety-six for two volumes published in 1838.

ation journeys during Oxford days' (35.218), and probably also for a watercolour of *Mount Pilatus* of 1835.[40] His appreciation of Turner's truthfulness to the material world was to find its first rapturous defence in his unpublished letter to the editor, *Reply to Blackwood*, of 1836 and was to effloresce in the first volume of *Modern Painters* (1843).

The Interdisciplinary Gaze

The Ruskins found themselves in the midst of evolving tourist practices. What distinguished their interests was the grooming of their son's natural precocity. In his autobiography Ruskin relished the recollection that at the age of five he 'was sending for [his] "second volumes" to the circulating library' (35.23). By 1837 John James was to position his son and heir as a Gentleman Commoner among the young aristocrats of Christ Church College, Oxford, destined to fulfil his parent's unbounded aspirations for him to become any kind of leading establishment figure: 'That I should [...] marry Lady Clara Vere de Vere; write poetry good as Byron's, only pious; preach sermons as good as Bossuet's, only Protestant; be made, at forty, Bishop of Winchester, and at fifty, Primate of England' (35.185). He himself conceived a more focused ambition to become President of the Geological Society, having begun to study rocks in Derbyshire at the age of ten 'with indescribable rapture' (35.75). As a boy he passed days in the British Museum, checking their mineral specimens against the descriptions in his copy of Robert Jameson's *A System of Mineralogy* (1821). Geological field trips accompanied more regular visits to historical sites and buildings. British cathedrals, castles, monasteries and great houses, especially those with picture galleries, were the staple programme, which the continental excursions extended, so that, as Ruskin wrote, he 'gathered curiously extensive knowledge, both of art and natural scenery' (35.33). John James actively organised the schedule, allowing 'unstinted time' to the search for interesting architectural remains, though significantly neither he nor Margaret was strong on historical detail: 'neither [...] could tell me enough history to make the buildings authoritatively interesting', complained Ruskin, so that he tended 'to animate them with romance in my own fashion' and to take them in visually and naively as 'a pleasant amazement [...] and panoramic apocalypse of a lovely world' (28.391). It was a demanding but fulfilling schedule, so that when Ruskin came to look back on the make-up of these studious vacations in 1875, he considered 'the tenour of [his] life happy, and the modes of [his] education, on the whole, salutary' (28.391).

The non-academic knowledge and talents his parents promoted were indeed liberalising in the comprehensive manner of the gentleman amateur. His pre-specialist but intense scrutinies of the natural world were held together holistically by an Evangelical discourse of natural theology which viewed the world as a revelation of divine creation, and were combined with a high degree of moral earnestness. John James had mapped out a grandiose mission for his ten-year old son:

> You are blessed with a fine Capacity & even Genius & you owe it as a duty to the author of your Being & the giver of your Talents to cultivate your powers & to use them in his Service and for the benefit of your fellow Creatures.

40 See below, p. 184.

> You may be doomed to enlighten a People by your Wisdom & to adorn an age by your Learning.[41]

Margaret, who supervised daily Bible reading as part of her programme to prepare him to become a clergyman, exacted a high degree of workfulness and was resolved to extract every benefit from their excursions. 'I have seen my own mother travel', Ruskin wrote, 'from sunrise to sunset, in a summer's day, without once leaning back in the carriage' (27.609). His parents were in effect conscientiously but unconsciously preparing him admirably for his as yet undefined role of cultural critic, and their travels were providing the requisite medium for his various interests and fields of knowledge to co-exist and interplay in a richly productive solution.

Historically, he occupied the position of a knowledge *totum*, before the disciplines had fragmented into professional disciplines. In the first part of his fragmentary novella of this tour, *Chronicles of St. Bernard*, 'A Night at Le Hospice', he satirises the alienated specialisms of the geologist and picturesque painter whose pedantic categorisations and techniques ridiculously miss an integrated response to nature. For example, he describes the artist's obliviousness of material reality in the manner of Thomas Rowlandson's caricature of 'Dr Syntax Tumbling into the Water', illustrating William Combe's *Tour of Dr Syntax in Search of The Picturesque* (1809) (Fig. 5):

> [...] the artist, who was just remarking to me that the landscape, though not exactly picturesque, was one well adapted for trying experiments of effect on, or, as he technically expressed it, "for tumbling about in," exemplified the truth of his opinion by slipping his foot and falling on hands and knees on a smooth, wet, round block of this foreground, as he called it. The geologist came up at the instant. "Good example of aqueous denudation and arrosion, that," said he, as the artist rose.[42]

He also pokes fun at his own tendency to detached poeticising.

More or less spontaneously, in his early records Ruskin was compiling the private archive that would in the course of time develop into pointedly planned research notebooks, while at the same time he was establishing key sites and terrains as touchstones for his religious, social and cultural teachings. It was to be a continuous process until, at the opening of his major work on geology, *Deucalion: Collected Studies of the Lapse of Waves and the Life of Stones* (1879), he wrote: 'I begin to ask myself, with somewhat pressing arithmetic, how much time is likely to be left to me, at the age of fifty-six, to complete the various designs for which, until past fifty, I was merely collecting materials' (26.95–96). The variety of literary genres and visual media representing his experience of art, architecture, landscape and scientific observations were already contributing to his holistic perception of nature and society which would have to accommodate the contradictory but interlinked perspectives which in later life he memorably referred to as 'polygonal' (16.187).

In 1858 he experienced an important 'un-conversion', 'an end to [his] "Mother-Law" of Protestantism' (29.90), deprecating the Evangelical discourse in which all the forms of his curiosity and studies from childhood had swum. But although his religious sense passed through several reformulations thereafter, he never relegated

41 *Ruskin Family Letters*, I, 209.

42 See below, p. 267.

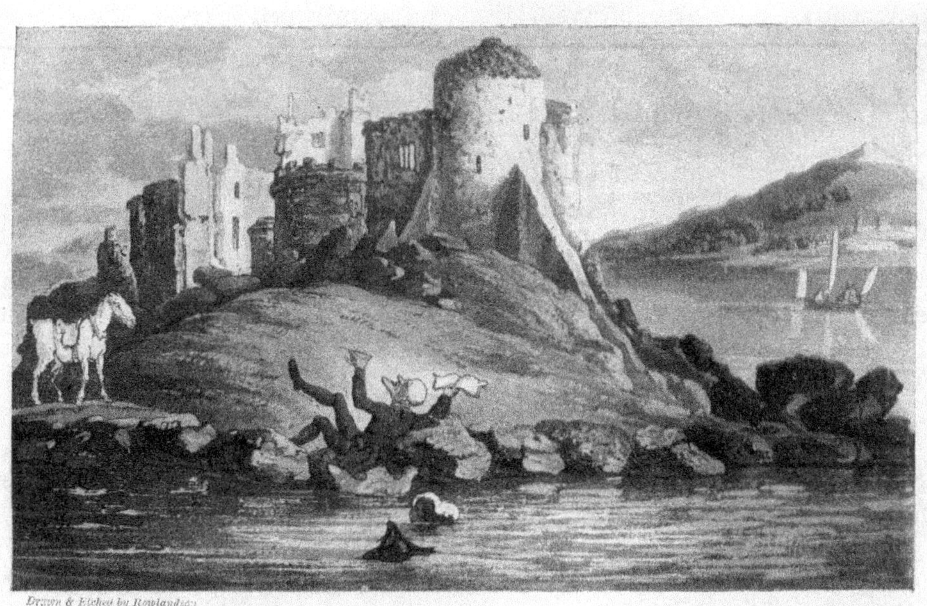

FIG. 5. Thomas Rowlandson, *Dr Syntax Tumbling into the Water.* From *The Tour of Doctor Syntax in Search of the Picturesque. A Poem* (London: Methuen, 1903), facing p. 68. Private copy.

his belief in the design of creation and the moral laws which inhered in it. As his preoccupations widened, from art and science, to architecture, to history and social criticism, they became layered in a cumulative process of interpretation which constituted a new and comprehensive practice of cultural criticism. Throughout its philosophical and ideological variations, it never lost touch at some point with an underpinning Christian world-view which he located most powerfully in the Middle Ages and feared was radically under threat by the industrialised capitalism of his own day.

On another level, all his enquiries served to orchestrate a journey of self-discovery which he narrates in his ultimate work, the autobiography *Praeterita*, 'Outlines of Scenes and Thoughts Perhaps Worthy of Memory in My Past Life'. There he shows how all his scattered experiences were *bound and blended together* by a pattern of recurrent destinations — symbols of a personal geography simplifying to the series of place-names which head most chapters: Schaffhausen and Milan, The Col de la Faucille, Roslyn Chapel, L'Hotel du Mont Blanc, etc. Such places stand for formative moments, when an actual scene becomes, at least temporarily, a metaphor for a state of realised selfhood. Ruskin shapes and is shaped by a structure of change and continuity attached to sites and scenes — travelling to the same places yet seeing more and different meanings in them over time, or indeed to different places and finding the same meanings — so that, as Elizabeth Helsinger writes, his 'constant traveling is never progress: it is the means by which he revisits the territory of a visually extended self.'[43]

Access to a vaster and richer cultural being was literally an eye-opening process. Again and again he notes his first self-enhancing sights: 'in the eastern light I well remember watching the line of the Black Forest hills enlarge and rise, as we crossed the plain of the Rhine. "Gates of the Hills" [Ruskin's title for Turner's *Pass of Faido*]; opening for me to a new life' (35.113), and the sensation of self-expansion over a widening visual field impelled his non-stop mobility for more than sixty years. Ultimately, his revisited destinations become for him symbols of unending self-augmentation. It is entirely appropriate that Ruskin named the three-volume collection of all his minor pieces, issued in 1885, *On the Old Road*, in allusion to what had been the recurrent map of his continental travels, 'from Calais to Dijon, Geneva and the Alps, and thence into northern Italy.'[44] In so doing, he made it a metaphor — though one retaining material reference — for the principle of coherence, his entire imaginative life, which bound together works produced throughout his writing career.

The interrelation between the visual and the word is core to the Ruskinian vision from the start. Underpinning the whole enterprise was an inchoate theory and practice of illustration relying on the intellectual use of the term 'illustration' as 'explaining', or serving to clarify. Ruskin's book illustrations are specifically designed to shed light on the inherent laws, or Truth, of nature, which never entirely loses the trace of a pre-evolutionary sense of deist design coupled with an evangelical reading of Biblical typology. Because of his founding belief in Natural Theology — seeing the material world itself as, in Aquinas's term, God's created Second Book, the natural world for Ruskin is already pre-mediated, or textualised. In that way, for him nature itself has commenced the process of mediation, and all intellectual endeavour and cultural creativity of the artist or scientist or critic is, from Ruskin's viewpoint, a collaborative project of 'illustration', seen as a belated attempt at re-mediation and interpretation in which the written and visual components are similarly engaged.

Ruskin's central role as an art critic made him a specialist in seeing. He came to judge that his parents' supervisory regime at home in his early years had restricted his field of visual stimulus, thereby helping to produce his exceptional 'thirst for visible fact', and developing 'that patience in looking, and precision in feeling, which afterwards, with due industry, formed [his] analytic power' (35.51). For him the primary medium is the visual, because, from his empiricist perspective, it is the hinge between sensation and idea, the material and the intellectual. All his journals and notebooks 'form a crucial nexus between [his] artistic philosophies, his social teachings and his personal experience',[45] containing the mixed media of notes, descriptions, drawings and sketches, as his finished works of art and

43 Elizabeth Helsinger, 'The Structure of Ruskin's *Praeterita*', in *Approaches to Victorian Autobiography*, ed. by George P. Landow (Athens: Ohio University Press, 1979), pp. 87–108 (p. 88).

44 Introduction, *Praeterita and Dilecta*, ed. by Tim Hilton, Everyman Library (New York: Alfred A. Knopf, 2005), p. xix.

45 Anne-Marie Millim, *The Victorian Diary: Authorship and Emotional Labour* (Farnham and Burlington, VT: Ashgate, 2013), p. 111.

architectural criticism are illustrated with prints which are an integral part, indeed often the clearest expression, of their purpose. John Dixon Hunt writes about Ruskin's 'hesitations about the primacy of the visual over [...] the joint endeavours of the visual and verbal tout simple', and points out how his adult letters 'will often switch from sentence to sketch and back again to complete his meaning'.[46] In *Praeterita* Ruskin even remarks on the advantages in his family's early travels of not understanding foreign languages so that they could take in more of their new experiences directly, 'and even in my own land, the things in which I have been least deceived are those which I have learned as their Spectator' (35.119).

Drawing, for example, provided him with, in his words, 'a power of notation and description greater in most instances than that of words' (16.143). His practice provides a constant interrogation of the possibilities of ekphrasis which evolved from the kind of awarenesses he puzzled over in the 1835 *Diary*:

> The opening to Airolo is beautiful, but what is the use of describing it. There were villages and fields, rocks and torrents, and grassy mountains and snow covered Alps, and we have had all that before. Objects on paper are always the same, it is by the disposition of them that nature gives variety. and therefore you can say no more than that — the opening to Airolo is beautiful.[47]

Words alone cannot represent the visual manifold, yet the limitation is precisely what spurs his rhetorical exuberances. He makes repeated statements like that in the third volume of *Modern Painters*: 'To see clearly is poetry, prophecy, and religion, — all in one' (5.333). For what he calls in the second volume of *Modern Painters*, 'The Theoretic Faculty', the mind's primary mode of contemplation, the eye provides a direct connection 'with the moral perception and appreciation of ideas of beauty' (4.35). Then, secondarily, the imagination is responsible for rearranging, in his words, 'the ideas it has received from external nature', performing 'the operations [...] which become in their turn objects of the theoretic faculty to other minds' (4.36). Ruskin writes that both primary and secondary modes offer what he defines as a 'true place for the intellectual lens and moral retina, by which, and on which, our informing thoughts are concentrated and represented' (36.4). The dialectic between the material and the moral is pictured as an eye, as Ruskin later elaborated in a lecture of 1877: '"Intellectual lens, and moral retina" — the lens faithfully and far collecting, the retina faithfully and inwardly receiving' (22.513), visual sensations becoming part of, and one with, the viewer's moral nature. His 'vision' is a moot term, but always visually grounded: 'All great men see what they paint before they paint it, — see it in a perfectly passive manner, — cannot help seeing it if they would; whether in their mind's eye, or in bodily fact, does not matter' (5.114).

A huge prospect was inflected in his youthful preoccupation with observation which was common to each of his practices. From his early scientific papers it is apparent that Ruskin was already scrutinising natural objects with a similar attentiveness to that he brought to Turner's vignettes. Ruskin could not understand why his writings on art attracted so much more attention than those on geology,

46 John Dixon Hunt, '*Ut pictura poesis*, the Picturesque, and John Ruskin', *MLN*, 93 (Dec. 1978), 794–818 (p. 803).

47 See below, p. 83.

'though precisely the same faculties of eye and mind are concerned in the analysis of natural and pictorial forms' (26.386). His scientific examinations of 'the native rock' (1.47) were guided by pre-specialist discourses of naturalism which relied on detailed topographical description, before the Geological Society began to publish its scholarly *Transactions*, and, overall, a religious insistence on Truth, the persistence of absolute values.

The word 'landscape' is, of course, ambiguous. It means either a real natural scene *or* a visual representation of one, and Ruskin's theories on art point up the peculiar continuities between the material actuality and representations of it. For him, visual representation looks both ways — back to the original sensory perception, and forward to the communication of Ruskin's unfolding interpretation. It is crucial to recognise the realist claim basic to Ruskin's vision which guarantees its promise to open communal access to all his readers who may share it, as seers, prior to intellectual elaboration. As long as naturalism lies at its base, art also is capable of providing a *lingua franca*, as in medieval religious decoration, for all levels of society, even the illiterate, just as it made possible Ruskin's own ready assimilation of international cultural phenomena. His assimilation of Romantic organicism, with its unalienated progression from nature to culture, was of a piece. Prout's Picturesque, for example, featuring crumbling domestic and historical buildings, merged easily with Wordsworthian naturalism, the sense of natural scenery blending with human constructions. It was a perception he had derived from Wordsworth's poetry reinforced by the 1835 edition of Wordsworth's *Guide to the Lakes*:

> These humble dwellings remind the contemplative spectator of a production of Nature, and may (using a strong expression) rather be said to have grown than to have been erected; the houses rise by an instinct of their own, out of the native rock.[48]

1835: Written Records and Drawings

In 1835, Ruskin equipped himself thoroughly and seriously by packing an array of equipment: 'I shaded in cobalt a "cyanometer" to measure the blue of the sky with; bought a ruled notebook for geological observations, and a large quarto for architectural sketches, with square rule and foot-rule ingeniously fastened outside' (35.152). He determined that 'the events and sentiments of this journey should be described in a poetic diary 'in the style of *Don Juan*, artfully combined with that of *Childe Harold*' (35.152), a development from his stylistic dependence on Rogers in 1833, and attracted by Byron's rhythm, 'Its natural flow in almost prosaic simplicity and tranquillity [...] in opposition alike to the symmetrical clauses of Pope's logical metre, and to the balanced strophes of classic and Hebrew verse' (35.151). In 'Verse Journal, A Tour Through France' two cantos of stanzas in a variant form of the Elizabethan sonnet were indeed completed, probably during the tour, taking him as far as Chamonix, 'where [he] broke down, finding that [he] had exhausted on the Jura all the descriptive terms at [his] disposal, and that none were left for the Alps'

48 William Wordsworth, *Guide to the Lakes*, ed. by Ernest de Selincourt (Oxford: Oxford University Press, 1977), p. 62. See Hanley, *Ruskin's Romantic Tours*, pp. 191–93.

(35.152). He also produced two verse letters: to his friend, Richard Fall (covering stops from Paris to Thun), and to a schoolfriend, Willougby Jones (a discursive summary from the St Bernard Pass to Venice).

To the playfully emulative roles of poet and artist was added, more seriously, that of geologist, and his notes became the basis of five scholarly papers for the *Magazine of Natural History*, owned and edited by John Claudius Loudon, in 1834 and 1836. His readings in the Romantic poets were mixed with his study of Horace Bénédict de Saussure's *Voyages dans les Alpes*, William Brockedon's Illustrations of the *Passes of the Alps*, issued in twelve parts between 1827 and 1829, and Robert Jameson's *A System of Mineralogy* (1804).

Other literary outcomes of this tour included a satirical dramatic sketch, *The Ascent of the St. Bernard*, which humorously sends up some of the tourists he and his family encountered at the hospice, including bad-tempered English guests and portraits of himself and his family and their harassed courier. The representation of his nurse is modelled on Sheridan's Mrs Malaprop. He also produced a fragmentary novella after Scott, *Chronicles of St. Bernard*, the first part of which , 'A Night at Le Hospice', is a detailed description of the monastic regime, tourist facilities, the environs, and the clientele, involving a shrewd and extended survey of the attitudes of his fellow visitors, a young Oxonian, English and other stereotypical Europeans, as well as professional experts who are blinkered by their narrow specialisms (ironically representing Ruskin's own interests). There are also some impressively detailed landscape descriptions and powerfully rhetorical evocations of his 'sensual gratification of the mind'[49] in attending mass and the Morgue. The second part, 'Valasquez, the Novice', also describes the contemporaneous tourists to Venice and Ruskin's first sustained representation of the city and the approach by sea.

The 1835 journal was the first of the diaries he was to keep during the rest of his life: as Hilton notes, it was here that Ruskin started 'a practice he continued for the next fifty-four years, until he could write no longer'.[50] It is an important document in the history of nineteenth-century cultural tourism, since it occupies a crucial position in the development and focusing of the interests and methods which were to find expression ultimately in his best known and variously influential publications.

It does not consciously conform to any literary genre, but is a diary-journal in the sense of being arranged by date, and its primary purpose is not one of self-expression, which is rather the object of the verse works, but recording observations. In the overall archive of his researches which the series of notebooks which he compiled over many years constitutes, it represents a distinct moment of definition. The miscellaneous curiosity he recorded in different media, clearly remarkable for its precocity, calls for serious scholarly attention, because the manuscript of this notebook is remarkable for being the only integral travel journal which Ruskin composed throughout his writing career, with the exception of the verse journal of 1830. It belongs to the sequence of records which became research aids and eclectic registers of facts, figures and discontinuous descriptions

49 See below, p. 266.
50 *John Ruskin: The Early Years*, p. 33.

— a range of treatment which, taken together, effectively created the paradigm for Ruskin's future practices of cultural tourism, with its multi-media representation of stratified scientific, evangelical, historical and aesthetical discourses. It established his composite Romantic, picturesque and scientific gaze which was sustained and elaborated throughout his future travels. It is factual in approach, though it adopts a first-person description for the first time in Ruskin's writings, and is largely preoccupied with geological, mineralogical and meteorological observations, which occasionally merge into the aesthetics of the picturesque and sublime, descriptions of some cultural sites, and rare personal comments, less concerned with his private feelings than the letters.

Recurrently he was to refer back to this tour which had first drawn him to crucial French sites of Gothic architecture, especially Abbeville and Rouen, and evoked the initial impact on him of Venice, prompting his first architectural descriptions and drawings. Perhaps it was influenced by his father's journal of 1833, to which he refers in *Dilecta* (1900), where he quotes it to illustrate his father's sang-froid at the religious insecurities of the time and his accounting 'with mercantile precision of entry day by day' (35.390) their first sight of Switzerland. John James continued in that style for his contemporary notebook version of the family's travels in 1835. The diary was eventually laid aside from late September, long in advance of the tour's termination in December, possibly to give priority to completing the forthcoming poetical publications for *Friendship's Offering*.

The mixed media ranged from verse to statistical data, with constant sketching and drawing. At this stage, Ruskin was separately assembling his various approaches to what became his amalgamated interdisciplinary method, while the verse which was designed as a Byronic pastiche expresses his personal responses and historical imagination. There are also a few lyrical poems from the tour which speak for his evangelical adaptation of Wordsworth's nature poetry. To add to his literary versatility, Ruskin penned a satirical dramatic sketch, *The Ascent of the St. Bernard*. The drawings constitute the foundation of his future draughtsmanship and architectural illustration, imitated from Turner's vignettes in Rogers's *Italy*,[51] and the lithographs in Prout's *Sketches in Flanders and Germany*, 1833.

All Ruskin's then reigning influences were to some extent in evidence in the pen-and ink-works which he produced each evening. He was now able to view the actual scene of Lake Como which Turner had depicted in Italy, but, as W. G. Collingwood comments, 'Turner was forgotten in the attempt to be Prout.'[52] In a verse letter to John James, Ruskin projected that he would emulate the styles of Copley Fielding's water colours and Prout's 'slight but grand' paintings in the Royal Academy of Arts on the forthcoming summer tour. It was Prout's architectural *Sketches in Flanders and Germany*, specialising in depicting continental towns, which was the dominant influence on Ruskin's draughtsmanship up to the later 1830s when he started to abandon Prout's technique of 'an acicular precision of sharp black line ending with a dot' as reductive of architectural detail and 'inconsistent with repose and consistency of flow in contour' (35.623) which he was later to discover in

51 Rogers's *Poems* (1834), of which Ruskin owned a copy inscribed to him by the author, also included the important engraved vignette from Turner, *The Alps at Daybreak*.

52 Ruskin Relics (London: Isbister and Co., 1903), p. 123.

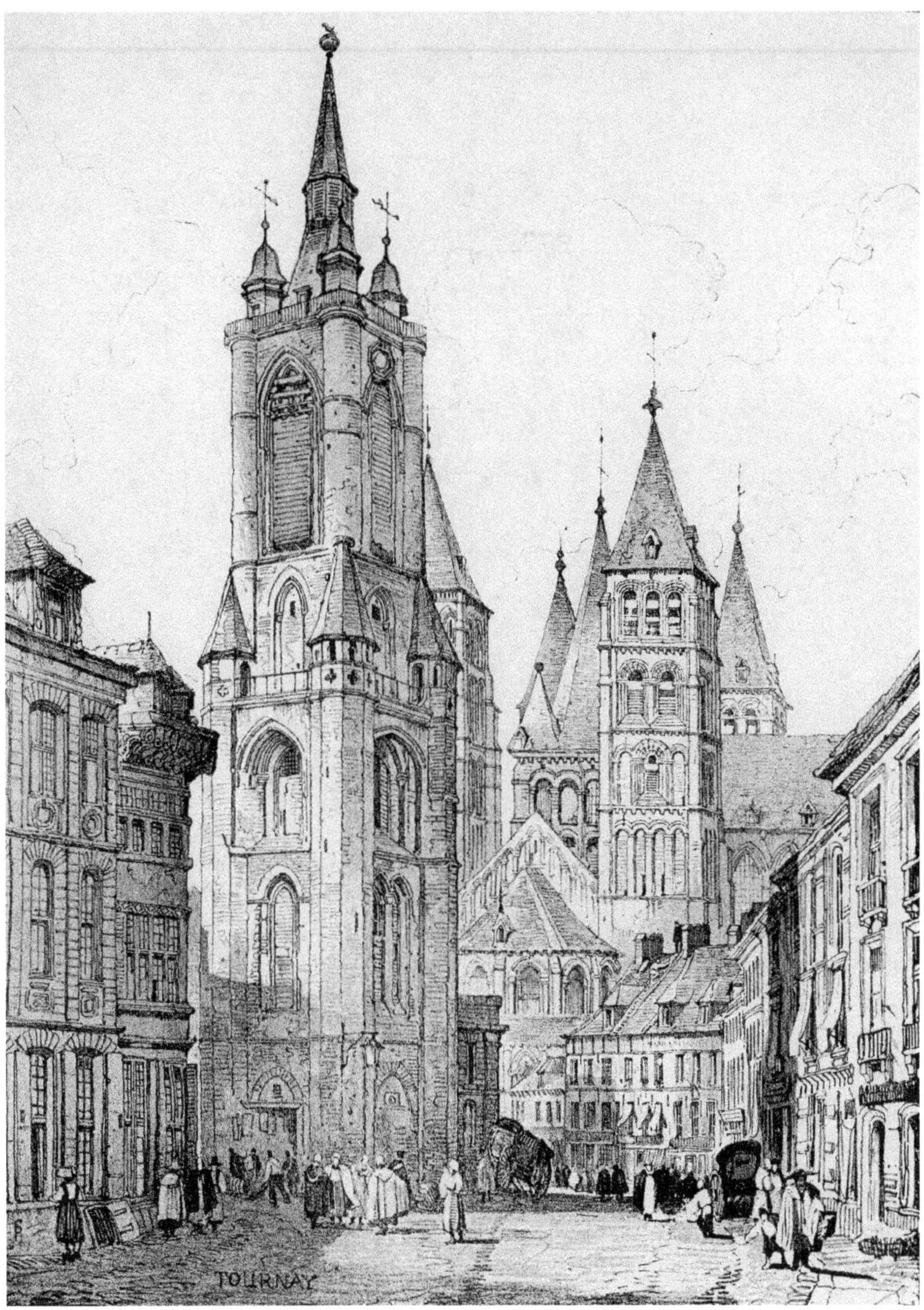

FIG. 6. Samuel Prout, *Tournai*. From *Facsimiles of Sketches Made in Flanders and Germany and Drawn on Stone by Samuel Prout F.S.A.* (London: C. Hullmandel's lithography, 1833). Private copy.

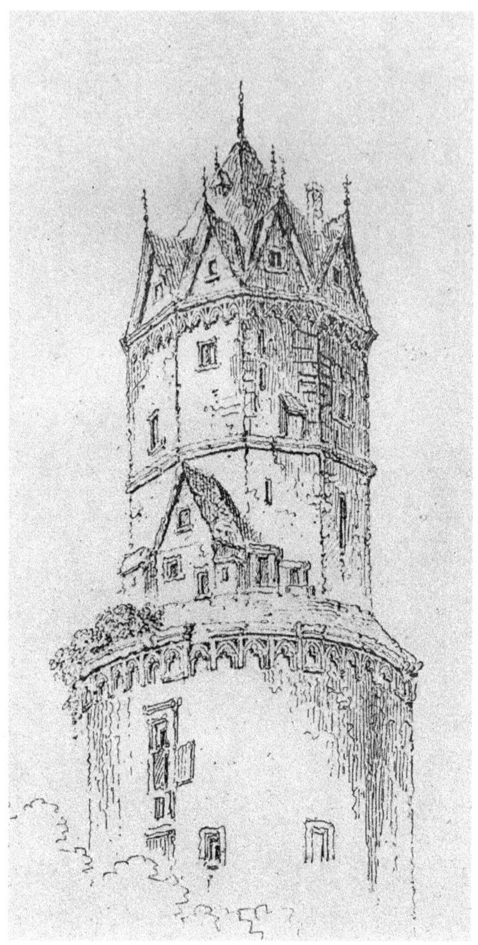

FIG. 7. John Ruskin, *Watch-Tower at Andernach* (1833). Photogravure of detail of a pen drawing. From *The Poems of John Ruskin*, ed. by W. G. Collingwood, 2 vols (Orpington and London: George Allen, 1891), vol. 1, facing p. 128. Private copy.

David Roberts's lithographic *Sketches in Egypt and the Holy Land* (1840).[53] In his first sketch book from the 1833 Continental tour he began to imitate Prout's facsimile plates (Figs 6 and 7) which are the models for the drawings of 1835. The line-and-dot Proutish style is represented by numerous drawings which Collingwood sees as also still overdetermined by 'the Cruikshank "style" of placing lines, without previously feeling about for them'.[54] They were both made 'on the spot with soft pencil upon grey paper' and later re-drawn 'in pen upon grey paper, touched with white'.[55] The latter were the majority, on small sheets, since, Paul Walton notes, '[h]e was still thinking of his art as an imitation of engraved travel illustrations, and did not yet have the confidence to loosen his touch and use the larger pages

53 Roberts's influence can most definitely be seen by Ruskin's *View of Oxford*, *c.* 1838.

54 W. G. Collingwood, *The Poems of John Ruskin*, 2 vols (Orpington and London: George Allen, 1891), vol. 1, p. vii.

55 Ibid.

characteristic of the newer, lithographed, books of the kind produced by Prout'; but his many drawings and sketches now revealed what Walton describes as 'a unity of style that reveals a much greater maturity of purpose and method than the work of 1833', and in particular individual features were emerging at this time which Walton characterises as

> [...] a liking for powerful effects of spatial recession, created by means of a wide angle of vision [...] a strong tension between receding diagonal accents and soaring vertical lines [...] [an] interest in the expressive possibilities of exaggerated perspective [...] [departing] from the more classical spatial balance of models like Prout and Fielding in favour of the dynamic and dramatic space that he had discovered at the heart of Turner's illustrations for Rogers's *Italy*.[56]

Turner had changed from copper-plate to steel engraving for the *Italy* series to explore the possibilities that had been created by this newly advanced medium, in which the art of the engravers had been called upon to match Turner's painterly effects (which they in turn encouraged). Turner's contribution to the evolution of the vignette took the device from a largely ornamental function to become 'in miniature the "elevated pastoral" and the "historical landscape" of the great canvases',[57] and for Ruskin they were a revelation that trained his eye in both observing exact natural effects and ways of representing them. He was similarly attentive to Prout's lithographic prints in *Sketches*. Referring to the period from 1835 to 1840, he explained the literalistic nature and background of his aims in his outline drawings of the time:

> First, I had the sense not to go on making bad drawings in colour, though occasionally by way of indulgence — or for fame in Cornhill — doing a vignette in imitation of Turner. And in the pencil work I retreated upon, did honestly try to carry away as much fact as I could, though I saw my way to very little. And here, be it observed in passing, that the method of outline drawing applied to landscape is an entirely modern scientific process, the landscape sketches of all early masters being merely notes of material to be immediately used in the backgrounds of pictures, and therefore merely painter's shorthand of fragments useful to him, each in his own manner. The idea of a mathematically accurate and attentive summary of the facts of an entire landscape or street view, for the sake of those facts, is essentially modern. Dutch in its origin — in the mere dulness of pleased imitations developed by the Early English water-colour school as preliminary to their attentive work, and explanatory of its rapid and too accidental work — it becomes afterwards a delight in itself, and pleasant insistence on the natures and forms of things, without proceeding to their realization. Turner and Prout perfected the system of it, and throughout their lives made ten outlines to one drawing — nine for their own sake. (35.624)

He had earlier described the dispassionate approach he sought in his own method of 'always working resignedly at the thing under my hand till I could do it, and looking exclusively at the thing before my eyes till I could see it' (35.217). His aim,

56 Paul H. Walton, *The Drawings of John Ruskin* (London: Oxford University Press, 1972), pp. 27–28. For Turner's illustrations, see the section 'Watercolours Related to Samuel Rogers's *Italy* c.1826–27' in the Tate Gallery's online research project, *J. M. W. Turner: Sketchbooks, Drawings and Watercolours*.

57 Jan Piggott, *Turner's Vignettes* (London: Tate Gallery Publications, 1993), p. 23.

as he was coming to view his skill in picture-making as increasingly subsidiary to his study of the power of art to reveal the created world, was simply to record:

> [...] it entirely refuses emotion. The work must be done with the patience of an accountant, and records only the realities of the scene — not the effects on them. Prout's towns are all in forenoon sunshine, mine in tranquil shade — Turner's outlined as it were with camera-lucida. (35.624)

The scenes which he encountered in 1835 were already invested with historical evocation derived from Rogers and Byron. Personal feelings, though subdued, did find some outlet. In 1836 he began to compose the dramatic tragedy of *Marcolini*, the prose narrative of which he had encountered in Rogers's *Italy*, which mixes Byron with Shakespeare, to give expression to his first infatuation with Adèle Domecq, the daughter of his father's partner, which became a grand distraction over the next years. She figures as Ada in the fragmentary novella, *Chronicles of St. Bernard*. Turning to love poetry after the 1835 tour may have distracted him from completing the *Verse Journal, A Tour through France to Chamouni*.

Bibliography

Primary Works (John Ruskin)

The Works of John Ruskin [Library Edition], 39 vols, ed. by Edward Tyas Cook and Alexander Wedderburn (London: George Allen, 1903–12)

Friendship's Offering and Winter's Wreath: A Christmas and New Year's Present, for MDCCCXXXV (London: Smith, Elder and Co., 1835)

The Architectural Magazine and Journal ... Conducted by J. C. Loudon (London: Longman, Orme, Brown, Green, & Longmans, vol. IV, 1837)

The Architectural Magazine and Journal ... Conducted by J. C. Loudon (London: Longman, Orme, Brown, Green, & Longmans, vol. V, 1838)

Poems J.R. Collected 1850 (London: privately printed, 1850)

The Poems of John Ruskin, ed. by W. G. Collingwood, 2 vols (Orpington and London: George Allen, 1891)

The Poetry of Architecture, ed. by W. G. Collingwood (Sunnyside, Orpington: George Allen, 1893)

The Diaries of John Ruskin, 1848–1873, selected and ed. by Joan Evans and John Howard Whitehouse, 3 vols (Oxford: The Clarendon Press, 1956–59)

Iteriad; or Three Weeks Among the Lakes, ed. by James S. Dearden, Newcastle upon Tyne: Frank Graham, 1969)

The Ruskin Family Letters: The Correspondence of John James Ruskin, his Wife, and their Son John, 1801–1843, ed. by Van Akin Burd, 2 vols (Ithaca, NY, and London: Cornell University Press, 1973)

A Tour to the Lakes in Cumberland: John Ruskin's Diary for 1830, ed. by James Dearden (Aldershot: Scolar Press, 1990)

Primary Works (other authors)

BYRON, GEORGE GORDON, LORD, *Childe Harold's Pilgrimage, a Romaunt [Cantos 1 and 2]* (London: John Murray, 1812)

——, *Childe Harold's Pilgrimage. Canto the Third* (London: John Murray, 1816)

——, *Childe Harold's Pilgrimage. Canto the Fourth* (London: John Murray, 1818)

EBEL, J.-G., *Manuel du Voyageur en Suisse*, new edn (Paris: Audin, 1830–31)

PROUT, SAMUEL, *Sketches in Flanders and Germany: Facsimile of Studies Made in Flanders and Germany and Drawn on Stone by Samuel Prout, PSA, Painter in Water Colors in Ordinary to His Majesty* (London: C. Hullmandels, 1833)

ROGERS, SAMUEL, *Italy, A Poem* (London: T. Cadell, Jennings and Chaplin E. Moxon, 1830)

——, *Poems* (London: T. Cadell and E. Moxon, 1834)

SAUSSURE, HORACE BÉNÉDICT DE, *Voyages dans les Alpes: précédés d'un essai sur l'histoire naturelle des environs de Genève*, 4 vols (Neuchâtel–Geneva: Samuel Fauche, 1779–96)

WORDSWORTH, WILLIAM, *A Guide through the District of the Lakes in the North of England* (Kendal: Hudson and Nicholson; London: Longman and Co., Moxon, and Whittaker and Co., 1835) [Reprinted as *Guide to the Lakes*, ed. by Ernest de Selincourt (Oxford: Oxford University Press, 1977)]

Critical Works

ALEXANDER, CHRISTINE, 'Play and Apprenticeship', in *The Child Writer from Austen to Woolf*, ed. by Christine Alexander and Juliet McMaster (Cambridge: Cambridge University Press, 2005), pp. 31–50

BIRCH, DINAH, 'Fathers and Sons: Ruskin, John James Ruskin, and Turner', *Nineteenth-Century Contexts*, 18 (1994), 147–62

BLACK, JEREMY, *The British Abroad: The Grand Tour in the Eighteenth Century* (Stroud: Sutton, 1997)

BURD, VAN AIKIN, 'Ruskin's Testament of his Boyhood Faith: Sermons on the Pentateuch', in *New Approaches to Ruskin: Thirteen Essays*, ed. by Robert Hewison (London: Routledge and Kegan Paul, 1981), pp. 1–16

BUZARD, JAMES, *The Beaten Track: European Tourism, Literature and the Ways to Culture, 1899–1918* (Oxford: Oxford University Press, 1993)

CLEGG, JEANNE, *Ruskin and Venice* (London: Junction Books, 1981)

——, and PAUL TUCKER, *Ruskin and Tuscany* (Sheffield: Ruskin Gallery, Collection of the Guild of St George, in association with Lund Humphries, London, 1992)

COLLINGWOOD, W. G., *The Art Teaching of John Ruskin* (London: Percival and Co., 1891)

——, *The Life and Work of John Ruskin*, 2 vols (London: Methuen, 1893)

——, 'Ruskin's Drawings', in *Ruskin Relics* (London: Isbister and Co, 1903), pp. 119–32

——, 'The Old Road', in *Ruskin's Relics* (London: Isbister, 1903), pp. 45–62

COOK, E. T., *The Life of John Ruskin*, 2 vols (London: George Allen, 1912)

DEARDEN, JAMES S., *John Ruskin and the Alps*, The Fine Art Society, 8th March–5th April 1991 [Exhibition catalogue]

——, *The Library of John Ruskin* (Oxford: The Oxford Bibliographical Society, 2012)

DE ROBIEN, GILLES, *Ruskin — Turner: Dessins et Voyages en Picardie Romantique* (Amiens: Musée de Picardie, 2003) [Exhibition Catalogue]

GULLY, ANTHONY LACY, 'Sermons in Stone: Ruskin and Geology', in *John Ruskin and the Victorian Eye* (New York: Abrams/Phoenix Art Museum, 1993), pp. 159–83

HALE, J. R. (ed.), *The Italian Journal of Samuel Rogers: Edited with an Account of Rogers's Life and Travel in Italy in 1814–1821* (London: Faber and Faber, 1956)

HANLEY, KEITH, 'Ruskin's Holy Land', in *Ruskin's Struggle for Coherence: Self-Representation through Art, Place and Society*, ed. by Rachel Dickinson and Keith Hanley (Newcastle: Cambridge Scholars Press, 2006), pp. 52–76

——, *John Ruskin's Romantic Tours, 1837–1838: Travelling North* (Lewiston, NY, Queenston, and Lampeter: The Edwin Mellen Press, 2007)

——, and RACHEL DICKINSON, *Journeys of a Lifetime: Ruskin's Continental Tours*, The Ruskin Library, Lancaster University, 2008 [Exhibition Catalogue]

——, Introduction, *Ruskin, Venice and Nineteenth-Century Cultural Travel*, ed. by Keith Hanley and Emma Sdegno (Venice: Le Bricole, 2010)
——, and John K. Walton, *Constructing Cultural Tourism: John Ruskin and the Tourist Gaze* (Bristol: Channel View, 2010)
——, and Brian Maidment, *Persistent Ruskin: Studies in Influence, Assimilation and Effect* (Aldershot and Burlington, VT: Ashgate, 2013)
Hanson, David C., 'The Psychology of Fragmentation: A Bibliographic and Psychoanalytic Reconsideration of the Ruskin Juvenilia', *Text*, 10 (1997), 237–58
——, 'Self and Revision in Ruskin's Revaluations of Romanticism, 1830–1880', *Studies in Romanticism*, 39 (2000), 255–302
——, 'Precocity and the Economy of the Evangelical Self in John Ruskin's Juvenilia', *The Child Writer from Austen to Woolf*, ed. by Christine Alexander and Juliet McMaster (Cambridge: Cambridge University Press, 2005), pp. 200–21
Hayman, John, *John Ruskin and Switzerland* (Waterloo, Ont., Canada : Wilfrid Laurier University Press, 1990)
Heaford, Michael, 'Between Grand Tour and Tourism: British Travellers to Switzerland in a Period of Transition, 1814–1816', *The Journal of Transport History*, 276 (2006), 25–47
Helsinger, Elizabeth, 'The Structure of Ruskin's *Praeterita*', in *Approaches to Victorian Autobiography*, ed. by George P. Landow (Athens: Ohio University Press, 1979), pp. 87–108
Hibbert, Christopher, *The Grand Tour* (London: Thames Methuen, 1987)
Hilton, J. A., '"Sailing to Byzantium": Ruskin's Imaginary Travel to Greece', in *Ruskin, Venice and Nineteenth-Century Cultural Travel*, ed. by Keith Hanley and Emma Sdegno (Venice: Le Bricole, 2010), pp. 361–79
Hilton, Timothy, *John Ruskin: The Early Years* (New Haven, CT, and London: Yale University Press, 1983)
——, *John Ruskin: The Later Years* (New Haven, CT: Yale University Press, 2000)
—— (ed.), *Praeterita and Dilecta*, ed. and intro. by Tim Hilton, Everyman Library (New York: Alfred A. Knopf, 2005)
Hindley, Geoffrey, *Tourists, Travellers and Pilgrims* (London: Hutchinson, 1983)
Hudson, Roger, *The Grand Tour, 1592–1796* (London: The Folio Society, 1993)
Hunt, John Dixon, '*Ut pictura poesis*, the Picturesque, and John Ruskin', *MLN*, 93 (1978), 794–818
Links, J. G., *Venice* (London: Lutterworth Press, 1967)
——, *Travellers in Europe: Private Records of Journey by the Great and the Forgotten from Horace to Pepys* (London: The Bodley Head, 1980)
Millim, Anne-Marie, *The Victorian Diary: Authorship and Emotional Labour* (Farnham and Burlington, VT: Ashgate, 2013)
Newall, Christopher, 'Ruskin and the Art of Drawing', in *John Ruskin and the Victorian Eye*, ed. by Susan Casteras (New York: Harry N. Abrams, in association with Phoenix Art Museum, 1993), pp. 81–115
Osborne, Peter D., *Travelling Light: Photography, Travel and Visual Culture* (Manchester: Manchester University Press, 2000)
Parsons, Nicholas T., *Worth the Detour: A History of the Guidebook* (Stroud: Sutton, 2007)
Penny, Nicholas, *Ruskin's Drawings in the Ashmolean Museum* (Oxford: Ashmolean Museum, 1988)
Piggott, Jan, *Turner's Vignettes* (London: Tate Gallery Publications, 1993)
Plumb, J. H., 'The Grand Tour', in *Men and Places* (London: Cresset Press, 1963), pp. 67–79
Porter, Dennis, *Haunted Journeys: Desire and Transgression in European Travel Writing* (Princeton, NJ: Princeton University Press, 1991)
Quill, Sarah, *Ruskin's Venice: The Stones Revisited*, 2nd edn (London: Lund Humphries, 2015)

Ruskin on Rocks: Art, Mountains and Mineralogy (Sheffield: Millennium Galleries, 2006) [Exhibition Catalogue]
SALAZAR, NOEL B., 'Tourism Imaginaries: A Conceptual Approach', *The Annals of Tourism Research*, 39 (2012), 863–82
SIGAUX, GILBERT, *History of Tourism* (London: Leisure Arts, 1966)
SPEAR, JEFFREY L., 'Ruskin's Italy', *Browning Institute Studies: An Annual of Victorian Literary and Cultural History*, 12 (1984), 73–92
THOMPSON, F. M. L., *The Rise of Respectable Society: A Social History of Victorian Britain, 1830–1900* (London: Fontana Press, 1988)
TOWNER, JOHN, 'The Grand Tour: A Key Phase in the History of Tourism', *The Annals of Tourism Research*, 12 (1985), 297–333
TREASE, GEOFFREY, *The Grand Tour* (New York: Holt, Rinehart, and Winston, 1967)
UNRAU, JOHN, *Looking at Architecture with Ruskin* (London: Thames and Hudson, 1984)
URRY, JOHN, *The Tourist Gaze*, 2nd edition (London: Sage Publications, 2002)
WALTON, PAUL H., *The Drawings of John Ruskin* (London: Oxford University Press, 1972)
WHITTICK, ARNOLD, *Ruskin's Venice* (London: George Godwin, 1976)
WILDMAN, STEPHEN, and CYNTHIA GAMBLE, *'A Perpetual Paradise': Ruskin's Northern France*, exhibition catalogue, The Ruskin Library, University of Lancaster, 2002. [Exhibition Catalogue]

THE 1835 ITINERARY

June 2 to July 2

From **Canterbury (June 2)** to — Dover — Calais — Montreuil — Abbeville — at **Rouen (June 9–10)** to — St Germain — at **Paris (June 13–16)**. Then to Soissons — Rheims — Chalons-sur-Marne — at **Bar-le-Duc (June 20–21)** — at **Nancy (June 23–24)** — Épinal — Plombières — Vesoul — at **Dijon (June 26–28)**. Then to Poligny — Champagnole — Les Rousses —

July 2 to Sept. 18

At **Geneva (July 2–4)**. Then to Sallanches — **Chamonix (July 7–10)**. Then to **St. Martin (July 11–12)** — St. Gingolph — Martigny — over the **Great St. Bernard Pass (July 15)** — Aosta — at **Courmayeur (July 17–19)** — back to Aosta and over the **Great St. Bernard (July 21)** — Martigny — at **Vevey (July 24–27)** — Yverdon — Neuchâtel — Soleure — at **Basle (July 31–Aug. 2)** — Stein — at **Schaffhausen (Aug. 4–5)** — Constance — Winterthur — Zurich — at **Zug (Aug. 10–11)** — Altdorf — through the **St. Gothard (Aug. 13–14)** — at **Fluelen (Aug. 15–16)**, at **Lucerne (Aug. 17–18) — the Rigi (Aug. 19)** — Alpnach — at **Meiringen (Aug. 22–23)** — **the Grimsel Pass (Aug. 24–26)** — at **Meiringen (Aug. 27–28)** — at **Grindelwald (Aug. 29–30)** — Unterseen in Interlaken — at **Thun (Sept. 1–2)**. Then to Berne — Fribourg — at **Lausanne (Sept. 5–7)** — back to Vevay — Friburg — Berne — Morgenthal — **at Baden (Sept. 12–13)** — Winterthur — St. Gallen — Feldkirch — St. Anton — Obermieming —

Sept. 19 to Sept. 23

At **Innsbruck (Sept. 19–20)**. Then to Landeck — Mals — over the **Stelvio Pass** —

Sept. 23 to Oct. 12

Bormio (Sept. 23) — Varenna on the **Lake of Como (Sept. 25)** — Milan — Verona — at **Venice (Oct. 6–12)**.

Return (dates not recorded)

Salzburg — Munich — Augsburg — Ulm — Stuttgart — Karlsruhe — Strasbourg — Metz — Verdun — Chalons-sur-Marne — Epernay — Meaux — Paris — Beauvais — Abbeville — Montreuil — Calais — **London (Dec. 10)**.

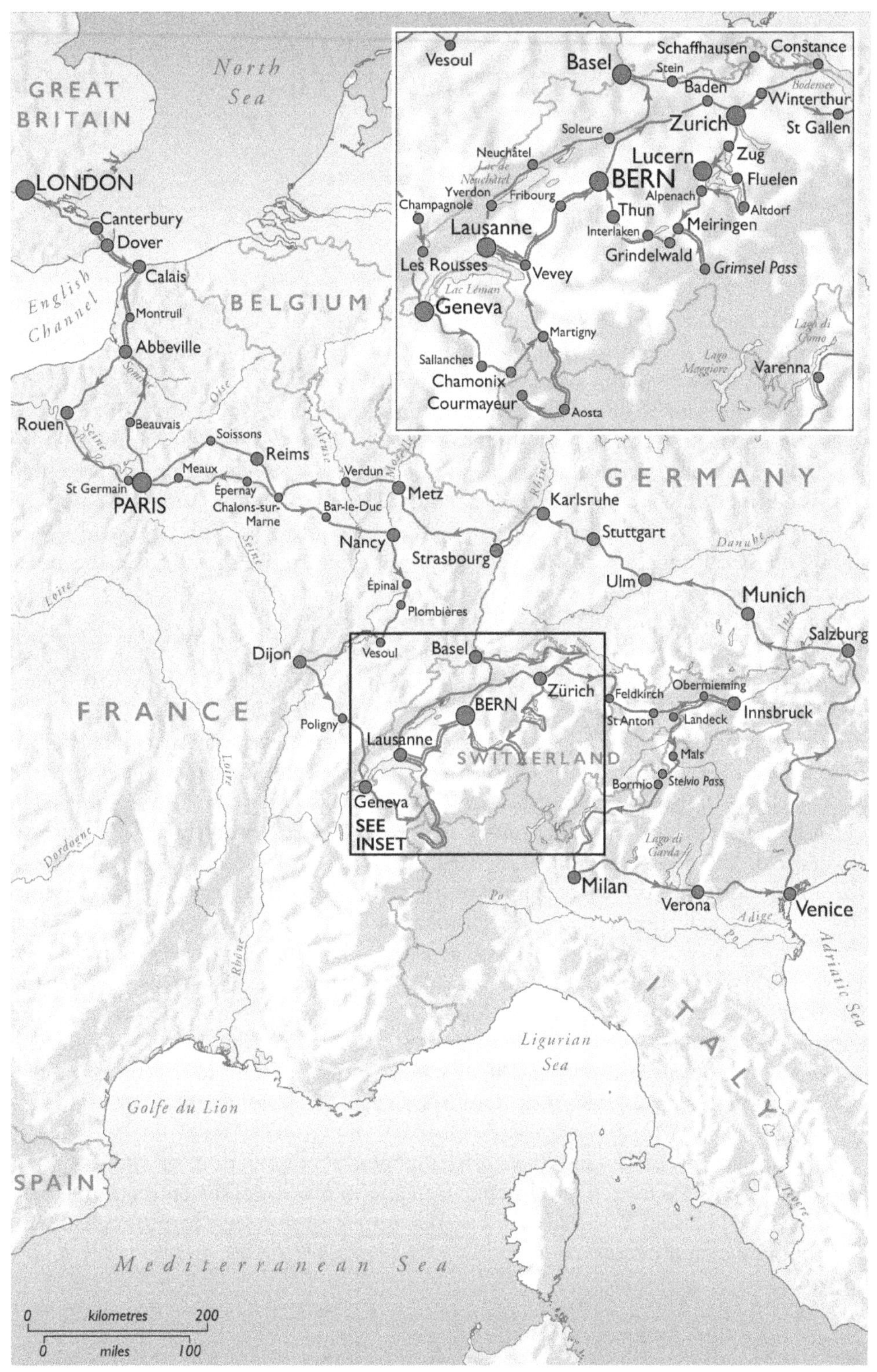

North Sea
GREAT BRITAIN
LONDON
Canterbury
Dover
Calais
English Channel
Montruil
Abbeville
Somme
Rouen
Seine
Beauvais
Oise
BELGIUM
Soissons
Reims
Meaux
St Germain
PARIS
Épernay
Chalons-sur-Marne
Meuse
Moselle
Verdun
Metz
Bar-le-Duc
Nancy
Strasbourg
Épinal
Plombières
Vesoul
Dijon
Poligny
FRANCE
Loire
Dordogne
Rhône
GERMANY
Rhine
Karlsruhe
Stuttgart
Danube
Ulm
Munich
Inn
Salzburg
Basel
Zürich
BERN
Lausanne
Geneva
SEE INSET
SWITZERLAND
Feldkirch
Obermieming
Innsbruck
St Anton
Landeck
Mals
Bormio
Stelvio Pass
Lago di Garda
Milan
Verona
Venice
Adige
Po
Adriatic Sea
ITALY
Ligurian Sea
Golfe du Lion
SPAIN
Tevere
Mediterranean Sea
0 kilometres 200
0 miles 100
Vesoul
Basel
Schaffhausen
Constance
Stein
Baden
Bodensee
Winterthur
Zurich
St Gallen
Soleure
Neuchâtel
Lac de Neuchâtel
Lucern
Zug
BERN
Fluelen
Yverdon
Fribourg
Alpenach
Champagnole
Thun
Altdorf
Lausanne
Interlaken
Meiringen
Grindelwald
Les Rousses
Vevey
Grimsel Pass
Lac Léman
Geneva
Martigny
Lago di Como
Lago Maggiore
Sallanches
Varenna
Chamonix
Courmayeur
Aosta

TEXTUAL NOTE

Previous editions

Nearly all the verse records of Ruskin's juvenile tours were first published, either fully or in part, in the first volume of W. G. Collingwood's 1891 edition of *Poems of John Ruskin*, in two volumes, based on MSS VIII and IX, as described in pp. 264–67 of that volume, and currently held in the Beinecke Library, Yale University. As well as 'Verse Journal, A Tour Through France to Chamouni', the 'Rhyming Letter, to Richard Fall, from Paris', and a series of poems from 1835, which are all presented in this edition, they include 'Passages from the Iteriad; or, Three Weeks Among the Lakes' (1830) and 'Account of a Tour on the Continent in 1833'. All these works were published again and in full, together with additions and extracts from the prose accounts of the 1833 and 1835 tours, in volume II of *The Works of John Ruskin*, ed. by Edward Tyas Cook and Alexander Wedderburn, in 39 vols (London: George Allen, 1903–12) (Library Edition). The 1835 prose diary was subsequently largely presented and transcribed in the first volume of *The Diaries of John Ruskin*, ed. by Joan Evans and John Howard Whitehouse, in 3 vols (Oxford: Clarendon Press, 1956–59).

A new version of *Iteriad, or Three Weeks Among the Lakes* was first published in full, edited by J. S. Dearden (Newcastle upon Tyne: Frank Graham, 1969), while *A Tour to the Lakes in Cumberland: John Ruskin's Diary for 1830*, also edited by J. S. Dearden, with an introduction by Van Akin Burd (Aldershot: Scolar Press; Brookfield, VT: Gower, 1990), is the first published prose account. Keith Hanley's reconstruction and critical account of Ruskin's British journeys as an Oxford student for which there are no written records, *John Ruskin's Romantic Tours, 1837–38: Travelling North* (Lewiston, NY, Queenston, and Lampeter: The Edwin Mellen Press, 2007), reconstructs those tours and also reproduces seventy-five of the related series of 170 drawings which it catalogues. A lucid evocation of the practices and approaches routinely adopted in later travels is provided by J. G. Links's *The Ruskins in Normandy: A Tour in 1848 with Murray's Hand-book* (London: John Murray, 1968), which comprehensively describes Ruskin's eleven-week continental tour with his new bride, Effie.

The project of producing the fullest scholarly presentation of the MSS for Ruskin's juvenilia is currently in preparation and in process of dissemination, edited by David C. Hanson: *The Early Ruskin Manuscripts, 1826–1842* <http://english.selu.edu/humanitiesonline/ruskin/>.

This edition

All Ruskin's known contemporaneous written materials related to the 1835 tour are gathered and documented in this edition in full. These chiefly comprise his prose diary, a verse journal in two cantos, and two verse letters to school friends. A selection of forty-three drawings of sites visited in pencil, pen and ink, and watercolour are here reproduced, mostly for the first time, together with a catalogue of all 124 known to be extant, including some newly identified. Forty are reproduced from the original drawings held in the Ruskin Library, Lancaster University, together with three from photographs also kept there. Appendix 1 collects a group of related topographical poems; Appendix 2 presents a dramatic verse dialogue and a fragmentary novel derived from the tour; Appendix 3 comprises the transcription of *John James Ruskin's Travel Diary, 1835*.

The present edition of the diary is based directly on the manuscript, RF MS 1, held in the Ruskin Library at Lancaster University in a separate red leather notebook for 1835, 18 cm x 10.5 cm, which contains a series of integrated sketches, mostly of rock formations. It offers an exact, full and annotated transcription of the entire 172-page notebook, occasionally correcting the only previously published version and adding new material, including all the original sketches in their original positions. Original ampersands, punctuation, and spellings are preserved; additions made with carets in the MS are so indicated; and legible erasures have been noted. Pages containing the original sketches are reproduced alongside the transcriptions.

The texts of 'Verse Journal, A Tour Through France to Chamouni', the 'Rhyming Letter, to Richard Fall, from Paris', and the appendicised poems are based on Collingwood's edition of 1891. That edition was the upshot of Ruskin's own original intention to print a companion volume of his early works in verse and prose to complement the privately printed *Poems* of 1850. The 1891 text of the verse journal omitted six stanzas from Canto 1 and two from Canto 2, with other missing parts (see note on Canto 2, stanza 19) which are here reinstated, based on the Library Edition's extended and corrected texts. '[At Verona]', which did not appear in *Poems* (1891), is based on its first printing in the Library Edition. The text of the rhyming letter to Willoughby Jones is transcribed and printed in full for the first time from the MS held in MS Vault Ruskin, in the Beinecke Rare Book and Manuscript Library, Yale University, according to the library's Public Domain and Fair Use policy. Cook's texts for the pieces in Appendix 2, Other Literary Outcomes, derive from the MSS identified in the notes to these items in this edition. *John James Ruskin's Diary* is transcribed and printed here in full for the first time from the manuscript, RF MS 32, held in the Ruskin Library, Lancaster University.

For the new transcriptions, Ruskin's own spelling and punctuation are given, and words which he crossed out included as indicated by a superimposed line. Erasures are noted in brackets. Uncertain readings are followed by [?], conjectural readings are contained within <>, editorially added words within [ ], and indecipherable words are represented by [...?].

6000
2
(2) 12000
100

J. Ruskin
1835.

The 1835 Diary

J. Ruskin
1835[1]

Canterbury. June 2nd. 1835 Weather. Sultry with little sun. Sky mostly covered with light clouds. At 12 o'clock. opposite the sun. 45° from the horizon. it corresponded with 7 of the cyan[r].[2]

Dover. June 3rd. Weather much the same. Cyan. 8. Beneath the chalk range of Shakespeare's cliff, there is a bed of stiff white clay. containing nodules of radiating pyrites. which are scattered over all the beach by the sea. I have found large masses of lustrous yellow pyrites, (in one specimen formed upon a nodule of blue iron-stone). This mineral on the least exposure to the air is decomposed, the pyrites becomes dull, and falls into dust at a touch, and a yellow sulphureous efflorescence appears upon the fracture, not on the exterior, which is usually renaform, and coated with brown oxide of iron. which I have found likewise on the beach in large masses. and sometimes even hematitic iron, and liver pyrites. Where a beach is composed of ~~whi~~ rolled flints, as the beaches on the south coast of England usually are, ~~ther~~ silex must now and *[page 2]* then occur in some of its more valuable forms. Accordingly, I have found two or three good specimens of pale milk blue chalcedony, and a fragment or two of cornelian on Dover beach, but only by a persevering search of an hour or two every day for more than a month.[3] Small crystals of quartz are very common everywhere in the cavities of flint.

Calais. June 4th. Rain in the morning. & dull all day. but warm. Wind N.N.E.

Montreuil. June 5th. Very misty in the morning. towards the afternoon became clear and beautiful. Cyan. 6. As we were going out of Calais, I noticed that the large plain in which that town is situated, is merely an extent of sea beach, being for miles composed of loose rolled pebbles, in some places covered with very thin vegetable

1 The signature and date are on the verso of the front cover. An introductory note, which is not in Ruskin's hand, precedes the text on the endpaper in the MS: 'Lent by Mr. Ruskin jun[r] to J. C. Loudon, and with Mr R.'s consent lent to Mr. Bakewell, to see if there is any thing in them adapted for M.N.H./ April 12. 1836.' John Claudius Loudon, 1783–1843, published various magazines, including the *Magazine of Natural History*, in which Ruskin's three earliest scientific papers had appeared in 1834. Loudon published the next, 'Observations on the causes which occasion the variation of temperature between spring and river water', derived from material contained in this diary, in October 1836, and was to bring out a series of Ruskin's papers on *The Poetry of Architecture*, which also incorporated observations from the 1835 tour, in the *Architectural Magazine* from November 1837 to December 1838.

2 Cyanometer. A simple instrument for measuring the blueness of the sky, probably invented by Horace-Bénédict de Saussure around 1787. Ruskin made his own for this tour, 'shaded in cobalt' (35.152).

3 On a summer holiday in 1832.

soil. which has been made capable of affording nourishment to a little corn, but more frequently entirely bare, tossed into low hillocks, and having every appearance of having just been abandoned by the ocean which deposited them there. The chalk downs between Calais and Boulogne run in long sweeping eminences nearly to Montreuil. sometimes covered by a few *[page 3]* beds of gravel and clay.

Abbeville. June 6th. A clear morning. with much thunder, accompanied by hail in the afternoon. Very sultry all day. Cyan. 5.

June 7th. Clear and warm morning, succeeded by thunder. In the evening there was much sheet lightening in the east, playing continually. During the night there was a tremendous thunderstorm. the lightning flashing ten or twelve times in a minute, and filling half the heaven with a sheet of lurid blue flame at every flash. accompanied by torrents of rain. Cyan. 7. In the morning we walked round the ramparts, serenaded by the melodious voices of a few thousands of frogs. congregated in the half dried up moat. Frogs have very strong voices in these warm countries and take great delight in exercising them. Where the water was deeper, and covered with reeds we heard the cry of a bird, (at least I supposed it to be so) somewhat resembling that of the corncrake, but more powerful, and shriller. I could not catch the least glimpse of the birds for they kept themselves concealed among the reeds.

[page 4] Rouen. June 9th. Arrived here yesterday. As usual when we left Abbeville the sun was hot, and the sky clear. There was a little thunder in the afternoon. and heavy rain, but [it] cleared up towards the evening. Cyan. 11.

The road from Abbeville to Rouen passes over a series of elevated plains, intersected by considerable vallies; These high, but level chalk downs, on the approach to Rouen sink suddenly down into a wide and richly cultivated plain which they surround on three sides, but which spreads away towards the south in uninterrupted distance. Round this champaign flows the Seine, skirting closely the bases of the hills, which it has washed away [in many parts] into lofty chalk cliffs, ~~which shut in~~ and in the centre of the horse shoe thus formed, at the bases of the hills, & between them and the river, lies the town of Rouen, one of the most beautiful out of all the beautiful cities of La belle France.

~~and which situated in an~~

The day was warm, rather cloudy. the evening beautiful. Cyan. 9.

[page 5] Rouen. June 10th. Warm in the morning. about 3 o'clock there was a severe thunderstorm. The evening was warm and beautiful. Cyan. 10.

Mantes. June 11th. Warm. thunder in the afternoon. Cyan. 7. The road from Rouen is beautiful, passing for some distance under the chalk cliffs, which, near Rouen, border the Seine. They are of a compact tolerably hard chalk, which supports itself in many singular forms, very different from the monotonous slope of the cliffs of Dover, by which however these [cliffs] are far exceeded in height.

St. Germain. June 12th: Day exceedingly warm. Sky without a cloud. Cyan. 6.

Paris. June 13. Still very warm. Cyan. 9.

June 14. Colder, day cloudy, without rain.

______15. Very warm. Cyan. 6.

______16. Still warm. Cyan. 6.

Soissons. June 17. Fine in the morning. the day cloudy, without rain. Some distance from Paris the road passes over an immense sandstone tract, which extends to a great distance in the direction of Fontainbleau. It consists of low rounded hills covered in *[page 6]* most parts with forest, but here and there heaving up naked summits of grey rock, ~~tinl~~ partially covered with turf, from among the trunks of the tall trees by which they are surrounded: The whole of this district, from here to Fontainbleau is covered with huge rounded blocks, apparently waterworn, of the sandstone by which the hills themselves are composed. These masses lie tossed among the trunks of the ancient trees, half buried ~~within~~ in the turf, covered with moss, or tinted with various lichens. I was at a loss to account for the appearance of a group of blocks lying near the entrance of the forest I mistook them at a distance for groups of gigantic Ammonites *[erasure beneath 'Ammonites']*, and indeed, even on a near approach could hardly believe them to be simple blocks of Sandstone. Their surface was worn into the most grotesque shapes resembling knots of serpents, or masses of aggregate fossils, and in some places even annulated, like ammonites. But this structure did not extend into the interior of the stone. I broke several of the blocks, the sandstone *[page 7]* was coarsegrained, and very soft, and on the fresh fracture nearly of a pure white colour. It crumbles down very easily, and the result is a very fine white quartzose sand, ~~wh~~ with which the road is a foot deep, where it passes through this part of the forest. None of the other blocks had this singular appearance, presenting only the usual forms of half flat half rounded masses.

June 18th. Rheims. Day fine. Cyan. 14.

June 19th. Chalons sur Marne. Getting cooler. Cyan. 17.

June 20th. Bar Le Duc. Cooler. Cyan. 16.

______21st. Bar Le Duc. Warm. Cyan. 13. Walked about the environs of this beautiful village. The whole extent of country from Rheims to Bar le Duc is a plain; ~~but~~ an immense extent of level, but still of considerably elevated country. This is intersected by narrow valleys, whose richly cultivated meadows are two or three hundred feet below the level of the surrounding plains. and in these vall~~ey~~ies are situated the principal towns and villages of this extensive district. To enter a *[page 10]* village is here a phrase synonymous with To go down into a hole, and "To leave a town" with "To go up a very steep hill.

Bar le Duc is situated in one of the largest of these beautiful vallies, through which flows a ~~large~~ small, but rapid river. The high plains break down upon the valley in the form of immense and regular bastions, whose summits are, of course, always flat, (being part of the surrounding plain), and whose sides have a very steep and regular slope. I could not perceive any correspondence between the angles of the hills on the opposite sides of the valley. ~~for both~~ These hills are composed, as far as I could see, of loose and friable loam. covering beds of very hard grey limestone. The loam is mixed with broken fragments of stones among which I found. 1st, the limestone of which the hills are composed. in great quantities 2nd, a fine reddish flint with a few fossils. 3rd (of which I found only 4 specimens,) a quartz rock. with fossils, which I believed to be vegetables, in abundance. and 4th, a dark grey ironstone, with a few fossils. *[page 9]* The sides of all these hills are covered with vineyards. which produce very good wine.

June 23rd. Nancy. Very warm in the middle of the day. Cyan. 8. The country from Bar le Duc has all the same character, of elevated plain. with intermediate valleys. In one, the ancient bed of a lake, the alluvial soil had been so smoothly and evenly deposited as to be perfectly level (to the eye). I could not imagine how the river which passed through it knew which way to run. From the top of a hill above Nancy. the north Jura, or those chains of mountains near Strasburg which run down to, and join the Jura, are distinctly discernible.

June 24th. Nancy. The weather here is always warm. I think. Cyan. could not be properly observed, the sky appeared quite mixed up, if I may so say, with white clouds.

June 24th. Plombieres. Day cloudy and remarkably cold. Cyan. 12. Road passes for some distance by the banks of the Moselle here only a clear and rapid stream. Above the village of Eppernel are some remarkable rocks of very thinly stratified sandstone. *[page 10]* which is exceedingly coarse grained, and of a dirty red. Through the mass of this stone are dispersed, ~~th~~ large quartz pebbles. which may be easier broken than detached from their matrix. They give the rock the appearance of a real breccia. They are not found in every bed of the sandstone, a few strata were entirely destitute of pebbles though not differing in other respects from the rest of the rock. I saw the rock on all sides, the beds were regularly deposited, and horizontal, or dipping very slightly to the east.

June 25. Vesoul. Day showery. Cyan. 14.

______26. Dijon. Day fine. Cyan. 10.

27, 28. Dijon. Very fine.

29. Poligny. Day beautiful. Cyan. 9. Poligny is situated at the extremity of an immense plain and at the base of the Jura. In most great ranges of mountains, the inferior chains, if they run parallel to the great central one, have their backs (so to speak) turned to the plains, and their escarpments towards the central range. The Jura, though it does not *[page 11]* run parallel to the Alps, is conformable to this general rule. The Dole, and most other high peaks of the Jura, rise immediately from the Pay's de Vaud. in steep grassy slopes, partly covered with forests of pines, so that they may be seen from Geneva from base to summit. But ~~when~~ on their northern side, they sink into elevated plains, or sloping valleys, surmounted by summits of far inferior elevation, and which gradually become~~ng~~ lower as you approach the plains; ending in a long and wide plain, which sinks suddenly into the cultivated champaigns of France. thus the highest summits of the Jura are not

11

run parallel to the Alps, is conformable to this general rule. The Dole, and most other high peaks of the Jura, rise immediately from the pays de Vaud. in steep grassy slopes, partly covered with forests of pines, so that they may be seen from Geneva from base to summit. But ~~when~~ on their northern side, they sink into elevated plains, or sloping valleys, surmounted by summits of far inferior elevation, and which gradually becoming lower as you approach the plains; ending in a long and wide plain, which sinks suddenly into the cultivated champaigns of France. that the highest summits of the Jura are not situated in the centre of the range, but at its southern border, as in figure 1.

1.

which a transverse section of the range of the Jura might present. Poligny is situated at the foot of the first slope of the Jura. whose rocks of grès are surmounted by blocks of grey granite, which present an appearance of stratification. as decomposing

12

granite very often does, from splitting into regular fissures. Past some very curious table beds of limestone, on the journey to Morez. a village situated in the centre of the Jura. between enormous rocks of magnesian limestone whose beds are in many places nearly vertical, and have not been made so without being twisted here and there in an extraordinary manner. fig 2 combines straight and curved beds, fig 3 is remarkable for its reversed contortions. The beds have commonly a dip of about 80°. Hence we ascended by a steep gallery bordered by a prec-ipice, to Les Rousses. and came suddenly in sight of the beautiful green heights of the Dole jagged with pines, and varied by a few thin

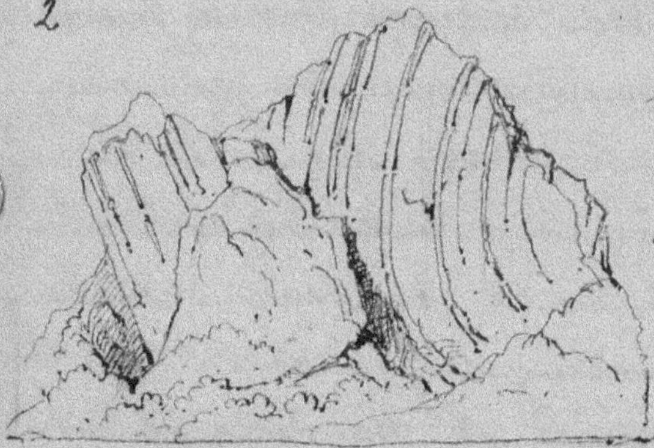

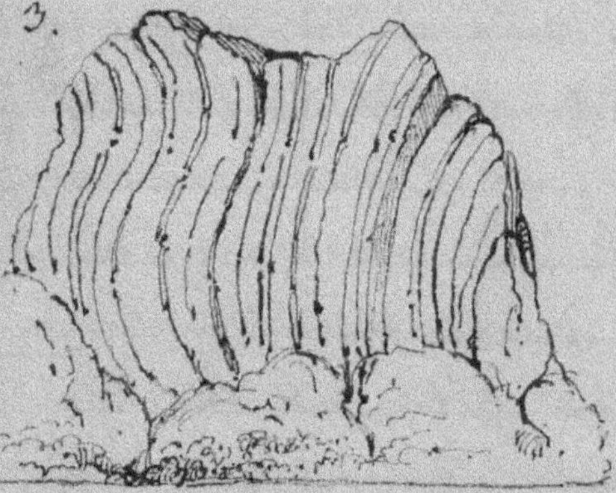

2

3.

situated in the centre of the range, but at its southern border, as in figure I, which a transverse section of the range of the Jura might present. Poligny is situated at the foot of the first slope of the Jura, whose rocks of grès are surmounted by blocks of grey granite, which present an appearance of stratification, as decomposing *[page 12]* granite very often does, from splitting into regular fissures. Past some very curious table beds of limestone, on the journey to Morez. a village situated in the centre of the Jura. between enormous rocks of magnesian limestone whose beds are in many places nearly vertical, and have not been made so without being twisted here and there in an extraordinary manner. fig. 2 combines straight and curved beds, fig. 3 is remarkable for its reversed contortions. The beds have commonly a dip of about 80°. Hence we ascended by a steep gallery bordered by a precipice, to Les Rousses and came suddenly in sight of the beautiful green heights of the Dole jagged with pines, and varied by a few thin *[page 13]* streaks of dazzling snow. The height at which perpetual snow commences on the Alps has been variously stated. Ebel[4] says at 8000 feet. one of the monks of St. Bernard told me at 6000 feet. which, as he most likely meant French feet makes 7000 English. The actual height is very difficult to determine. This year the Jura had snow upon it in considerable quantities at the end of June. but it was after remarkably cold weather in the plains, and was not the winter snow remaining, but the remains of a fresh fall, which frequently occurs in stormy weather even on such minor elevations as these. When I saw the Jura in September their highest peaks, (4,500 Eng[li]sh ft.) were entirely free of snow. But on the high Alps snow is met with much lower, glaciers at 3000 [x *in pencil]* feet. because they are continually supplied with fresh ice and snow from the superior heights, and force their way into the low valleys by their own weight. being of too considerable a mass to be rapidly melted. Thus, among the Alps you never see a mountain slightly capped with snow. If its height be less than [*page 14*] about 6000 English feet; it will retain no snow during the summer, if its elevation be greater so as to render it capable of retaining a little snow during summer, it will be coated with glacier to perhaps 2000 feet below its summit. From Les Rousses we past along the beautiful pasturages which extend along the Jura from the base of the Dole, rich with a thousand flowers, dark with forest, or green with young corn, and dotted with detached cottages, here and there sprinkled along the heights, or gathered into small clusters. The hills became more peaked and more sprinkled with snow as we advanced, until, after passing along an immense gallery, high upon the precipices of the Dole. we turned that illustrious corner. that looks across the broad & beautiful valley of Geneva to the eternal ramparts of Italy. to the "redoutables aiguilles," and glittering aetherial elevation of Mont Blanc. I have seen no view of it equal to this, yet. I believe the Breven is a little too near. Sallanche is grand; Chamouni shows nothing of the height of Mont Blanc, which is quite foreshortened when *[page 15]* you look from such a near valley. No station shows the ~~elevation~~ height and sublimity of the Alps so well as an elevation of 2000, or 3000 feet at a distance of about 80 or 60 miles, especially if you get a good sunset. The sky, at the highest part of the pass, (3,000 ft) was about 18 of the cyanometer. the air fresh, but not

4 Johann Gottfried Ebel, 1764–1830, in his *Manuel du Voyageur*, Paris, 1830–31, which John James Ruskin owned in 1835.

cold, the sun hot. a light haze about the horizon. The distance from the plains of France to this highest part of the pass is about 57 miles. the descent to the plain of Geneva about 10. Nothing could better illustrate the form of these minor ranges of mountains. Got to Geneva about 4 o'clock. 1st of July.

July 2nd. Geneva. Weather very fine, and very hot. Cyan. 12. New bridge built over the beautiful blue Rhone. The colour of this river appears to me to vary with the season. When I was here in September,[5] it was of an indigo blue colour, especially when you looked upon it with your back to the sun. I was afterwards much surprised to hear it called by many people 'sea green.' Now it appears *[page 16]* to me of a much paler blue than it did later in the season. It is, certainly, a steady blue tinge in the water. for all the stones at the bottom look blue through it. How other rivers would look if they were equally clear, we cannot tell, even this water does not look very blue where it is shallow. But the Rhine is green, not blue, and therefore there must be some cause, which tinges clear water in the one case emerald green, in the other indigo blue.

Mont Blanc was beautifully clear. Before it was ascended it was thought to be ice, not snow, which blanched its summit, why, I cannot tell, no ice could assume the sweeping, rolling, luxuriously wreathed outline which at once shows the depth, as well as the substance of its mantle. The aiguilles look very low beside it. I think either their height must be over estimated, or that of Mont Blanc under estimated. Argentière is said to be 13000 feet. Now Mont Blanc looks one third higher; I should think Mon^{r} de Saussures estimate of 17000 feet was ~~a~~ more correct ~~one~~ [*page 17*] than the usual one of 15000.[6]

July 3rd. Geneva. Very fine. and sultry.

______4th. The same, continued fine to the 5th.

July 6th. Sallenche. Cloudy and warm. Set off from Geneva, on the Chamouni road at 6 o'clock. At first you pass over the wide plain of Geneva. composed of alternate sand and rolled pebbles. and pass the base of the Saléve, where its beds dip beneath the plain. The side of this precipitous hill next Mont Blanc, is covered with forest, or scattered plantations or beautifully cultivated, and sprinkled with cottages and chalets, and then a beautiful and wide view opens, showing the conical rise of the Mole. and the woody slopes of the Voirons and the jagged crests of the Brezon. and the Mont du reposoir, which fall back to heights sprinkled with snow, and to the dazzling triple peaks of Mont Blanc. Perhaps the best point of view is from the top of a hill which descends into a deep ravine to a bridge across a torrent which joins the Arve. It has worn its way far down, through steeply inclined [*page 18*] limestone beds, which are covered by about a hundred feet of debris, ~~masses~~ composed of sand, rolled pebbles of all sizes, and huge blocks ~~of limestone~~ of granite. This debris is one confused mass, not disposed in beds There is a very fine bridge thrown over the torrent. Hence you pass for a small distance along the plain, and then skirt the Base of the Mole, as you enter the valley of Bonneville. This mountain, a long

5 On the 1833 tour.

6 In his *Voyages dans les Alpes*. Mont Blanc is now measured at 4,810m/15,780ft high.

79.

4.

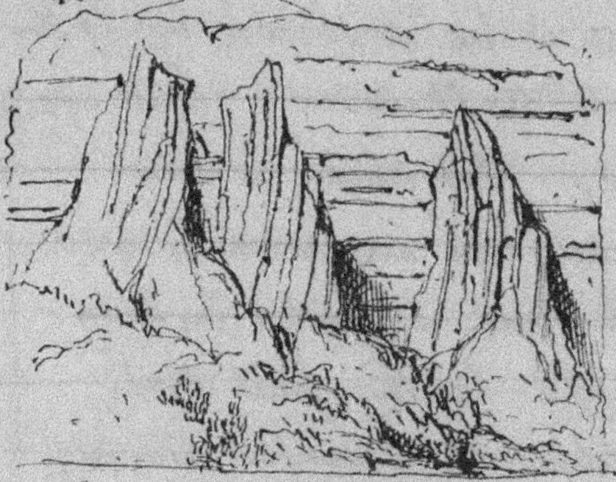

fig 4. They are of the same substance as the horizontal beds. and appear to have been torn from them, and forced into their vertical position by some tremendous force from below. The Mole is only precipitous at its north western extremity. opposite Bonneville it appears in green and beautiful heights, covered at their base with pines. On the other side of Bonneville rises the Brezon. in steps of alternate turf and forest; and bare precipitous, inaccessible rock. It has no snow. not being above 4500 feet above Mediterranean. I could not make out the direction of its beds. or their substance. which however I suppose to be the same as that of the Mole. After passing through Bonneville and crossing the Arve, the road lies through an immense alluvial plain, deposited by the Arve and not long since subject to dreadful inundations

and regular ridge, presents its end to Geneva, and its long steep side to Bonneville. and separates two transverse valleys, which run at right angles to the chain of the Alps. the one of which is bounded by the Brezon. the other by the Voirons. The limestone beds of the Mole appear from Bonneville to be horizontal. whether they are or not I cannot say, it requires to see strata on two sides at least, before you can determine if they dip at all. and on many before you can tell what the dip is: Against these apparently horizontal beds. are raised huge ~~beds of~~ buttresses of vertical beds. slightly curved, *[page 19]* fig. 4. They are of the same substance as the horizontal beds. and appear to have been torn from them, and forced into their vertical position by some tremendous force from below. The Mole is only precipitous at its north western extremity. opposite Bonneville it appears in green and beautiful heights, covered at their base with pines.

On the other side of Bonneville rises the Brezon in steps of alternate turf and forest, and bare precipitous, inaccessible rock. It has no snow. not being above 4500 feet above Mediterranean. I could not make out the direction of its beds, or their substance which however I suppose to be the same as that of the Mole. After passing through Bonneville and crossing the Arve, the road lies through an immense alluvial plain, deposited by the Arve and not long since subject to dreadful inundations *[page 20]* from that river, as ~~ha~~ is shown by a pillar erected at Bonneville to Charles [ ][7] qui aggeribus flumina coercuit;[8] This plain is now beautifully cultivated, hops are grown in great quantities, and the road is shaded by long avenues of large and healthy fruit trees. It is however subject to dreadful storms of wind, as most flat valleys are if surrounded by lofty mountains. When we passed here in 1833 the hops were all laid flat on the ground poles and all, by a late storm. And though subject to such attacks from air and water it is not exempt from those of fire. In this plain, as well as in one or two other parts of Switzerland, the roots of the trees during an excessive drought took fire under ground and it was in vain that the peasants. endeavoured to stop the devastation by digging deep trenches and filling them with water. The mountains which surround this plain are all calcareous. After skirting their bases for some time you reach the village of Cluse, which is situated at the entrance of one of the most superb vallies or rather ravines, of the Alps, that of Maglan. *[page 21]* It is bordered by enormous precipices of limestone, from 800 to 2000 feet in height, veiled with pine forests of immense extent; above which rise peaks of enormous elevation, loaded with dazzling snow, and broken into fantastic forms. Here the limestones begin first to yield to the ~~slate~~ clay and mica slates, here accordingly the mountains increase in elevation, ~~and~~ lose the rounded sweeping outlines of the calcareous rocks, and break into tremendous precipices and singular peaks. The limestone beds on each side of this valley, are ~~singu~~ confusedly disposed, sometimes curved, particularly at and near the Nant D'Arpenaz. After passing this cascade the road enters a much wider valley in which is situated the village of Sallenche. This valley, where the mountains slope down into it, is beautifully cultivated, ~~and on it~~ but in its centre it is very flat, and subject

7 Left blank in the MS.

8 Translated as 'who checked the river with ramparts'. The king was Charles Felix of Sardinia, 1821–31. See note 64 to 'Verse Journal, A Tour Through France to Chamouni, 1835'.

to terrible devastation from the floods of the Arve, which even when it is low flows in a hundred different channels, divided by wide beds of sand and gravel, with a few wild shrubs twisting their roots among them. *[page 22]* These stony beds are perfect mineral treasuries, they are composed of specimens of every mountain in the course of the Arve from the Col de Balme. 1st. large masses of clay slate, and very red mica slate with brown mica: these come from the mountains which extend from hence to Servoz. These slates sometimes contain nodules and veins of quartz passing into 2nd. Foliated Granites, whose composition is the same as those of true granites but having the plates of mica disposed in parallel and sometimes curved, folia, which gives the stone the appearance of being thinly stratified which it is not. it does not even break in the direction of its folia rather than in any [X *in pencil*] other. These come from the hills near Servoz. and from some of the aiguilles of Chamouni. 3rd. True Granites. such as those of the Mont Blanc itself. and of many of its needles, coarse grained, with chlorite instead of mica. sometimes in nests. sometimes with distinct veins of quartz. This is a white granite. That of the Midi, Blaitiere, and most of the aiguilles *[page 23]* near the glacier du Bois, and of the aiguilles rouges on the Mont Breven is red, and I think foliated. 4th. Quartz rock, in nodules very white, half crystallised. with chlorite. compact, and of a dirty green. 5th. Hornblende rock, which however is not plentiful. We arrived early at St. Martin. The summit of Mont Blanc was not clear, but the Dome du Gouté, and aiguille du Goute were clear and beautifully lit up by the evening sun. and the peaked outlines of the mountains round the valley rose magnificently against a broad and lovely sunset.

June *[sic]* 7th. Chamouni. Morning rainy. Cleared up. and we started. Past the fine bridge thrown over the Arve. and after crossing the plain for some distance began to wind up a steep hill into the narrow defile which leads to Servoz. In these mountain valleys there is no gradual rise from the valley till the hill becomes ~~f~~ steep. The gravel and alluvial matter are deposited by water, and are as level as water and stop at the edge of the valley as sharply *[page 24]* as water, and the hills dip down beneath them as they would beneath water. In fact so sudden is the change from plain to precipice that near Cluse I saw a man lying sleeping with his head and shoulders comfortably supported by the slope of the mountain and his feet and legs delightfully deposited upon the level surface of the plain.

Up the hill therefore, we wound, among beautiful fruit trees; and entered a narrow defile between immense slaty mountains along which rush~~e~~ or rather down which tumble the turbid waters of the Arve. At the top of the hill a small and beautifully clear streamlet enters a small reservoir and forms a pretty little quiet pond, which is elevated to the dignity of being called the lac de Chede. Its waters are beautifully clear. and have a very slight but steady tinge of green. This tinge I should suppose to be an indication of the presence of Copper. For the whole bottom of this lake is covered with a coat of bright verdigris blue which however I could not get conveniently ~~get~~ at, *[page 25]* not liking to go over head and ears. The colour of this lake is quite different from that of the Rhone, for the latter is coloured but makes no deposit, and the former is very slightly coloured, yet deposits a strongly coloured sediment. I should have at once considered the waters of the Lac de Chede to be cupriferous, had it not been for their excessive clearness, and for the presence of numerous water serpents, one of which we caught as it was twisting about among the grass and reeds near the shore, holding its head well above water. About 14 inches long. (I believe there are some nearly a yard.) belly yellow. back yellow with green chequers. head ~~yell~~ green with a yellow ring round its neck, and two black triangular spots on the ring with their points directed down the back. Said not to be venomous. No watersnakes are, indeed. This little lake is surrounded by beautiful trees, and its clear water reflects the summits of Mont Blanc, which are seen far down the piny valley. After passing *[page 26]* this lake the road winds along the side of high slaty mountains at a great height above the ravines of the Arve. As you descend towards Servoz the summit of Mont Blanc sinks behind the rounded mass of the Dome du Gouté. Above Servoz there are yet seen the ruins which fell from an overhanging mountain of mica slate.[9] Three days the masses of stone continued falling and the dust was so great and so thick that at Turin ~~th~~ it was supposed that an immense volcano had broken out among the Alps. The whole side of the mountain is a ruin, but its fragments did not cover the valley like those of the Rossberg. After passing the village of Servoz you cross the Arve where it issues from a deep and narrow ravine, cut right through the ridge which separates the valley of Chamouni from that of Servoz. Over this ridge beside the ravine passes the road. over masses of compact*[erasure beneath]* granites, which certainly appear to be stratified. ~~But~~ They *[page 27]* are a good deal veined with quartz. From the summit of this ridge are first seen the green meadows of the valley of Chamouni and the dark forests of the Breven and Montanvert. and the peaks of the Glacier de Bosson, and the huge frozen waves of Bois. After crossing the Arve a second time you arrive at the Prieure, which is situated very nearly in the centre of the Valley of Chamouni and at equal distances from its two principal Glaciers. Went to the source of the Arveiron in the afternoon. which is fine, but almost all glaciers have such an arch. that is they are all melting below. and their water must find an outlet. The source in Argentiere is very fine. in Bossons very poor. because there are two or three others higher up.

Chamouni. July 8th. Morning cloudless. Mounted and off for Col de Balme.

Crossed the Arve, and past the Glacier du Bois. The Valley of Chamouni is divided into two distinct parts. The largest is that in which is situated the Prieure, and *[page 28]* into which descend the Glaciers of Bois, and of Bossons. But this valley is terminated near the Glacier de Bois, by a hill two or three hundred feet high, where cultivation appears to cease. yet after surmounting this hill another distinct but narrower valley opens which is still called the valley of Chamouni and in which is situated the village of Argentiere. The pine-covered mountains on the south eastern side of this valley conceal upon your entrance the whole range of the aiguilles of Chamouni, except the red granite of Midi and the white snowfields of Mont Blanc; The valley however opens again towards Argentiere. whose immense glacier comes ~~fou~~ apparently rushing down the mighty valley between the huge masses of the aiguilles Verte and Argentiere, and on the other side opens the ravine ~~a~~

9 In the landslide of 1751, also evoked in 'Verse Journal, A Tour Through France to Chamouni, 1835', see note 80.

through which lies the passage of the Tete noire. After this the mountains become sterile. The torrent descending from the Col de Balme has worn itself a channel deep down among the slaty beds of that mountain which are *[page 29]* here, and in no other part, exposed. The slate does not lie in fine, compact well formed beds such as I have seen in Wales. But it is of a dirty black, and of a crumbling friable nature, falling into small fragments and totally unfit for ~~quarrying~~ roofing, as is shown by the houses in Chamouni being all roofed with wood. It is quarried however for another not less useful purpose, for which it is peculiarly adapted. As the snow in Winter falls frequently three or four feet deep in the valley of Chamouni, and gets frozen quite hard it would not melt for some time after the fine weather had commenced, and until it was too late to sow corn. The peasants therefore spread this black and powdery slate in heaps over the snow, which so increases and reflects the heat of the sun that the snow is melted in a very short time. After passing this slate rock the mountain is covered with fine green turf to the very summit. where we arrived at about 12 o'clock. The Col de Balme is a high ridge which separates the valley of Chamouni from that of the Rhone, in *[page 30]* which is situated the village of Martigny. As it thus commands the Bernese Alps on the one Side, and the Glaciers of Savoy on the other, there cannot be imagined a better observatory, or a more magnificent panorama to be observed. Beginning with the Aiguilles of Chamouni. The two nearest are the Aiguilles de Tour et d' Argentiere. They are very perpendicular and are in consequence slightly sprinkled with snow. From their granite bases descends the beautiful glacier de Tours, which is not between high mountains in a steeply inclined ravine, as most of the glaciers are, but spread out on the side of a broad hill, and therefore preserves the snow whiteness of its surface and the beautiful blue of its Chasms unsullied by granite dust. Beyond these mountains and far above them, rises the aiguille Verte. an excellent example of a structure very general among such granite mountains. Its summit, a, fig. 5, is, or appears to be, the summit of an immense perpendicular mass of solid unstratified granite. tapering slightly to the top. Which *[page 31]* is covered with thick, white, and beautiful snow. On each side of this central mass are deposited huge folia of granite. those nearest to the centre being vertical, or nearly so, the next more sloping, the slope increasing as the folia retire from the centre. The tops of these side beds rise up in detached pointed peaks. frequently surrounding the aiguille like the leaves of a rose. Such a structure gave the Monte Rosa its name. One of these peaks on the aiguille Verte rises up in a beautiful and regular pyramid. b. which from Chamouni appears higher than the aiguille Verte. towering above the Mer de Glace under the name of the Aiguille Dru. The rest of the Aiguilles of Chamouni cannot be separately distinguished from *[page 32]* the Col de Balme, for they are all lost in the huge mass of the Mont Blanc. from whose near side they rise, jagged black snowless, perpendicular peaks, up, up, up one over another, Charmoz lost in Blaitiere and Blaitière in Midi, and Midi in the bright, dazzling summit which crowns the whole. Mont Blanc is curiously regular in its form. Its summit is ~~summits~~ supported by three grand Buttresses, each of which have two summits. They are seen best, one from Geneva, one from Sallenche, and the other from the Col de Balme. That from Geneva, has three peaks Mont Blanc du Tacul. aiguille sans Nom. and Mont Blanc.

31

is covered with thick, white, and beautiful snow

a b

5

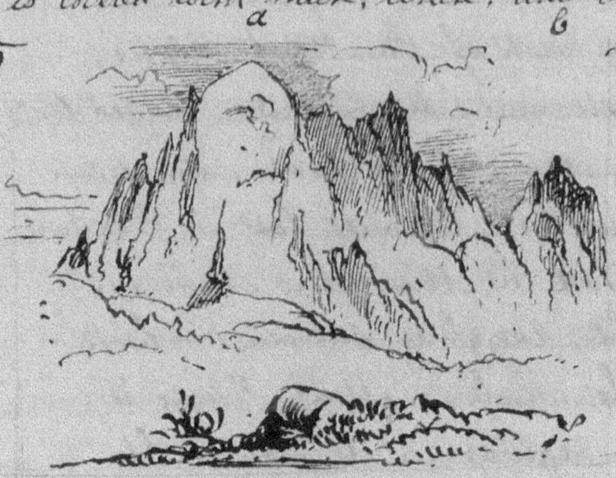

. On each side of this central mass are deposited huge folia of granite. those nearest to the centre being vertical, or nearly so, the next more sloping, the slope increasing as the folia retire from the centre. The tops of these side beds rise up in detached pointed peaks. frequently surrounding the aiguille like the leaves of a rose. Such a structure gave the Monte Rosa its name. One of these peaks on the aiguille Verte rises up in a beautiful and regular pyramid. b. which from Chamouni appears higher than the aiguille Verte. towering above the Mer de Glace under the name of the Aiguille Dru. The rest of the Aiguilles of Chamouni cannot be separately distinguished from that from Sallenche three. and that seen from the col de Balme three. the aiguille du Goute. the Dome du Goute. and the Mont Blanc. The first of these, which is the lowest descends steeply into the valley of Chamouni. which is seen lying along the base of Mont Blanc. with the Arve *[page 33]* twisting about backwards and forwards among its green meadows. to the right of this valley rise the Aiguilles Rouges, of the Mont Breven. their granite is very coarse grained: the plates of Mica are brown red and very large. They are laid parallel to one another thus rendering the granite foliated, and so completely so that it looks like a mica slate. The forms of these aiguilles are beautiful. particularly from this point. They are not very lofty, but they appear as if they were. To the right of these appears the Buet: a calcareous mountain. It presents its steep, precipice side to the col de Balme and its sloping side sheeted with snow to Geneva. This half of the panorama from the aiguille de Tour to the Buet, was cloudless. but over the Bernese Alps, which are almost all visible from the Col de balme, over the Simplon, and the whole range of the high Alps, floated masses of thick white clouds. not rain clouds. which entirely concealed the summits. The height at which the clouds float on a fine day causes them to crowd about the mountain summits, contin*[page 34]*ually tantalizing you with the view of their bases. For though the vapour at the ordinary temperature of the air may be so much diffused as not to be visible, yet it is often condensed by the cold, when it approaches a snowy mountain, and becomes visible under the form of a light white cloud, adhering closely to the summit. Such clouds I have watched for hours. hoping that they would pass away. because they were the only cloud in the sky. but though always in motion, these troublesome vapours keep continually in the same place and conceal the summits far more effectually than rain clouds, for these latter are so low that they do not actually envelope the summits, which they suffer you to see every now and then through their openings. Accordingly all view in this direction was concealed. by tantalizing fairweather clouds. ~~all~~ It was fortunate that they were confined to this quarter, and left the Mont Blanc unobscured. At the Cabinet of Natural history on this *[page 35]* mountain I obtained what I had long wished for. a large, octohedric crystal of rose fluor. Returned to Chamouni. And watched the sun go cloudlessly down upon Mont Blanc.

Chamouni. July 9th. This would have been a peculiarly day in any climate, much more so among mountains. From dawn till night there was not a single atom of a cloud to be found out by the most telescopic eye in the whole blue dome of the sky; not a mist nor a shadow. Off for Montanvert at 10 o'clock The ascent begins very steeply zigzagging among blocks of granite and mica slate. tossed about among pines of immense height. which twist their long rough roots among the stones. Path, a series of stumbling blocks and staircases. Capital animals, these mules, marvellous, quite incomprehensibly surefooted. You soon get to a great height above the prieure and get two or three beautiful views of the valley of Chamouni. There is a curious specimen of natural grafting on this *[page 36]* part of the road. An immense pinetree has been torn up by the roots by a tempest, and as ~~the~~ it was ~~plo~~ growing on a steep slope the root was lifted up in the air and the top laid low on earth. Being however not totally torn from its moorings this root was capable of affording nourishment to such seeds as might happen to fall on it. and it now presents the singular spectacle of five different trees growing from one root with a large broken trunk projecting from the same root down wards. I could not understand the French names of the trees, there were sapin and meleze,[10] both firs, beech, a broad leaved shrub, and a tree resembling mountain ash. The Montanvert is chiefly composed of mica slate with quartz which is rich in minerals. It has been deeply excavated near a small fountain about half way up. where are found beautiful crystals of quartz in the cavities of the veins; and flexible asbestus (amianthus) in considerable quantity. I found some good specimens growing, or rather appearing *[page 37]* to grow on a piece of detached rock. Sometimes the amianthus is found twisted among and ~~ho~~ adhering to the crystals of quartz. then forming very beautiful specimens. Chlorite is plentiful here in the quartz, as indeed every where in the valley of Chamouni, and that, not in minute dark green crystals, such as occupy the place of mica in Mont Blanc granites, but in large, compact, and beautiful masses. After passing this rock you come in view of the source of the Arveron far below. and of the precipices of ice which terminate the Mer de Glace under the name of the glacier du Bois. These ice waves descend on one side in an unbroken sheet into the valley, but on the other approach the top of a high and craggy precipice~~s~~ over which they fall in loud avalanches. which you see and hear excellently from the Montanvert. About this spot I found a crystal of quartz with Titanium. After a little more climbing ~~and~~ you com~~ing~~e in sight of the magnificent pyramid of the aiguille Dru and then reach the brow of the montanvert. The glacier as it is seen *[page 38]* from this spot, retiring backwards among innumerable aiguilles, appears immense and wonderful, but as the near part of its surface is very flat it is by no means beautiful. but after advancing a little way towards the Jardin, the mountains and blue precipices of ice become beautiful and astonishing, broken into shelves and columns and perpendicular cliffs. with streams of green water pouring in thunderous cascades into the chasms. The road towards the Jardin lies between the granite moraine, brought down from the higher aiguilles, and highly inclined beds of mica slate lying back in beautiful half grassy slopes, with a few of the most hardy species of pine clinging to their crests Then you approach some steep stratified rocks, les Ponts. which you have to cross in going to the Jardin. They were said to be calcareous. but I think that they, as well as most of the Montanvert were composed of mica slate, or if not, of a foliated granite. And beyond this, all is *[page 39]* granite, far as the eye can reach, a wilderness of inaccessible peaks and unsullied snow. among which the overhanging peak of the Geant, and elephant like immensity of les Jorasses, are pre-eminent. The Alpine rose[11] grows on the Montanvert beautifully, but it is rather too low for it On the passage of Splügen. at a height of 8000 feet, close to the snow, yet sheltered from very cutting winds by superior mountains, the whole breast of the hill blushed red with roses, heaped like cushions upon the grey rocks beautiful. The road to Chamouni is rather rough on the descent, but ~~still~~ very fine, affording beautiful views of the valley. Cyan. on Montanvert about 20.

10 The silver fir and larch.

11 Or snow rose, a type of rhododendron.

Chamouni. July 10th. To the Glacier des Bossons. which is far superior in beauty to the Mer de Glace. broken into splendid pyramids of dazzling ice, quite free from Granite dust Its moraine however is very large. and all moraines are very ugly. for owing to the constant motion of the glacier the moraine is kept in motion *[page 40]* too, and in consequence not even grass can grow upon its moving mass. The great shoulder of Mont Blanc, the Dome du Goute. which rises above this glacier. is here the principal mountain, and a beautiful field of unbroken snow it is. The summer of 1834 was very hot here. the snows were very much melted, and in consequence a slip of snow has taken place on the Dome du Goute above the Glacier du Taconay, and an immense crevice has been formed, ~~whose sides~~ which enables you, even from Chamouni to judge of the depth of the snow on this magnificent mountain. Its sides cannot be less than 400~~0~~ feet of perpendicular height. and this is not glacier, but unfrozen snow. or snow just so much frozen as to be able to separate into crevices with perpendicular sides. certainly not the dry and fine powder which I have seen rising from the summit of Mont Blanc like dust. and which I took at first for a fine white cloud, till a guide told me it was a wind avalanche.

Among these mountains, if the clouds in the *[page 41]* morning be white, and have a distinct outline, even although they are very small, and very high, and though they may not be numerous, yet they always increase fast, and rain follows in the afternoon, but though they ~~b~~ may be large and even low, yet if they are of a rose colour, and broken like spray, fading off into the sky with no outline, they do not increase and usually entirely disappear towards the evening. This day there were a few white clouds in the morning. they spread rapidly and came down about the middle of the day in a heavy shower. During a clear interval we walked up the side of the Breven to a considerable height. with Mont Blanc and the Line of aiguilles on the opposite side of the valley pushing their pointed summits through the rolling lines of cloud, breaking out among the vapour like visions appearing in the heaven, with no relationship to the low earth. and appearing higher and higher every step we went. Found some beautiful brown mica. and foliated granites. not chloritic. and descended sorrowfully from the last walk, for *[page 42]* this time, in Chamouni.

St. Martin. July 11th. Started, just as the clouds broke that had been raining all the morning. and the blue sky looked out over the Dome du Goute as we climbed the hill which separates the valley of Chamouni from that of Servoz. The granite of which this hill is composed I *[dark blot]* found not to be foliated; it is compact, and contains little chlorite, and much quartz. Breaking a piece w in which were very large half crystals of quartz I found two small grains of gold. The sand of the Arveiron contains a good deal of gold. I got some out of an eddy which was very fine, and in which I found several grains. Instead of going directly to St. Martin we wound round the base of the precipice which borders the valley of Sallenche to the north. and went to the baths of St. Gervais. which lie beneath cliffs of sand, ferruginous, with alternate layers of pebbles. about 300 feet in height. They seem the remains of a deposit which must formerly have covered the whole valley of Sallenche. *[page 43]* for there is a hill of the same nature on the opposite side of the ~~river~~ valley, which would therefore present such a section as fig. 6. a, a, *[text inked*

43.

for there is a hill of the same nature on the opposite side of the river. valley. which It would therefore
(6.) present such a section as
fig 6. a, a. ~~[struck out]~~.
gneiss, with quartz veins
(which I saw better after-
wards) which beds dip to the north west
and therefore appear horizontal looking from to the
south east. b b, beds of sand and pebbles.
which are horizontal, appearing to have been
deposited during a long series of years by the
peaceful waters of some immense lake, and
to have been swept away in their centre by
the current occasioned, when they retired.
c, a recent alluvium, deposited by the Arve.
The mineral waters of St Gervais are of two
kinds. the first spring is sulphureous, beautifully
clear, and very warm, just cool enough to be
drank. within three yards of this spring rises
another, perfectly cold, and strongly impregnated
with iron. The juxta position of the hot and
cold springs is not singular; for a bed of iron
pyrites may be supposed to lie very close to one
of iron ochre. the former would furnish to the first

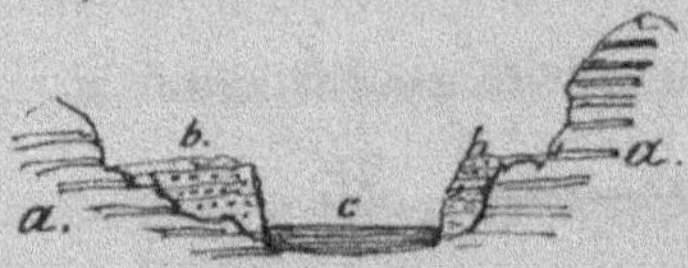

out] gneiss, with quartz veins (which I saw better afterwards) ~~which~~ beds dip to the north west and therefore appear horizontal looking from ~~to~~ the south east. b b, beds of sand and pebbles. which are horizontal, appearing to have been deposited during a long series of years by the peaceful waters of some immense lake, and to have been swept away in their centre by the current occasioned, when they retired. c, a recent alluvium, deposited by the Arve. The mineral waters of St. Gervais are of two kinds. the first spring is sulphureous, beautifully clear, and very warm, just cool enough to be drank. within three yards of this spring rises another, perfectly cold, and strongly impregnated with iron. The juxtaposition of the hot and cold springs is not singular, for a bed of iron pyrites may be supposed to lie very close to one of iron ochre. The former would furnish to the first *[page 44]* spring its heat and its sulphur, and the red banks and steely taste of the latter spring at once show over what mineral beds it flows. A rather severe shock of an earthquake was felt here ten days before we arrived. The Bath house is situated in a narrow ravine opening into the valley of Sallenche. and echoing with the roar of a noisy torrent, which forms, a little higher up, a very beautiful cascade. but the place is sombre. and I was glad to get out of it into the sunny valley of St. Martin.

Out we went in the afternoon. up the dry bed of a torrent, which never fails to bring you to something good, and indeed is very good in itself. After stumbling for some time over fragments of primitive rocks, I came to a large piece of slate, thoroughly and beautifully coated with stalactitic carbonate of lime, very hard, semi-translucent, and of a fine yellowish brown colour. where this fragment had come from I know not, I found no more of it. I was soon stopped by a wall of rock, the site of a cascade. only *[page 45]* there was no water. but the rocks were very remarkable, hard, black, slaty rock, in alternate beds with quartz, or rather alternate veins. for very few of the beds were more than three or four inches in thickness. The quartz was very full of cavities which were full of beautiful but very small crystals. These beds were steeply inclined and where they were laid open at the cascade they had the appearance of being curved, in a direction parallel to their planes, or rather, since this is impossible, of having been channelled by torrents of falling water into their present form, that of a wall with ~~round~~ semicircular towers on it at irregular distances. fig. 7. Correspondent strata appear on the opposite side of the valley near Sallenche, but they are not channelled in this singular manner. The hills above Sallenche appear to be slate surmounted by what I supposed to be limestone but I cannot be sure.

[*Page 46*] St. Martin. July 12th. Showery, but clear in the morning and evening... Warm.

St. Gingolph. July 13th. a lovely and burning day. Set off early. for Bonneville The curve of the crags over which falls the Nant d'Arpenaz, is huge, but the ~~curve is a~~ depth of the curve is slight. while a little farther on there are some contortions, on a smaller scale, but much more remarkable. fig. 8. This piece of rock is about 30 feet broad. After passing Bonneville and going some distance on the Geneva road, we turned off for Thonon. from the brow of a hill on this road the view is splendid. On the right the Buet, and its surrounding peaks. the Mont Blanc. and its

45.

there was no water. but the rocks were very remarkable, hard, black, slaty rock, in alternate beds with quartz, or rather alternate veins. for very few of the beds were more than three or four inches in thickness. The quartz was

7

very full of cavities. which were full of beautiful but very small crystals. These beds were steeply inclined and where they were laid open in at the cascade they had the appearance of being curved, in a direction parallel to their planes. or rather, since this is impossible, of having been channelled by torrents of falling water into their present form, that of a wall with ~~round~~ semicircular towers on it at irregular distances. fig 7. Correspondent strata appear on the opposite side of the valley near Sallenche. but they are not channelled in this singular manner. The hills above Sallenche appear to be slate surmounted by what I supposed to be limestone but I cannot be sure.

46.

St Martin. July 12th Showery. but clear in the morning and evening.. Warm.

St Gingoulph. July 13th. a lovely and burning day. Set off early. for Bonneville The curve of the crags over which falls the Nant d Arpenaz, is huge, but the ~~curve is a~~ depth of the curve is slight: while a little farther on there are some contortions, on a smaller scale, but much more remarkable. fig 8

8 This piece of rock is about 30 feet broad.

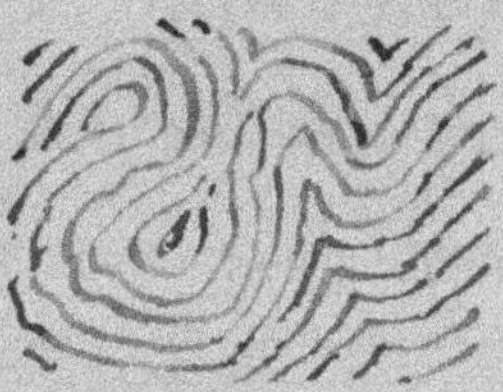

After passing Bonneville and going some distance on the Geneva road, we turned off for Thonon. from the brow of a hill on this road the view is splendid. On the right the Buet, and its surrounding peaks, the Mont Blanc. and its aiguilles. the Mole, the Brezon. and the Mont du Reposoir. In front the Voirons, and the summits of the Dents de Midi and de Morcles. and on the left the blue waters of the lake of Geneva. and the long hazy line of the Jura.

aiguilles. the Mole, the Brezon. and the Mont du Reposoir. In front the Voirons, and the summits of the Dents de Midi and de Morcles. and on the left the blue waters of the lake of Geneva. and the long hazy line of the Jura. *[page 47]* Our ride was beautiful during the whole day After coming down upon the borders of the lake, and passing the beautiful rocks of Meillerie, we arrived at St. Gingoulph, one of the most beautiful villages on the lake of Geneva.

Martigny. July 14th. very fine. The rocks which you pass ~~amou~~ immediately after leaving St. Gingoulph are exceedingly remarkable: The first are composed of calcareous tuffa. and are moistened by a hundred dripping streamlets, which deposit their carbonate of lime in beautiful translucent brown stalactites, which in some places coat the original rock entirely. some in the progress of formation. instead of being soft and crumbling like lumps of brown sugar, as some stalactites are, were flexible something like a rather tough paste. The rocks which are below this tuffa break out soon afterwards. Ironstone, veined with quartz, in thin layers, divided by lamina of indurated blue clay. rendering the rock easily ~~fra~~ separable. In one piece I found a quartz *[page 48]* vein pierced through by a long cylindrical hole, quite filled with blue clay.

Soon after passing these rocks the road leaves the beautiful borders of the lake of Geneva to enter the flat and marshy plain deposited by the Rhone where it enters the lake. The delta of this river continues to increase rapidly, as indeed it must, for I have seldom seen a river more foul than the Rhône at Sion. Martigny, &c. and all this calcareous matter is continually being deposited by its waters when they enter their resting place in the calm lake of Geneva. I would that the land would not encroach any farther, indeed it has encroached too much already. Deltas are most disagreeable things, for ~~since~~ from their nature they cannot rise above the level of the water they remain marshy, low, half cultivable lands. The causes of ague in cold countries, and of malaria fever in warm. These marshes are at last terminated by the sudden closing of the valley at St. Maurice, where a magnificent bridge strides over the *[page 49]* compressed Rhone. and the ~~letting~~ raising of a drawbridge, or the turning of a key would be ~~qui~~ sufficient to shut you out from the whole Canton Valais. Passing under the huge overhanging rocks we entered the immense, and I think beautiful valley which is the only territory of one of the largest cantons of Switzerland. The part of this valley which extends from St. Maurice to Martigny, is bordered on each side by huge limestone cliffs, which far [*out*]rival in beauty and singularity the rocky bulwarks of Cluse. These veteran crags remain, and will remain, telling to every traveller a wonderful ~~and well r~~ tale of ancient convulsions. Such coiled crags I never saw, whole mountains twisted like macaroni, as if they had been tortured on the rack and broken on the wheel of the world for ages. I sketched three dispositions, and could have had a hundred *[page 50]* but these are sufficient for illustration. Fig 9. is a crag just above St. Maurice, remarkable for the immense scale of its contortions, since from th the height of this crag is not less than 2000 feet perpendicular. The curve of this crag is rendered conspicuous at a glance by the disposition of the pines, which grow in belts, upon the ledges formed by the projection of the strata from beneath one another. Fig 10 is a still more remarkable instance. It is a chain of calcareous peaks which you come in sight of on the right

49..

compressed Rhone. and the letting raising of a drawbridge, as the turning of a key would be qu sufficient to shut you out from the whole Canton Valois. Passing under the huge overhanging rocks we entered the immense, and I think beautiful valley which is the only territory of one of the largest cantons of Switzerland. The part of this valley which extends from St Maurice to Martigny, is

(9)

bordered on each side by huge limestone cliffs, which far rival in beauty and singularity the rocky bulwarks of Cluse. These veteran crags remain, and will remain, and will telling to every traveller a wonderful tale of ancient convulsions. Such coiled crags I never saw, whole mountains twisted like macaroni, as if they had been tortured on the rack and broken on the wheel of the world for ages. I sketched three dispositions, and could have had a hundred

55

but these are sufficient for illustration. Fig
9. is a crag just above St Maurice. remarkable
for the immense scale of its contortions, since
~~from St~~ the height of this crag is not less
than 2000 feet perpendicular; The curve
of this crag is rendered conspicuous at a glance
by the disposition of the pines, which grow
in belts, upon the ledges formed by the
projection of the strata from beneath one another.

(10)

Fig 10 is a still
more remark-
able instance.
It is a chain
of calcareous
peaks which
you come in
sight of on the right half away between St
Maurice and Martigny. I was at first struck
by their beautiful outline, which exactly resembles
that of a granite mountain. which indeed I
should have been mistaken them for, had it
not been for their finely marked strata.
These, it will be observed are not only curved
but bent completely round upon themselves.

54

being perfectly straight both before and after this singular bend, and the rest of the mountain bearing no traces of contortion. Below these

(11)

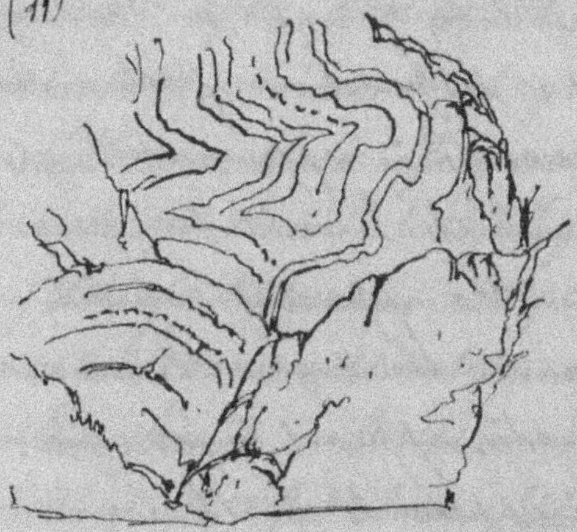

peaks, rather nearer St Maurice, is a more isolated rock whose beds are most singularly twisted. fig 11. These sketches are all taken from the rocks on the east side of the valley. those on the opposite one are much distorted, but not on so large a scale.

The cascade of the Pissevache near Martigny is a sort of split the difference between the immense body of water and small height of the cataract of the Rhine, and the enor- mous height and dribbling stream of the Nant D'Arpenaz. It is, I think, one of the finest falls in Switzerland, with its head buried in spray, and its feet planted on the rainbow. These high cascades fall like reversed half way between St Maurice and Martigny. I was at first struck by their beautiful outline, which exactly resembles that of a granite mountain. which indeed I should have ~~been~~ mistaken them for, had it not been for their finely marked strata. These, it will be observed are not only curved but bent completely round upon themselves. at a, *[page 51]* being perfectly straight both before and after this singular bend, and the rest of the mountain bearing no traces of contortion. Below these peaks, rather nearer St. Maurice, is a more isolated rock whose beds are most singularly twisted. fig. 11. These sketches are all taken from the rocks on the east side of the valley. Those on the opposite one are much distorted. but not on so large a scale.

The cascade of the Pissevache near Martigny is a sort of split — the difference between the immense body of water and small height of the cataract of the Rhine, and the enormous height and dribbling stream of the Nant D'Arpenaz. It is, I think, one of the finest falls in Switzerland, with its head buried in spray, and its feet planted on the rainbow. These high cascades fall like reversed [*page 52*] rockets in spearpoints of water, hissing as they come down. You can never judge of the height of cataracts by measuring them with the eye, their body of water, or the height of the mountains or disposition of the rocks around, all influence their apparent height The only way by which I could ever judge was by observing the apparent rapidity of the fall, Of course, the higher the cataract the slower the water appears to fall, ~~of a~~ some high falls appear to walk down the rocks, while the low fall of the Rhine seems to whiz by you like lightening.

Hospice of Great St. Bernard. July 15th. Set off from Martigny on a cloudless morning. Crossed the bridge over the turbulent Drance, and plunged into a narrow defile, losing sight of the beautiful valley of the Rhone, and confined between immense slaty mountains, whose beds, on the right side of the valley, at least, were principally vertical. intersected here and there in a most remarkable manner by a horizontal group so distinct from the rest as to resemble huge heaps of quarried slate laid upon the side of the mountain. *[page 53]* Through these rocks is cut the only gallery, or rather tunnel, on the passage of the Great St Bernard, which, however, is a long and beautiful one: After passing this gallery the road rises rapidly, on rocks of gneiss, with here and there a block of quartz, with very much chlorite, and in which I found two or three crystals of titanium. Up to Liddes the cornfields and cultivated meadowlands continue although you quit the walnut and chestnut trees at five hundred feet above Martigny. but every thing yields to pine forest and flowery mountain turf immediately beyond Liddes. The rocks continue very monotonous. nothing but gneiss. We arrived early at L'Hospice. This convent is, I believe, the highest dwelling constantly inhabited, in the known world. and a mournful habitation it is; It is situated in a narrow valley on the very highest part of the passage, and close beside a small lake. The building is very substantial. no ornament. formerly supported by ~~many~~ immense buttresses, which a few years ago were taken down, and the *[page 54]* building totally renewed. There are three buildings, the first is a sort of storehouse, then the principal building, and close to the hospice for the living is a narrow and small hut built against the crags of Mont Mort, the dwelling place of the dead; ~~for~~ and there the bodies are laid side by side, and they perish not, for the cold blast of the day, and the keen frost of the night are their preservers. It is a strange museum, a revolting rareeshow for every chance comer to peep into, and wonder at, and come away from, complaining that he came before breakfast and has lost his appetite. The old bones might be let lie uncrunched by the thoughtless feet of staring hundreds; the corpses might be let sleep unoffended by their gaze.

Above this melancholy habitation rise the crags of Mont Mort, ~~wh~~ loaded with f masses of thick snow. The grey steep rocks which remain uncovered are thinly greened with moss and lichen to a certain height, the limit of all vegetation *[page 55]* except that of lichens. There is a dead stop. The green bunches of moss cease suddenly. They flourish where they are, it is death to them to crawl an inch higher. This line looks remarkable seen from below the mosses coat the mountain like a belt and appear as green at the utmost limit of their territory, as they do far down. The line of demarcation is a foot or two higher on Mont Mort than on the opposite crags, because that mountain has a south exposure. Above this line all is monotony, grey rocks, bare on the precipice side, lifting up coronets of snow upon their foreheads, climbing up on one another's backs into the deep, blue, silent heaven, gathering themselves around you on every side, gleaming in a pure, liquid crystal, frosty sunlight or with their white summits shining out, themselves like suns, from oceans of invidious cloud, white misty wreaths ~~driving~~ billowing beneath you, and whirling past you, and eddying above you, like the wings *[page 56]* of mountain spirits.

~~The S~~ Beneath the sloping flanks of Mont Mort, at about twelve feet below the Hospice, rests a small, deep, calm, transparent lake. Ice is lighter than water, and I should suppose that snow, even when half melted, and thoroughly penetrated with water, would float, and therefore I was surprised to see the snow in some places sloping down beneath the water of this lake; It however was an excellent test of the colour of the water; It had not the bluish, verdigris green of the lac de Chede. but a rich olive sort of green, like the green of phosphate of copper. Nevertheless it is beautifully transparent, fed by snow water, chiefly, and by two or three springs, one of which is conducted for more than a quarter of a mile in pipes to supply the hospice. Its waters descend on the Aosta side, a tributary of the Po. Beyond this lake the valley appears to be terminated by peaks of gneiss of a great elevation, sloping towards the mountains of Cormayeur, and on the Valais side, the view is checked by the *[page 57]* immense bulk of Mont Velan, a series of dark aiguilles, connected by flat masses of snow. When we were at the Hospice, (middle of July, remember) the masses of snow around and beneath the hospice were universal and large. but the heats of August and the beginning of September usually melt almost entirely, sometimes altogether, the snow in this valley. Yet this is no proof that the line of perpetual snow on the alps is above eight thousand feet. There is a great difference in temperature between two spots of the same elevation, if the one be a valley, and the other a summit. The snow which lies in the valley of the Hospice, is between two walls of rock, by which the heat of the sun is doubled, and it is also sheltered on two sides from severe winds. How much colder would a summit be, of the same elevation, with no reflected sun, and no shelter from cold winds — the snow on such a summit would be, and is known to be, perpetual. Witness the summits behind the Mont Breven, the Dent du Midi above Bex, nay, many *[page 58]* peaks which from the Hospice you may look over, are yet loaded with perpetual snow. The snow here in summer is partially saturated with water, and in very large crystals, which causes it to be very unyielding, and to support itself in arches, often very wide, over the torrents Mounted mules ~~ric~~ pass over this snow, and do not sink at the most above a foot. When I past here in 1833 there was very much red snow, lying in patches upon the white; not a fine crimson, as it some-times is, but a pale and delicate pink, as if the colouring matter had been very much diluted. I wished to examine it, but damp clouds, tired mules, coming night, and friends in a hurry, are great enemies to philosophical experiments.

GREAT ST BERNARD July 15th *[this heading added in pencil]* The afternoon which we spent at L'Hospice was beautifully clear. The sunlight on these heights appears to me less fouled by the air than below, it is so clear, so bright so lovely not very hot, certainly, but warm, compared with the air, and really a sunny afternoon up here is a very delightful thing, just cold *[page 59]* enough to put you in spirits, when the sun goes though, you begin to feel queer, the cold is a sort of unwholesome starveling cold that communicates itself to every inanimate object, and makes you jump at the touch of table or chair, or wall, spoon, dish, knife every thing; This cold is unwholesome to ~~every~~ human beings, and to most brutes, but to the St. Bernard dog, it is life, they cannot live in a warmer climate, Short haired, lion limbed, dewlapped like Thessalian Bulls, I should not like to try a fall with an old one. but from what I heard from one of the Fathers, both the strength and sagacity, though not the usefulness, of these dogs have been considerably overrated. Their muscular strength is, I believe, for a certain time considerably greater than that of a man, but it is not so durable. They delight in the snow, scamper to the nearest as soon as they are let out and tumble and roll and romp on it as if it were grass; Summer is their play time in the winter they begin to work. In the cold seasons, all the rocks about the convent *[page 60]* are completely buried in snow, one white unbroken sheet, thirty or forty feet deep. This snow is exactly like dust, loose, yielding to the slightest ~~drye~~ pressure, so that a man sinks almost up to his middle, and a dog has to swim making way by pushing with its strong limbs and just holding its head out of the snow; Thus, the dog becomes sooner tired than a man, it is forced to remain still to get breath and strength much oftener than its follower. Nevertheless, when not only all trace of the path itself is lost, but when there is not a single landmark near, since every rock in the winter time is covered, when there is nothing but an illimitable waste of ~~is~~ dazzling and guideless snow, the dog keeps above the regular path, as the monk said, from habit. but though an animal may have a habit of keeping to a discovered path, it cannot be said to have a habit of discovering, the path; which it can only do by instinct and by a very wonderful instinct. Their scent too is excellent. and thus if any traveller be lying among the snow to the ~~east~~ right or left of the path, they discover him. I believe the *[page 61]* supposition that they carry provisions tied round their necks, or go out alone in search of travellers, bring children in on their backs, &c., are altogether false. Every day ~~with~~ in winter a courier, accompanied by a dog, goes down half way to St. Pierre on the Swiss side, and as far on the Italian, shouts loudly, and waits for ten minutes or a quarter of an hour before he returns. This is an office of no small danger for though he runs no danger from the cold, being thoroughly inured to it, it is impossible to escape the danger of avalanches. When fresh snow falls on the smooth beds of old snow, a certain quantity of air is enclosed between the two layers, which is compressed to a certain degree by the weight of the superincumbent snow. As long as the frost continues, all is well, all remains firm, but, as the monk expressed it, le premier coup de serac, est le coup de mort pour les voyageurs. With the first thaw the air within the snow expands, bursts the upper layer with a noise which echo's like thunder along the illimitable waste's, and in so doing entirely loosens the upper layer; Now there are, as I mentioned *[page 62]* before, no rocks project~~ed~~ing from the snow to support these ~~loose~~ masses, but on the contrary loose smooth and slippery slopes for them to slide on, and thus whole snow fields slide down from every mountain side, with a rapidity and force which can be compared to nothing but to a cannon ball of equal size. They give no warning, and they are not seen to fall, for their fall is too swift. Spring and summer avalanches (when the snow is more moist,) do not slide, but roll. They descend much slower, and it is possible to avoid them. And even in winter time, after a thaw, until snow again falls, travelling is safe as far as regards avalanches. Many more travellers perish from not being able to resist the temptation to sleep, which the cold always occasions and from which sleep they never waken. The cold is, to say the least of it, unhealthy for those even who are used to it. Very few of the brothers of St. Bernard live ~~tw~~ more than twelve years in this desolate region. although after they are inured to it, the heat of Italy would be more suddenly pernicious to them, than the most severe cold of the Alps.

[page 63] Aosta. July 16th. Left the Hospice on a fine clear morning. passing along the side of the small lake, and then passing over the site of the Temple of Jupiter, a round flat spot among the rocks with an ascent cut through the rock to it, which still bears the marks of chariot wheels. A beautiful moss grows on these gneiss rocks, bearing pink starry flowers, a beautiful species of gentian too, which delights in the neighbourhood of the snow. It is a little too high for the Alpine rose. A small and delicate forget me not is found in great quantities. Having past this spot you come in sight of a very remarkable gneiss mountain, fig. 12. An immense cavity resembling the crater of a volcano separates the body of the mountain from two detached pinnacles a, and b, which appear at some time to have been connected both with each other and with the mountain behind them. Their beds correspond, and they rise with a comparatively *[page 64]* gentle slope from the outer valley, overhanging the interior cavity in terrific precipices. This cavity is full of débris; some fragments appeared to have fallen recently. Descending from these crags, you pass beneath the steep slopes of Mont Mort; the most dangerous spot for avalanches on the St. Bernard. It was at this spot that the avalanche descended in September, 18[ ][12] which ~~destroyed~~ overwhelmed two domestics of St. Bernard, and a traveller, ascending from Aosta. Two dogs were with them, one of which, the oldest, by its enormous strength extricated itself from the snow and went to the Hospice. But the intelligence it conveyed was in vain. assistance was ~~hop~~ impossible. The bodies were found when the snow melted in the following summer, swept many hundred feet down, in the bottom of the valley.

12 Left blank in the MS.

63.

Aosta. July 16. Left the Hospice on a fine clear morning. passing along the side of the small lake, and then passing over the site of the temple of Jupiter. a round flat spot among the rocks with an ascent cut through the rock to it, which still bears the marks of chariot wheels. A beautiful moss grows on these gneiss rocks, bearing pink starry flowers. a beautiful species of gentian too, which delights in the neighbourhood of the snow. It is a little too high for the Alpine rose. A small and delicate forget me not is found in great quantities. Having past this spot you come in sight of a very remarkable gneiss mountain, fig 12.

12

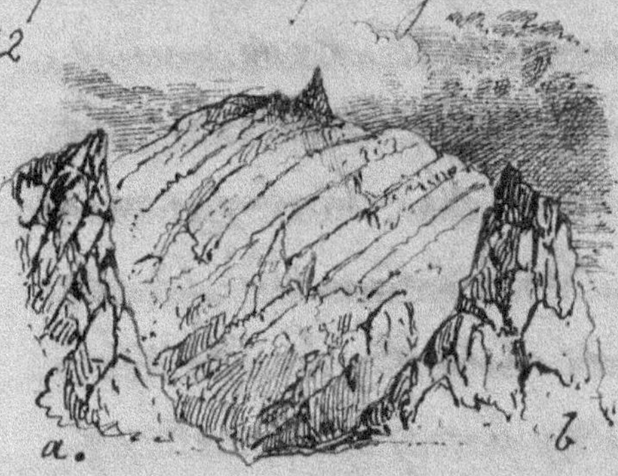

a. b.

An immense cavity resembling the crater of a volcano separates the body of the mountain from two detached pinnacles a, and b, which appear at some time to have been connected both with each other and with the mountain behind them. their beds correspond, and they rise with a comparatively

The descent to St. Remy is steep, but short, and easy. The fragments de of the mountains above, which lie in confusion by the road side, are very interesting. Quartz uncrystallised, mica slate. gneiss. earthy red iron ore; very rare; *[page 65]* found a few crystals of arseniate of lead in the quartz and a globule of native copper. The road from St. Remy to Aosta is beautiful. passing along the brows oflofty and pinecovered precipices, with Mont Velan, and mont Combin glittering on the opposite side of the valley; and descending gradually from pineforest to cornfield and pasture, which become gradually enriched with walnut trees and then with the sweet chestnut, and then you come down upon the Val d' Aosta, covered with vineyards, with here and there a tall fortress rising from among them. and the whole garden is walled in with enormous and cloudcovered Alps. The population of Aosta are by no means healthy or cleanly. I suppose two or three dozen wash their faces once a week, two or three score once a fortnight. the generality once in two months, or so. a dozen or two of them have not goitres. and the half of them are idiots. It is much worse than in the Haut Valais. and that is bad enough. Nobody can say what it is owing to, or at least nobody agrees upon it. Great heat, great idleness, *[page 66]* filth, malaria and bad water, have a good deal to do with it. but whatever may be the cause, Aosta is a very bad place to begin Italy at.[13]

Courmayeur. July 17th. The road from Aosta after leaving the great valley passes through a narrow ravine bordered by immense precipices of gneiss. and then enters a well cultivated mountain valley, terminated by Mont Blanc. In this valley are situated the ~~imm~~ baths of St. Didier. and the village of Cormayeur. I found a very large mass of tolerable plumbago built into a wall! Savages, ignoramuses! At Cormayeur there are two mineral waters. one is sulphureous and warm, ~~and~~ by holding your nose you are enabled, with courage, to force your way through the Tartarean stench of the pump room, and to taste the delicious stream. which is like ten concentrated Harrowgates.[14] The other spring is contains much fixed air, and a little iron. and is really a very pleasant drink. like Seltzer water. Twenty to thirty glasses is the morning dose for a drinker. [page 67] Several springs near this one deposited travertin in abundance. In a bed of a stream near these springs, I found a large block, 3 or four feet in diameter, of a black foliated rock, with quartz Through the quartz ran a rich vein of copper pyrites, accompanied by sulphuret of silver. It was a large stream, none of the rocks around resembled this fragment, it had been brought from a great distance, and I gave up the thoughts of finding the place whence it had been detached. We had thunder in the afternoon. Cormayeur, though a little higher, is much warmer than Chamouni, but it is on the Italian side of the Alps.

Courmayeur. July 18th. Day fine, so set off for the Alleé Blanche. There was a bridge destroyed upon the usual road, so we were forced to cross the Col du Cramont. The road ascends through a narrow ravine, among fragments of cipolino, quartz, and a fine white mica slate. and presents beautiful views of the valleys of Cormayeur, and Pré St Didier. The Mont Blanc is not seen till you arrive at the summit of the Col. which *[page 68]* though not so elevated as the Breven, yet has the

13 See John James Ruskin's Diary, Appendix 3, for a comparable denunciation of this region.
14 Harrogate is a spa town in North Yorkshire.

same opposite position, and I should think was quite as fine a station for observing the monarch of mountains. With the exception of Mont Breven it is almost the only point from which Mont Blanc can be compared with its aiguilles. There are two ranges of these granite pyramids. which diverge from the Mont Blanc; (a) [fig. 13]. the northern and lowest one consists of the Mont Blanc du Tacul, (c), the aiguille du Midi, (d) that of Blaitiere, (k), of Charmoz, (e) and terminates in the huge bulk of the aiguille Verte, (f), and its dependent Dru, (l). Now this range of aiguilles is seen from the Jura, Geneva, Chamouni, and other points of view to the north, and conceals the principal range, in which are the Aiguille du Geant, (g) and the Grande Jorasses, (h), &c., and the Mont Blanc appears, ~~therefore~~ from the north, to be a more insulated mountain *[page 69]* than it really is. From the col de Balme the aiguilles make part of Mont Blanc and therefore cannot be compared with it. But from the Cramont, the Mont Blanc is compared with its range of highest aiguilles. which indeed add more to its bulk and beauty, than they diminish its comparative height. It appears from the Cramont at least twice the height that it does from Chamouni. for instead of retiring in long perspective of sweeping snowfields, it falls down in an uninterrupted precipice of aiguilles, whose rocks shake the snow from their perpendicular sides like noble vessels cleaving a foamcovered ocean; The eye drops down into the depth of the valley, and climbs laboriously up the wall of granite, of which it seems unable to reach the summit. I wonder that Saussure, and other travellers who have ascended the Mont Blanc, have not spoken more of the terror of looking down this precipice which must be from 11000 to *[page 70]* 12000 feet high. For the Alleé Blanche itself, which is not blanche, it is a desolate ravine, a sort of reservoir for the refuse of Mont Blanc, in the shape of dirty ice, fouled water, and powdered granite. I think there could not have been a more fortunate accident than the breaking down of the Bridge in the Allee blanche. The view from the valley cannot be comparable to the magnificent panorama seen from the Col du Cramont. The Cramont itself is an uninteresting mountain, except from the number of Chamois upon it. || In several places the snow was covered with the traces of their light steps. Rain in the afternoon.

Courmayeur. July 19. Cooler and Rainy.

Aosta. ______20. Showery. but clear in the evening. Roman antiquities at Aosta are very well preserved. very interesting.

Hospice of St. Bernard. July 21. As we were climbing in clear sunshine up the Italian side of the mountain, a large thundercloud was coming up from Martigny. It began to thunder a little while after we were housed. Thunder does not sound well at such a height *[page 71]* the air is too thin to convey sound well. Sky, at 9 in the morning, opposite the sun about 22 cyan.

Martigny. July 22. Fine clear morning. a drop or two of rain in the afternoon.

Martigny. July 23. Very clear. Started for the Tete noire The road, after it has extricated itself from the immense walnut and chestnut trees which continue for some distance above the valley of Martigny, winds up a small and prettily cultivated valley, ascending rapidly and commanding splendid views of the deep blue valley

68

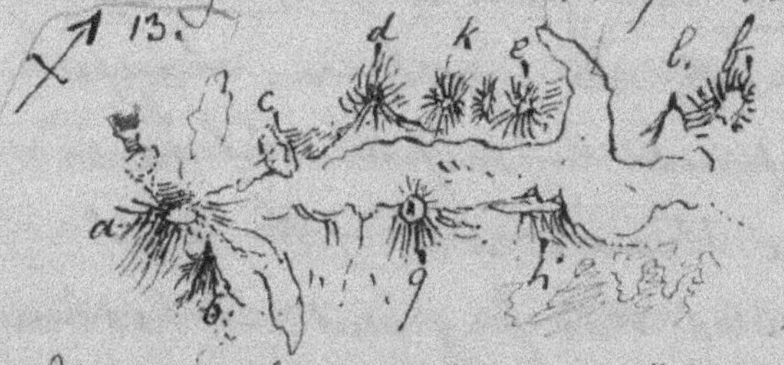

though not so elevated as the Breven, yet has the same opposite position, and I should think was quite as fine a station for observing the monarch of mountains. With the exception of Mont Breven. it is almost the only point from which Mont Blanc can be compared with its aiguilles. There are two ranges of these granite pyramids. which diverge from the Mont Blanc (a) fig 13 the northern and lowest one consists of the Mont Blanc du Tacul, (c) the aiguille du Midi, (d) that of Blaitière, (k), of Charmoz, (e) and terminates in the huge bulk of the aiguille Verte, (f,) and its dependant Dru (l.) Now this range of aiguilles is seen from the Jura, Geneva, Chamouni, and other points of view to the north. and conceals the principal range, in which are the Aiguille du Geant, (g) and the Grandes Jorasses, (h) &c. and the Mont Blanc appears, therefore from the north, to be a more insulated mountain of the Rhcne, with the river coiling about in the middle of it, and beyond, the Gemmi, the Altels, the Blumlis alp the Breithorn, and to crown all, the magnificent mass of the white Yungfrau. The passes of the Col de Balme, and the Tête Noire, descend on the Martigny side, into a long transverse valley, which is separated from Martigny by a col of considerable height, ~~to~~ being entirely surrounded by high mountains except at its north eastern extremity, where the stream, which *[page 72]* flows from the Glacier du Trient through this valley, finds an issue between walls of perpendicular crag, forming a tremendous chasm, which is broad enough to permit the passage of the river, and no more. This chasm opens into the valley of the Rhone near the Pissevache, but as no road can be carried through it you are compelled to pass over the col which separates the valley of the Trient from Martigny. thus obtaining a magnificent view of the Valley of the Rhone on the one side, and of the Glacier du Trient and the surrounding peaks on the other. The descent into the valley of the Trient is very steep, but not long. the mules go down wonderfully — beautifully After this descent you pass beside the banks of the Trient, ~~loaded~~ through a pine forest which had been visited (when we past it) by a hurricane. which had uprooted and shivered the immense trees, played with them as if they had been straws, and tossed them about among a wilderness of enormous rocks It is a thoroughly picturesque road. a most beautiful ruin, a superb desolation. *[page 73]* a most admired disorder and after passing through this forest you come out upon a narrow gallery hung up five or six hundred feet above the bed of the roaring ~~Dri~~ Trient, and ~~which~~ turns sharp round upon the beautiful rock to which the name of the Tete noire is given par-excellence. The bold outline of of the aiguilles rouges in the distance, and the pinecovered crags which rear themselves up ~~against~~ above the great gallery, form a beautiful landscape, but the great interest of these rocks consists in their remarkable composition. They look, on the first glance. like a slate, but they are composed of nodules of quartz, and felspar, with little or no mica. passing into what I should call a regularly stratified granite, not foliated granite, a mass, with its component minerals disposed in parallel lines, but a granite, unfoliated, disposed in thin and distinct beds. I never saw granite resembling this before. It is much veined with a fine white quartz which was not parallel to, or between, the folia of the granite but cutting them at an *[page 74]* angle, usually very large. yet without any apparent distortion of the granite beds. The whole appearance of the rocks was very picturesque, their contours at a distance resembling that of a f stratified sandstone. Nearer Martigny the same rock occurs, but with much brown mica. We returned by the same road to Martigny.

Vevey. July 24th. Very warm. Past by Bex, where we wished to see the saltmine but a dark walk of a league and back, under ground is no joke. I have several pieces of the salt, well crystallized, white, and pure, but it is all mixed with a calcareous rock, no fine beds of rock salt. The brine springs which rise from this rock, are not only impregnated with salt, -but with carbonate of lime. Several high, ~~the~~ roofed sheds are erected near the mines, which are filled with thorn faggots, built up and compacted in a substantial manner. The brine is conducted in pipes to the top of these sheds, and is suffered to trickle slowly down among the twigs. on which it deposits the whole of its carbonate *[page 75]* of lime, and flows out at the bottom clear, and thoroughly saturated with salt, having been a good deal evaporated in its progress. It is then evaporated in boiling houses as at Droitwich, and other places. The incrustation on the twigs is yellow, semitranslucent and tastes slightly of salt. The twigs only require to be changed once in four years.

Vevey. July 25. The view from this town is exceedingly fine. ranging from the blue line of the Jura to the bold outline of the Dent de Midi, and the white distance of Mont Velan. But the whole time that we were at Vevay, the opening of the valley of the Rhone was full of mist, not enough to conceal the mountains, but enough to throw them to a great distance, appearing as if the air of the valley was thoroughly adulterated, and unwholesome, whether it is so. or whether the ~~b~~ill health prevalent in the valley is owing to this bad air must be difficult to determine. I should think it likely, especially considering how little circulation the air obtains, being confined between *[page 76]* immense and unbroken chains of mountains, without a single opening except the narrow gorge of St. Maurice. There was a breeze on the lake of Geneva, which added to the beauty of its sapphire blue, and a remarkable line, like the red part of a rainbow, ran along the whole opposite side of the water yet without rendering the objects seen through it indistinct. I have several times seen red stripes on the distant blue water of the lake of Geneva, but not this remarkable red haze rising above it. Walked up a hill behind Vevay where I found a ~~curr~~ conglomerate of silicious pebbles, and fine white travertin, which was very hard.

Vevey. July 26th. Warm. with a cool wind. Cyan. 10.

Vevey. July 27th. Very warm. Cyan. 9. Breeze in the morning. Walked among the walls of the vineyards, which are white, hot, and monotonous, and fine fields of exercise for the small, brown, and green lizards which abound in warm countries. The most rapid in movement of any animal I know *[page 77]* (that does not fly or leap), dashing up the walls with an undulating motion, turning their pointed ~~eye~~ heads and bright eyes about in every direction and running into the first crevice ~~of~~ in excessive terror on your near approach Large snakes too are frequently found. saw one near Aosta four feet long, mottled green and yellow. and another of the same kind here, not quite so large.

Yverdon. July 28th. Passed through Lausanne. Yverdun is marshy, but I should think not unhealthy. situated at the base of the Jura. Much sandstone rock in the vicinity.

Neuchatel. July 29th. This town, and more especially the hills above it, command one of the most extensive views of the Alps in Switzerland. comprising the whole range of the Bernese Alps, the Gemmi, Diablerets, etc. and then the chain of the high Alps as far as Mont Blanc. Snow from its whiteness and brightness is of course seen much farther than the grey rock of distant Mountains so *[page 78]* that from the distance of a hundred or more miles it appears to be suspended in the air We saw Mont Blanc very plainly indeed in the morning, though at a distance of 93 miles in a straight line.

Soleure. July 30th. Ride from Neuchatel to Soleure by Bienne is very beautiful. alps in sight all the way, though their range decreases in extent, (as you lose sight) of Mont Blanc and the High Alps), it increases in size ~~of~~ and beauty of Form. There cannot be imagined a more splendid range of crags, than the Jungfrau, Blümlis Alp, Breithorn, Eigers, Wetterhorn, Shrĕckhorn, and Finster-aar horn, seen by a good setting sun from Soleure.

Basle. July 31st. Soon after leaving Soleure you turn away from the plains, and lose sight of the chain of the Alps as you enter a gorge of the Jura, a rent in enormous limestone cliffs, which is, as far as I know the only entrance to a large longitudinal valley of the Jura, in which is situated the village of Balstall. The strata of these cliffs *[page 79]* dip considerably; about 25°, and are torn into many detached and beautiful pinnacles, half clothed with wood, and usually having their tops concluded by large and picturesque fortresses. It is a very fine study of limestone. The ascent begins soon after leaving Balstall, but is very short and not steep, for the Jura in this part of its range is exceedingly low. Many beautiful fossils are found in it, and a little iron. Basle is finely situated on the Rhine, just where it turns north, and it sweeps round through the town with a cool, determined velocity which is quite astounding. Very hot day, and cloudless. Cyan. on top of Jura, 16.

Basle. August 1. Very fine city, interesting cathedral of old red sandstone, very durable and curious, if it be ~~drew~~ true that the older it is, the harder it grows. The sculpture on the tombstones on the floor of the church is hardly worn in the least, though very old and constantly trod by hundreds.

Basle. August 2. Splendid thunderstorm and deluge of rain it absolutely appeared to *[page 80]* chastise the Rhine. Double rainbow dyeing the distant hills of the black forest with its glorious belt of colours, and magnificent forked lightening very near.

Stein. August 3rd. Pretty place on the Rhine. which wears its way among horizontal beds of red sandstone. Rainyish, and much cooler.

Schaffhausen. August 4th. Set off early on a morning of white thick mist, which gradually gathered itself up into heavy rainclouds, but they broke after a shower or two and left us a fine day. Laufenbourg, a curious picturesque town, fine covered bridge, built over the Rhine where the huge roaring river is squeezed along between great elbowing rocks, such a current, such a rush. such a sweeper. Road to Schaffhausen is a little monotonous. except on a near approach to the town.

Schaffhausen. August 5th. This beautiful town is built on the slope of a hill rising from the Rhine, surmounted by an ancient Swiss fortress which rises opposited to tall *[page 81]* and beautifully wooded rocks. There is not a city more finely situated in Switzerland. Started for the falls. Old wooden bridge was undergoing repairs ~~at~~ we were obliged to cross the Rhine per ferry. lovely, transparent, bluish green yet not copper green water. crowded with large fish. Hill beyond this affords a magnificent view of the chain of the Alps when it is clear. it is covered with vines, which are not cut short enough, and produce nothing but vinegar.

Standing on the Gallery at Laufen you feel as if you were being sucked down into the abysses of an Atlantic. The mountains of foam which are relieved whitely against the blue sky appear to be closing ~~of~~ over you and the thunder of the cataract drowns every sound of the world, and its voice is heard alone.

The bright green colour of the water is seen admirably among the white churned foam. bright as the green zone of the rainbow that bends lovingly and peacefully, and silently, over the turbulent *[page 82]* crash of the ceaseless billows. Why is it green and not blue, answer me that. We did not cross the Rhine. this time view from the other side is nothing, unless you want to see how low the fall is. The water is not rough below the cataract, the impetus carries it down into the abyss below the falls, and the upper water is but slightly agitated.

Constance. August 6th. Pretty ride by the smaller lake of Constance. fine expanse of water, but no hills. Town of Constance in a marshy situation, yet appears healthy, and larger lake splendid. chain of Alps in Distance. ~~with~~ beyond a wide sealike horizon.

Winterthur. August 7th. Fine forests and fine views. Weather breaking a little. rain in the afternoon.

Zurich. August 8th. Lake very pretty. Albis range well seen from the town. horizontal beds of sandstone and sand furrowed curiously into sloping regular buttresslike transverse ridges. The Limmat as it flows out of the lake is transcendently clear. and of a sort of sickly pale green like that of the olive leaf. Every river *[page 83]* here appears to have its own regular, constant colour.

Zug. August 10th. Got up to the beacon of Albis by an abominable road, view magnificent &c. Zug a very pretty place. Fine fore-shortened range of Bernese Alps.

Zug. August 11th. Rested on a ~~fr~~ cloudless day. Very hot.

Altdorf. August 12. By the valley of Goldau, Mont Rigi and Mont Rossberg are huge fragments of an immense deposit of breccia remarkable more for its depth than its extent. The hill immediately beyond Zug is limestone, and the remarkable junction of the two rocks is seen between Zug and Art. The limestone beds dip southeast. as far as I could ascertain, and soon begin to alternate with thin beds of breccia. which is composed of siliceous pebbles, but united by a calcareous paste. so that the pebbles (especially where the rock is exposed to the attacks of wind and weather) may be more easily separated from their matrix than broken. which is not the case with a true breccia. *[page 84]* The breccia beds become thicker, and more frequent till at last the limestone entirely disappears, leaving only strata of conglomerate from 50 to a hundred feet in thickness. deposited with great regularity, although on a considerable slope and rising in the Rossberg 4,100, in the Righi 5300ft above the Mediterranean. Such an immense isolated deposit, for there is not an inch of conglomerate beyond Schwytz, is a most remarkable memorial of a series of successive and powerful deluges; successive they have been. for the beds of breccia, distinct though they be, are only separated from each other by thin layers of red clay, enormous they have been, how else could they roll up heaps of debris to the height of 5000 feet, how far they have extended cannot be determined, we shall see some vestiges of their action all along the lake of Lucerne.[15] and these two summits are apparently mere remains of a deposit formerly much larger. As you advance, towards Art you have an excellent view of the steep precipices which descend from Rigi Kulm, laying bare the thick beds of which the mountain is composed. *[page 85]* and which present their escarpments to Lucerne and which descend steeply into the lake of Zug. After passing Aart, and going for some distance through a sultry and well cultivated plain, you begin to ascend the side of that desolate ridge which is the grave of the unfortunate inhabitants of Goldau.[16] The strata of Rossberg and Righi are (as I before remarked) very steeply inclined, and those of the former mountain sloped down towards the village of Goldau and the lake of Lowertz. The year 1805 was exceedingly wet and the winter was cold and there was very much snow. The water insinuated itself among the layers of clay, which separate the beds of conglomerate, and gradually loosened the structure of the whole mountain. Terrible crackings were heard on the morning of the 2nd of September 1806. *[marginal notation: y 18o6]* many of the inhabitants fled. and about 5 oclock P.M. a mass of the mountain from 3" to 400 feet in thickness, and of enormous width slid from the sloping side, and at once filled up one third of the lake of Lowertz, and separated it from that of Zug by a hill 200 feet in height. *[page 86]* The side of the Rossberg appears now as it did just after the fall, a ruinous cavity of bare breccia without a single tree ~~of~~ or the slightest tint of verdure, and covered with a ruin of broken fragments. The hill of fallen masses, although grass and moss have clothed the rocks is still like the summit of some lofty, uncultivated, treeless mountain conveyed into the plain. and it is melancholy to ride over the three buried villages of which there is not a single vestige remaining. Then you wind along the side of the Lake of Lowertz, having come in sight of the beautiful pyramid of the Mythen. The lower part of these crags is whitish, without any distinct vestiges of stratification. which is terminated in a sloping line like the surface of an inclined bed, and is surmounted by a red rock, of the colour of the Righi breccia. I believe these rocks are inaccessible, or nearly so, and it requires a practised eye to distinguish rocks from a distance. but it is most likely a detached pyramid of the same limestone which forms the base of the Rossberg, with a remnant *[page 87]* of conglomerate on its summit. The junction of the two rocks is very distinct and rather striking. The opening from Schwytz to the lake of Lucerne presents a splendid view of the Rothstok and its surrounding Alps, which becomes more extensive and beautiful as you approach Brunnen, where you embark for Altorf. The lake of Lucerne between Altorf and Brunnen is confined between tall and perpendicular limestone cliffs, with openings here and there into green Alpine valleys at which openings only it is possible to land. The strata of these cliffs, after continuing for some distance nearly horizontal, are suddenly bent back upon themselves, without the least fracture, and

15 At this time, Ruskin shared the then prevalent catastrophist theory of geological change which regarded the Biblical deluge as the most recent geological cataclysm to reshape the surface of the earth.

16 In 1806 the mountain of Rossberg had buried the village of Goldau, killing 457 people. Ruskin was subsequently to see hints of the disaster in Turner's painting, *Goldau*, 1843.

87.

of conglomerate on its summit: the junction of the two rocks is very distinct and rather striking. The opening from Schwytz to the lake of Lucerne presents a splendid view of the Rothstok and its surrounding Alps, which becomes more extensive and beautiful as you approach Brunnen, where you embark for Altorf. The lake of Lucerne between Altorf and Brunnen is confined between tall and perpendicular limestone cliffs, with openings here and there into green Alpine valleys at which openings only it is possible to land. The strata of these cliffs, after

14.

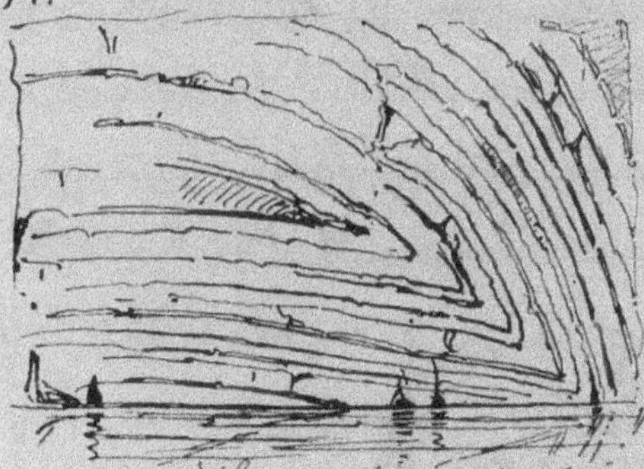

continuing for some distance nearly horizontal, are suddenly bent back upon themselves, without the least fracture, and with such perfect continuity as could have been preserved only under the operation of an immense and widely extended power. (fig 14) But it is remarkable that the beds on the opposite sides of the lake exactly correspond with each other. They con-

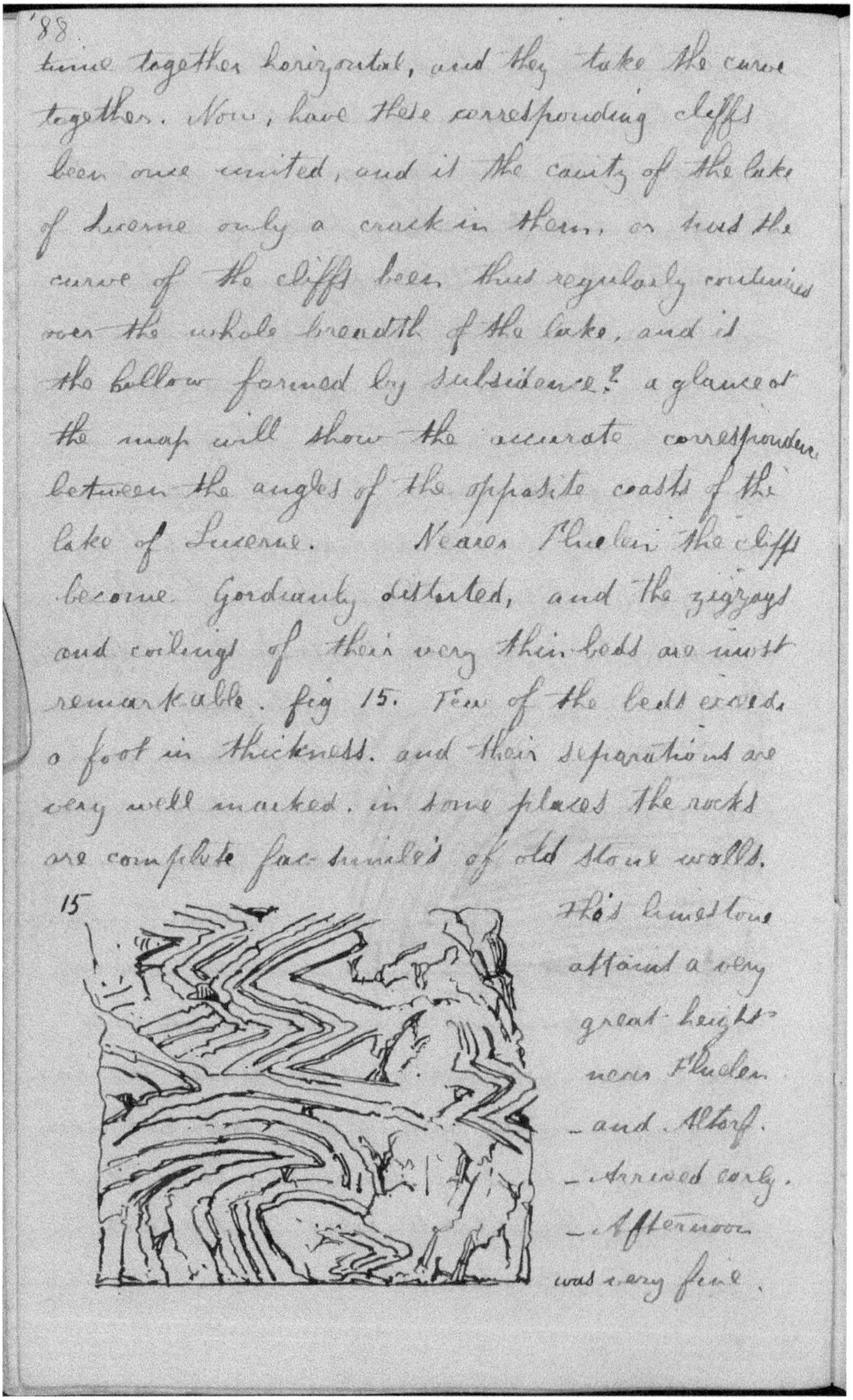

88.

time together horizontal, and they take the curve together. Now, have these corresponding cliffs been once united, and is the cavity of the lake of Lucerne only a crack in them, or has the curve of the cliffs been thus regularly continued over the whole breadth of the lake, and is the hollow formed by subsidence? a glance at the map will show the accurate correspondence between the angles of the opposite coasts of the lake of Lucerne. Nearer Fluelen the cliffs become Gordianly distorted, and the zigzags and coilings of their very thin beds are most remarkable. fig 15. Few of the beds exceed a foot in thickness. and their separations are very well marked. in some places the rocks are complete fac-similes of old stone walls.

15

This limestone attains a very great height near Fluelen and Altorf. – Arrived early. – Afternoon was very fine.

with such perfect continuity as could have been preserved only under the operation of an immense and widely extended power (fig. 14) But it is remarkable that the beds on the opposite sides of the lake exactly correspond with each other. They con*[page 88]*tinue together horizontal, and they take the curve together. Now, have these corresponding cliffs been once united, and is the cavity of the lake of Lucerne only a crack in them, or has the curve of the cliffs been thus regularly continued over the whole breadth of the lake, and is the hollow formed by subsidence? a glance at the map will show the accurate correspondence between the angles of the opposite coasts of the lake of Lucerne. Nearer Fluelen the cliffs become Gordianly distorted, and the zigzags and coilings of their very thin beds are most remarkable. fig. 15. Few of the beds exceed a foot in thickness and their separations are very well marked. in some places the rocks are complete facsimiles of old stone walls. This limestone attains a very great height near Fluelen and Altorf. Arrived early. Afternoon was very fine.

[page 89] Hospital. August 13th. Set off on a fine morning. The hollow valley, in part occupied by the lake of Lucerne, continues for a considerable distance beyond Altdorf. Enormous cliffs of limestone border it on each side rising shelf above shelf, and precipice above precipice (with pines clinging upon the narrow shelves, and fringing their summits,) becoming bare and red, and shattered as they rise, and indenting the clear blue sky at last with lines of jagged peaks with remnants of white snow on every point where it can lie. The valley itself is a flat bed of alluvium deposited by the Reuss. and apparently *[erasure]* a mere delta. very marshy near Fluelen. This long mountain valley continues for three leagues beyond Altdorf before the ascent commences. crossing the Reuss by a splendid bridge. and not long afterwards the granites of St. Gothard commence.

The rock which separates the limestones from the granite at this part of the road is met with much higher up, lying upon the granites between L'Hôpital and the summit of the pass. It is a reddish brown mica slate. *[page 90]* here in almost vertical beds, shaly and soft. It is full of quartz veins running parallel with its beds, and in these quartz veins are nests of good crystal, accompanied by white & green amianth, and rutile, both which are often imbedded in the interior of the crystal, the rutile not only in its usual delicate hair form, but in considerable crystals, forming very beautiful specimens and the quartz is quite full of fine green compact chlorite. The granites commence in half flat, half rounded, masses, breaking up into picturesque and pinecovered cliffs frequently with table formed tops. beautifully striped and variegated by the trickling of the mountain streams, but no aiguilles, here, at least. the limestones form by far the finest pinnacles. but on you wind, up rise the granites as you go, and become pointed and bare and snowy, and then you look up a narrow valley to the prodigious glacier and granite peaks of the Mont St. Gothard, or at least of the highest point of the group of St Gothard. And after that, you are in a wilderness. *[page 91]* The road zigzags up a narrow ravine down which rushes the Reuss in one long cataract and on each side rise up perpendicular cliffs of solid granite, bare and lichenless. But this granite is certainly stratified, lying in steeply inclined and distinctly marked beds, and these beds are again divided by a regular fracture into parallelograms, the fissures being straight and parallel. These granites are white, containing no chlorite, and very little mica, and being chiefly composed of feldspar and quartz. They contain large veins of this latter mineral which run usually parallel to the regular stratification of the rock. it is fine white transparent quartz rock running into good crystals.

The fall at the pont du diable is wonderfully fine, especially when belted with its morning rainbow, and after crossing the enormous bridge and rumbling through the dark gallery beyond it, you suddenly emerge from the shadowy chasm between the granite cliffs, and the plain ~~of~~ or valley of Andermatt lies open before you, level, and little cultivated, but beautifully green, and surrounded by magnificent aiguilles, and full of a crystal air, elastic, and inspiring like a spirit of life. *[page 92]* There are two villages in this singular mountain valley. Andermatt. and Hospital. both picturesquely placed. Afternoon became gloomy as we arrived at the latter village and we had some thunder. It will clear the air for tomorrow.

Hospital. August 14th. Started for Airolo. As you wind up the zigzags above Hospital you look back on the whole valley. and on the ravines which diverge from it. The first of these is terminated by beautiful aiguilles, rising out of fields of thick snow, and marking their granite composition by their spiry summits and jagged sides. Then comes a long range of mossy turf of great elevation, ~~co~~ crowned by a fringe of rock; and then a rounded mountain breaking down on its side into huge cliffs of grey granite, with the sun gleaming and glancing along their rugged sides, catching points and shelves of glittering rock, until they sink down into the dark and deep and narrow gorge of the Pont du diable and there the rays are checked, and can penetrate no farther. And beneath these mighty crags lies the level and green valley, with its two small villages shining in the sunshine, and the grey rocks lifting *[page 93]* up their heads from among its pasturages, or lying bedded in thick cushions of emerald moss. and the sky above is so blue, so beautifully blue, there is so little air between you and it. There is nothing half so delightful as a 5000 feet high summer morning.

I should think the valley of Andermatt, or as it is sometimes called of Urseren. had been formerly occupied by a lake. It is a circular bason, I should think from the steepness of the surrounding crags very steep, full of alluvium (smoothly deposited, consisting in part however of the debris of the granites round) and having only one narrow opening to the north where the Reuss after tumbling from the col de St. Gothard, and taking a rest of a quarter of an hour while it flows through the valley, finds its cataract issue. ~~on~~ It is on the first ascent from the valley of Urseren that you again meet with the mica slates. A small group of them lies upon the granite, ~~of~~ containing quartz veins &c., like those near Altorf. and resembling the mineral rocks of the Montanvert These do not continue long, and you again come *[page 94]* to the solid granites winding along their sides in galleries built up against the rock The col St. Gothard is a plain, small, and elevated and on which are five lakes, green, and clear, and rock bordered. There is a small marsh within a fathom of the highest, and the stream which trickles from it falls into the Reuss, and the Aar, the Rhine, and the German ocean. while the little lake within a fathom of it empties its waters into the Tessin, and the Po and the Gulph of Venice.

Vegetation ~~is~~ still flourishes on the mountains round the Col St. Gothard. That is to say, there is a little moss and lichen, and a few gentianellas and so forth, but they are very desolate, they won't do without clear sunshine, and though not so high as the col of St Bernard, this pass is almost as dreary. The descent on the Italian side commences with twenty nine zigzags, one beneath another, carried along on the top of a wall. sometimes leaning against the cliff, sometimes for a short distance entirely detached from it. While the Tessin, already swelled to a considerable torrent *[page 95]* falls by its side in six or seven fine cataracts. The opening to Airolo is beautiful, but what is the use of describing it. There were villages and fields, rocks and torrents, and grassy mountains and snow covered Alps, and we have had all that before. Objects on paper are always the same, it is by the disposition of them that nature gives variety. and therefore you can say no more than that — the opening to Airolo is beautiful. Yet there is a peculiar character in the Italian sides of the Alps and it is difficult to say exactly in what it consists. First there is less snow on the higher mountains, ~~as~~ which strikes you very much when you look at the chain of the Alps from Opposite points such as Berne and Milan, Geneva and Turin, &c. then the pasturage is more sunburnt, there is a peculiar yellow glow upon it a harvest like richness, which is wanting in the fresh green pasturages on the swiss side. Looking down the long valley from Airolo to Bellinzona, the prevailing colour is brown. looking down The valley towards Altorf the prevailing colour is green. The villages too are more thickly scattered on *[page 96]* the Italian side — it is Amazing what a distance you may see all full of *[erasure 'f']* villages and shining with the roofs of chalets. Airolo is not far distant in a straight line from the Col St. Gothard. but it is much lower than Hospital, and in order to get down the steep flanks of the mountain above it you are forced to treble your distance in zigzags, now nearing and then retiring, going over the same ground half a dozen times, it is quite a relief to go straight forward for ten minutes before you arrive.

The valley of Airolo is confined on three sides by Alps of enormous height, and on the fourth by a low line of rocks, of picturesque and beautiful forms. with a narrow passage, pierced through them by the Tessin. These rocks are of a fine, whitish brown mica slate. in vertical beds. and rich in minerals. They contain, first Common garnets, dodecahedral. in great quantities. size varying from small and very small to an inch in diameter. The colour of these garnets is usually good, a fine deep lake red. and they are transparent on the edges and translucent. The crystallization is bad. *[page 97]* they are not easily detached from their matrix, & they are full of flaws and very brittle. so that it is difficult to obtain a good specimen. 2nd. Kyanite. in middlesized and large crystals. not plentiful. but good specimens may be found with little trouble. 3rd. Glassy and common Actynolite, of which I found very fine specimens. Feldspars, common and adularia, are found near the same spot. For rock crystal, it is found every where. in the granite pure and with amianth, and in the mica slates with beautiful crystals of iron forming splendid specimens. The rocks look most tempting about the middle of the descent from the summit to Airolo, where the slates are exceedingly soft and in a state of half decomposition and the road which was based on them has been a good deal washed away by the torrent, and the quartz veins stand out white and beautiful mixed with green chlorite and running into imperfect crystallization. After mastering the troublesome zigzags on the Italian side you soon trot down to Hospital. Day had been clouding over gradually, and set in for a wet evening after letting us in.

[page 98] Flüelen. August 15th. It is very disagreeable to poke your nose out of bed into very cold air on a very wet morning. Melancholy was the dawn of the 15th of August on St Gothard, pitiless was the rain which cascaded from the eaves, and cataracted from the spouts. and thick and grey and impenetrable was the rolling vapour that mantled round the mountains. Speculations continued until half past eight. and then the clouds, after a little thunder, broke in an instant and the blue sky became bright, and ~~of~~ out looked the mountain peaks, and away went we. Above us is blue aether, and round us is rock, living with cascades, and turf, glistering with the gentle rain, and below us, like the smoke from a field of battle, roll the white rainclouds along the bottom of the valley, now bright and rosy as the mountain snow, now shadowed by the overhanging crags into pale grey veils and the tall pines stand out against them in dark relief, and seem to fear to enter into the cloud.

[page 99] It is curious to observe the strata of cloud while a storm is clearing. Up in the opening, The thin, white, streaky lines of cloud run across the blue sky, half mingling with it. the highest of all visible clouds, soaring far above the most ambitious summits of the Alps. Then come clouds like spray, thin and white, but not streaky, much lower, and sometimes touching the highest tops before rain. I have sometimes, especially among mountains, seen these spray clouds appear and disappear alternately without moving from the same spot~~;~~ perhaps shadowed by higher clouds. Then come the heavy white masses which portend rain and are seldom above 7: or 8000 feet ~~hi~~ above the plains, and then the real raincloud, which sometimes floats at less than 1000 feet above you I like to watch the different beds of cloud passing. each other, often driven by contrary currents. While we were above the lowest clouds, the scenery of the sky was beautiful, but when we got below them the cloudline became monotonous on the mountains, and the afternoon became dull as we arrived at Fluelen.

[page 100] Flüelen. August 16th. Cloudy and wet. every thing dull and stupid. Lake grey. Clouds grey. Hills grey, tops invisible, very disagreeable.

Lucerne. August 17th. By Schwytz and Aart. Day dull. clouds low. I asleep. Nothing interesting.

Lucerne. August 18th. The view from this city is superb, commanding the whole chain of mountains round the lake, from Righi to the magnificent calcareous crags of Pilate, one of the most beautiful mountains (allowing for its want of height) in Switzerland. ~~(~~Wherever you see it, its form is always beautiful, and the pineforests on its sides, and the turf out of which rise the tall peaked crags give it a variety of colour and form which is met ~~whi~~ with in few detached and low mountains.

Top of Righi. August 19th. Over the lake to Waggis. pretty and pleasant. The ascent begins among fine pastures and cornfields rising among broken masses of breccia. and gradually presenting beautiful views upon the Lake of Lucerne. It soon becomes tolerably steep going along the perpendicular sides of huge beds of conglomerate. dip about 25° towards Brunnen. *[page 101]* After this the ascent becomes less steep, passing amongst enormous blocks of breccia, heaped on each other in marvellous confusion, in one spot wedged into a natural arch. and then you wind through pasture land to Kalt Bad. Under a huge rock of breccia a small spring flows out of a narrow cavity. putting your ear to which you hear the ~~moan~~ gushing sound of an immense torrent flowing in the interior of the mountain part of its waters filter through the rock, forming this small spring. I am not aware that these waters have any issue below.

After passing this spring the clouds came round us white and thick, and confined our view to a few yards of rock and turf. We arrived at the Kulm about 3 o'clock. and until 7, the clouds did not once break After a few low growling thunderclaps, the mist opened for an instant, and a lurid smouldering sun looked out on the wide plain that appeared through the mist as if immeasurably beneath us. and then the clouds closed and the sun went down together, and darkness came upon the mountain.

All that evening the lightning blazed continually [*page 102*] apparently close to us with a vividness which was perfectly blinding. the thunder following on the instant rattling like a near discharge of musquetry. But the thunder of the plain is usually much louder, even when the storm is more distant. and that for two causes. first on a mountain there are ~~here~~ no objects around you that can either confine the sound, or return the echo of it. you are on an isolated point and the sound dissipates itself around you. Then the greater rarity of the air cannot even convey, much less form, a sound of strength and body. The thunder is neither so loud, nor conveyed so far, as thunder in a plain or valley. Lightning as near to us as these flashes were, would have produced, in a plain a sound like the discharge of a battery of great guns, while the feeble rattle of the thunder on the mountain top was drowned by interior din.

Went to bed speculating on the chances for tomorrow. looked out at half past three. the air was clear, the sky blue and full of stars. there was a faint golden tinge in the east, and the long chains of the Alps lay along *[page 103]* the south horizon, faint and dream like and aetherial, silvered by the pale light of the waning moon.

So we got up before the sun, and were ready on the Kulm to watch his rising, which was very much like any other sun rise, except inasmuch as it rose upon a scene which was like no other scene that I ever saw. The chain of the Alps immediately to the south is not, at this season completely sheeted with snow except a few very high summits. Titlis rises conspicuously, sloped gradually on one side, and sinking down in a vertical precipice on the other, on which no snow can rest. affording an excellent opportunity of judging of the depth of the snow on the mountains summit, which is broken off sharply at the edge of the precipice, about 200 to 250 feet in thickness.

Farther to the right, a good deal foreshortened. rise the whole range of the Bernese Alps. Sheeted with thick and unbroken snow, and beneath these appears the valley of Sarnen. (with its small lake), which opens out towards *[page 104]* the lake of Lucerne); then the magnificent peaks of Pilate, and the wide range of immeasurable plain. Low clouds in many places lay down upon the plain, appearing just on a level with it, and resembling lakes so nearly as to deceive the eye completely before the sun was up. Perhaps they were higher than they appeared. but a few tree tops came up through the cloud, where there were no mountains, perhaps on the top of low hills, otherwise not distinguishable from the general flatness of the plain. Then above the lake of Zug rises the heavy mass of the Rossberg, with its long line of desolation and at its foot the melancholy valley of Goldau. with remnants of the Lake of Lowertz glittering among its ruins. and then beyond the beautiful rocks of the Mythen, again commences the silver chain of the Alps. Off at 7 o'clock to walk down to Kussnacht. Road rather steep, down the escarpment of Rigi. and repeated our ride from Kussnacht to Lucerne.

Alpnach. August 21st. Sailed over the lake. Form of Pilate changing but always beautiful

Meiringen. August 22nd. Morning very fine. passed by the valley and lake of Sarnen. the valley luxuriant. lake with little variety. Then climbed a long hill with magnificent limestone cliffs on the right. It is amazing what beautiful forms the Alpine limestone assumes. in the Jungfrau rising 12,800 feet above the sea, and even in lower mountains breaking into a variety of peaks, which render limestone scenery the finest, with the exception of granite, among the Alps. Here the peak on the right is of a beautiful form. and finely wooded with dark pines. From the Top of this hill the Wetterhorns are seen rising, with their triple crest and precipice side. above the beautiful woods of the Brunig, and beneath, the small lake of Lungren, blue, or green or of a very beautiful between colour. shadowed by the steep hills which hang over it, but with a verdant shadow, an emerald reflection, set like a transparent jewel among raised work of mountains chased with forest. Passed this small lake, and began the ascent of the Brunig on beds of clay slate much decomposed. not variegated or tinged with iron *[page 106]* quite unfit for quarrying. The Brunig is very low, not above 3000 feet above the sea but its scenery is rich, varied, and luxuriant. Summit commands the whole valley of Hasli, the village of Meyringen and lake of Brientz, and-the beautiful limestone Alps which surround the valley. Descent steep, gets upon the limestones, apparently remains of an old eboulement, for they are tossed about in large and beautiful blocks, loaded with moss and turf with scattered trees, ashes, sycamores, alders, and lower down walnuts and chesnuts.

Meyringen. August 23rd. A dull, disagreeable, rainy day.

Hospice of the Grimsel. August 24th. The morning came brightly upon Meyringen, and we set off early, before a single light vapour had broken the beauty of the blue of the Alpine sky. The vale of Meyringen is closed at its upper extremity by a range of beautiful rocks. little wooded but with fresh green meadows upon their tops. through which the Aar has washed itself a passage, deep and narrow, just enough to allow the river to squeeze itself through — no room for mule path or any other path. so you are forced *[page 107]* to zigzag up the rocks, which are not very high however and then you pass through a lovely glade of oak upon cool greensward, from the end of which you look down on a valley, a small, hill bound solitary valley. It is on the same level as the vale of Meyringen, from which it is only separated by the low line of rock which I have just mentioned; formerly very probably the dyke,

108

distinctly stratified the near rocks were something between a limestone and an adhesive slate, hard, very thinly stratified, in laminae seldom more than half an inch in thickness, of a whitish grey colour, brittle, adhering slightly to the tongue. Then you begin to ascend again and after passing over a few slates, you arrive at the granite near Guttannen, a small village the last on this side of the Grimsel. situated beneath enormous hills. This valley is walled in by ranges of immense granite buttresses, between every one of which you look up to the higher peaks which they support. Both the buttresses and the alps behind are composed of granite beds with a dip of about 75° towards the ~~north~~ south east; so terminating in long and jagged ridges fig 16. which descend towards the north east to into the valley of Guttannen The beds of these ridges lie against one another like high steps and appear at the top to be

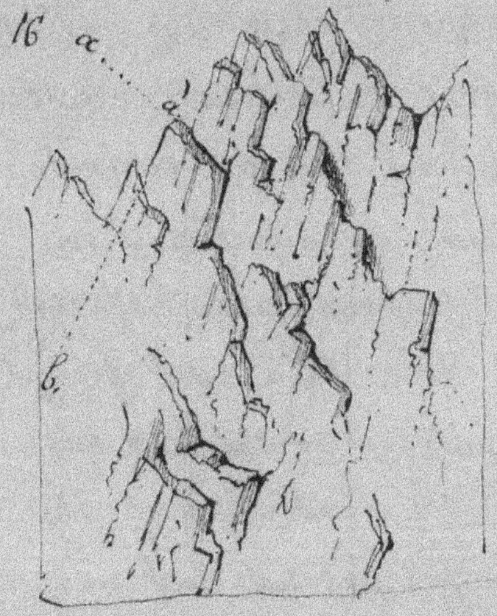

16 a.

b.

109.

terminated by planes at right angles to their dip.
17. 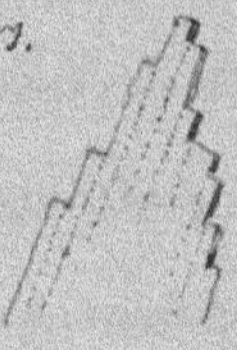 that is, by planes dipping to the north
west about 25°. so that if one of
these ridges were to be intersected in
a direction at right angles to the direction of its
strata, it would present the profile given in fig 17.
broken and confused of course, but in the main
such a regular profile, the dotted lines marking
the ~~direction~~ dip of its beds. These mountains
appear very remarkable from Guttannen where
this structure is seen to great advantage. Fig
16 lies to the west of Guttannen. The
buttresses which project almost at regular
intervals into the valley are more heavy and
rounded masses, presenting no thin and edgy
ridges, but composed of the same beds as
the higher mountains, and inclined in the same
manner. The granite is white, compact, with
little mica.
After passing Guttannen the road winds gradually
up a narrow mountain ravine, with little variety
of scenery, always confined by a succession of
similar buttresses, but the Alps behind gradually
increase in elevation, large glaciers are seen hanging

confining the waters of a lake which might have occupied this small valley. until the channel for their escape was cut down among the limestone rocks.

Into this valley open two mountain ravines, the one conducting you to the Grimsel, the other to a mountain pass leading to Altorf. The hills which separate these two vallies terminate in a ridge of limestone, whose peaks are as beautiful as they are curious, rising in pyramids, — no — in aiguilles from 3 to 4000 feet high, perpendicular, detached, inaccessible, with pines like thin dark fringes variegating their summits. I could not tell whether the rocks near the road were of the same substance, the cliffs did not look very *[page 108]* distinctly stratified The near rocks were something between a limestone and an adhesive slate, hard, very thinly stratified, in laminae seldom more than half an inch in thickness, of a whitish grey colour, brittle, adhering slightly to the tongue. Then you begin to ascend again and after passing over a few slates, you arrive at the granites near Guttannen, a small village, the last on this side of the Grimsel, situated beneath enormous hills. This valley is walled in by ranges of immense granite buttresses, between every one of which you look up to the higher peaks which they support. Both the buttresses and the alps behind are composed of granite beds with a dip of about 75^{0} towards the ~~north~~ south east, ~~so~~ terminating in long and jagged ridges fig. 16. which descend towards the north east ~~to~~ into the valley of Guttannen. The beds of these ridges lie against one another like high steps and appear at the top to be *[page 109]* terminated by planes at right angles to their dip, that is, by planes dipping to the north west about 25^{0} so that if one of these ridges were to be intersected in a direction at right angles to the direction of its strata, it would present the profile given in fig. 17. broken and confused of course, but in the main such a regular profile, the dotted lines marking the ~~direction~~ dip of its beds. These mountains appear very remarkable from Guttannen where this structure is seen to great advantage. Fig. 16 lies to the west of Guttannen. The buttresses which project almost at regular intervals into the valley are more heavy and rounded masses, presenting no thin and edgy ridges, but composed of the same beds as the higher mountains, and inclined in the same manner. The granite is ~~a~~ white, compact, with little mica.

After passing Guttannen the road winds gradually up a narrow mountain ravine, with little variety of scenery, always confined by a succession of similar buttresses, but the Alps behind gradually increase in elevation, large glaciers are seen hanging *[page 110]* from their peaks or couching on their sides, all traces of cultivation vanish, the loose stone walls which are twisted about the mountain pastures marking that they are available for something and belong to somebody, and which somewhat distract your attention to the scenery, by compelling you to make continual observations of the longitude of your toes, at last disappear, being replaced by huge blocks of granite, and, lesser debris, tossed about the mountain by ancient eboulements, Huge masses of rock lift up their heads from under the turf and the Aar rushes and roars by the side of the road in a perpetual whirl. a small distance farther on, after a steep zigzag, you turn off the road to see the fall of the Aar.

This is the very finest fall in Switzerland, not excepting the fall of the ~~to~~ Rhine. It is true. this latter has a greater body of water, it is a wider fall, it occupies more space in the landscape, it bears a greater ~~and its~~ proportion to the objects around, and its height (80 ft) is sufficient to give the water the velocity of lightning, and the whiteness *[page 111]* of snow. only varied here and there by the lovely emerald tint of its most pure waters. it is a superb cataract, and there is no occasion to disparage it in order to praise the Handek whose beauty indeed is rather of a different Character than of a superior degree. Two mountain streams, one indeed, even here, a considerable river, approach together the brow of the rock, they take the leap together, a leap of 270 feet, they join halfway down, choking the air with their spray, and raising a whirlwind with their velocity, and they plunge into an abyss where the sun cannot penetrate, but ever above it with fluctuating beam the double rainbow bends, now becoming pale when the drift of spray is too strong from the cataract, or the beam of the heaven fades, then brightening again into its beauty as the yellow light rekindles along the broad branches of the pines, and the soft, dewy, mist rises gently from the rush of the river. The rocks around the fall are remarkably chiselled by its spray, not only worn into a ~~d~~ sort of tunnel by the wash of the water itself, but *[page 112]* polished, and full of circular cavities, apparently formed by the beating back of the spray only, water against granite, water and time against very obstinate solidity, very particularly unaccommodating durability.

Looked at the great splash from above it and before it, but not from below it, for the river which has scooped out a narrow channel for itself has taken no pains for any body else, and there is no seeing the fall from below, for good quiet respectable people at least who do not choose to liken themselves to cats or monkeys.

Left the Handek as the light clouds that had lately covered the sky began to concentrate themselves and darken, and touch on the top of the mountains. The road scenery becomes savage, and the air exhilarating You pass over an eboulement. blocks of solid white granite looking as fresh as if they had been broken only yesterday from the mountain; Noticed that the form most frequent, and which indeed the rock seems to have a tendency to divide into, is that of a parallelopiped. Curved fractures comparatively rare.

[page 113] From hence to the Hospice, the road, taken as a whole, is what you would call a bad road. That is, it ~~was~~ is sometimes ? only perceivable by steps chiselled in the solid granite. sometimes passes along the top of a loose stone wall, sometimes crosses bridges, built over magnificent waterfalls, without any fence, not six feet wide, and sometimes disappears altogether in a bed of a torrent, or a wilderness of turf and rock. After crossing the Aar several times and climbing up into a desert, which although ~~as~~ less lofty, is more extensively desolate than even the col St Bernard, woe arrived at L'Hospice. By the side of a small lake, under magnificent granite peaks, beneath several glaciers, stands the small, strong, Hospice, built against the side of a high rock, which protects it from the swirl of the wind, a pleasant place to arrive at, after a ride in the clouds.

The granites of the Grimsel are to me the most interesting I have yet seen. I think that any person carefully examining them will find almost certain grounds for supposing that the regularity so frequently apparent *[page 114]* in granite is crystallization, not stratification. For there is this difference between granite and other stratified rocks, that granite beds are always vertical, or nearly so. I never saw any with a less dip than 75°. Again, in observing granites even from a distance~~s~~,

114.

in granite is crystallization not stratification. For there is this difference between granite and other stratified rocks, that granite beds are always vertical, or nearly so. I never saw any with a less dip than 75°. Again, in observing granites even from a distances, they have two palpable – what shall I say – cleavages, the first, of the mass into strata, the second of the strata into foursided columns. These two cleavages are very distinct in fig 16. the first in the direction a, á. occasioning the step like appearance of the rock. the second in the direction á. b. occasioning its apparent division into inclined columns. These two cleavages are of course at right angles to each other.

I was again struck with this structure in riding over the top of a large block of granite

(18.) near the Handeck. fig 18.

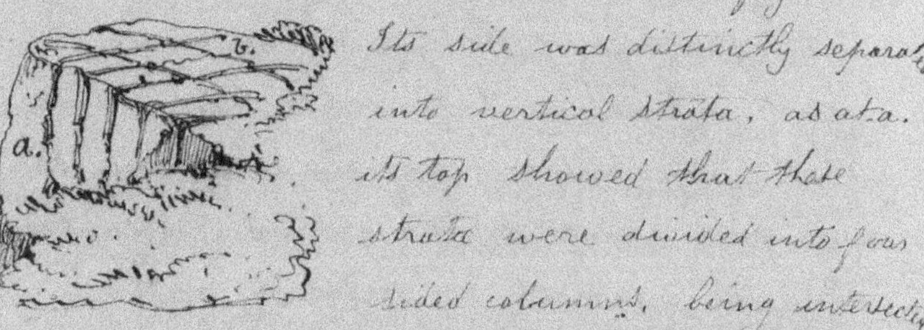

Its side was distinctly separated into vertical strata, as at a. its top showed that these strata were divided into four sided columns, being intersected

115.

by fissures running at right angles to each other. as at .b.

But these are not the only cleavages of granite, it has a third. The quadrilateral columns which are the result of the two cleavages above mentioned, are divided by another into joints, at irregular distances. Where these three cleavages are distinct the rock has frequently an exact resemblance to quadrilateral basaltic columns. I met with

19

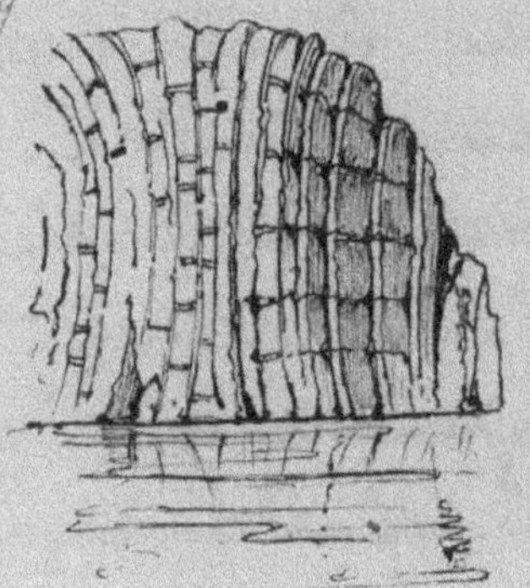

a remarkably fine instance of this structure very near the Hospice of the Grimsel fig 19. in the columns here are not only extremely distinct but they are regularly jointed, and they are jointed at different places, not intersected by a general and continuous fissures. But the great peculiarity of this group of columns is, that they are curved. and it will be observed that the joints continue at right angles to the curve showing that they are real joints. not a third cleavage.

they have two palpable — what shall I say — cleavages, the first, of the mass into strata, the second of the strata into foursided columns. These two cleavages are very distinct in fig. 16, the first in the direction a a' occasioning the steplike appearance of the rock, the second in the direction *a'. b.* occasioning its apparent division into inclined columns. These two cleavages are of course at right angles to each other. I was again struck with this structure in riding over the top of a large block of granite near the Handeck, fig 18. Its side was distinctly separated into vertical strata, as at *a.* its top showed that these strata were divided into four sided columns, being intersected *[page 115]* by fissures running at right angles to each other. as at *b.* But these are not the only cleavages of granite; it has a third. The quadrilateral columns which are the result of the two cleavages above mentioned, are divided by another into joints, at irregular distances. Where these three cleavages are distinct the rock has frequently an exact resemblance to quadrilateral basaltic columns. I met with a remarkably fine instance of this structure very near the Hospice of the Grimsel fig. 19. ~~w~~ The columns here are not only extremely distinct but they are regularly jointed, and they are jointed at different places, not intersected by ~~a~~ general and continuous fissures. But the great peculiarity of this group of columns is, that they are curved and it will be observed that the joints continue at right angles to the curve. showing that they are real joints. not a third cleavage. || *[page 116]* Now, as we meet with compact and columnar basalt, so I think we meet with compact and columnar granites. although perhaps there is very little compact granite, so called in which we shall not discover some vestiges of a tendency to divide itself into quadrilateral columns. (I say quadrilateral, because I have only seen them so formed, they may sometimes be met with pentagonal or hexagonal:) The Mont Blanc granites I never came to close quarters with, except in broken masses. ~~b~~ and I can only say that their distant contour differs not in the least from the peaks above the hospice of the Grimsel, whose bases are so distinctly columnar. The remarkable formation of fig 16 is much more rare, but I think that an instance of it may be found in the aiguille du Bochard. I have been speaking it must be remembered, exclusively of compact granites, and have used very incorrectly the word cleavage to denote crystallization, for compact granites have no cleavage. If one of these columnar masses fall, or be blown up with gunpowder it will fall into parallelopipeds as I have often *[page 117]* seen granite do. I have seen it on the Grimsel itself. the result of a large eboulement. But the granite falls into this form, because it has been previously crystallized in it, the joints of the columns are detached, and they are parallelopipeds and therefore the mass falls into parallelopipeds. Half frozen snow falls into the same form. the natural cubes are known by the name of Sorac, the large cubes break into smaller, and the smaller into the very small, as calcareous spar will break into rhomboids. But granite will not do this. Break one of the large parallelopipeds into smaller one's if you can. It has no cleavage, ~~it will~~ its fracture will be rounded or angular, just as your blow has been given. With foliated granites the case is different, they will usually break into folia. those of the Breven for instance break like slates. Their distant outline however is much the same as that of compact granites, a little more edgy. I think, but am not sure, that another specimen of columnar construction may be found in the Granite rocks, called les Bouts, (if they be granite.) between the Montanvert and Jardin.

[page 118] Hospice of the Grimsel. August 25th. Oh what sights and sounds saluted our eyes and ears on first awaking Patter of innumerable drippings through indiscoverable and unstoppable holes on floor and bed and habiliments. Plash of streams falling from the housetop, murmur of perpetual heavy rain, roar of the river rushing by, swoln with accumulated waters. sights, first wet window panes that would not let us see, secondly granite bare, ~~d~~ cold uncomfortable granite. and beyond, and above whole sheets of fresh snow that had fallen a little higher up during the night, dimly seen through the falling rain. rain with us, but snow there, accompanied by wind of excessive violence. it came in successive waves against the house. beat, beat, beat, bringing the sleet with it like the drift of foam from a cataract, and the wind hushed not, and the rain ceased not throughout the whole long monotony of that do-nothing day and in the evening the auguries were worse and worse, and the cattle were brought in out of the snow, and another stormy night came darkening down.

[page 119] Hospice of the Grimsel. August 26th. It was vain to attempt to persuade ourselves that the sudden gleam of light which chased away our darkness when the shutters were thrown open, was sunshine, or that the plashing murmur outside was only the hum of the swoln river. Oh, the leaden certainty of conviction that today out Heroded yesterday.

Matters were changed in some respects, not much for the better, the wind, less constant was if possible more violent when the swirl came, the thick, melancholy, sleety rain was changed into large flakes of cheerful snow, drifting down continually, melting on the granite, but covering every inch of turf, and a few feet higher up blanching every thing indiscriminately, which presented a surface whereon it could lie.

It was certainly no day for fighting our way down the worst road in Switzerland and so we prepared for more monotony. warmth, smoke and idleness. I wonder why snow should lie on grass when it will melt on rock. the one must be as cold as the other.

[page 120] Meyringen. August 27th. This morning the wind had abated, the snow was turned into a slight drizzling rain. which ceased as soon as we got out of the clouds. The sight even of the stunted pines was pleasant to our desolated eyes. Afternoon very doubtful.

Meyringen. August 28th. The morning was too cloudy to allow of our starting for the Scheideck. but it cleared up enough to let us have a pleasant walk to the Reichenbach &c. The valley of Oberhasli is a transverse valley, running northwest and southeast, that is, at right angles to the chain of the Alps, and is bordered, like many other large Alpine vallies, by enormous and beautiful cliffs of Alpine limestone, which are yet so much broken and varied as to prevent your experiencing that sense of being in a hole, which you feel almost painfully at Lauterbrunn.

The strata of these cliffs are not much disturbed, except at one spot, on the east side of the valley, just above Meyringen where they are bent sharply round. There is no corresponding turn on the opposite side. *[page 121]* and indeed no perceptible correspondence between the sides of the valley at any point. The cliffs on the western side are the finest, and over them tumble several magnificent cascades, the chief of which is the Reichenbach, a series of splendid falls, none of which however are at all equal to the Handek. but every fall has its own particular beauty, the infinite variety of fall, and the beauty of the green banks and tall trees which adorn the Reichenbach might be more pleasing to some tastes than the sombre and tremendous plunge of the Aar into the invisibility of its pine shadowed abyss.

There are many fine cascades on the opposite side of the valley; which would be wonders in any other part of the world but are little prized here. ~~This~~ Their beds are very uninteresting, limestones, a few clay slates from the Brunig, and plenty of calcareous spar are the only minerals they bring down I believe the Reichenbach, above its falls, contains a considerable quantity of gold.

[page 122] Grindelwald. August 29th. The morning was cloudless; Oh, the comfort that there is in an hour or two of blue sky and sunshine after a day or two of rain. Started for the Sheideck, Wound up the green banks between the cliffs of limestone, down which tumbles the Reichenbach, and at last got up to the sun, while the valley, far below, remained in deep shadow. Then, after skirting for a minute the dark gorge of the Reichenbach, the valley opens towards the Sheideck, closed by the redoubtable peaks of the Wellhorn, and pointed snow of the splendid Wetterhorn. On winds the path among the pines, higher at every step rise those magnificent mountains, the one snowless, the other dazzling with unbroken glacier, and by their side rolls down the huge glacier of Rosenlaui into the green pasturage of the Sheideck. and the sun was very brilliant upon its ice, but it was very early, and we were 2500 feet high, and it was excessively cold and delightful. The inn of Rosenlaui is near the foot of the glacier at the base of the Wellhorn and commands a wonderful view, of the limestone peaks of that *[page 123]* mountain (they say they are limestone; may be so,) and of more distant and mightier elevations that rise whitely over the green waves of the glacier and over the fields at the base of the Wetterhorn, a green, soft elevation, which yet doubles the height of the most famous English mountain. Up upon those fresh green pastures we wound, emerging from the shadow of the ~~green~~dark forests which encircle Rosenlaui. and above our heads rose walls of perpendicular rock, red and bare, without the presence of the least cool tint to denote an atom of vegetation, up they go, higher and higher, immeasurably high, with perhaps hardly a hundred feet of inclination from the perpendicular, in 5000 of direct elevation and over them, as the foam of a breaking wave hangs over its smooth and polished side, impends an enormous precipice of ice, relieved splendidly against the dark blue of the Alpine sky, that seems to rest on as ov it like the dome of a mighty [*page 124*] temple on a Corinthian column of Marble. The whole of the Wetterhorn, and of its companion, the Wellhorn, are said to be ~~granite~~ calcareous rock. I do not believe it. The part of the Wetterhorn which is come-at-able from the Sheideck is certainly limestone, but the summit of the Wetterhorn has never to my knowledge been ascended, and it is believed without any farther evidence, that because the bottom of the mountain was ~~granite~~ calcareous, the top must be so. One might as well affirm that Mont Blanc was not granite, because the Montanvert was mica slate.

In the first place, the appearance, and the form of the summit of the Wetterhorn is not that of limestone rock, from whatever point it may be viewed. from the east, it is a majestic and regular pyramid, with a point as sharp as a needle and with a few jagged rocks *[page 125]* projecting from its sides, fig 21, from the west a pyramid with a jagged, not pointed summit, rising from a crown of the sharpest aiguilles. fig 22. Neither of these forms are often, or perhaps ever assumed by calcareous rock There is a difference between the colours of the base and summit of the Wetterhorn the base is reddish brown, the summit black, or nearly so. another distinction between limestone and high granites. Again, the limestone strata of the Wetterhorn, seen from the Sheideck, have a very remarkable appearance fig. 23. At the first glance they appear horizontal, slightly curved. on a nearer approach you perceive them to be vertical, quite vertical, running east and west, and terminating in steps or rather forming ledges by their terminations which are of course horiz *[page 126]* ontal, and give the rock the appearance of being horizontally stratified, as at *a,* and *b.* Now, I think it is seldom, or never that limestone, unaccompanied by any other rock is found in beds, evenly, undisturbedly, and perfectly vertical, and that on an immense scale. its beds may be distorted, broken, twisted or steeply inclined, they are seldom uniform still seldomer uniformly vertical, except where they immediately rest on primitive rock.

The Sheideck, which is beneath these limestone rocks, is of a black mica slate, much decomposed, indeed passing into clay in some places. It is difficult to ascertain the direction of the beds of such a rock, but as far as I could see, they appeared to be nearly vertical, dipping north, and consequently lying against the Wetterhorn at its base just as the limestones do against its side. The position of these rocks I think affords strong grounds for believing that they lie on an immense mass of granite which is only developed at the summit of the Wetterhorn, and that fig. 20, would be a tolerably accurate section of the whole group. *a,* ~~mic~~ clay *[page 127]* slate, forming the Sheideck, *b,* vertical beds of limestone, lying on the slate, forming the side of the Wetterhorn, and *c,* granite supporting both slate and limestone, and forming the pointed summit of this magnificient mountain. Thinking that such might be the case, I looked for granite debris as I walked down the Sheideck, and was disappointed at finding none. But *[it]* is impossible that any granite debris can fall upon the Sheideck, (*d*) because this pass is overhung by the shoulder of the Wetterhorn (*b*) which is wholly limestone and must altogether intercept the granite debris falling from the summit itself. If no granites are carried down by the upper glacier of Grindelwald, which is immediately beneath this summit, it would settle the matter at once; I did not visit this glacier, but I believe its moraine is in great part composed of granite, thus offering another ground for believing that the summit of the Wetterhorn is composed of granite, and the Jungfrau is a solitary instance of the great elevation which limestone sometimes attains. *[page 128]* The summit of the.Sheideck is a low ridge which connects the Wetterhorn with the Schneeberg, terminating on the one side the valley of Grindelwald, a longitudinal valley, opening into the transverse valley of Lauterbrounn, and on the other the longitudinal valley of Rosenlaui, opening into the transverse one of Hasli. The panorama discovered from it is not extensive and it has little variety, but is perhaps, nevertheless one of the most magnificent in Switzerland. To the north rises the Sch^{n}eeberg, so called (I believe) because being of little comparative elevation it is

28

temple on a Corinthian column of Marble. The whole of the Wetterhorn, and of its companion, the Wellhorn, are said to be ~~granite~~ calcareous rock. I do not believe it. The part of the Wetterhorn which is come-at-able from the Scheideck is certainly limestone, but the summit of the Wetterhorn has never to my knowledge been ascended, and it is believed without any farther evidence, that because the bottom of the mountain was [calcareous] granite the top must be so. We might as well affirm that Mont Blanc was not granite, because the Mont-anvert was mica slate.

In the first place, the appearance and the form of the summit of the Wetterhorn is not that of limestone rock, from whatever

71.

point it may be viewed. From the east, it is a majestic and regular pyramid, with a point as sharpe as a needle, and with a few jagged rocks.

125

projecting from its sides fig 21. from the west a pyramid with a jagged not pointed summit; rising from a crown of the sharpest aiguilles. fig 22. Neither of these forms are often or perhaps ever assumed by calcareous rock

There is a difference between the colours of the base and summit of the Wetterhorn the base is reddish brown, the summit black, or nearly so another distinction between limestone and high granites.

Again, the limestone strata of the Wetter horn seen from the Sheideck, have a very remarkable appearance fig 23. At the

22

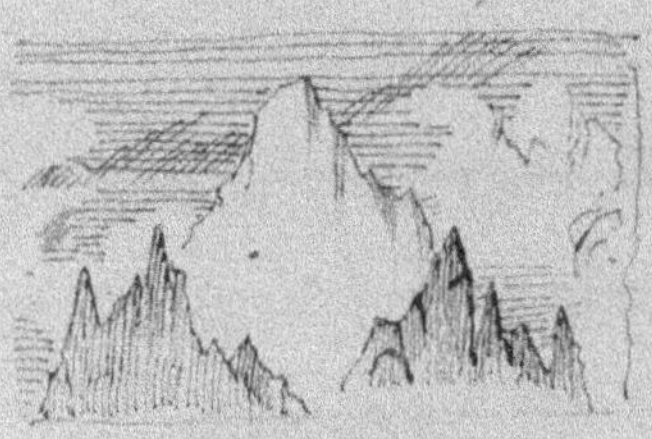

first glance they appear horizontal, slightly curved. on a nearer approach you perceive them to be vertical, quite vertical, running east and west, and terminating in steps or rather forming ledges by their terminations which are of course hori

23.

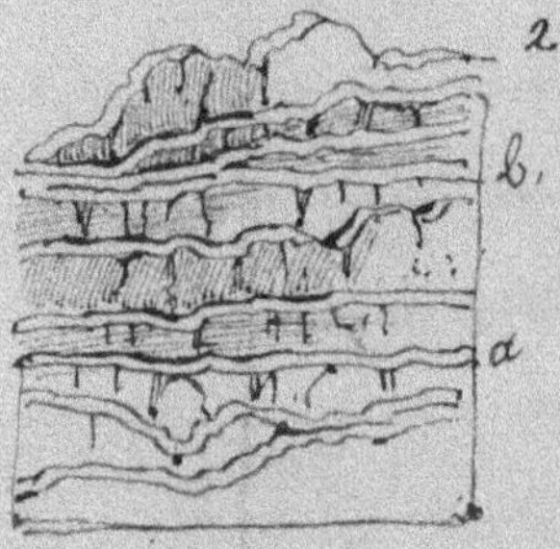

b.

a

more sheeted with snow than the surrounding peaks, on account of its form being more adapted to retain it. to the east the range of beautiful Alps on the other side of the valley of Hasli *[four dashes inserted about these two words]*, farther ~~to~~ round, a long chain of granite aiguilles, connected with the huge mass of the Wetterhorn which rises on the south, and on the west the luxuriant valley of Grindelwald with its two glaciers shining amidst the green of its meadows and above the edgy summit and precipice sides of the great Eiger, rising unimaginably high into the silent heaven.

[page 129] As you descend towards Grindelwald you pass by the upper glacier, thought to be the finest; which rolls down between the Wetterhorn and Mettenhorn, and above it are seen the steep crags and jagged summit of the Schreckhorn, rising like a small island amidst the immense extent of frozen ocean, which lies between the Finsteraarhorn, Wetterhorn, Eiger's, and Jungfrau. The side of the Sheideck next the Grindelwald is composed in great part of marshy and boggy land, ~~co~~ alternating with ugly black rocks of decomposing slate. by no means a foreground fit for such a magnificent distance, at least until you come down among the cornfields and pasturages of Grindelwald. a splendid valley, not a narrow strip of cultivated land lying between steep hills, like Chamouni, nor an extent of rich plain between high mountains like the Valais, or the Hasli but a valley composed of beautiful undulating hills, becoming higher and higher as they recede from the banks of the stream that flows from the two glaciers through the valley, until they are lost *[page 130]* in the immense bulk of the mountains which border it on each side and gradually decreasing in luxuriance, passing from fruittrees to cornfields and from cornfields to pasturage. which degenerates into velvety turf, broken higher up by grey rocks, ~~and f~~ which are gradually concealed by snow.

Grindelwald. August 30th. The morning came without a cloud upon the brilliant snows of the Eiger and the Wetterhorn, too fine to last, and by 12 o'clock there was little blue sky to be seen, and the clouds were dark and heavy, though without rain. Walked a little way up the road of the Wengern Alp, the first part of which is monotonous, passing immediately beneath the precipices of the Eiger, and though it commands the valley of Grindelwald, and gives a good idea of its form and position, yet the view from the valley itself is to my taste infinitely finer. It Looked rainy, so we descended, but started again for the lower glacier. the most easy of access of any. that I have seen. At the source of the Arveron you have to stumble for *[page 131]* half a mile over the large, rolled, loose, blocks of granite which form the bed of the stream at Bossons you have to climb a mountain of moraine; the glacier du Rhone is worse still. the glaciers of the Allée blanche, if not difficult of access may be said to be disagreeable of access. here, you walk through successive cherry orchards and meadows, the last covered with a forest of pine, and stumble on the glacier as easily — it does not exactly touch the meadows, but you may go within twelve yards of the ice without ever leaving the beautiful green level turf. The ice of the glaciers has been often described and still it remains very incomprehensible ice. The beautiful blue or green colour of its chasms is optical, because it is only in its chasms, and the lump of broken ice which you take up and examine is always transparent and colourless, or rather of all colours for its prismatic colours are most vivid and beautiful; Why then should the mass reflect only one colour, while the morsel reflects all? The arches in the glaciers whence run the streams *[page 132]* formed by their melting are remarkable, because they do not resemble passages torn by the violence of the waters, but beautiful and regular arches melted away around them and high over them, as if by a warm air rising from the water itself. which indeed may be the case, for the glacier streams are not what you would call bitterly cold, ~~but~~ not much colder indeed than running water in general, and in winter, when the water is colder, the arch is not only smaller in proportion to the diminished quantity of water but barely enough to let the stream out, its relative size is much smaller than in summer.

Interlaken. August 31st. by Lauterbrounn a secondary day, among secondary formations. We wished to cross the Wengern Alp, but some how or other, I know not why, we found ourselves going by the valley. which is a very tiresome, and stupid valley. very monotonous and all limestone. we shall have nothing else for a long time. They say the Eiger is limestone, but I think the same of it that I do of the Wetterhorn. its limestone strata are likewise vertical, rising in *[page 133]* immense sheets above the Wengern Alp, and terminating in a ridge, which, from Grindelwald. appears as sharp as the blade of a knife. I should have mentioned above, that I found much granite debris brought down by the lower glacier of Grindelwald, which descends between the Mettenberg and Eiger. The morning was fine. although it was treacherous. clouds came up very fast but they did not conceal the mountains till pretty late. which was fortunate. for Lauterbrounn would be nothing in wet weather except inasmuch as the Staubbach would be magnified thereby.

The valley which connects Grindelwald with Lauterbrounn is, as I before said, tiresome enough. hills sloping down on each side with no break or variety of outline. rocks of limestone ~~is~~ partially concealed by pine forests. I had seen so many instances of twisted strata that I was little interested in the numerous and remarkable contortions of these strata till I observed one very peculiar. fig. 24. The apparently horizontal strata, at *[page 134]* this point little distorted, were cut in two by a dyke of perpendicular beds of the same rock which appeared to have been thrust down from above, because the horizontal beds were bent a little downwards on each side of them. The limestone was brownish. The valley of Lauterbrounn, where this one opens into it is narrow, a ravine rather than a valley, but it opens out a little higher up. and enables you to view the heights of the Jungfrau and Silberhorn. Yet at the best Lauterbrounn is but a sort of moat or fosse with steep walls of limestone on each side fine cliffs certainly, but not the sort of thing that I admire. The Jungfrau rises whitely and beautifully, marked calcareous by its wavy domelike outline. although such an outline is not always a certain criterion of the composing rock, for I should have applied the same epithets to the contour of Mont Blanc, as seen on two sides at least. But among the Bernese Alps the ~~all~~ form *[page 135]* of the Jungfrau is peculiar, for they are mountains of straight lines, and sharp angles, and inaccessible peaks, the highest is a regular, but craggy and inaccessible cone, the wetterhorn a pyramid pointed, and surrounded by aiguilles. the Shreckhorn a bare and perpendicular rock, the Eigers are sharp ridges formed by precipices almost vertical, but the Jungfrau is all curves and lines of beauty, presenting in the ranges of the Silber horn that figure assumed by the waves of a rippling sea under the influence of opposite

134

this point little distorted, were cut in two by
24. a dyke of perpendicular
beds of the same rock
which appeared to have
been thrust down from
above, because the hori-
zontal beds were bent a little downwards on each
side of them. The limestone was brownish.
The valley of Lauterbrunn, where this one
opens into it is narrow, a ravine rather than
a valley, but it opens out a little higher up,
and enables you to view the heights of the
Jungfrau and Silberhorn. Yet at the less
Lauterbrunn it but a sort of moat or fosse
with steep walls of limestone on each side fine
cliffs certainly, but not the sort of thing that I
admire. The Jungfrau rises whitely and
beautifully, marked calcareous by its wavy
domelike outline, although such an outline
is not always a certain criterion of the
composing rock, for I should have applied
the same epithets to the contour of Mont
Blanc, as seen on two sides at least.
But among the Bernese Alps the [illegible] form

currents, that of ridges with regular concave sides, which quite prevents any of that lumpishness which spoils the Chamouni view of Mont Blanc.

Over the cliffs on the left or western side of the valley tumbles the Staubbach the highest cascade in Switzerland, I believe in Europe, would be much the better of a little more water. which comes down at an apparent snails gallop, minced into a veil of gauze before it gets to the bottom. and acting to the near shrubs, ~~a~~ grass and *[page 136]* trees as a perpetual watering pot. The ride towards Interlakken is pretty enough, not very interesting. The Jungfrau rises as you approach Interlakken. appearing far down the long perspective of Lauterbrounn. Interlakken is placed as its name implies, between two lakes, which have been formerly connected, and the piece of ground which now separates them is, especially near the lake of Brientz, even now little better than a marsh, but rich and fruitful near Unterseen. and watered by the Aar, clear and beautiful purified by its repose in the lake of Brienz and very different from the turbid waters which torment the rocks of Handeck. Rocks around all calcareous, and with little variety of form, especially on the Brientz side.

Thun. September 1st. Sailed per steamer down the lake of Thun, 15 miles in an hour and a quarter. very good sailing quite another thing from the boats on the lake of Geneva, which go 6 miles an hour. The head of the lake is fine, its borders not [*page 137*] striking. Mont Niesen is a fine calcareous pyramid, but formal. Day splendid but coldish in the morning.

Thun. September 2. a pleasant place enough, and view magnificent especially from a low hill above the town where you command the broad lake and its surrounding Alps, Eigers, Jungfrau, and Blumlis Alp, which we saw a clear purple sunset upon. The different effects of light on the Alps are as remarkable as they are beautiful, on a clear day they change continually in the morning the dark sides are of a pale silvery grey, exactly the colour of the sky. so that the outline is scarcely discernible except by the scattered touches of brilliant light which catch the eye in an instant and drag ~~s~~ it down to the horizon wherever it may be looking. as the sun rises the dark sides become darker and the lights become broader, and as the sun gets to the meridian they assume a tinge *[scribble]* which is not *[page 138]* white, nor golden, nor pink, but an inexpressibly rich tawny colour made out of the three, which nevertheless is far brighter than the pure ~~col~~ silver white of the morning. They become more golden towards the evening, and if the sky be clear, just before the sun sets when he is about a degree from the horizon they suddenly, very suddenly change to the most beautiful pink possible, pale certainly but dark for snow, and inexpressibly beautiful. and at the instant when the sun touches the horizon they assume a rich purple which after remaining for a minute or two fades away, and leaves the mountains faint and white and lustreless, yet remaining a long time visible when every thing else is lost in the shadow of night.

I have thought sometimes that though there always appears a richness, a melancholy, a fatigue if I may so say, in the light of the afternoon, and a freshness, coldness, cheerfulness and vigour ~~of~~ in that of the morning, yet that these changes were more in our feelings than in the light itself, and that *[page 139]* a person waking from sleep in the evening would not be able to distinguish it from the morning and this is true to a certain extent but these changes of light on the Alps show that it is not altogether so. The purple tint is difficult to account for, the more so as it is always brightest and purest when there is no haze about the horizon When there is any distinct haze or cloud in the west (however red it may be) it never appears at all.

Berne. September 3rd. Ride here very pretty, and chain of Alps lengthening in the distance. The view from the cathedral terrace is splendid. It is curious that seen from here the Wetterhorn appears a considerable distance from the great Eiger. and the Shrekhorn appears between them yet the two former mountains are only separated from each other by the Mettenberg, and rise at opposite extremities of the valley of Grindelwald. The Shrekhorn is between them, certainly but so far behind that it cannot be *[page 140]* seen from Grindelwald and its summit appears over the upper glacier only upon mounting towards the Sheideck. yet here it appears to be between them and in their chain. Our old friend the Aar rolls round the city, sadly muddy. very different from the river of Thun or Interlakken.

Fribourg. September 4th. Road pretty Alps in sight all the way. Finsteraarhorn very fine. why should they call it Finster. it is loaded with snow. Fribourg is a remarkable city built on high cliffs composed of sandstone in thick horizontal beds, through which a rapid river, one of the tributaries of the Aar has cleft a deep and precipitous channel. The suspension bridge ~~I~~ over it is marvellous. finer or at least more wonderful than our Menai.

Lausanne. September 5th. Here we are again after a good round of Switzerland. Road hilly and prettyish. nothing after what we had seen Lausanne I never liked and never shall, There is too much of lake, and *[page 141]* the town is a town of Beau Sejours and Bon Repos-s and about it there is nothing but dead walls.

Lausanne. September 6th, 7th. Blank.

________ 8th. Vevey. Wet.

Fribourg. ________9th. Farewell to the lake of Geneva. The road from Fribourg to Vevay is as far as we could judge from glances got ~~H~~ in a day which never ceased pouring, one of the most beautiful in Switzerland. the vegetation luxuriant, the near country magnificently cultivated as if every farmer were a landscape gardener. and the Alps in the distance. on which snow fell today, as it often does during wet weather at this season.

Berne. September 10th. Weather still very disagreeable. They keep bears here. for bears are the supporters of the national arms, as indeed they ought to be, for of a bear and a Swiss or German, I consider the bear to be by far the politer animal Here indeed they are exceedingly polished brutes and beg to you for a piece of bread with a good grace.

[page 142] Morgenthal. Sept 11. Road among low hills covered with forest with distant views of the Alps. Country about Morgenthal luxuriant.

Baden. Sep 12. Scenery rather finish, pretty hills, and fine views of the Alps, the same almost ^{as} only more distant than, that of Rigi who rises below them very black or blue or a sort of hobbletehoy[17] between colour *[erasure]*

Baden. Sept 13. Pretty place on the Limmat among limestone rocks of distinct and thin strata dipping southwest about 30°, richly wooded in some parts and bare and fantastic in others. meadows around green and beautiful and town picturesque enough ~~co~~ This day it stopped pouring for an hour or two in the afternoon, so we took a paddle, and called it a walk.

Winterthur. Sept 1~~3~~4. By Zurich. Buckets full of rain. cats and dogs.

St Gall. Sept 1~~4~~5th. Morning misty and beautiful. a complete silver morning. The light mists coagulated and gathered themselves into white and excessively low ~~hills~~ clouds which lay *[page 143]* here and there sprinkled along the plain country and touching the tops of its very lowest hills They first thickened, so much so as to threaten rain, then gradually disappeared and left a cloudless sky over very beautiful scenery of its sort. alps as usual in distance.

The evening sky opposite the sun was today of a most gorgeous purply pink like the colour with which the Alps are emblazoned at sunset, and which I never saw at home. I noticed that every house in St Gall, with perhaps one or two exceptions, though I do not recollect any, had two or three lightning conductors, and connected with each other frequently with those of the next house by cross rods. so that the houses were- surmounted by interminable railings. yet I should not have liked to have been here ~~ano~~ in a thunderstorm. I saw a few days before that 3 houses had been struck here in one storm, and indeed I should have thought by their appearance that these irons were rather attractors of *[page 144]* the fluid to the house than conductors of it away. Instead of being connected with the house by glass rings, or not at all, they ~~cam~~ are carried up from the ridges of the gables. where they are usually connected by iron with the roof, then proceed to the eaves and down the side of the house, close to it, and joined to it frequently, and by iron too, so that it is twenty to one that the lightning gets to the ground without an explosion. I suppose, however, that there is some cause for this for I never saw so many thunder conductors there must be some mineral, perhaps a great quantity of iron in the soil, which serves as an attractor.

Feldkirch. Sept 16. An interesting day. descended first a steep hill among rich meadows and woods to the borders of our old friend, the lake of Constance. which looked as boundless as the sea in the mist of the morning, which mists soon cleared and showed us Lindau shining white and beautiful on the opposite shore. We soon reached the extremity of the lake and were ferried across the Rhine which appeared very muddy *[page 145]* indeed it is said it can be traced nearly the whole way through the lake of Constance. but this is impossible. it has deposited and continues to deposit~~e~~ an immense delta, which is worse than the delta of the Rhone for it is much larger. Soon after crossing the Rhine an immense view opens upon you suddenly, the high Alps of Splugen and St. Bernardino bounding an immensely long and immensely wide valley, which is all delta, and through the midst of which

17 Hobbledehoy = an awkward or clumsy youth.

flows the Rhine the higher part of this large valley, which you pass on the road to the Splügen is like most other Alpine Vallies, indeed in some parts not so flat, and there are some parts as beyond Werdenberg, and near Ragatz and Coire, which are exceedingly beautiful, shelving up to the mountains in smooth slopes of green turf not jagged with monotonous pine, but tufted with various and beautiful trees. but hereabouts. it is an unbroken flat, which sailors would call between wind and water. for it is exactly on the level of the water, so that there is not *[page 146]* an inch of dry land in the whole plain ~~nor~~ and nothing which you could fairly and truly denominate water, it is a sort of bastard element, of amphibious land. on which or in which, the peasants plash about like so many frogs, yet I believe there is not much malaria here, and the people look tolerably healthy. Crossed this marsh and wound along the base of limestone cliffs to Feldkirch which lies prettily and is nearly surrounded by high hills. Evening was cloudless. but not so pinky as yesterday evening.

<u>St Antoine</u>. Sept 1~~8~~7. The morning was at first cloudless, but before we left the suburbs of the town I saw clouds which always bring rain in mountainous countries. They are small, but distinct clouds, in streaks, but solid not in streaky streaks, distinctly outlined, of a pale reddish brown colour and lying on the horizon in the direction of the wind. They are unfailing signs of rain before long, though all the rest of the sky be cloudless. I saw them on a fine morning ascending from Cormayeur, the evening of that day, the whole of the next *[page 147]* and the morning of the next were wet. I saw them ascending the St Gothard on an otherwise cloudless morning from Hospital the evening was wet, and was followed by much wet weather. with few interruptions. I saw them before our most unfortunate arrival at the hospice of the Grimsel. again on leaving Berne for Fribourg, when the following series of wet weather seemed interminable. and we shall see what weather they will bring us here.

Our commencement however was most delightful, passing first through a narrow Ravine, worn by the waters of a large and strong river, one of the tributaries of the Rhine. which opened into a most lovely and secluded valley, a delightful specimen of the Tyrol to begin with. It was bordered by limestone mountains, and limestone mountains are the most delightful things in the world I do not mean the limestone flanks, of high mountains of different composition, which are always monotonous and sometimes ugly take for instance the borders of the vallies of *[page 148]* Hasli, Lauterbrounn, Interlaken, or that of the Rhone below Martigny, but mountains wholly composed of limestone, though of inferior elevation, are always beautiful, their outline is varied and their colouring magnificent. as may be seen in some parts even of the Jura, in the calcareous cliffs of Cluse and St Martin, in the mountains of Altorf and of Alpnach, and Lungren; and, a better instance than any, in the beautiful form of the celebrated Mont Pilate. This valley was bordered by such mountains, and it was beautiful in itself, though not what you would call richly cultivated it had been taken great pains with by nature and she is a good landscape gardener. it was not rankly luxuriant but it was fresh, green and gay and glittering with a heavy morning dew, lit up by the morning sun, shining through morning mist, and every thing looks beautiful in the morning. Pludens lies prettily towards the extremity of this ~~morn~~ valley. The ascent of the Vorarlberg begins soon afterwards, very gently, you can hardly tell you are ascending. but there is not an inch *[page 149]* of level ground; and you get up gradually pretty high The scenery is very fine, and very much varied. but not in character. In Switzerland you go a long way without [a] change, but when you do get a change, it is a real one, but here the scene changes every mile. but it changes to the same thing. the same sort of mountain and valley, and the same height, and the same general character.

Rock mostly limestone, with a few slates. a little white quartz. and no interesting minerals. My clouds have been true prophets. the sky was very gradually overclouded, and about 5 oclock the clouds as if by general consent stooped down upon the mountains. we ascended and they descended till they wrapped themselves about us, and began to rain heavily. Fresh snow had fallen lately too, and we got up among that, it was pretty thickly sprinkled on the south side of the valley, where the sun could not get at it but it was not very cold Just when we were at the top the clouds broke and the setting sun shone through upon the mountain tops. and down *[page 150]* a long valley towards Landek. it set before we arrived at St Antoine. a small hamlet on the hillside. could not get any farther.

Ober Miemingen. Sept 17.[18] Started from St Antoine on a melancholy cloudy morning, could see nothing of the hills on the road to Landeck. but I should think from a glance down the valley last night that the scenery was fine. I caught one glimpse of a large glacier through the cloud. Were benighted. nice starlight ride into another little shabby place, with a long name. Ober Miemingen. ———

Inspruck. Sept 1~~8~~9. The morning was full of low, ~~li~~ but light rosy clouds above which rose the mountain tops in a full blaze of sunlight. it just doubles a mountains apparent height when it is seen only at its top and its base is concealed by cloud. wonder why. I recollect seeing the Eiger in this way from Grindelwald. one of the most sublime sights and most astonishing possible magnificent, incredibly high. and here our morning view was very wonderful even though the mountains were only moderate.

[page 151] Sept 20. Inspruck. It is curious to look down the great square of this town, fine, very fine houses. like those of some large German city. and above the enormous bulk of some of the most magnificent hills in the Tyrol. sprinkled with snow, The climate here was at this time magnificent, the sky cloudless, the sun blazing and hot, the mountains round glowing gorgeously beneath it. the indian corn growing round, and the excessive heat like that of Italy. I could hardly think we were on the north side of the Alps. we shall have a change.

Landeck. September 2~~0~~1. We go ~~a~~ back on the same road today, which is the more agreeable as ~~w~~ the mountains were partially concealed by cloud before. We started on a cloudless morning. You pass first under enormous cliffs of limestone ~~where th~~ hanging over the Inn, at a small distance from which is the little village of Zul. whence the view is magnificent. ascending a hill a little farther on, we looked up the broad and beautiful valley of the Inn. *[page 152]* bordered by its noble limestone

18 Actually Sept. 18. See *The Diaries of John Ruskin, 1848–1873*, ed. by Joan Evans and John Howard Whitehouse, 3 vols (Oxford: The Clarendon Press, 1956–59), vol. 1, p. 63, n. 1.

mountains which consist almost entirely of rock without being veiled by turf or forest; they are rather gigantic crags than mountains, they are also too low for perpetual snow, and ~~are ob~~ their limestone is of a yellowish red colour, which is exceedingly bright when the sun shines on them and gives a character to the scenery of the valley of the Inn quite different ~~to~~ from any thing I have seen elsewhere. The valley itself is not monotonously flat but varied by low and gently sloping hills among which the Inn winds backwards and forwards now washing the rocky bases of the higher mountains, now winding away into the middle of the valley among green pasturages and fields of maize.

The valley of the Inn is about 50 miles long. and of the form of a bow *a* *b* but the road from Inspruck. *a.* to Landeck. *b.* ~~is~~ follows the dotted line, crossing a low mountain so that you leave the valley of the Inn 5 or 6 leagues beyond Innspruck, and rejoin it two or 3 farther on, descending through Ober Inn Thal, which is an elevated marsh, considerably *[page 153]* above the level of the Valley of the Inn, but far flatter, and drowned in water, and I should think unhealthy. Rejoining the lower valley you look westward up it, and southward down it, on ranges of noble hills, or rather clusters, for the mountains of the Tyrol are far more insulated than those of Switzerland and therefore in some instances produce a grander effect. one ~~in~~ pyramid of limestone projects like a promontory into the upper valley, compelling the river to make a long circumbendibus,[19] rising in perpendicular crags, wooded at their bases, into an isolated, apparently inaccessible pinnacle, which is crowned, a thousand feet above the rivers bed, by a tall and solitary tower. and opposite to it are walls of rock. rising 4000, and 5000 feet above the Inn. into massy, rounded summits. without a blade of vegetation from base to summit Immediately opposite the pyramid above mentioned, the rocks are composed of perfectly vertical beds of limestone, which have been blasted away in sheets *[page 154]* in order to make the road and now rise in massy walls beside it, and rise above it in fantastic and lofty pinnacles, which seem to set the laws of gravitation at defiance. but nearer Landeck the mountains look like a slate. black, loose, and shaly. and their bases, which otherwise would go plump down into the fiat alluvium of the valley, are rounded off into it by immense heaps of debris, which tire the eye by the monotony and regularity of their slope, and the desolation of their appearance, though a few few barberry bushes have rooted themselves into the restless and inhospitable soil. and have resisted the fall of the rock, and the sweep of the avalanche and the rush of the torrent all wreaking their rage on them.

A few clouds ~~a~~ darkened across the evening sky, but the horizon, red as a fire opal, seemed to promise well. and it spoke the truth. as did ~~a~~ the lovely, lovely, red sky or rather purple, which shone over our heads at Inspruck yesterday evening.

[page 155] Mals. Sept. 22. Rose on a clear starlight morning. and the sun rose without a cloud. Left the valley of the Inn. going up a much narrower valley between hills of limestone. in thin strata. but variegated very beautifully. a fine marble if it could be had in blocks. Beds horizontal. This ravine opened into a beautiful little valley. running east and west, that is, parallel to the valley of the Inn, and at right angles

19 An indirect or roundabout course.

to the one we had entered it by. Mountains round it were high, but still nothing but limestone.

Out of this valley we again entered a sublime ravine. or rather chasm. cloven between steep calcareous hills whose crests were broken into massive pyramids of a brownish red colour. but easily distinguished from granite by their solidity, their want of splinteriness. Opposite to these pyramids rises the road, high above the torrent, (one of the sources of the Inn. which tumbles beneath in a perpetual cataract,) & turns sharply round the angle of a lofty cliff which hangs over it, gloomy with pines, and opens on the instant into a wide, elevated *[page 156]* melancholy plain, the highest part of the pass of the Finstermunz.

The situation of this plain is remarkable. it seems formerly to have been a wide and elevated hollow. fig. 25. surrounded by limestone peaks forming altogether one gigantic mountain. shaped somewhat like a mural crown. This hollow is filled now by alluvium, *a.* and is partly occupied by two small lakes. from the borders of these the near limestone peaks are seen rising jagged and red and precipitous all round partially sprinkled with snow, in their intervals appear more distant and loftier mountains, and through a wide opening to the south rise the immense glaciers and snowcovered ridges of the great Orteler, and the mountains on the border of the Valtelline. The southernmost of the two lakes is rather pretty. the rest of the valley is bare and desolate. here a few pines fringe the mountain sides and come darkly down to the edge of the water. After passing this lake, at the brow of ~~a~~ the descent to Mals, a view opens very beautifully. *[page 157]* the broad valley ~~of th~~ which descends from Mals to Botzen, here rather marshy, mottled by tufts of pine and alder, glistening with detached pieces of water, and walled in by high ranges of mountains the highest in the Tyrol, coated with snow upon the summits, and surmounted by the higher crest of the Orteler.

The fortresses of the Tyrol are usually beautifully placed, and they generally mark an interesting piece of geology because they are always on pyramids of rock rising out of plains, or sides of mountains, and therefore generally point out a piece of secondary rock rising through tertiary beds, or of primary through secondary. a considerable castle here on the left is erected, I think, upon slate, rising in vertical beds out of limestone. but an unlucky torrent prevented access to the junction of the two rocks, and certainty of their nature Another lovely evening, not a cloud shadowed the beautiful rosy sides of the Orteler.

[page 158] Bormio. September 23. Another magnificent day. Descended ~~in~~ from the village of Mals into the lower valley, gleaming with white villages and fortresses, and passing over it by an embankment whose long straight line showed over the flat plain long before we approached it, entered a confined ravine, beyond whose vista of pines showed an enormous glacier. This ravine is at its lower extremity walled in by high sandhills, the remains of a deep alluvial deposit, washed away at their bases by the mountain torrent, furrowed by the minor streams which dash down into it they remain in fantastic forms and precarious pinnacles, sometimes a shelve of sand hanging over its base like a high breaker before it falls and at its very edge a pretty little Swiss cottage. which ~~th~~ is sometimes surrounded by small models of cornfields and potatoe grounds, the tout ensemble, cornfield, potatoe ground

156.
melancholy plain, the highest part of the pass of the Finstermunz.

The situation of this plain is remarkable. it seems formerly to have been a wide and elevated hollow. fig. 25. surrounded by limestone peaks forming altogether one gigantic mountain. shaped somewhat like a mural crown This hollow is filled now by alluvium, a – and is partly occupied by two small lakes. from the borders of these the near limestone peaks are seen rising jagged and red and precipitous all round sporting sprinkled with snow, in their intervals appear more distant and loftier mountains, and through a wide opening to the south rise the immense glaciers and snow covered ridges of the great Orteler and the mountains on the border of the Valtelline.

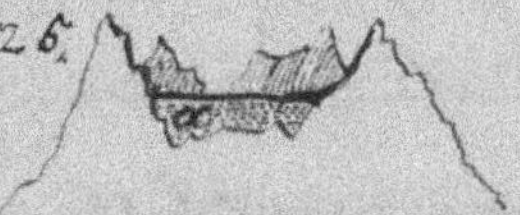

The southernmost of the two lakes is rather pretty. the rest of the valley is bare and desolate. here a few pines fringe the mountain sides and come darkly down to the edge of the water. After passing this lake, at the brow of a the descent to Mals, a view opens very beautifully.

dwelling house, and appurtenances appearing in imminent danger of being floated down to Botzen ~~as some~~ by the next flood which may come down from the Stelvio. [*page 159*] The road here ~~commences~~ begins to ascend. I believe the inclination is very slight. 8 feet in the hundred but ~~as~~ it is perpetual not an inch of level, not a line of descending ground from hence to the summit The bridges here are numerous and noble. not very high like those on the Via mala at the commencement of the passage of Splugen, but massive and beautifully built fit to resist an ocean. The valley widens, widens but gradually the glacier becomes nearer, more of it is seen, ~~to~~ and ~~a~~ its extremity rises from the pines, a precipice of ice nearly 150 feet high. The slates commence here, very shaly. black and bad. I do not recollect having seen a morsel of good slate in all Switzerland and the Tyrol. I am sure there is not a good quarrying bed.

After winding on a few miles farther you come in sight of the huge peaks of the mountains of the Valtelline, only separated from you by a valley rendered apparently narrow by its immense depth; slightly jagged by the stunted pines that climb up its precipices *[page 160]* disputing every inch of ground with the snow and the glacier, which lie above in dazzling and interminable fields, tossed into rounded and wreathed masses like the foam of a rock beating sea. appearing to have dashed its surf against the mighty pyramids which rise beetling over its billows, until they drip with its whiteness. remaining black and robeless only where the sheer perpendicular crags afford not a single resting place even for the light foot of snow. Down came two glaciers hanging from the snow above in such vertical ravines, that they look like two ultra-gigantic icicles radiant at their roots with blue chasms and glancing pinnacles, sapphire and silver, but black as ink at their extremities. charged and surcharged with the black debris that the foul slate pinnacles above them have shaken from their loose and shaly summits, not nailed together by a root of pine, or bound by one tuft of moss or lichen or lowest vegetation. till the miserable glaciers beneath them are buried beneath a load of black dust, and are only distinguishable here and there by a fractured pinnacle, a solitary ~~bit~~ morsel of melancholy blue *[page 161]* The Orteler rises close to you on the left but so directly above you that its summit is concealed by its shoulder, and it therefore does not appear so high as the more distant mountains which are altogether seen. After passing Trafoi the zigzags commence, the only way in which the road can be carried up the precipice slopes of the mountain, most of them are long, and in number, hence to the top of the pass more than 50. sometimes with long sweeps of ascent, not in zigzags, but ascending as rapidly, intervening, which of course add considerably to the height attained.

Soon after having mastered the first set of zigzags, you quit the pines, at a point where the valley turns round and directs itself away from the Orteler and parallel to the mountains of the Valtelline, so that the former mountain rises every instant in its apparent elevation. You pass another immense glacier very near, the same which is seen from the valley of Mals, and whose broken sides permit so accurate an estimate of the immense depth of its ice.

[page 162] The upper valley which you now enter, is one of desolation. There is a little grass in the bottom of it on the sunny side. The rest is bare rock, ~~at it~~ with here and there a sprinkling of snow. It began to appear to by the roadside in detached

and dirty heaps, which though the sun appeared to beat on them warmly did little more than damp the ~~road~~ dust for a yard or two round them. The last zigzags which ascend the highest ridge of the pass, terminating this desolate valley are most wonderful, twelve or 14, one above another, ascending beside a fearful precipice, which is so loose and shaly that it appears as if the whole line of zigzags might go down at a slip; The road is I should think about twenty feet wide. one half of it, that next the rock is covered by a ~~th~~ strong sloping roof, supported by huge upright beams rising from the middle of the road at intervals of about 6 feet with strutts. This part of the road being near the top of the ridge, it is not exposed to large avalanches and the smaller ones, bound over this penthouse roof without materially injuring even the outer and exposed part of the road. Either part of *[page 163]* the road thus divided is excessively narrow, underneath the roof you every now and then graze against the wall or posts, and a great part of the outer road was even at this late season obstructed by snow which lay in heaps 7 or 8 feet deep. and hung melting on the sloping roof through which a perpetual shower was kept up. These zigzags are the last, emerging from under the highest gallery we arrived at the most elevated point of the pass of the Stelvio at about 4 oclock in the afternoon. This point of ~~the~~ land, the highest to which a carriage road was ever carried is 9,230 English feet above the level of the Mediterranean sea. and is therefore higher by more than 700 feet than even the Hospice of St. Bernard. The sky was cloudless the air cool but not cold, the sun agreeable, feelably warm, and every object around at distances of I suppose 80 and 90 miles w[as] splendidly clear, looking close to you, the near hills as if you could touch them. The sky, opposite the sun was 28 of the cyan. at 12 oclock, although we were much lower it appeared to me considerably *[page 164]* darker, but I could not then measure, and I suppose it was only a deception for the darkest part of the sky was then seen over snow, while now it was over grey rock excessively beautiful nevertheless.

The panorama ~~t~~ which is seen from the summit is very grand, and remarkable for the desolation of its beauty. from the summits of most other passes, though the mountains round may be snowy and savage enough, and plenty enough yet there is always or generally some green patch of pine and pasturage, or a bit of some distant and luxuriant valley, an oasis in the desert to relieve the weariness of the eye. the St Gothard is an exception but even there, if you go on for a quarter of a mile you have the whole long valley of Airolo and Bellinzona. If you walk to end of the lake of St Bernard you command the green fields of St Remy. from the Simplon the valley of the Rhone and city of Brieg, from the Splugen the beautiful ravine of Campo dolcino. here a waste of snow, beautiful and bright, rises in enormous peaks. ~~rising~~ far and near, the Orteler seeming *[page 165]* to sit upon ~~the~~ a throne of them, like an elected candidate chaired, and their bases, although without snow, lose its brilliancy and beauty without an equivalent, for not a stunted pine varies the ~~s~~ universal monotony of the red rocks. Snow is beside you, deep as a glacier, the accumulation of winters. [as if] luxuriously couched on their snow cushions the rocks here and there start up out of it, ~~as~~ and the whole scene, foreground (or foresnow,) and distance astonish as much as they delight the eye that is not accustomed to the scenery of such elevations. and the more so, because this singular landscape has been obtained by a few hours' ride in your carriage instead of the discouraging fatigue, which is experienced by some persons even on a mule excursion, and must be undergone on attempting the ascent of the Buet, or any other point among the Alps of equal, or even inferior elevation to the f_r snow surrounded ridge which you ride over at your ease on the pass of the Stelvio.

[Page 166] On the Italian side, the mountains are far less elevated, although ~~their~~ there are some noble summits among them. The Orteler, which is entirely on the Tyrol side, and all its glaciers with the hills of the Valtelline, are lost sight of as soon as you begin to descend, and the mountain tract is uninteresting as far as Santa Maria. the rocks around seem a link between the slates and foliated granites. but beyond Santa Maria you again find yourself among limestones. which form the sides of a vast opening in the hills, wide enough to be a valley, but so deep as to become a ravine, into which you descend by a range of sharp zigzags. Far down this enormous chasm the promontories of perpendicular ~~d~~ rock jut out from behind one another, like the side scenes of a theatre, their bases lost in an abyss ~~at~~ in whose depth the river is not seen, their summits rising so high above you, and so steeply, that you feel as if the convulsed earth had yawned and let you down into ~~an~~ a chasm from which there was no egress. *[page 167]* and the road is carried along their sides in a fearful ~~go~~ terrace, passing through the ~~soft~~ rocks, which are ~~clou~~ cut out into long caverns, or under vaults built to bear the burst of the bounding avalanche The rocks on one side of this ravine are limestone apparently hard, and red, in thin distinct beds sometimes much distorted sometimes vertical down which the ~~Aro~~ Adda tumbles into the bottom of the gulph in a staircase of cataract, on the other they are of a soft shaly clay slate, passing into adhesive, of a pale grey colour, which renders the road very liable to be washed away by the torrents or torn down by the avalanches in spite of its protections. The junction of these rocks would be interesting, but it is uncomeatable. Farther down the Adda is reinforced by a large torrent which gushes from a cavern in the calcareous rocks. beyond this you come upon the baths of Bormio stuck upon the precipice as if the mountain were balancing them upon its nose, and then after passing through a *[page 168]* long gallery, and thundering over a high and noble bridge the valley of Bormio opens, ~~wh~~ bounded by mountains nearly as lofty as those from which you are emerging and with its thoroughly romantic, Italian, beautiful picturesque, filthy and abominable village of Bormio lying amid its mountain meadows which you had better hold your nose on first entering that you may be treated gradually and not by surprise.

Morbegno. September 24th. Left our unwashed and miserable sleeping place as early as possible Entered another valley, confined enough, but less sombre than the descent on Bormio. Villages all in ruin, all dirty, all miserable making you melancholy to look at them, yet perfectly Italian, beautifully situated, and exquisitely ~~placed~~ picturesque. Morning mountain air was at first refreshing, but as we were going down, and Italian drivers are noble fellows, and go like comets on any ground, and as four horses on a declivity just enough to make the carriage follow easily and a magnificent road beside are capable of going at a great rate. as every mile might *[page 169]* be calculated at a degree higher temperature Fahren. and as the sun was rising, without a cloud his rays being reflected from the mountain sides, and as Autumn was not yet passing into Winter, we found ourselves by twelve oclock in a climate considerably differing from that of 4 oclock yesterday. top of Stelvio, and to me by no means an agreeable alteration, for the lassitude and fatigue which are produced by the immoderate the blasting, furnace like heat, are far more unbearable than any keen breeze or frosty air over the glacier and snow of summer. Grapes were ~~ae~~ hanging about us in festoons rich ripe and plenty as blackberries. mulberry trees and olives sometimes afforded a little shade, but the dead brown of the perpetual Indian corn is tiresome. Malaria district among the marshes before entering Morbegno, formed by the Adda. galloped over it, and reached a cleaner and beautiful village, a healthy wider, and ~~beautiful~~ luxuriant valley, and a capital hotel. Geology today calcareous and nothing interesting.

[page 170]. Varenna. September 25th. After an hour's ride through the widening valley of the Adda we came upon the lake of Como, behind the Fort de Fuente, having on the right the magnificent crags which rise above the extreme end of the lake to the north, which is connected ~~adj~~ with the principal lake by a narrow channel, and is called sometimes the Lake of Riva or Chiavenna. It is the most sombre and sublime part of the lake of Como. the mountains round it are limestone, but are broken into Aiguilles like granites. ~~sl~~ separated by deep and gloomy chasms. One of these narrow vallies ~~is~~ seems to have gradually worn to an immense depth by a terrible mountain torrent, which has deposited where it at first fell into the lake an immense heap of debris, forming a large elevated hill projecting into the lake, ~~*a.b.* fig. 26~~, now covered with pasturage and cottages, and which is the only smiling and cultivated piece of ground to be found, on the borders of this immense well. *[page 171]* The quantity of debris which forms this delta must be immense, for the depth of the lake, which is very great, has been to a certain extent filled up before this hill of alluvium could rise out of its waters. Passing the village of Colico the road skirts the borders of a natural harbour forming in itself a beautiful little lake. I believe it is called the lake of Colico, likewise connected by a narrow strait with the principal lake whose opposite shore is exceedingly beautiful, glittering with white villages green with myrtles oranges and olives which clothe to a considerable height the sides of the noble mountains which retire in ~~wa~~ far perspective towards the southern extremity of the lake.[20]

The side on which the great road of the Stelvio is continued to Lecco is ~~on th~~ here far more precipitous. although its rocks are beautifully adorned with olives, cypresses, and vines. They project in some places into the lake while the road is carried through them in ranges of long and magnificent galleries lighted by openings blasted through the~~ir~~ sides ~~wit~~ which startle you with ~~the~~ a sudden burst of light and beauty of landscape as you pass *[page 172]* them. The rocks themselves are composed of thin strata of a fine hard, greyish black marble, capable of receiving a fine polish, but not generally applicable, because the thinness of its strata renders it entirely impossible to obtain a useful ~~block~~ massy block, while its colour being seldom perfectly black, but greyish and shaded not variegated in distinct marks, but blotchy, is perhaps one of the ugliest that a good marble ever assumes. The strata

20 This is the view illustrated in Turner's vignette for 'Como' in Rogers's *Italy*.

170

Varenna September 25th. After an hours ride through the widening valley of the Adda we came upon the lake of Como, behind the Fort de Fuente, having on the right the magnificent crags which rise above the extreme end of the lake to the north, which is connected ~~only~~ with the principal lake by a narrow channel, and is called sometimes the Lake of Riva or Chiavenna. It is the most sombre and sublime part of the lake of Como. the mountains round it are limestone but are broken into Aiguilles like granite. & separated by deep and gloomy chasms. One of these narrow vallies ~~is~~ seems to have gradually worn to an immense depth by a terrible mountain torrent, which has depotited where it at first fell into the lake an immense heap of debris, forming a large elevated hill projecting into the lake, a.b. fig. 26 now covered with pasturage and cottages. and which is the only smiling and cultivated piece of ground to be found on the borders of this immense well.

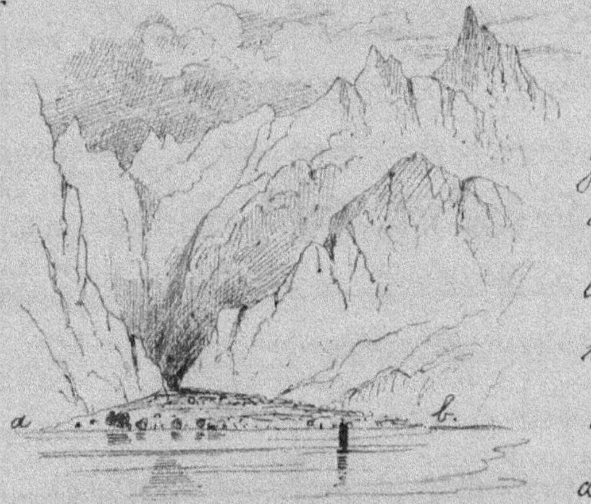

26

a

b.

are very steeply inclined, usually about 50° or 55° but sometimes nearly vertical, and in some parts curved, distorted and broken but only on a small scale. Their general contour is exceedingly beautiful and picturesque. These rocks compose the greatest part if not the whole of the mountains on this side of the lake of Como. Those on the opposite side I should suppose to be composed of common limestone, but could only judge by the ~~broken~~ colours of the rocks projecting from the turf and the general contour of the hills. The head of the lake, looking back, is exceedingly fine, bordered by a chain of splendid hills, which decrease in height towards the middle of the lake where it increases in breadth. Arrived early at Varenna. The day was burning, and the cool apartments grateful.[21]

21 There is a sketch of an unidentified building inverted at the foot of the back cover.

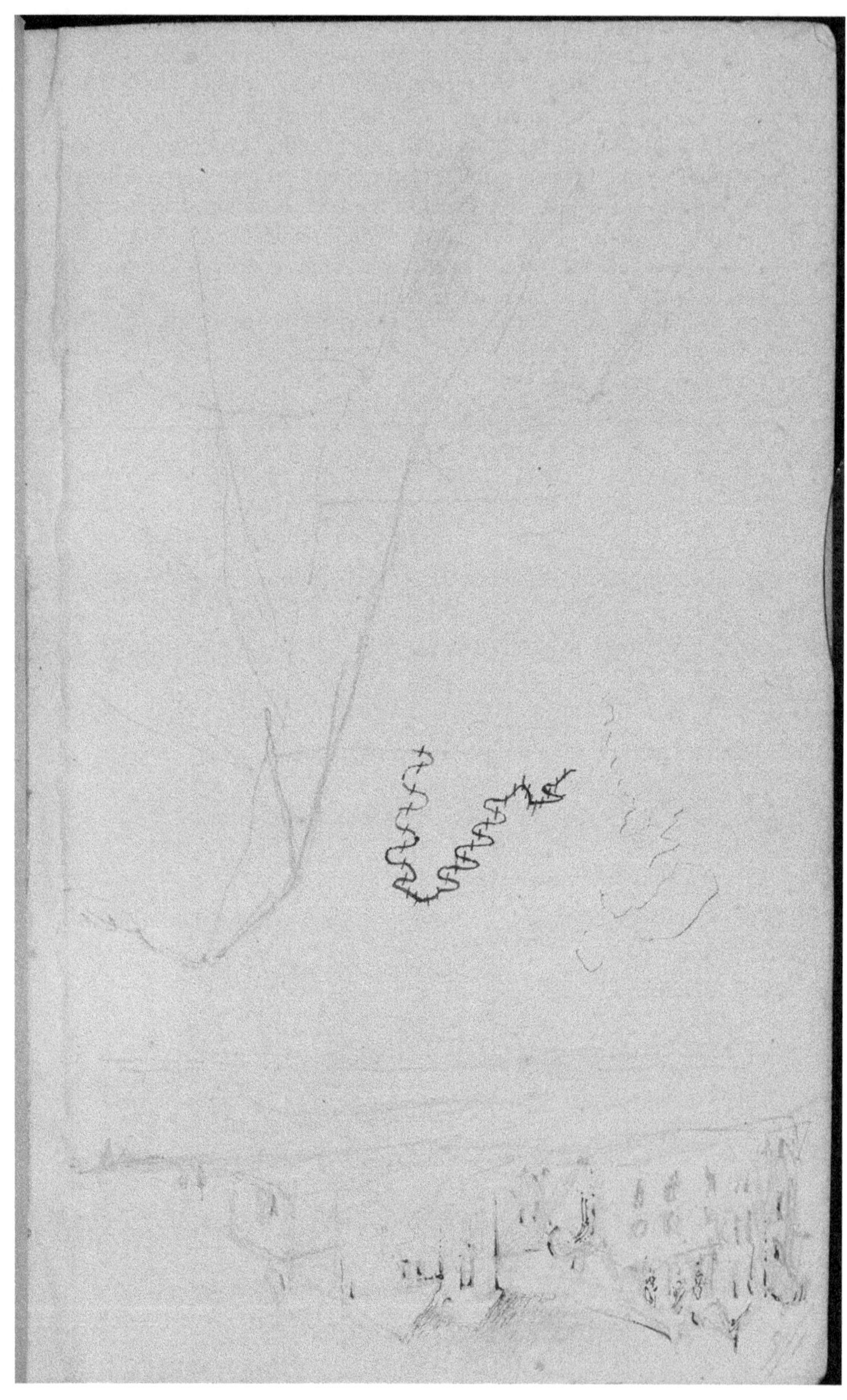

A Tour through France to Chamouni[1]

CANTO I

1

"Now, as you need not ride with whip and spur, I
  Beg very seriously to advise
That you should never travel in a hurry."
  Thus slowly spoke the doctor,[2] looking wise,
We took the hint, and stopped at Canterbury.
  Then in the morning early did we rise,
But not to see the place where old Tom Becket is,
  Nor where the monks have heaped such heaps of bones—
I'm sure, enough to make any one sick it is—
  Under the old cathedral paving-stones,
Nor any other like[3] antiquities,
  Nor the Museum, rich by gifts and loans:
But 'twas to trot to cliff encircled Dover,
And think how we could get the carriage over.

2

For that, they chained and swung it in a minute,
  And down the steps we went, and soon were seated,
The boat was pretty full, I wish you'd seen it,
  Then we heard such odd sentences repeated,
La, what green water. Bless us, what's that in it?
  Why that's a fish, ma'am. No, it's only seaweed.
I wish the water were not quite so rough,
  I feel a little curious inside.
Steward, some brandy; No, that an't enough.
  Ask him—Oh dear! I thought I should have died.
Call you that brandy—never saw such stuff.
  Then poke your head over the vessel's side.
One rates[4] the cabin stairs, which he can't go up,
Another hopes the boiler will not blow up.

1 The title is W. G. Collingwood's, from *Poems* (1891). Written from June to December, and later.

2 Ruskin had been withdrawn from school in spring suffering from pleurisy.

3 The Library Edition notes: 'So in MS. The ed. of 1891 reads "similar" for "like," and in stanza 3 inserts the words "curious" before "set" and "very" before "hot."'

4 Scolds.

3

I'm sure enough to fluster any body 'tis
  To step upon the stones of Calais quay;
You meet with such a set of oddities;
  This way and that you turn yourself to see,
And then you bawl out, "Dear! how hot it is!"
  Then you're hauled off—for they make very free,
Those interfering officers of custom—
  For they will search, ay, and they will examine;
—It's very impolite, but then, they must, ma'am!
  "They should not be so rough, and rout,[5] and ram in
My things so!"—but they're used to it; only trust 'em;
  You will make all things right by dint of cramming.
—Now, sir, I hope you've finished with that box;
See, here's the key; and that's the way it locks!

4

There is a monument beneath the wall
  Of Calais, as you pass along the pier,—
A plain, unsculptured, low memorial;[6]
  Yet pass not by it, stranger; for 'tis dear—
A thing most precious in the sight of all
  Who dwell upon the deep. There lie not here
The bones of those whose names thereon you see;
  But 'tis a tomb for such as have no tomb,—
Memory of those who have no memory,
  Nor even a burial-place, except the gloom
And ceaseless roll of the relentless sea;
  For whom no hymn was sung except the boom
Of waves innumerable, and the roar
That their grave makes upon their native shore.

5

Weep not for those who in their honours die,
  Whom fame forbids to perish,—for the brave,
The mighty and the glorious, all pass by,
  All must go down into the voiceless grave.
Weep not for those for whom whole nations sigh,—
  But we will weep for those who died to save

5 Search through.

6 A monument was erected on the quai Auguste Delpierre in 1791 to the memory of two citizens of Calais who had died while saving survivors from drowning.

The stranger perishing. Approach and read!
   There's not a name upon yon simple stone
But of a hero. What although the dead
   Have all gone down into the deep unknown,
And what although their bones be scattered
   All underneath the deep, salt surges thrown?
They speak, for whom their being was surrendered:
They have been wept, and they shall be remembered.

6

Now as I stood beside the tomb, thus thinking,
   There came some perfumes o'er the pier — thinks I—
This is not very sweet, I won't say stinking,
   Then as I saw some ancient fish close by,
I sentimentally departed winking,
   There was a tear, or something, in my eye;
Perhaps the wind had blown the dust into it,
   It broke upon my train of sentiment,
I saw the ancient portal, and walked through it;
   I need not say to which hotel we went,
But 'twas the best in Calais, and we knew it;
   Our trunks were from the custom houses sent,
And then we dined on many a savoury stew
And then we—what is what we did to you?

7

Then by Montreuil to Abbeville we went,—
   An ancient place, and picturesque indeed all;
The ramparts round enclose a large extent.
   We put our noses into the cathedral[7]
(Much tempted by the outside) with intent
   To wander through the naves,[8] and see it all;
But started back, and instant sought the door,
   Nought seeing there but dirt and dirty people.
—The marble chequers of the ancient floor,
   Oh, citizens of Abbeville, why not sweep well?
We stared about, the Gothic front before,
   Surveyed the porch, and criticised the steeple,
Marvelled to see the carving rich, and talked of
The figures standing with their noses knocked off.

7 The mostly fifteenth-century Saint-Vulfran Cathedral was never completed.

8 The Library Edition notes: 'So in MS. The edition of 1891 reads, "To wander through the nave inside and see 't all."'

8

And so we wandered on, until the Seine
  Glistened along the distance mistily,
Floating among the azure of the plain
  Like milky way along the midnight sky;
Which wooded hills surrounded with a chain
  Of silver cliffs; and Rouen's minster high,
Uplifted in the air its Gothic light[9]
  In rich array of spiry pinnacle.
The river, that we looked on from the height
  Was full of islands green, and wooded well,
Like fairy dwellings in the misty light
  That o'er the city and the waters fell,
Throwing a beautifully golden shower
On minster grey and tall St. Ouen's fretted tower.[10]

9

Now, every street in Rouen without fail is
  Traversed by gutters of enormous size;
(The joke about the Grecian quite stale is),
  But, in such occupation of your eyes
Beware lest you endure the fate of Thales
  —Ditched in philosophizing on the skies.[11]
For, as you pass each antiquated street
  Diverging from the Place de la Pucelle,
Over your head the Norman houses meet,
  Black with old beams, and ornamented well
With huge, broad roofs to shade them from the heat;
  And you enjoy variety of smell
Quite infinite,—in fact, you can't suppose
Better amusement for the eyes and nose!

10

Rouen is full of holes and corners curious;
  What thing you are to see next, there's no knowing;
And churches two, applied to use injurious,
  Sounded with anvil stroke and bellows blowing.
The rascally canaille!—it makes one furious!
  What English mob would ever think of stowing

9 *Poems* (1891) reads 'Flight'.

10 The abbey church of St Ouen was to become the object of Ruskin's later bitter censure exemplifying the excesses of the flamboyant style. See 8.42 and 64–65.

11 Thales, *c.* 624–*c.* 546 BC, was a pre-Socratic Greek philosopher from Miletus in Asia Minor about whom Plato narrates that one night, while gazing at the sky, he fell into a ditch.

Old iron 'neath the Gothic portals grey
  Of holy shrine, whose niches, statueless,
But carved and sculptured in a wondrous way,
  Remained to tell how sacred once the place?
Indignant at the deed, we turned away
  Towards the huge Cathedral's western face.
I stood, upstaring at the lofty steeple
—And ran against a dozen market people!

11

It is a marvel, though the statues cramp[12] are,
  How beautifully rich the tower is!
But 'tis amazing what a sudden damper
  Of all enthusiasm a shower is!
Down came a thunder-cloud, which made us scamper
  Under the arch that shows what hour it is.
—I don't admire the plan of elevating
  A clock upon a steeple huge and high,
Where really nobody can see it, bating
  Those who have got a very practised eye;
And people in a hurry can't stand waiting
  Until the clappers tell how time goes by:
Besides, on Gothic work, the great, flat face
Looks quite incongruous, and out of place.

12

So, as the Rouen architects thought fit
  To go upon a plan entirely new,
They built an arch on purpose every bit;
  Chiselled it over, till gay garlands grew
Beneath their hands, where'er their mallets hit,
  And open flowers along the granite blew
Unwitheringly. On the arching wide
  Stood up the dial, bridging over quite
The narrow Norman street from side to side.
  Long distance down the street the dial white
By every passer-by might be espied,
  And looked exceeding picturesque and light.
In fact, there never was a plan projected
By which a clock could better be erected.

12 Difficult to make out.

13

So, as I said before, past this we ran,
  (For, in this clime, when thunder-clouds come blowing,
Always retire as quickly as you can);
  Reached the hotel, and scarce had time to go in
Before the thunder and the rain began;
  So we sat at the window, and cried "Oh!" when
There came a brilliant flash along the sky.
  We, from the next day's morn till day departed,
Went up and down in Rouen constantly;
  Admired, and wondered that in every part it
Presented rich street-pictures to the eye.
  And then we ordered horses, and we darted
Many a long look at beautiful St. Ouen,
Climbing a verdant hill, the last that looks on Rouen.[13]

14

St. Germain is a pleasant place to mope at—
  Uninteresting as a place may be.
There's a fine view 'twould be as well to stop at
  Near the old palace; and they say you see
Beyond the spires of Paris; and I hope that
  It's true, but it is only an "*on dit*."[14]
When you've walked up the Rue la Paix at Paris,
  Been to the Louvre, and the Tuileries,
And to Versailles, although to go so far is
  A thing not quite consistent with your ease,
And—but the mass of objects quite a bar is
  To my describing what the traveller sees.
You who have ever been to Paris, know:
And you who have not been to Paris,—go!

13 In *Praeterita*, Ruskin writes: 'The sight of [Rouen and its Cathedral], and following journey up the Seine to Paris, then to Soissons and Rheims, determined [...] the first centre and circle of future life-work. Beyond Rheims, at Bar-le-Duc, I was brought again within the greater radius of the Alps, and my father was kind enough to go down by Plombières to Dijon, that I might approach them by the straightest pass of Jura.' (35.158)

14 'it is said': a popular claim.

15

By Soissons, and by Rheims,—which is much spoken of;
There's very little in it to admire,—
The statues' heads are not all broken off,—
The thing is well preserved, from porch to spire;
And clean and neat, which is a token of [15]
Good order here. But many spires are higher:
The carving is not rich, the Gothic heavy;
The statues miserable,—not a fold
Of drapery well-disposed in all the bevy
Of saints, and bishops, and archbishops old
That line the porches grey. But in the nave I
Stared at the windows, purple, blue, and gold:
And the perspective's wonderfully fine,
When you look down the long columnar line.[16]

16

So on by Chalons, where no lions are
Save four on the Hotel de Ville, we past
Plains in abominable flatness far
Extending westward, till we dropped at last
Down in a hole upon the town of Bar.
I love to see a streamlet flashing past
Down some still valley, in a sportive mood;
Where the winds come to bathe themselves, and sing,
And dip their breezy tresses in the flood.
'Tis sweet to stand and watch the quivering
Of wave-embarrassed beams, where pebbles strewed
Brightly along the bottom of the spring
Fling back and forward flashes — constant play
Of silver sunbeams that have lost their way.

15 As Collingwood notes in 1891, this and several lines throughout are not complete dactyls and he inserted extra words, but here they are left in the original state.

16 In *Praeterita*, Ruskin notes: 'By the "carving" I meant the niche-work, which is indeed curiously rude at Rheims; by the "Gothic" the structure and mouldings of arch, which I rightly call "heavy" as compared with later French types; while the condemnation of the draperies meant that they were not the least like those of either Rubens or Roubilliac. And ten years had to pass over me before I knew better [...].' (35.349)

17

Therefore we went along the river's bank
  Shaded by many a broad tree, branching wide
Where the cool ripple made the waters dank.
  And everywhere along the valley-side
The hill, upon its brown and sunburnt flank,
  Bore full and verdant vineyards in the pride
Of fruitfulness. But though we hear a deal of
  Italian vineyards, and the juice delightful
Which Spanish peasantry make every meal of;
  And though a glass looks pretty when 'tis quite full
Of sparkling wine; and though we like the feel of
  A bunch of grapes just gathered with a slight pull;
And though the Grecian poets praised a foamer
Of wine, when they were thirsty (witness Homer);—

18

Yet, sir, you would by no means think it fun,
  And all your fine romantic feelings fly off,
When you are stewed beneath a burning sun
  Panting with heat which you are like to die of,—
The stones beneath you scorching, every one,—
  The walls around you white and hot,—a sky of
Untempered, sultry, and continual blue,—
  The air without a motion or a sound ;—
'Twould put a salamander in a stew[17]
  To feel the dry reflection from the ground!
Vine, vine, still vine,—the only thing in view,—
  All vine, monotonously roasting round!
'Twould make you cry, as up the hills you scramble,
"Oh, for an English hedge of shady bramble!"

19

From Bar-le-Duc we made a dash at Nancy,
  Whose beautiful arcades we walked about.
Its buildings are, as any body can see,
  By revolutionists much knocked about.
There are two fountains spouting on a plan we
  Admired, and the triumphal arch is talked about.[18]

17 Salamanders were legendarily believed to withstand any heat and extinguish fires.
18 Collingwood points out in 1891 that lines 2, 4, and 6 are also irregular.

But if you wish to see a foreign town,
Look out for every narrow, dirty street,
As you walk diligently up and down;
Pop into it directly; you will meet
Such combinations,—houses tumbling down,—
Old fragments,—Gothic morsels, quite a treat,—
Columns and cloisters,—old *boutiques* which stink of
Garlic, and everything that you can think of!

20

Thus here, there's such a bit, in such a lane
A gate, with curious carved Gothic niches
Where statues were, but where they don't remain,
Those men of taste, those Gemmen without breeches[19]
Considering all such monuments a stain
Upon their city, broke the statues, which is
A monstrous pity. Then the centre square
Is well designed, by numerous arches ended,
The gardens such as you see everywhere,
The church is tol lol,[20] and its organ, splendid—
On carved wood work lifted up in air
High o'er the nave the branching oak is bended.
Thus we examined all things, high and low,
Then we left Nancy to the southward, ho!

21

Long had I looked, and long I looked in vain
For the pale mountains in the distance showing.
It was a hill that we had climbed: the plain
Beneath lay brightly, beautifully glowing.
Is it a cloud, that yon pale, azure chain
The whole, wide, low horizon round is throwing?
Oh no! the peaks are high on Jura's crest,—
The plains do worship to their distant might,
The clouds by day couch, drowsy, on their breast,
And the stars gleam along their flanks by night;
There comes the storm to dwell, the mist to rest;
There, like communing spirits, from their height
They echo at the thunderbolt's behest,
That gleams[21] with lightning eye from east to west.

19 Gemmen = gentlemen. The reference is to the French Revolutionary *sans-culottes*.
20 Tolerable.
21 Collingwood in 1891 notes that this word is Ruskin's father's correction for 'looks'.

22

We saw them all the way to Plombières,
  Which is a pretty place; but it is not that
Which makes the crowds of invalids go there.
  The springs are so abominably hot, that
They steam and bubble in the open air,
  Which makes the place look like a boiling pot, that
Smokes from the valley. There the baths are seen,—
  The water, through distilling drop by drop there,
Fills four large tubs with liquid warm and green.
  There sit the social invalids and pop their
Thin yellow noses out like lobsters lean
  Boiling for dinner. Hour to hour they stop there,
Sleeping an[d] reading,—subjects lean and bony,
Engaging in a conversazione.

23

I'm on the Jura. Lo! the rocks are dun,
  Although the opposite of heaven is[22] bright,
And all the glare of gaudy day was done;
  And there is shadow mingled with the light.
The dazzled world is weary of the sun;
  Her eyes are shaded by the hand of night.
  Yet beautiful, oh! beautiful the beam
  Along the azure of the plain was sleeping:
The distant hills are veiled as with a dream
  Of mist, of dewy mist, their foreheads steeping.
The heaven is parting with the dying gleam,
  And lo! the heaven is sad, the heaven is weeping.
The voice of streams is hushed[23] upon the hill ;
No murmur from the plain, and all the world is still.

24

Farewell, ye plains; ye champaigns wide, farewell!
  The cloud, the storm, the mountain now for me!
Mine be the deserts where the chamois dwell,
  And the wild eagle soars at liberty!
For meditation on the pinnacle
  Of the lone mountain sits, and loves to see

22 The Library Edition notes: 'So in the ed. of 1891; "was" in the MS.'
23 *Poems* (1891) reads 'heard'.

The beauty of the living solitude;
  And music floats around; the mountain air
With a rich spirit of music is imbued;
  And every sound becomes harmonious there;
The streamlet's plash, the thunder of the flood,
  The flock's low tinkle o'er the pastures bare,
And the long roar and echo never ending
Of distant avalanches terrible descending.

25

This isn't humbug; no, you feel quite odd when
  You climb an elevation hugely high;
Step after step goes hop upon the sod then,
  Lightly as if you were about to fly;
Mile after mile with merry heart is trod then,
  Enjoying all things with unwearied eye.
Then you feel hungry, eat a double ration
  Of viands, don't despise your what you call it,
It is a member of imagination,
  And of much sentiment, and, after all, it
Is pleasant in romantic situation
  To fall upon your dinner or forestall it
With half-a-dozen breakfasts, rolls and eggs
To vivify your mind, and fortify your legs.

26

So, on the heights of Jura, as I said,
  I stood, admiring much the setting sun
Taking a bath before he went to bed
  Out of the mists, that, indistinct and dun,
And dark, and grey, and colourless as lead
  Along the horizon's farthest outline run
Like velvet cushions for his weary head;
  Or like a sort of scene, for him to slip off
Behind: and a long line of ruby red
  Zigzag'd along their summits, like a strip of
Dutch gold[24] upon a piece of gingerbread
  After the happy urchin's gnawed the tip off
The finger, after long deliberation
Between his appetite and admiration.

24 Edible gold leaf.

27

So, on the heights of Jura, as I said,
 I stood, and rocks around in quantities,—
In cliffs quite high enough to turn your head,
 And make you cry "how very grand it is!"
Especially after coming through the dead
 And stupid plains of France, where scant it is[25]
Of beauty, and monotonously low.
 These are those famous rocks by which the stone-
Examiners have all been puzzled so.
 For here and there the granite blocks are strown
Over the bending mountain's softer brow;
 And some affirm that here they have been thrown
By mighty floods, quite large enough to heave a
Mountain across the valley of Geneva![26]

28

When o'er the world the conquering deluge ran,
 Rolling its monster surges, far and wide,
O'er many an ancient mountain's lordly[27] span,
 And when upon the all devouring tide
Wallowed the bulk of the leviathan
 Where cultivated plains are now descried;[28]
And when the toppling peaks of mountains old
 Were shook from their foundations into ruin,
Like shingle at the ocean's mercy rolled,
 That worked, and worked,—ever its work undoing,—
Heaping up hills beneath its bosom cold,
 Then wide again the devastation strewing,—
Then the dark waves, with nothing to obstruct 'em,
Carried these blocks from far, and here it chucked 'em!

29

Such are the dreams of the geologist!
 He sees past ages of the world arise;
Strange sounds salute his ears, prepared to list,[29]
 And wondrous sights, his rock inspired eyes.
Before him solid mountains wave and twist,
 And forms of life within them fossilize;

25 Collingwood notes that lines 2, 4, and 6 are all short.
26 See the diary (Altdorf, August 12th) for the contemporary diluvian theories.
27 *Poems* (1891) reads 'lofty'.
28 Collingwood notes in 1891 that lines 2, 4, and 6 are all short.
29 Listen.

The flint invades each member as it dies,
And through the quivering corse[30] on creeps the stone,
Till in the mountain's hardened heart it lies,
In nature, rock,—in form, a skeleton;
Much for the feature valued by the wise,
Or in some huge museum to be shown,—
A mystery, as wonderful, at least,
As that of apples conjured into paste!

30

Thus on the Jura dreamed I, with nice touch
Discriminating stones; till, which was teasing,
The evening mists rolled round, with dampness such,
That, though they brought a coolness not unpleasing,
They made me sneeze! Now, nothing half so much
Disturbs a person's sentiment as sneezing:
It takes you impudently by the nose;
Throws your component parts into confusion;
And shakes you up, as doctors shake a dose
In which they've put some villainous infusion;
And the shrill echo in at both ears goes
With such a sharp and[31] startling an intrusion,
Like a fell thunder clap by tempest brought,
Breaking the deep, still silence of your thought.

31

And so I wished myself good luck, you know,
As many people do on like occasion:—
The Swiss takes off his hat with a low bow
To you, though in the midst of conversation;
And if you've caught a little cold or so,
You keep your friend just in the situation
Of the caparisoned dragoon, with sword on
His side, well carved in wood, with wooden steed,
Placed the extremest limit of a board on:
Still up and down he goes, by ball of lead
Which slowly swings beneath him, ever spurred on:—[32]
Thus at each sneeze your friend still bows his head;
In fact, the courteous Swiss puts off and on his
Hat, like a master of the ceremonies.

30 Organic remains.
31 '[so]' in *Poems* (1891).
32 The allusion is to a wooden toy.

32

A mountain walk by moonlight, people say,
  Is interesting and poetical.
Some like to walk while twilight wastes away;
  Some choose to be a peripatetic all
Night, and a very Stoic during day.
  I am not given to be ecstatical
When I can't see, and therefore I descended;
  Although the night that came was scarcely night,—
So softly with the air was starlight blended,
  Like the sea's phosphor lustre, coldly bright;
The peaks above me, as I downward wended,
  Grew misty in the ray so faint and white;
You could have thought, as, veil-like, you did view them,
That the moonbeams were shining through and through them.

33

O redly broke the morn, and Jura smiled,
  And all the plains awoke them from their slumber.
The morn! the morn! I heard along the wild
  The torrents shouting with a voice of thunder.
Under the cliffs fantastically piled
  We wound and left the city couching under:
Up on the mountain where the breeze is free,
  Up on the mountain where the wild flowers grow,
Up on the mountain where with melody
  The cataracts sing and tempests loudly blow,
Up on the mountain, where quick rushing by
  Leaps like a lion the lavange,[33] we go.
Farewell, ye plains, the rocks around I see,
The cloud, the storm, the mountain now for me!

34

Thus[34] did we leave Poligny, and to Morez
  We went, which is an odd place in a hole,
Under huge cliffs built in successive stories
  Of limestone, very pretty on the whole,
Swiss-ish, and picturesque, and so on: nor is
  It far from the green summit of the Dôle

33 French synonym for an avalanche.
34 'Then' in *Poems* (1891).

Which groves of tall and spiry pine embrace,
  Which[35] like a mantle of the deepest green,
Shadow its sides and darken round its base:
  But grassily doth rise its crest; between
Its ridges and in every sheltered place
  The wavy lines of whitest snow are seen: —
Through the first summer months it wears them yet,
Like a large emerald in silver set.

35

Reader, if you are trigonome—, no! I
  Can't manage that long word, which is a bother;—
Trigonometrical, I'll tell you how high
  It is above the Medi—, there's another!—
Mediterranean; and that will show why
  The snow, although it melts some time or other,
Continues there so long. I've calculated
  It is 3000 and 900 feet
Above the sea:[36] a summit, insulated
  So high, is seldom subject to much heat,
And therefore, as above I have related,
  Although the sun's rays may appear to beat
Warmly upon the grass with tow'ring glow,
They cannot melt the hard heart of the snow.[37]

36

And when the day is hot, at two o'clock,
  And trees and flowers are loaded with the heat,
And walnuts tall give shelter to the flock
  That crowds[38] beneath their branches, then 'tis sweet
To seek the shadow of some lofty rock
  With a cool streamlet gurgling at your feet;
And when you've scaped the power and the might
  Of the fierce sun, and coolness fills your breast,
Then, to look up to some enormous height
  Where winter sits for ever, and whose' crest
Is lovely with the kisses of the light,—
  The ruby light that loves on it to rest,
And to feel breezes o'er your features blown, is
Like eating raspberry ices at Tortoni's![39]

35 'And' in *Poems* (1891).
36 In fact it is 5505 feet above sea level.
37 See the 1835 Diary,
38 *Poems* (1891) reads 'cowers'.
39 A café on the Boulevard des Italiens in Paris.

37

The meadows of these hills are like the robe,
  Bedight with gems, of some high emperor:
There's not a spot in all this lovely globe
  That's more abundant in its flowery store.
The Alpine rose along its ridges glowed,
  The mountains burning with the fiery flower.
Queen of the blossoms in the fields below,
  The silver lily lifted its pale head,
The emulation of the mountain snow.
  Fresh emerald moss along the rocks was spread,
And hare bells trembling as the breezes blow,
  And many another flower, of blue and red,
Purple and gold, too numerous to mention,
Half-drowned in dew, solicited attention.

38

—Attention difficult to give, when we
  Saw such a scene of loveliness around;
Yet 'twas not much amiss to stoop, and see
  The beauty of that flower enamelled ground:
First, to behold the mountain's majesty,
  Then, the fresh green of yonder mossy mound.
As when you enter some enormous pile—
  Gothic cathedral very ancient,
First, you admire what people call the style
  And massive wholeness of the monument,—
Magnificent effect of dome and aisle,—
  And next, you view the lavish ornament
That's carved on every part, but all intended
To make the general effect more splendid.

39

Thus on the Jura did we gaze, beholding
  A monument enormous everywhere:
The hills, that on their shoulders seemed upholding
  The high blue dome that looked above the air;
Groves of dark pines their scarped crags enfolding;
  Rocks raised like castles from their summits bare,

In many a varied form: and then did look
  At the most rich and intricate detail;
The coloured marks in yonder marble rock,—
  The green moss that hangs o'er it like a veil,—
The turf inlaid with flowers,—the crystal brook
  That ever tells its never varied tale
Unto the air, that sporteth with its spray,
And sings, and sings, [and sings][40] to it all day.

40

Give me a broken rock, a little moss,
  A barberry tree with fixed branches clinging,—
A stream that clearly at its bottom shows
  The polished pebbles with its ripples ringing;—
These to be placed at nature's sweet dispose,
  And decked with grass and flowers of her bringing ;—
And I would ask no more; for I would dream
  Of greater things associated with these,—
Would see a mighty river in my stream,
  And, in my rock, a mountain clothed with trees.
For nature's work is lovely to be seen;
  Her finished part as finished whole will please;
And this should be a mountain-scene to me—
My broken rock, my stream, and barberry tree!

41

I'm going to turn a corner,—which I've done
  A hundred or a thousand times before!
But this is really a distinguished one,
  And needs a little preparation, for
The shock of it is quite enough to stun
  You, like a box upon the ear, and floor
Your very feelings, that you will not move
  A muscle of your body, nor will dare
To breathe the breezes that about you rove.
  You could chastise the movement of the air
While drinking in the beauty that you love!
  Some cannot that delicious rapture share;
Those who feel little, talk, and rant, and vapour,
Kick up their heels, prance, frisk, curvet, and caper.

40 So in *Poems* (1891); blank space in the MS.

42

Mighty Mont Blanc, thou hast been with me still
  Wherever I have been![41] In the dark night
I've walked upon thy visionary hill,
  And have been filled with infinite delight:
And when I woke, it was against my will.
  Though then I did not have thee in my sight,
Still wert thou like a guiding star, and all
  My hope was to be with thee once again,
Hearing thy avalanches' fearful fall.
  I was bound to thee by a pleasant chain,
And I am here in answer to thy call!
  I see thee rise o'er yonder lordly plain,
Like nothing else i' the world; for thou hast stood
Unrivalled still, thine own similitude![42]

43

Nobly the hills are set on Leman's shore,[43]
  Like to a dark and most tempestuous deep
Petrified into mountain; and the power
  Of silence on the lake laid it asleep
In the arms of the mountains, evermore
  Embracing it. Down, down the torrents leap
In[to][44] the calm waters, with a rush immense,
  Like headlong passion which appeased is straight
When it is met by gentle patience.
  And on the other side, in purple state
The plains spread out their broad magnificence,
  And gorgeous[45] enrobed, and all elate
With corn, and vine, and forests deeply green:—
It was a lovely sight and beauteous to be seen!

44

The Alps! the Alps! though in the lap of night,
  Lit by the lightening[46] silvered by the moon,
Or purple with the evening's beacon bright,
  Or blazing in the fiery glance of noon,

41 First seen by Ruskin in 1833.

42 In *Praeterita*, Ruskin writes: 'I have never seen that view perfectly but once — in this year, 1835; when I drew it carefully in my then fashion [see Catalogue 27], and have been content to look back at it as the confirming sequel to the first view of the Alps from Schaffhausen' (35.167).

43 Lake Geneva.

44 The Library Edition notes: 'the MS, has "into" apparently altered to "in."'

45 'gorgeously' in *Poems* (1891).

46 *Sic*, for 'lightning', as also below in this stanza.

Or shivering in the morning's colder light,
  Or veiled in tempest and in cloudy gloom.
Still are they noble, as the monarch is,
  Whether he wraps himself around in wrath
Or with benignity do[th] charge his eyes,
  Joying all those who wait upon his path.
I see them far: their battlements arise,
  And lightenings from their glaciers go forth,
Blinding as if a chain of suns were there,
Burning and dazzling all the ambient air.

45

Now down the hill we heard our carriage roll,
  In our enthusiasm sent away.
—Enthusiasm is a parasol
  When the sun's hot; and on a rainy day
As[47] umbrella doth the rain control:—
  A carriage, on a long and weary way,—
A cloak when it is cold,—a fan in heat,—
  Patience when you are out of patience.—Oh!
Down the hillside with still delaying feet
  How merrily and lightly did we go!
Although the sun did fiercely on us beat,
  And though it was some seven miles or so,
Our hearts were merry, and our limbs elastic,
Only because we were enthusiastic!

46

Thus we went down the Jura, and before
  Our road had led us a long way past Gex, it
Showed us the villa, beautiful no more,
  —Voltaire's,—and the low, humble chapel next it,
With this inscription placed above the door
  Conspicuous, *Deo Voltaire erexit,*[48]—
Which reads a little oddish! This we past;
  The hills increasing, nearer as we drew,
Till fair Geneva raised its spires at last,
  Sitting beside the waters bright and blue,
On which, though trembling with the noontide blast,
  Mont Blanc from far his silver image threw;
And, nearer us, the waters did receive a
Clear image of the city of Geneva.

47 *Poems* (1891) adds '[an]' here.
48 'Voltaire built it for God'.

47

Geneva is a rather curious town,
And few its public edifices are. How
The streets upon each side come sloping down,
Too steep for carriages, and rather narrow.
It has two bridges o'er the double Rhone,
Which darts beneath as swiftly as an arrow:
Forth from the lake it comes, with swirl and sweep,
Fed by the distant glaciers on high—
The reservoirs that hang on every steep—
And giddily the billows dance you by.
Thirty or forty feet the stream is deep;
Strong as a giant; azure as the sky;
And clear and swift as a tempestuous wind they go,
And very like a painter's pot of indigo.

48

Many a philosopher has scratched his pate,
Pronouncing it incomprehensible,
While standing on that bridge, and looking at
The waters passing by with ceaseless swell,
So richly, so intensely azure, that
You could imagine,—ay, and very well,
That heaven 'neath the sun's excessive ray
Was melting! All the pebbles may be counted
Thirty feet down, it is so clear; some say
That even from the river's icy fount it
Preserves its azure colour all the way.
—By this, the circumstance is not accounted
For,—that green (like the sea-green beard of Neptune)
Is nothing but an optical deception.[49]

49

In fact, it cannot be accounted for;
And nothing on the subject can be said!
There is no reason for it, any more
Than that a cherry should be white or red,
Or a plum blue. On all Lake Leman's shore
The waves beat bluely, save just at its head,

49 See Ruskin's article, 'Enquiries on the Causes of the Colour of the Water of the Rhine' (I.191).

Where the Rhone rushes from its glacier-fountains,
  It is a little turbid; that's no matter,—
Only a little granite from the mountains,
  Which torrents wear and tear, and lightnings shatter.
The river is soon cleared, nor far around stains
  The purity of Leman's crystal water.
I'd say 'twas like a sapphire,—but I've more
Than once used that similitude before!

50

The scenery about Geneva's rich.
  On one side is the Jura, blue and bare;
Opposite, is a valley, out of which
  From huge Mont Blanc and tall Argentière
Rushes the Arve, as dirty as a ditch.
  And if you ask for it, they'll take you where
The river, in romantic situation
  Between high banks of gravel, gushes down,
By its most foul evil communication
  Corrupting the good manners of the Rhone,
Which holds aloof from all the perturbation
  Of its foul neighbour, and goes down alone.
Some time it so continues: long it can't,—
Which I could moralise upon, but shan't...

51

And in this valley which I have just spoken of
  Appears Mont Blanc, with silver summits three,
Whose wavy, domelike outlines,[50] broken off
  Into aiguilles, which by his side you see
Splintered, and crushed,[51]—a direful token of
  Ancient convulsions of their majesty.
There is Jorasse, Midi, and spiry Dru,
  And the Géant, and high Argentière:
And dark and scowlingly they look at you.
  There's not a spot of vegetation there—
Even where the hand of winter cannot strew
  Snows on the sides, so splintered and so bare,
With granite points upon their rugged flanks,
Like spears of the archangels' military ranks.

50 *Poems* (1891) inserts 'finish' here.
51 *Poems* (1891) inserts 'and rent' here.

52

But on your left a softer scene appears,
  Where the lake spreads out its metallic glow.
No mountain there its scraggy outline rears,
  But all is peaceful,—beautifully so!
Some little bark in distance fades, or nears
  With forked canvass flitting to and fro
Over the dimples of its polished face.
  Many a field and many a garden gay
Bedeck the Voirons' gently sloping base;
  At these you look and wonder, day by day,
So that Geneva is a pleasant place
  Whereat to make a week's or fortnight's stay,
To rest and to enjoy yourself at; and to
End a long journey, and a tiresome canto.

CANTO II

1[52]

You who are tired of journeying with me
 May stick here if you like, nor read my rhyme.
You who desire a few more sights to see,
 Cities more splendid, scenery more sublime,
Come on, I'm going to start, and instantly—
 No stopping, no delaying, I've no time.
I will invoke no muses: I can do
 Without 'em, and my Pegasus[53] goes first;
I'm not upon Parnassus,[54] it is true,
 But soon midst higher mountains shall be lost.
And, gentle reader, I will carry you
 Where upon frozen ocean's Alpine coast
Are streams as sweet as any Heliconian,[55]
Fit to inspire the soul of a Maronian![56]

2

We left Geneva. 'Tis against the grain
 From such a lovely place yourself to sever,
Knowing that you will not be there again
 For a long time at least,—and perhaps never.
I must confess I crossed the bridge with pain,
 The bridge that arches o'er a rushing river.
But up my heart leaped with a bound once more
 When, full in front, increasing as we went,
The ancient mountain stood, with glaciers hoar.
 And entering the valley, which is rent
Between the Môle and Brezon (I before
 Have spoken of it),[57] I grew quite content,
And ceased to sigh, though I no more could see of
Geneva's spires, which there are two or three of.

3

Our road fast brings us nearer to the Môle,
 And we shall pass beneath it presently.
The Môle—now don't confuse it with the Dôle,—
 There is a difference between M and D—

52 This stanza is omitted in *Poems* (1891).
53 A winged horse in Greek mythology.
54 Referring to the Greek mountain associated with Apollo and a symbol of poetry.
55 On Mount Helicon, home of the Muses.
56 Devotee of Virgil.
57 Canto I, stanza 50.

The Môle, I say, sir, is upon the whole
 A lovely mountain as you'd wish to see.
Those who for height alone inclined to stickle are
 May say that it is nothing of a height;
[Six][58] thousand feet, or something, perpendicular:
 That's quite contemptible!—and they are right!
But I[59] am not at all particular,
 So that a mountain's aspect please the sight;
And even to look up so high makes one feel
Stiff i' the neck, from such a place as Bonneville.

4

They told me things about the Môle, on which
 I was incredulous, and quite refractory.
They said 'twas shaped exactly like the ridge
 Of some spare, lean old gentleman's olfactory[60]—
A sharp and regular and well-formed ridge,
 You scarcely could believe the fact, nor I.
Seen from Geneva, 'tis a pyramid,
 Sharp, high, and pointed, for beheld from thence
Its back by its extremity is hid.
 But here the ridge is lengthened and immense,
Furrowed by avalanches, which have slid
 Down its steepsides, and with magnificence
Of verdure robed; indeed, there's not a spot on
Its sloping flanks of snow from top to bottom.

5

And on the other side appears the Brezon,
 A lofty precipice of limestone hoar.
Monsieur Saussure,[61] who used to lay much stress on
 Necessity of practising, before
You venture into danger (and with reason),
 Used to climb up, and poke his numskull o'er
Couched on his breast,—a ticklish situation
 For those who are not thorough mountain bred!
Oh, Shakespeare! when the paltry elevation
 Of Dover's promontory filled thy head
With dizziness and instant inspiration,[62]—
 Oh, Master Shakespeare, what would'st thou have said

58 3000 feet in the MS. Collingwood notes in *Poems* (1891): 'The Môle is 6125 feet above the sea, and 4665 above Bonneville: the Brezon is 6142 feet above the sea, and 4682 above Bonneville.'

59 *Poems* (1891) inserts 'myself' here.

60 Nose.

61 Horace-Bénédict de Saussure (1740 –1799), the Swiss physicist and Alpine traveller.

62 As described by Edgar in *King Lear*, IV. 6. The allusion continues into the next stanza.

If, 'stead of poor four hundred, as at Dover
Thou hadst looked down four thousand feet, and over?

6

Tell me of crows and choughs,—a pretty thing!
   Why, man, you could not see a flying cow
A quarter down!—or samphire gatherer swing,—
   Such nonsense!—here were room and height enow
To hang a dozen of 'em in a string,
   Nor see the topmost from the mountain's brow.
"Not leap aloft[63] for all beneath the moon?"
   —No, nor leap backward from the verge of fear
For all beneath the shine of stars or sun.
   "Not hear the sea?" why, here you could not hear
The echo of the chamois hunter's gun
   Fired at the bottom of the cliff so sheer![64]
The vallies lying in the mountain's lap
Look like a pretty little pocket-map!

7

Onward we went; and as we went, the cloud
   Fretted the sunny sky with silver white,
Like Gothic carving on a temple proud;
   Pale at the first, and shadowy, and light;
Then darker and distincter, like a shroud
   Stooped upon each surrounding wintry height.
For these, where'er in heaven the clouds are tost,
   Do gather them together, and wrap over
Their naked sides, all comfortless with frost.
   Above us, wreathed like smoke the cloudy cover,
And half-way down the higher hills were lost;
   But here and there by chance you might discover
A spire of ice, incredibly on high,
Start like a meteor through the misty sky.

63 *Poems* (1891) reads 'upright'.
64 See *King Lear*, iv. 6:

Edgar. Hark! Do you hear the sea?
Gloucester. No, truly.
[...]
Edgar. [...] How fearful
And dizzy 'tis, to cast one's eyes so low!
The crows and choughs that wing the midway air,
Show scarce so gross as beetles. Half way down
Hangs one that gathers samphire, dreadful trade!
[...]
[...] For all beneath the moon
Would I not leap upright.

8

Onward we went, in—what's the name of it?—I
  Really don't know if it has any name,
The vale 'twixt Cluse and Bonneville, which looks pretty
  At summer's early glow; though at the same
Time it is liable—which is a pity—
  To the attacks of water, wind, and flame.
You ask, at its wild beauty wondering,
  How can the place be such a flat as to
Permit the Arve its turbid waves to fling
  Over its greenest fields, and to renew
An annual devastation? till some king[65]
  (A monument's built to him) passing through
Bonneville (just at the bridge-end mark you it?)
"*Aggeribus haec flumina coercuit.*"[66]

9

But when the fierce and unrelenting heat
  Of summer doth oppress the weary stream,
Along the hills the rays, all burning, beat,
  And the hot valley pants beneath the beam.
The glowing soil beneath you fires your feet
  And tires your eyesight with an arid gleam.
Once,—'twas a marvellous and fearful thing,—
  The trees took fire beneath the glowing soil;
Wide Conflagration spread his purple wing:
  Vainly the frighted peasants pant and toil,
Vainly dig channels for the crystal spring;—
  The helpless waters in their channel [boil],[67]
And a red Autumn in an instant came,
And Nature withered 'neath her glance of flame.

10

But when, in furry robe of whitest snow,
  The Winter spreads his[68] desolate dominion,
Forth come the winds, and loudly do they blow,
  And, like an eagle poised on threatening pinion,
Swoop in wide circles round the plain below.
  And when a tempest once begins within one

65 Collingwood, *Poems* (1891), identifies the king as Charles Felix of Sardinia.

66 'Checked these waters with banks'.

67 Corrected in *Poems* (1891) from 'came' in the MS.

68 *Poems* (1891) reads 'her'.

Of these low mountain-vallies, many a tree
  That long firm-rooted in their earth have stood
Bow their old heads[69] before it painfully;
  And all the plain, obscured with hoary wood,
Undulates like the variable sea:
  The very river backward rolls his flood,
Shakes the far mountains with his echoing roar,—
Heaves his white crest on high, and deluges his shore.

11

And now the bridge of Cluse is gained and past:
  Sharp turns the road to enter the ravine
Cloven in the hills as by some weapon vast.
  The river takes his rushing path between;—
I would not be the Arve, to fly so fast
  Through the variety of such a scene!
From side to side, from crag to crag rebounding,
  Sheeted with foam, as is the spurred war-horse,
So leaps the river, that the rocks around him[70]
  Are formed and chiselled by his constant force.
With bursting echoes quake the cliffs resounding,
  No deepness stills, no barrier checks his course;
On, ever on, the maddened billows sweep,—
Rest in no pool, nor by their border sleep.

12

The castellated cliffs stand o'er your head
  Broken, as is the war worn battlement.
But, as if its defenders were not fled,
  Bristle the pines above their summits rent
Like a well-ordered army. Bare and red
  Gleam their high flanks, and beautifully blent
Are moss, and turf, and crag, wet with the spray
  Of yon aërial stream, which long ago
We saw in distance glittering down, and gay
  With its broad, beautiful, perpetual bow
Belted about its column, as the ray
  Shoots through the dissipated drops below,
Like dew descending, or soft April showers
Bathing in sunshine the delighted flowers.[71]

69 *Poems* (1891) reads 'Bows his old head'.
70 So in the MS. *Poems* (1891) reads 'surrounding'.
71 *Poems* (1891) notes: 'The waterfall of Nant d'Arpenaz'.

13

Oh, gently sinks the eve, and redly [sets][72]
 The sun above Sallenches' mountains blue;
Like regal robes, the purple clouds beset
 Mont Blanc; but on his crest, still breaking through.
The last bright western rays are lingering yet,
 And the white snow glows with a rosy hue.
And now it fades, and now is past away;
 The highest dome among the stars is white;
It seems to wake, and watch the night away[73]
 And kindle at the first gleam of the light,—
A mighty beacon, to proclaim the day,
 A beacon fit to meet the gladdened sight
Of half the world, from Gallia's[74] plains of vine
Unto the distant ridge of the blue Apennine.

14

The morning came; delightful was the weather.
 Up to the door with rattling rumble daundered
Those very strange compounds of wood and leather:—
 Oh, *char-à-banc,* thou vehicle most honoured
Of all the vehicles e'er put together!
 What though thy cushions be to sit upon hard,
And though they scarce can hold their well-squeezed three,
 And though thou lookest ancient, worn and brown,
What coach and chariot can compete with thee,
 That knead the mud of Pall-Mall up and down,
Or traverse and re-traverse constantly
 The loud monotony of London town,
With gilded panels, arms upon the door,
Footmen behind and coachmen cocked before?

15

I love to see, with stately gait advancing,
 The city coach, that vehicle historical,
With golden glare the vulgar eyes entrancing!
 I love to see the darting gig or curricle,
With pawing greys and harness brightly glancing!
 I love to see, with swiftness meteorical,

72 The MS has 'set'.

73 *Poems* (1891) reads 'decay'.

74 Latin: the region of Western Europe now occupied by France, Belgium and neighbouring countries.

The mail coach spurn the dust like clouds behind,—
  Eyes watching for it, expectation strung,
When "Troo, taroo, turuw!" comes on the wind!
  I love to see a chariot float along
On softest springs for luxury designed,
  Yieldingly firm, and delicately strong,—
With whirling wheel divide the lagging air,—
Steeds pant, dogs bark, boys shout, and rustics stare!

16

But thou, of all to me the sweetest sight,
  Made for the mountain, servant of the hill,
Contemner of bad roads, who tak'st delight
  In crushing rock and stone, be with me still,
Friend of my wearied limb, for visions bright
  Rise on me when I see thee; by the rill,
The river, and the precipice I've past
  Safely and most delightfully in thee!
—Thus thought I, while around me progressed fast
  Bustling and packing :—"Where could that thing be?
And where could this have got to?"—till at last
  The things must be tied on, and steadily
Some twenty minutes were at last allotted
Ere the last cord was stretched, and tightly knotted.

17

For the interior—how we could pack into
  So small a space so many things, I can't tell:
Baskets, and covered things that bore one's back into
  Boxes and bundles,—everything one can't well
Want, or may possibly require: twines cracking, too,
  Things tumbling down because they cannot stand well:—
And "tie that there," and then, "tie" that thing to it,
  And tie this on the top of them; and that thing
Must go between your legs;—ay, so you'll do it;—
  And this behind your back, it is a flat thing;
This on your knee."—No, thank ye; I'll give *you* it!—
  "This in your pocket."—How that bottle's rattling!
"Dear me, it's loose; how lucky you have spoken!"
Smash! "That's the tumbler; hope it is not broken!"

18

We'd sixteen miles to go, or thereabout.
  That, among hills, is something appetising.
Hadst seen us, you'd have said, I make no doubt,
  Our provend[75] preparation was surprising;
With lemonade (you cannot get brown stout,
  The creamy bubbles through its crystal rising),
Bottles of wine and brandy, butter, bread,
  Cheese of the finest,—cream and rich Gruyère;
Strawberry jam upon our crusts to spread,
  And many a purple plum, and golden pear,
And polished apples, blushing rosy red;
  Ham, beef, and bacon, slices rich and rare;—
We found our knives and dishes useful; you
On carrying them may find them useful too.

19[76]

Thus from St. Martin's gate we made our[77] start, I
  Following in the second *char-à-banc.*
Behind us in a third there came a party
  Who, dashing down for Italy point blank,
Here from their route had ventured to depart; we
  Found them agreeable, and free, and frank.
There was a sort of middle-aged old lady,
  And a not very young young lady too;
A miss beginning to be sage and steady,
  And advice-giving, and her brother, who
Was younger, had a great deal in his head; he
  Knew Greek, French, Latin, had not time to dally in
  What he left to the ladies—the Italian.

20

Thus from St. Martin's gate we rolled away;
  We found at first the motion rather tiring,
Loquacious we as crickets are, and gay,
  Arranging, rearranging, and admiring.
Poking our heads this, that, and every way,
  Murmuring and pushing, packing and perspiring.
The day was very hot, and quite a smotherer,
  That makes one drowsy, which is very odd.

75 Provisions.

76 *Poems* (1891) omits the second half of this stanza (which has one line short), and the first half of the next stanza.

77 *Poems* (1891) reads 'a'.

Those[78] who inclined to make a pother were,
  Quite disturbed those who were inclined to nod
By playing at bopeep with those in t'other *char,*—
  Popping behind the leathern curtains broad.
I was ashamed, and told them—"no more gammon![79] I
Think that a shocking way of going to Chamouni!"

21

There is a little and a quiet lake,[80]
  And lovely are its waters, hardly seen,
Lying beneath the shelter of a brake,
  Like the spring turf beneath its foliage green;
And where the sunbeams through the leavage break
  They dive beneath its waters, with a sheen
Such as the moon sheds on the midnight deep,
  When mermaids, issuing from their coral caves,
With shelly voices sing the seas to sleep,
  And scatter wayward lustre o'er the waves.
Forth the stream issues with a hurried leap
  Down its rock-girded channel, which it paves
With many a ball of alabaster white,
And marble gay, and crystal clear and bright:—

22

Not clearer than its waters, which receive
  The image of Mont Blanc upon their breast,
Nor, with the motion of one ripple, heave
  The quiet snow on his reversed crest,—
So beautiful the scene, you might believe
  A limner, 'mid the fairies deemed the best,
Had painted it with natural colours fair,
  And put the water o'er it for a glass,
And framed it in, with fretwork rich and rare
  Of jewel-flowers, and moss, and daisied grass.
How sweetly sounds the gurgle through the air
  Of the cool, dancing streamlet, as you pass:
There is no music pleases you so truly
As gush of waters in the heat of July.

78 So in the MS. *Poems* (1891) reads 'Some of us'.
79 Slang: stupidity.
80 *Poems* (1891) notes: 'The Lac de Chède, now destroyed.'

23

By slow degrees and winding pathway mounting,
Onward we went the ancient pines among;
By many a trickling stream and gushing fountain
O'er the rough bed of many a torrent strong,
Amid the wreck of Servoz' ruined mountain,[81]
So beautiful in ruins. Far along,
And up the ridge, amid whose granites grey
Struggles the Arve, you hear the constant cry
Of waters, though unseen they wind their way
A hundred fathom down. In front, on high
The glacier flashes in the noontide ray,
In the deep azure of the Alpine sky.
And now the ridge is won: rest, rest, and see
What lies beneath you now; for there is Chamouni!

24

Like the Elysian fields where rove the blest,
Though round them reaches the Tartarean[82] wild,—
Thus lies the enchanted vale, and all that's best
Of spring and summer's lavished on their child."
While, round the space where those green meadows rest,
Is mountain chaos, like a barrier, piled,
And Winter holds an undisputed reign;
The chilly fingered tempest winds that go
On waving wings along the hills amain[83]
Shake not a blossom in the fields below;
And every sunbeam that, with effort vain,
Strikes on the cold and unrelenting snow,
Seeks the sweet covert of the sheltered plain,
And lies delighted upon flowers again.

25

The King of mountains, clothed in cloudy veil,
Asserts his rule upon the meadows green,
And lays his sceptre on the subject dale—
Sceptre of silver ice, whose spires were seen
And many a minaret of crystal pale
Rising above the pines with silver sheen.

81 *Poems* (1891) notes: 'The landslip of stanza 23 is [...] that which happened in 1751; and the lake, described in stanzas 21 and 22, was destroyed by another landslip only two years after Mr Ruskin's visit.'

82 Referring to Tartarus, the abyss in which the Titans are imprisoned in Greek myth.

83 With great speed and force.

Oh, beautiful, how beautiful to see
  The summer sun on tower and bastion beaming,—
Their bases beaten by a frozen sea,—
  The moveless foam upon its breakers gleaming;
And from a mighty portal constantly
  A sparkling river through the valley streaming;
For here's the company of glaciers, that is
Supplying all the world with water, *gratis!*

26

Then we descended, through the valley going,
  Till the small village in the front was seen
With its low spire conspicuously glowing,
  (For here they cover all their spires with tin,
Which makes them sparkle in the distance, showing
  Like diamond in gentleman's breast-pin).
Here there are several hotels; but which of them
  May be the best, is difficult to say.
Accommodation may be found at each of them;
  But don't believe those fellows on the way,—
They'll recommend the worst, if you trust speech of them!
  The Union seems the largest and most gay;
Of which I'll give you an exact description,
Because it was the place of our reception.

27

The Union is a building large and strong,
  And somewhat English; and its side is[84] graced
With triple row of windows broad and long;
  But at its end are wooden galleries placed,
Well carved and ornamented all along;—
  The Swiss in such things have a deal of taste.
And there the guides assemble, when the sun
  Is red upon the mountains' topmost snow,
And all their[85] labours of the day are done,
  To smoke a sociable pipe or so,
Telling their feats of *peril,* one by one;
  And happiest he who oftenest below
His foot hath trod that crest where none can stand
Save in a shadow of death, his life laid in his hand.

84 *Poems* (1891) reads: 'sides are'.
85 *Poems* (1891) reads: 'the'.

28

In the interior are lobbies three
Above each other, windows at each end,
From which—I will not tell you what you see
At present,—in a minute I intend
To take the panorama properly.
And in these passages I'd recommend
A walk for exercise in rainy weather,—
They are so long, they're quite a promenade.
I've tramped away in them for hours together,
And measured miles before I dreamed I had.
And in them there are pictures which are rather
Well executed, or at least not bad,
Of ibex, deer, and chamois, bisons, buffaloes,
Which those who hunt 'em say are rather tough fellows.

29

From this the bedrooms open, clean and neat,
Well furnished; and which often furnish you
With much amusement. It is quite a treat
When you have nothing in the world to do,
Close to the window oped to take your seat,
And feast upon the magic of the view.
I went to one; 'twas at the lobby-end,
Full opening on the gigantic hill,
Up went the casement: there I took my stand,
Stupidly of the scene to take my fill:
My head dropped somehow down upon my hand
Sleep-like; and I became exceeding still.
Sometimes, when such a glory you espy,
The body seems to sleep,—the soul goes to the eye.

30

The noonday clouds across the heaven were rolled,
With many a lengthened vista opening through,
Where many a gorgeous wave of white and gold[86]

86 The MS ends here.

A Letter from France[1]

PARIS, 14 *June.*

DEAR RICHARD[2]

AT Paris, in the Rue la Paix,
Last Midsummer I sit reviewing;[3]
And think of you, now far away,
And wonder what you may be doing:—
If after church at school you stay,
Not yet come back from Wales;
Or if at Herne Hill glad and gay,
Returned from Doctor Dale's.[4]
I love to write to you, and so,
Our journey hither well digesting
I write, altho' I hardly know
What may be chiefly interesting.
You'll guess the time went very slow
While I was being dosed[5] and stewed up,[6]
But then there was a pretty go
When I escaped from being mewed up!
The day was fine as day might be;
We cantered down to Canterbury;
Then on to Dover; crossed the sea;
Stopped, as we were not in a hurry,
At Calais; walked about to see
The Gothic steeple,[7] and the people:

1 The title is W. G. Collingwood's. Written between 14 June and 2 September 1835. Copy of the original sent to Richard Fall.

2 Richard Whiteman Fall was Ruskin's closest boyhood friend, who was the son of close neighbours on Herne Hill and a pupil at Shrewsbury School. The two embarked on a tour to Wales in 1841, though Ruskin, who was showing signs of consumption, was recalled by his father: see *The Diaries of John Ruskin 1848–1873*, selected and ed. by Joan Evans and John Howard Whitehouse, 3 vols (Oxford: The Clarendon Press, 1956–59), II, 210–11.They took a last walk together, to Chamouni, on Ruskin's Swiss Tour of 1849.

3 Collingwood notes in 1891 that the two boys had spent that period together at Herne Hill.

4 As Collingwood notes elsewhere in 1891, this is a different schoolmaster from "the Mr. Dale to whom the author went to school in 1834, and to lectures in 1836."

5 Corrected in the Library Edition from 'closed' in *Poems* (1891).

6 Ruskin had been withdrawn from school in spring suffering from pleurisy.

7 Église Notre-Dame de Calais.

I sketched, in manner bold and free,
A sketch at which you'll like to peep well.
Next morn was dark and thick[8] with rain;
But on the next we braved the weather.
Thinks I, "Oh, this is just the same,—
Their harness is as bad as ever!
Their horses still, in tail and mane,
Uncombed, unornamented brutes!"
But soon I saw, and saw with pain,
There was a falling off in boots!
And so to Rouen down we went,
By many a hill full gay and green;
The evening was magnificent;—
The noble city, like a Queen,
Sat in silence on the Seine
That here and there about was bent,
With islands bright his waves between,
Like an emerald ornament.

HOSPICE OF GREAT ST. BERNARD: *July 21, 9000ft. above sea.*

And there I sketched me sketches three,[9]
Though Mr. Prout has nearly spent all!
Two of his pictures you may see
In the Annual Continental.[10]
Up to Paris next we went all,
Seeing many an English face;—
No wonder that they there are bent all!
'Tis a wondrous pleasant place.
On we went, enjoying rarely
Soissons, Rheims, and Bar, and Nancy,
—'Tis quite an itinerary;—
We saw all that people can see.
But nothing pleased so much my fancy
As when we went to Plombières;
—Far as the quickest eye could scan, we
Saw the Jura, blue and bare.
And now the sun is shining bright
On many a lofty crag of grey;

8 'Dark' and 'thick' are reversed in *Poems* (1891), but the Library Edition adopts the corrected order from the MS.

9 There are in fact four sketches: Catalogue 8, 9, 10 and 11. See Stephen Wildman and Cynthia Gamble, *'A Perpetual Paradise': Ruskin's Northern France*, exhibition catalogue, The Ruskin Library, University of Lancaster, 20 April–15 September 2002, pp. 10–11.

10 See *The Continental Annual, and Romantic Cabinet for 1832. With Illustrations by Samuel Prout*, ed. by William Kennedy (London: Smith, Elder, and Co., 1832). It contains two drawings of Rouen.

And sheets of deep snow, silver white,
Beating back the flashing ray.
Mont Velan in his white array
Looks o'er the little lake of blue,
Whose verdant waves transparent play
With ice and blue snow shining thro'.

SCHAFFHAUSEN, 5 *Augt.*

The afternoon was clear and fair;
The sun shot warm along the snow;
The clearness of the mountain air
Like crystal gleamed, above, below.
And nearer drew the Velan's glow;
While on the mountain side were seen
Mosses most rich, of emerald green,
Sprinkled o'er with fairy show
Of Alpine flowers; you cannot think
How sapphire-like the gentian blue
Mixed with stars of paly pink!
How humbly, and how low they grew
On every shadowy spot!
And I did think of home and you,
When from beneath a rock I drew
A young *forget-me-not.*
The dogs all out,—ay, every snout,—
Upon the snow they romped and rolled;[11]
How they pulled each other about!
How the young did plague the old!
They can't bear heat, as we were told,
But love to feel the constant cold.
They welcome you, altho' they're mute,—
There's such a manner in the brute!

Aosta! oh, how thick it is
With buildings, ancient, strange and rare:
—I know you like antiquities;—
Full twelve feet thick of brick laid bare,
The ancient city-walls are there,
With a marble ornament
By the chisel sculptured fair.
Broadly are the arches bent;
Tho', as the facings are defaced,
The old inscription is replaced.[12]

11 The famous St Bernard dogs from the Hospice.
12 *Poems* (1891): 'Ruskin is here describing the Porta Praetoria (now called the Porte de la

It runs in French, to this intent:—
"Stranger, respect this monument!
Augustus Caesar in the space
Of three short twelvemonths built this place,
And called it by his name. Pass on!"
An arch of most triumphal span
Is there, of brick as hard as stone,
With this inscription thereupon
—I give it you as best I can;—
"Rome, in many a weary fight
O'er the Salassians victorious,[13]
Built this arch, remembrance glorious
And memorial of her might."
Much were we pleased, you may be sure,
When we set off for Cormayeur;—
Fortresses arising round;
Rocks, with ruined castles crowned;
Vineyards green with trellised rail;
Villages in every vale;
Alps on high of granite grey
(Snow on every point appearing),
That, capped with cloud, seem far away,
Or vision-like, in heaven clearing.
Oh, the wild and [worn][14] array
Of the huge aiguilles you see,
Waiting on the majesty
Of their monarch! Oh, the gleam
Of his silver diadem!
With a thousand glaciers set
In his summer coronet;
All the mountain's brow, they span it,
Barred about with spires of granite.
Avalanches, one and all,
Down they fall in what they call
—'Tis a sort of lonely valley
Full of ice—which they call "Allée
Blanche," but blanche it an't at all!
Mont Blanc is lifted up on high
And shakes his snowy head into it;
Broken ice and granite strew it,—
'T'is confusion constantly.

Trinité), through which the road still passes. Aosta was captured by the Romans in 24 B.C., and rebuilt by Augustus.'

13 Ruskin notes in the MS: '*Anno urbis 724.*'

14 Ruskin later filled an original blank with this word.

TOP OF RIGHI.

I hope all this is entertaining!
I think, if lesson-time's gone by,
And play-time come, and it is raining,
It may be so, at Shrewsbury.
But if the sun is shining bright,
And games agog, when you receive it
Then fold it up,—say "that's all right,"
And take your cricket bat, and leave it.
When you're knocked up, and wickets down,
And when you panting, tired, and warm[15] are,
Then in the school room pray sit down
In that comfortable corner.
Then will you read, while you repose,
All that I am going to tell you,
Nor think the letter is verbose,
Nor say that I'm a tiresome fellow.[16]
From Cormayeur we backward bore,
O'er St. Bernard's Alps again,
Down upon Lake Leman's shore
Where [blue][17] waves on Chillon roar.
Round by Neufchâtel we came,
By ancient Granson's towers of fame;[18]
And where the Rhine for evermore
'Mid columnar rocks of grey
Thunders down with lightening spray,
Underneath an iris bright,
That arches o'er with trembling light.
'Tis sweet to see the peaceful thing
Around the warring waters cling,
With a sort of fearful quivering!
Then to Zurich,
Where I grew sick,—
Almost thought I should have staid a
Day on purpose, but we made a
Dash at Zug, and heard fine music
Played by landlord and landlady.

15 As in the MS. *Poems* (1891) reads 'worn'.

16 In *Praeterita*, Ruskin writes: 'Richard Fall was entirely good-humoured, sensible, and practical; but had no particular tastes; a distaste, if anything, for my styles both of art and poetry' (35.139).

17 Later substituted by Ruskin for 'the' in the MS.

18 *Poems* (1891): '"Granson" (Grandson), on the Lake of Neuchâtel, was the scene of the decisive victory of the Swiss over Charles the Bold, March 3, 1476; interesting to the author from the description in Sir W. Scott's *Anne of Geierstein* (chap. xxxii.).'

Mont St. Gothard next we drew nigh,
By Altorf and the lake of Uri.
The Swiss, as you know very well,
Are yery fond of William Tell:
To show they've not forgot him,
A chapel's built where from the prore[19]
Of [Gessler's][20] boat he leaped ashore,
And *ditto* where he shot him.
Up we went, wondrous high
In the midst of the beautiful dark blue sky,
'Mid St. Gothard's granites tall.
Down we went,—'twas fair and fine,
Down by zig-zags twenty-nine,
Built upon the top of a wall
Close by a torrent's flashing fall.

HOSPICE OF THE GRIMSEL, 6000 *feet high.*
25 Augt—a terrible day.

I wonder much what sort of day
This 25th of August may be
In dear old England far away![21]
Perhaps the sun is shining gaily,
And you may see, by Severn's stream,
The city basking in the beam,
And sloping fields with harvest white,
And distant mountains, bluely bright.
Now turn your gladdened eyes away
From all this landscape warmly gay;
And read, and think, and try to see
The scene that August brings to me.
I see around me, far and wide,
A weary waste of mountain-side,
Strewed with blocks of granite bare,
With scanty grass blades here and there.
Above, the summits tall and proud
Are buried in a veil of cloud;
But through the misty mantle show
The frosty fields of new fallen snow.
Thick and constant everywhere
The snow flakes ride the rolling air.
The mountain torrents loudly call

19 Prow, and changed to that word in *Poems* (1891).
20 So corrected in *Poems* (1891) from 'Gesner' in the MS.
21 Collingwood notes in *Poems* (1891) that 'R. Fall would have returned to school by the 25th of August, according to the time of the old-fashioned holidays.'

And fret the crags with constant fall.
The river that receives them all
Lifts up his voice on high:
On, onward still, with downward gust,[22]
The foam-flakes on his billows rush
Monotonously by.
The fire is bright; the window pane
Is thick with mist, and wet with rain.
My corner-seat, quite warm and cozy,
Makes me feel talkative and prosy.
So, where was I? Can't tell at all,—
So long and tiresomely I've pottered!
Oh yes, descending the St. Gothard,—
"Close by a torrent's flashing fall."[23]
The interest of that pass to me
Lay in its mineralogy.
Will take you to the top of Righi.

The vapours came with constant crowd;[24]
The hill was wrapt up in the cloud.
Hour after hour 'twas misty still,
As evening darkened on the hill.
Before the sun had left the sky
The wind stretched out his mighty hand,
And back recoiled the clouds, and nigh
Out looked the sunset luridly,
Like smoulder of a dying brand;
And white-edged thunder clouds around
Gave forth a hollow, groaning, sound.
Then onward came the cloudy tide;
Again it met from either side;
And darkness came, and darkness dire,
But cleft by constant sheets of fire.
Broad blazed the lightening's blinding flash,
With following thunder's instant crash:—
A pleasant night on which to be
Five thousand feet above the sea!
At half-past three we first looked out;
The stars were sprinkled all about;
The sky was blue, the air was clear,

22 *Poems* (1891) alters to 'constant gush'.

23 Quotes the last line of the previous section.

24 Collingwood notes in *Poems* (1891) that Ruskin's experience of this storm in the middle of August 1835 lay behind the elaborately extended description in volume one of *Modern Painters* (1843) (3.415–19).

And the white moon looked wondrous near![25]
The golden streaks of breaking dawn
Across the smiling east were drawn.
Relieved against the brilliant light
Dark purple outlines met the sight;
Which, brighter still as grew the flame,
Darker and purpler still became.
Round all the south, eternal snows
On dark horizon [paly][26] rose;
And it was beautiful to see
The light increasing constantly,
To search the gloom in vallies deep,
And wake the flowers on mead and steep.
Come, stand upon the Kulm[27] with me!
The sun is up; on what shines he?
Mountain on mountain rosy red
With glacier helmet lifts his head.
Oh, the long chain of snow-fields white,
Like the pale moon of summer night,
Peak over peak with wondrous glow!
While wreathing vapours [brew][28] below,
And on the other side were seen
Innumerable champaigns green.
Far, and more far, and faint they grew,
Expansive, beautiful, and blue!
Many a large lake beneath us set,
Without a breeze its waves to fret,
Like silver mirror distant lay
In many a lovely creek and bay;
Reflected, sank beneath its strand
Dark woods and flowery meadow land,
And farther down the mountains high,
And underneath the morning sky
By Pilate's[29] side you might discern
The glittering towers of fair Lucerne.
City, and hill, and waving wood,
Blue glaciers cold, and sparkling flood,—
All that was marvellous or fair
Seen at a single glance was there.
It was a landscape wondrous rich
In countless lovely scenes, on which

25 Later corrected from the MS 'clear'.
26 Later substituted by Ruskin for the original 'clear' in the MS.
27 Hill: a German toponym.
28 Corrected in *Poems* (1891) from 'brow' in the MS.
29 Mount Pilatus, overlooking Lucerne.

My paper in a well filled state
Forbids me to expatiate.[30]

THUN, 2 *September.*

I sit me down to make a whole
Of this long winded rigmarole:
To put in order its confusion,
And bring the tale to a conclusion.
I've written it at different stations,
From very different elevations.
By writing as the journey goes on,
My dates are wondrously well chosen.
You see I've taken in its turn all;
In fact, I've kept a sort of journal;
Hoping it may be in my power
To interest some[31] leisure hour,
And make your fancy cross the sea,
And roam in Switzerland with me.[32]

30 The last four lines omitted in *Poems* (1891).

31 As in MS. *Poems* (1891) reads 'a'.

32 There is a prose postscript in the MS: '*P.S.* — Perhaps you do not care about Switzerland, and it would have given you more pleasure until I could fill my paper with an account of Rome and Naples; but I am of opinion that what is said of giving may as well be applied to writing, that he who writes quickly writes twice, and is very likely to write twice too; and I am now glad that my letter is ready to despatch, for, from the cholera's having appeared in Italy (where I am afraid it is likely to prevail to a terrible extent), and from some other circumstances, I think there is not the least chance of our getting the length of Rome. We think of passing the Simplon to Milan, perhaps to Venice, crossing the Stelvio, and through the Tyrol to Vienna, and then home by Paris, so that I expect to be at home to receive you at Christmas. It is very wrong of you, the fonder you are of me, the more you will exult in my disappointment. Sketches innumerable I have which you must not yawn over, poetry interminable I have which you must not sleep over; and we will go over Switzerland very comfortably together on the green chairs in the study; and I have some splendid minerals of St. Gothard and Mont Blanc to shew Eliza [Richard's younger sister], and now for the present farewell. I will write again before I return, where from, I know not. My best regards to all at home. Dear R., etc., etc."

Letter to Willoughby Jones[1]

❖

Dear Willoughby[2] Hospice of Great St Bernard. July 15th[3]

9000 ft above the sea.

We commenced our journey delightfully, and it has continued delightful.
We came by Calais to Rouen, a beautiful city, then to Paris, a bustling
city, then to Rheims, a dull city. then to Nancy, an odd city.
then to Dijon, a picturesque city, then we mounted the Jura, and
jumped down upon Geneva amidst such a blaze of Alps and lake
as held us fast for four days. Then we went to your favourite Sham
money,[4]
Since we had planned a nice long trip nor thought to end so soon it,
when letters were sent off let slip full many an opportunity
Because I hoped to write from Rome an excellent epistle
But cholera and plague have come and plagued it: we have missed all
And now indeed we're all in doubt and none of us can know
How long we shall roam about or whither we shall go[5]
Our route we ve hardly planned as yet, and such suspense is horrid, we
Are like the man whom Sancho met with insular authority[6]
As when we first laid out our track to Italy the fair
We little thought of turning back afraid to breathe its air,
But all enjoyment would be gone if there were any fear in us
And twould be foolish to go on, for things look very serious,
The cholera quite savage is, and easy tis discerning
It will make dreadful ravages, Italians are such vermin.
~~But~~ Though, if the doctors weren't afraid the people would think less of it,
But frightened doctors, they have made a very pretty mess of it
And so, we turn, because they say the Tyrols very fine.
By Inspruck,[7] Munich, & that way, and homewards by the Rhine
And if you near us chance to be, if Fortune shall assist us
I think It very likely we shall meet again at Christmas.

1 Transcribed from MS XI. The holograph is in ink. It is quoted from in the Library Edition and in *John Ruskin and Switzerland*, ed. John Hayman, Waterloo, Ontario: Wilfrid Laurier UP, 1990, p. 2.

2 Jones was Ruskin's fellow pupil at Thomas Dale's school, 1834–36: see 35.82–83 and 381.

3 In pencil, '1835' is added.

4 That is, Chamouni.

5 See the postscript to 'A Letter from Abroad', n.32. The original plan had been to travel to Rome.

6 Sancho Panza, who in Part Two of *Don Quixote* is made the governor of the fictional island of Barataria.

7 Innsbruck.

But I'll go back to Englands shore, when joy fully we thence went
Nor speak about the end before I've told you the commencement
Which wondrous pleasant was, and gay as setting off could be
~~I am~~ Driving down the Dover way and dancing oer the sea
Then by Montreuil to Boulogne may be more than 60 mile
For a long day tis not too long, and we went in fine crack style
The morning sun enlightening half dewily it shone
On ocean mists that weltered in the valley of Boulogne
And there were country houses fair, erected sir, upon a part
Of elevated downs that bear the pillar built by Bonaparte.
And I tried by instinctive sense, which you'll say Im a zany for
To guess which was the residence in summer of Dunsane[?] Law[?]

[end of page 1]

In France, although the towns you see ~~would need~~ require descriptions florid,
Theres really no fine scenery, and the roads are very horrid.
Rouen is grand, well worth your pains, then Paris, not worth stopp <ing in>
But the interior at Rheims will strike you on your popping in.
It was a day, oh, such a day, when from ~~Geneva~~ the Jura down
We came upon the valley, gay with glitterring lake and town
Oh, can you dream the ~~wonderous~~[?] magic burst that through the chasm came on us
The very thoughts were hushed at first, Oh marvellous, oh marvellous
There stood Mont Blanc, his cloudy height most beautifully prest[?]
By the eternal snowwreaths white, thick drifted on his crest.
They look up to the bright sun still they look from day to day
They glitter with his light, but feel no ~~splendour~~ glowing from his ray
There shone the lake, the lovely lake, the mountain girded ocean
His mirror was without a break, his billows without motion
Oh happy, happy lake, that bore, reflected far below,
The mountain wonders of its shore, [~~....?~~] the dazzling summer snow
Like flowery sapphire brightly blue, there lay the wide champaign
And greenly grew the forests there, and goldenly the grain
~~Oh~~ would you find the rich repose of Arcady tis there
The dreams of Mars[?] never rose more magically fair
It was an introduction meet to Switzerland the bright
It was an earnest very sweet of many a future sight
So at Geneva waited we, and when the days became sunny
Expended plenty real money at your old favourite Sham money
Which is a place beset with ice, a narrow valley, cut on
A mass of mountain, like a slice out of a leg of mutton
And, to pursue the simile, the pyramid up stuck alone,
The snow enwreathed Mont Blanc would be a tolerable knuckle bone
And in excursions rich and rare the valley did we span it
Here and there and every where among the dents of granite

My father wished that all the dents were far enough, I know,
Because he got the mal aux dents among the ice and snow.
We saw all there was to see, and then we turne'd us about
By the rocks of Meillerie, which Rousseau made a fuss about[8]
Lake and rock and field and tree are beautifully blent all
You really feel inclined to be a little sentimental.
Then Chillon came, but there the feasts of fancy could not drag us in,
Because they've turned it, oh the beasts, into a powder magazine[9]
One time indeed is quite enough to see the rings of iron
Last time we might have been blown up because we loved Lord Byron[10]
At St Bernard did we aspire to elevation high
<A>nd gathered closely round the fire although twas in July
We blew our fingers on the height, which in the morn we crossed, oh,
And almost turned to toast as night lay panting at Aosta
Then through the whole of Switzerland as merrily went we
[at bottom left:] Felds.[?] with bow.

[end of page 2]

I took my pencil in my hand, my Horace on my knee
And now I sketched a mountain scene, or any thing that me did please
And then I puzzled out a sentence of the cramp Thucydides.
Since too much work, the doctors say will make your brains quite muddy
I mingle in the wisest way amusement with my study
And first I read, and then look up in passing through a town,
Look out a word or two, and pop my dictionary down
Then Granson towers did see, where by his fortune fickle
Poor Charles the bold of Burgundy was put in such a pickle[11]
Though in Swiss towns in general theres little to be seen
They models are of neatness all and beautifully clean.
You may, at turn of every street, on fountains, tower and gate see
~~Stone statues~~ The Swiss s greatest favourite in marble tall and stately
~~Swiss~~ Because the Tyrant fierce and fell abused the people greatly
And William Tell shot very well and touched him off most nately[?]
Of which you see a monument upon the lake of Uri
Where hop upon the shore he went, and scaped the Tyrants fury,
Which with the most consummate art is by some clever fellow
Painted oer in every part with figures red and yellow

8 In a letter in volume three of *La Nouvelle Héloïse* (1763), St Preaux describes taking Mrs Wolmar to the rocks in luxuriant summer and describing to her his solitary visit there amid the horrors of winter which he had found congenial.

9 The Vaud government had turned the Castle of Chillon into a military storeroom.

10 See Byron's 'Prisoner of Chillon':

> And in each pillar there is a ring,
> And in each ring there is a chain;
> That iron is a cankering thing (36–38).

11 See 'Letter from Abroad', n.18.

The beauty of the scenery incited us to go on
By Meyringer and Grindelwald, and Lauterbrown, and so on
Rode 4 and 20 miles a day, and on such places, bless you
I really do not like to say for fear it should distress you
With precipices by our side a thousand feet or so
[...?] tumbling tossing alpine ride careering on below
The path itself not 4 feet wide, the mules, how well they go
With out a slidder[?] or a slide oer rock and turf and snow.
Hast ever seen an apple bob in agitated ocean
Now down into abysses drop with heavy plunging motion
Then rise on some high billows crest, and shake the floam[?] away
And show the red streaks on its breast all glittering to the day,
Then down again, ~~pressed~~ whelmed woefully beneath the surges all,
It plunges but to rise on high it rises but to fall
Sir we, ~~were~~ now in deep valley ~~deep~~ stuck[?], between huge mountains riven
And now on some tall summit made acquaintance with the heaven.
And when we reached the fair Vevay from Lemans inland sea
From Italy we turned away and sorrowful were we
And Tyrol next did we espy a country very comical
What with their hills so very high, and caps so very conical.
When we to Insperuck got, you know how small the distance then is
We thought that we might venture by Verona down to Venice
So started for the mountains brow and whither did we go
Oh Hannibal my man,[12] if thou hadst seen the Stelvio
Up we went 9000 feet (thats tolerably high)
And all above a dark blue sheet of lovely Alpine sky
And east and west and south and north the mighty peaks arose
With blinding brightness shooting forth the dazzle of their snows
In many a richly ~~wreathéd~~ drifted hill, in precipice dread
Three thousand feet above us still the ~~gla~~ summer snows were spread
And here and there the rocks looked out, the greenless rocks, above them
The glacier clasped them all about, the glacier seemed to love them
It was not cold, the sun was higher, and yet there seemed a spell
That froze it into powerless light on every pinnacle.

[end of page 3]

There was deep silence every where, and lifelessness of sound[13]
A sort of deadness dulled the air, and froze the rocks around
There is a contrariety your every sense between
You feel a summer air, your eye beholds a winter scene
You feel the sun, or seem to feel nor can imagine why
The snow beside your carriage wheel is 7 or 8 feet high
The evening sun shot ruby flame along that desolation

12 Hannibal famously crossed the Alps in the Second Punic War.
13 Page 4 is written between crossed-out lines written in Greek.

We travelled when the morning came in novel situation
The[r]e in a wilderness were we, a wilderness most fine
A wilderness of olive tree, of mulberry and vine
The indian corn was brown and tall the which we wound among
The olive[?] blossomed on th[e] wall when like a star it clung
And Bacchus seemed to revel on the sunny rocks around
The purple clusters bent down and grovelled on the ground
And when we went still farther south, fore fear the heat should bore us
On Comos lake we sailed about where Pliny sailed before us
And ate some trout, remembring that he used to poke his nose over
The lake to catch his dinner, pat amusement for philosopher
~~An~~ There in our bedrooms twas not hard to study well zoology
The animals sent in no card and made us no apology
One morning, jumping out of bed I saw, my nose before
A Tarantula on the wall, a scorpion on the floor
Then at Verona, sweet Verona, did we spend a day
And saw by moonlight silver glow a Roman ruin grey
~~Les~~ Row on row of massive stone, a noble amphitheatre
More perfect than the one at Rome although the last may be greater
There Master Shakespear wheedled us a long way to behold
A very old sarcophagus in cemetery old
I could believe the tale was true Verona is a scene
Where many, many a Montague and Capulet have been
There may have been some fact on which the mighty mind could weave
That broken stone may not have been her tomb, but oh, believe it.
And now I'm in the halls so high of oceans lovely daughter
The gondolas are gliding by, like arrows on the water.
Here and there they dart about where far around I see
The palaces arise from out the blue waves of the sea.
[...?] of marble, marble wondrous white, they fairly[14] like arise,
The Doge's is upon my right, and near the bridge of sighs
Oh Venice is a place to make a tortoise quite ecstatic
Ive crossed her lake, her ocean lake, and seen the Adriatic
A place of terror and of gloom, which very much is talked about
Ive tred St Marks by midnight moon and on Realto walked about
The Gondolier has rowed me by the House where Byron took delight
The palace too of Foscari is very nearby opposite[15]
But 4 days more, and we go forth and fast we sail away
And oer the Alps direct we north, a [~~...?~~] delightful way.

[end of page 4]

~~For~~ though here the air be mild and sweet and though I love to roam
I feel there dwells enchantment yet in the [~~...?~~] dear name of home

14 For 'fairy'?.
15 See Byron's *The Two Foscari* (1821).

And when we meet, soon may we meet, Ill let your eyes gaze then upon
Such sketches as I used to make in spare leaves of my [...?]
Of Gothic windows fair and tall, and rich cathedral spire
Italian scenes, and Alps, and all which you will much admire
Believe me Sir I do remain your faithful friend, I do.
And hope you'll welcome back again — the travelled —

V. Angelroo[?]

THE DRAWINGS

Caroline S. Hull

There is a body of around 124 drawings related to the 1835 tour which can be divided into seven or eight types by medium and technique. The group as a whole represents a systematic approach to recording Ruskin's experience of the places he visited on the tour, and to his plans to rework certain drawings at a later time for possible publication. The watercolours, whether derived from known drawings (*Mount Pilatus*, Catalogue 44, *Lake Thun*, Catalogue 69, and *Landeck*, Catalogue 97) or not directly related to a known drawing (as with *Stelvio Road from above Trefoi*, Catalogue 101), together with such 'finished' ink drawings as *St Gall*, Catalogue 95, and *Verona*, Catalogue 111, are unlikely to have been made during the journey itself.[1] As a whole the series constitutes the adolescent output of the artist, a fascinating mixture of youthful and adult goals, aspirations and methods of making sense of natural and built surroundings. As with all the records of this tour, they are formative in character.

Paul H. Walton points out the remarkable advance in technique in this series: 'Some pencil sketches in pure line achieve an almost professional standard of touch and composition.'[2] Timothy Hilton comments on the new 'artistic competence'[3] of the drawings which Walton had selected for illustration (*Mount Pilatus*, Catalogue 13, *The Jungfrau*, Catalogue 65, and *Friburg*, Catalogue 79). Though it is evident that Ruskin is still occasionally employing his early imitation of 'the [George] Cruikshank style' of 'placing lines, without previously feeling about for them',[4] while emulating Turner vignettes and even more exactly Prout's lithographs,[5] the development from the copying approach of the 1833 series, as Walton notes, shows the influence of Ruskin's new drawing master, Copley Fielding, on a closer observation of nature. He was now actually viewing the places which previously he had only seen in mediated form. His eye for architecture also had been engaged by his editor, J. C. Loudon's detailed interest in picturesque buildings, and there is a noticeably pronounced preoccupation with technique:

> [...] a liking for powerful effects of spatial recession, created by means of a wide angle of vision [...] a strong tension between receding diagonal accents and

1 I owe these comments to Stephen Wildman.

2 Paul H. Walton, *The Drawings of John Ruskin* (London: Oxford University Press, 1972), p. 27.

3 Timothy Hilton, *John Ruskin: The Early Years* (New Haven, CT, and London: Yale University Press, 1983), p. 34.

4 W. G. Collingwood, Prefatory Notes to the Plates, *The Poems of John Ruskin*, 2 vols (Orpington and London: George Allen, 1891), vol. 1, p. vii.

5 See W. G. Collingwood, 'Ruskin's Drawings', in *Ruskin Relics* (London: Isbister and Co., 1903), p. 123.

> soaring vertical lines [... an] interest in the expressive possibilities of exaggerated perspective [...] [departing] from the more classical spatial balance of models like Prout and Fielding in favour of the dynamic and dramatic space that he discovered at the heart of Turner's illustrations for Rogers's *Italy*.[6]

He was in transition to the freer and more assured larger formats of the 1837–38 drawings, in part inspired by a wider exposure to Turner's art and his introduction to that of David Roberts.[7] Characteristically Ruskinian features are already emerging from his scrutiny of the different kinds of architecture depicted in towns and especially alpine scenery, where the complementary interrelationship between natural and constructed forms prefigures the themes of his first extended analysis in *The Poetry of Architecture* (1837–38), for which some of the illustrations derive from the 1835 tour.

The different types of approach in the 1835 series are a sign of self-conscious and not yet resolved experimentation. His compositions are indicative: in virtually every single drawing of this period (including those from 1833 — only less refined at that point), Ruskin thinks in planes rather than compositions. He has a (borrowed) method for constructing the foreground or frontal plane of each drawing, and a separate distinct method for the background. There is very rarely anything approaching a midground to give a believable sense of progression through space, so that one's eye is given the more detailed (still 'black dots and Proutish breaks', 35.611) foreground — whether it consists of buildings or natural formations — and then a sketchier, less-defined rear plane. Sometimes the two planes run parallel to each other with the foreground a stripe across the bottom of the composition; sometimes they wrap around each other in some degree with the frontal plane occupying less than the full width of the composition, and with the background method used across the rear plane and partially across the front of the composition as well.

Ruskin's playing with perspective is not fully controlled, as he is still working on getting things just right. The bedroom drawing (Catalogue 13) is the most obvious example of this — presumably he is sitting on the floor (though the perspective system is inconsistent). He seems not to like this exaggerated angle as it is about the only time it appears throughout the drawings — he tends to avoid extreme linear perspectives elsewhere. This is a notable achievement given the gigantic proportions of mountains and vistas that he is trying to capture. It makes for an odd mixture of a vast and wondrous space somehow seen through an even wider eye, tending to reduce the vastness of effect. There is also a recurrent slant — more often slightly to the left, but sometimes to the right.

Though there would appear to be no principle behind the difference, at this period, or for the purposes of this tour, he has two main methods of defining his pictorial space. He uses a double-ruled frame (usually in ink) with a straight inscription, or he uses a composition with a curved 'step' in the foreground, and here the inscription curves around that 'step'. The inscriptions speak of a similar need to control by cataloguing. Ruskin went back in later years to inscribe or

6 *The Drawings of John Ruskin*, pp. 27–28.

7 See Keith Hanley, *John Ruskin's Romantic Tours, 1837–1838: Travelling North* (Lewiston, NY, Queenston, and Lampeter: The Edwin Mellen Press, 2007), p. 131 ff and pp. 143–45.

re-inscribe many of these drawings, though occasionally misremembering dates and places. He was effectively mapping out his own artistic development.

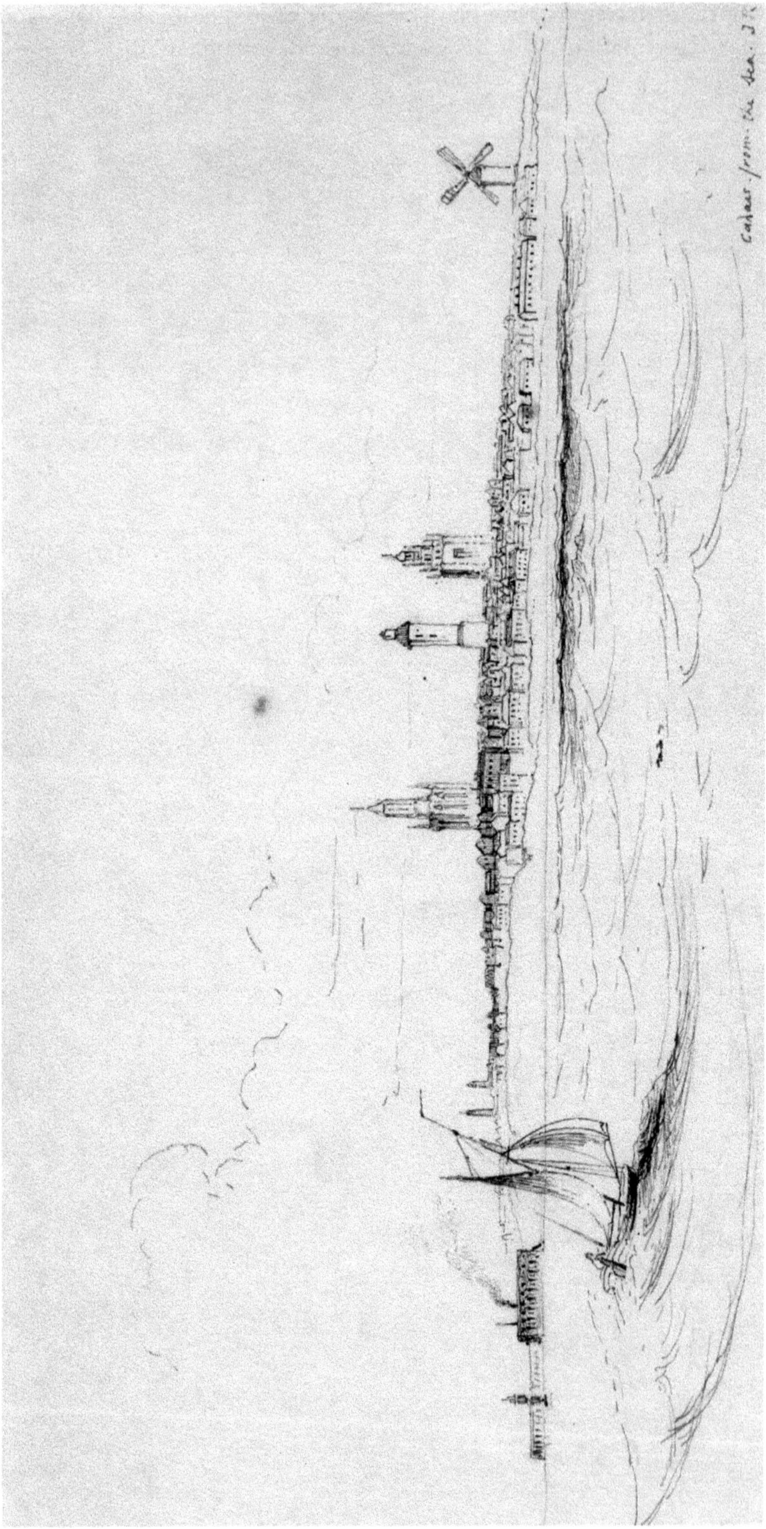

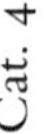

Cat. 4

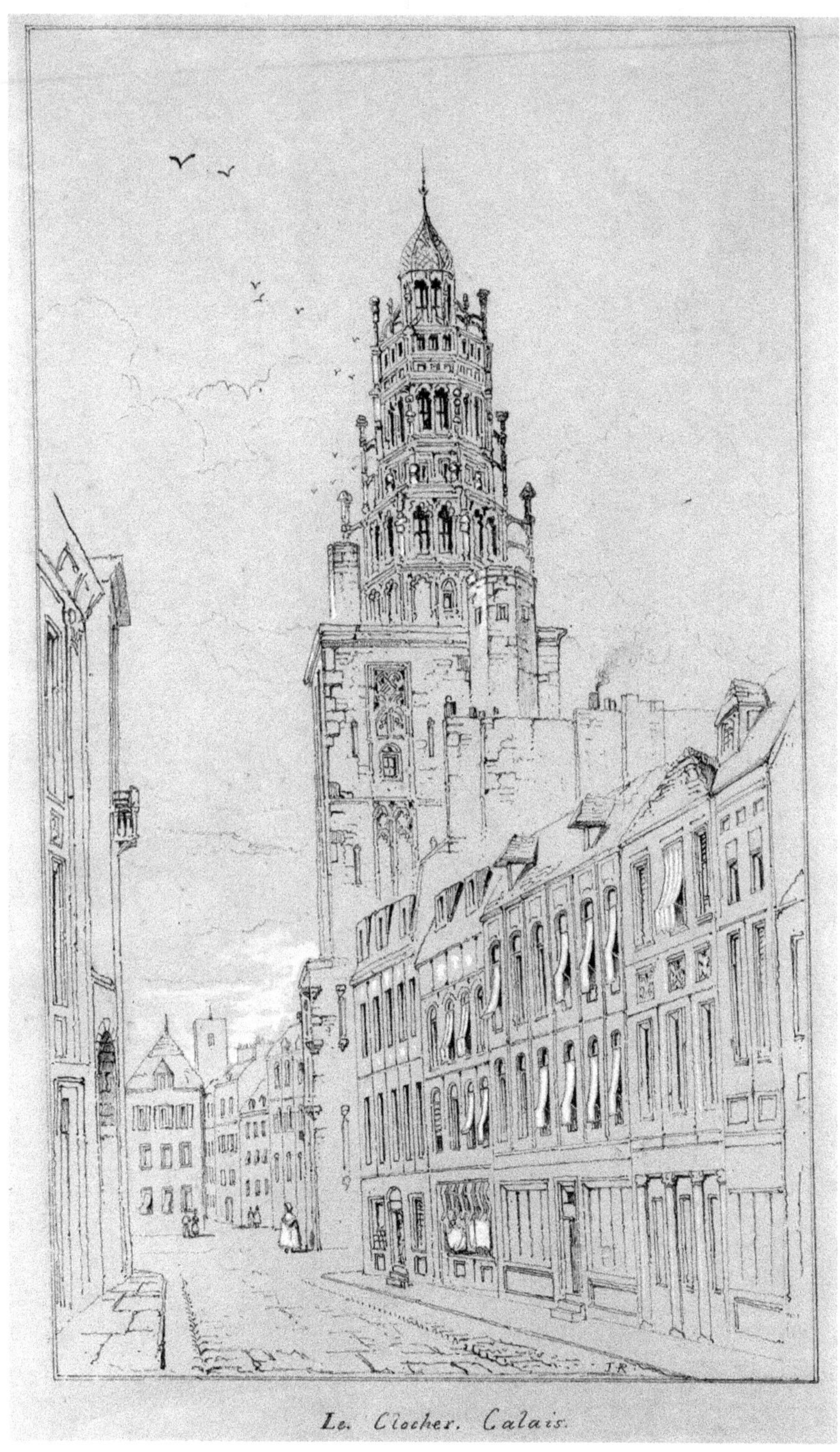

Cat. 5

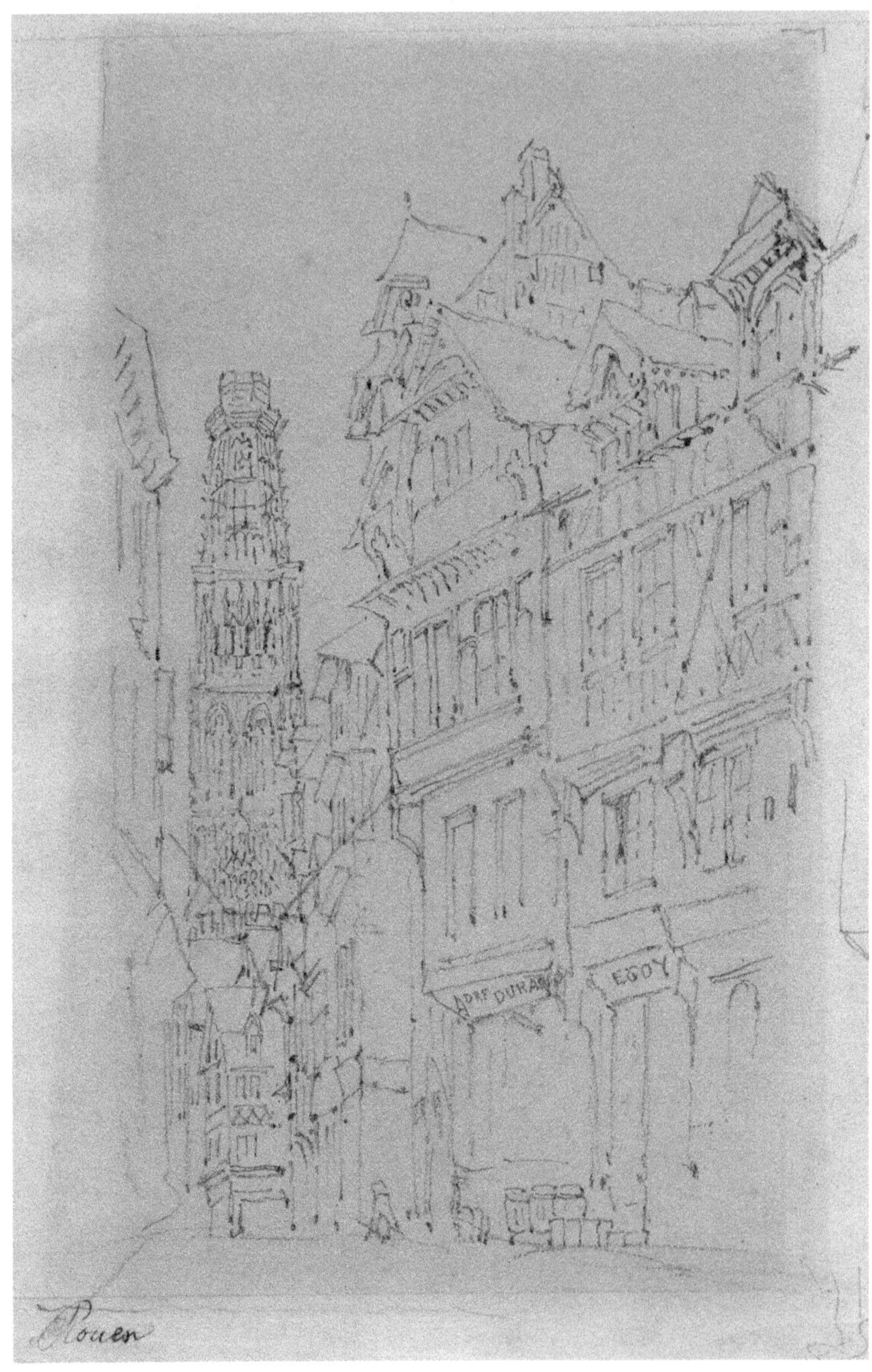

Cat. 8

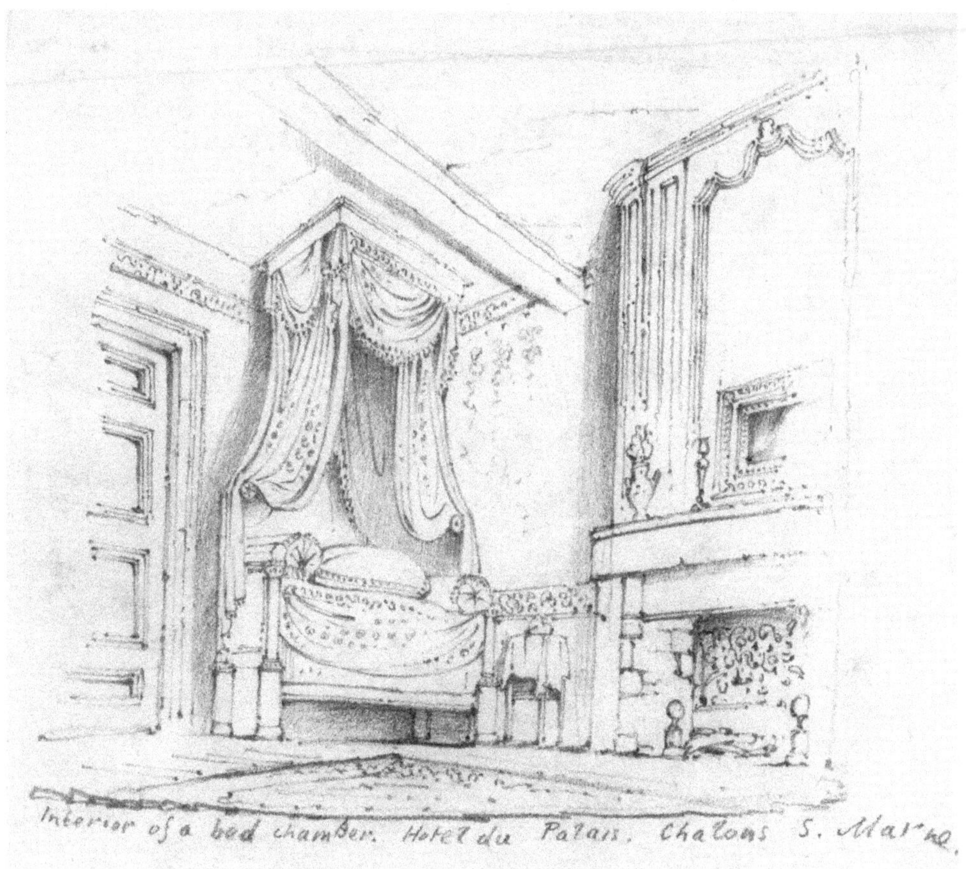

Cat. 13

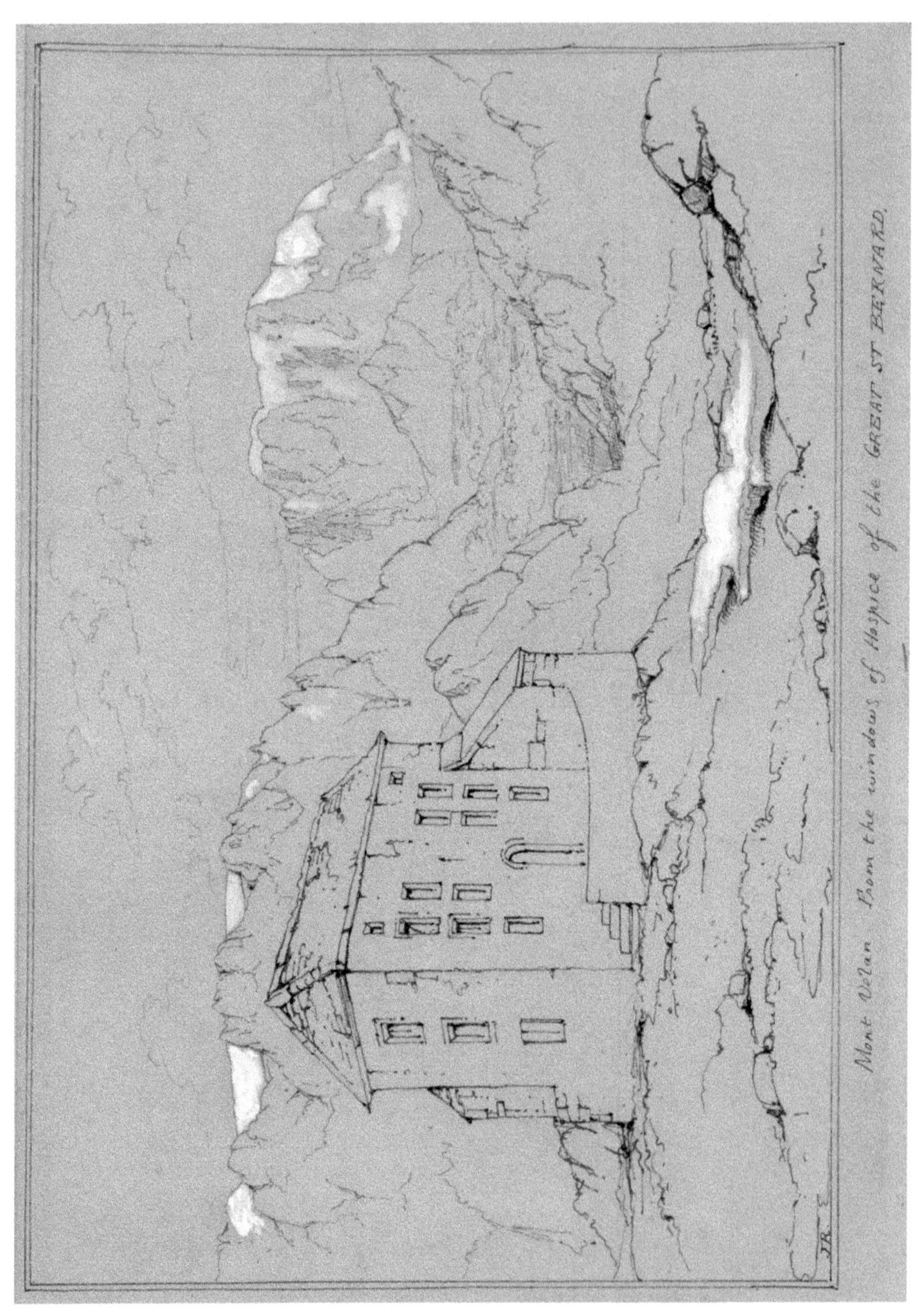
Mont Velan From the windows of Hospice of the GREAT ST BERNARD.
JR.

Cat. 21

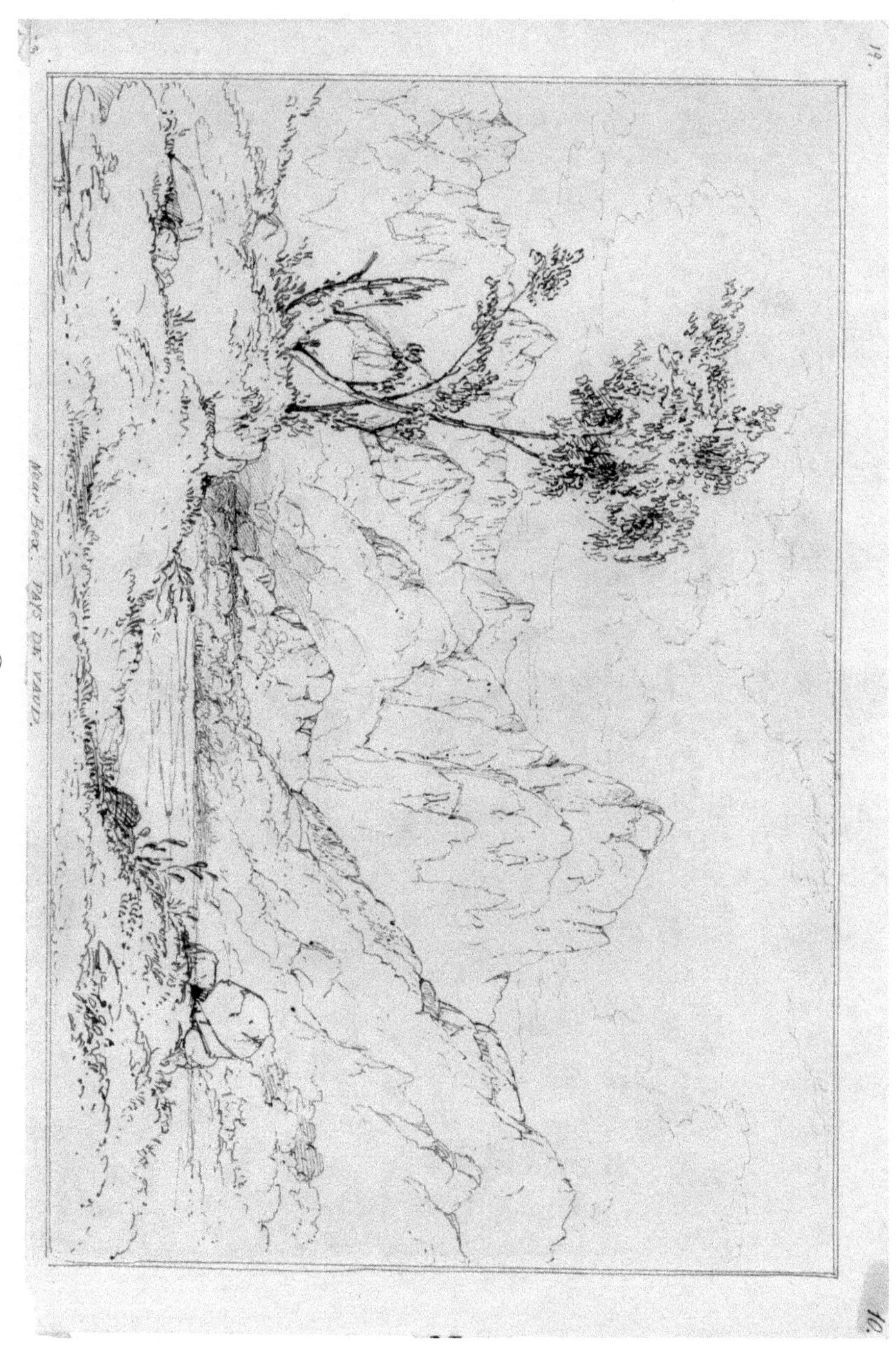

Cat. 25

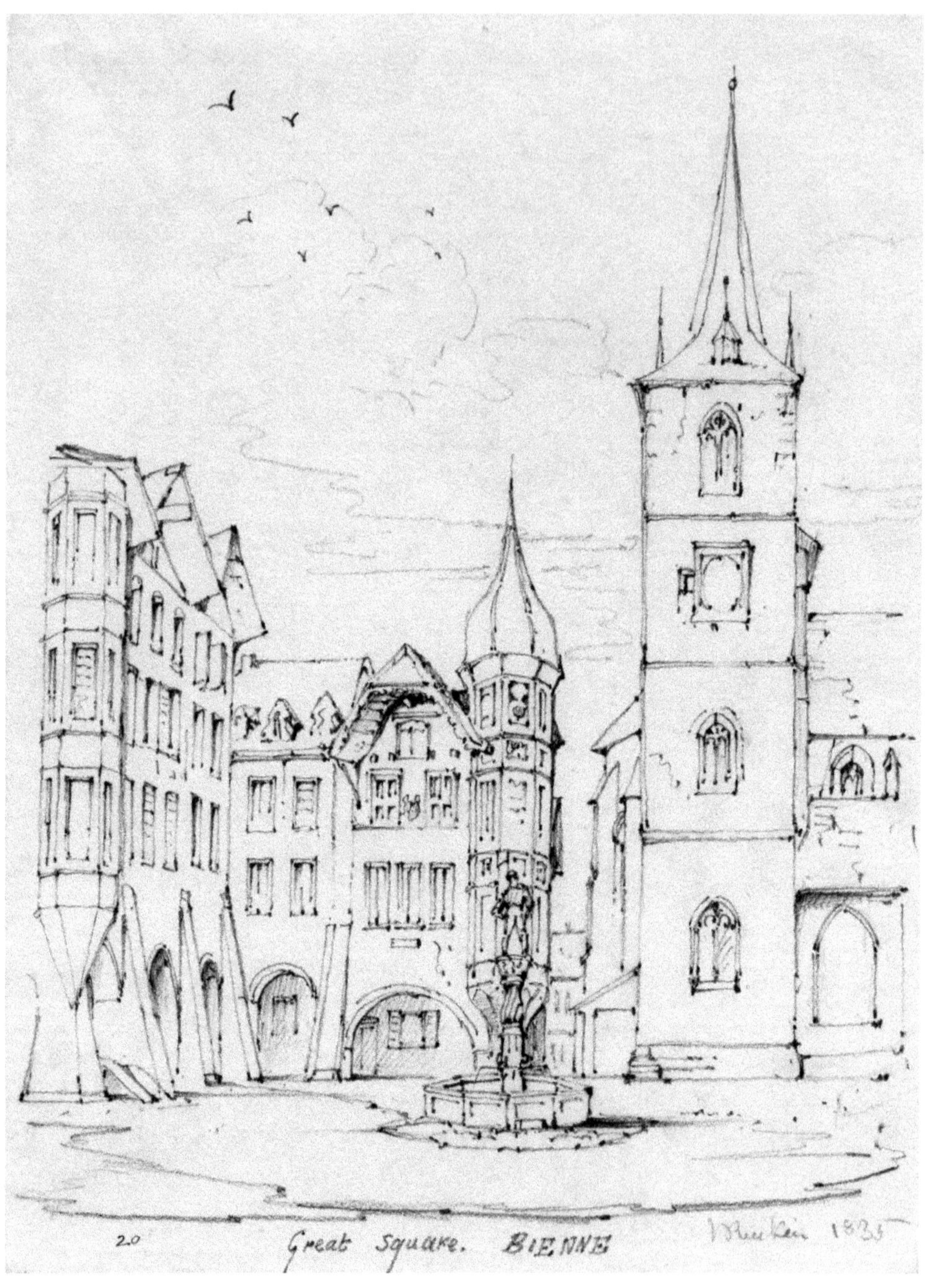

Cat. 31

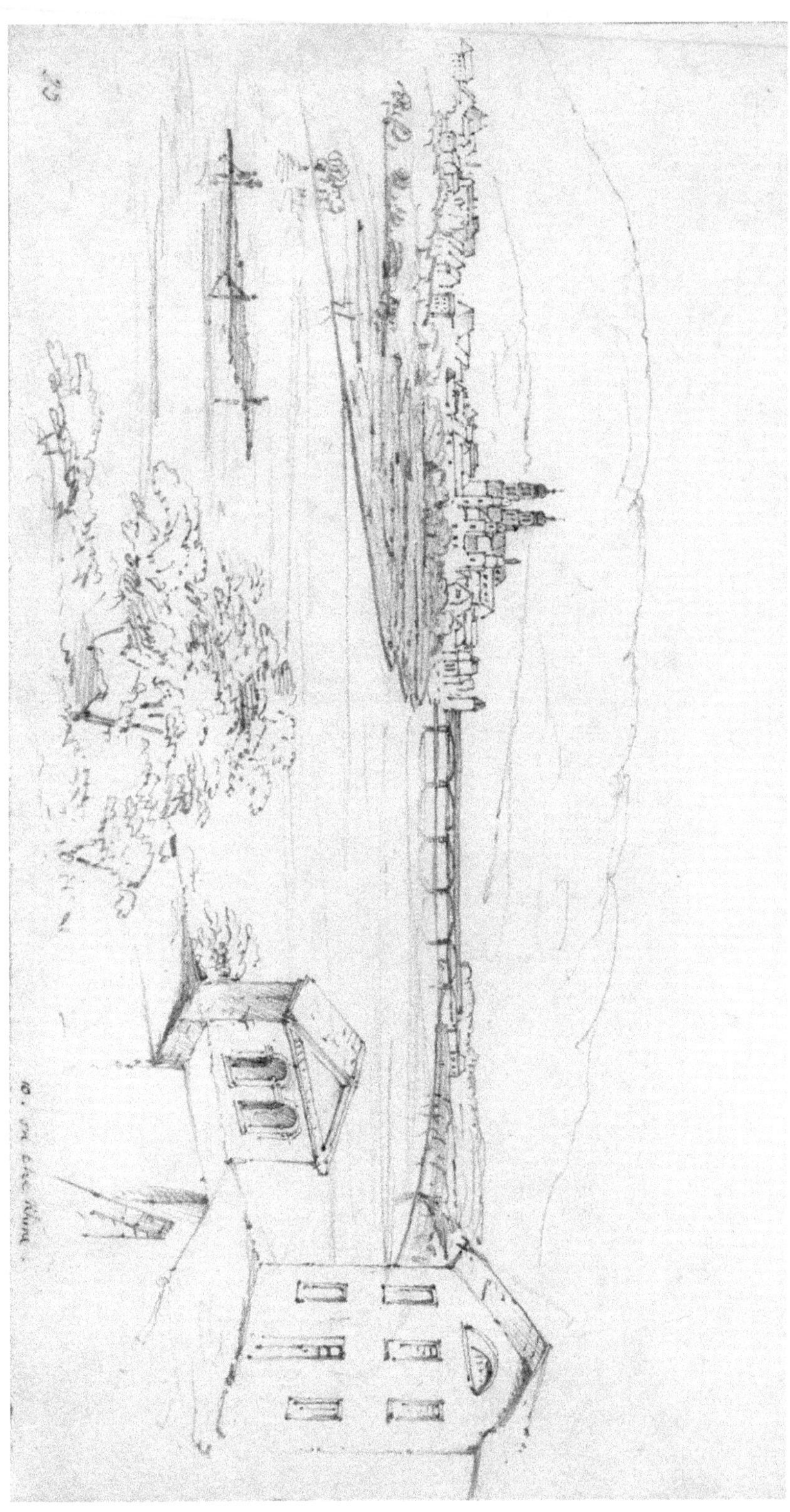

Cat. 32

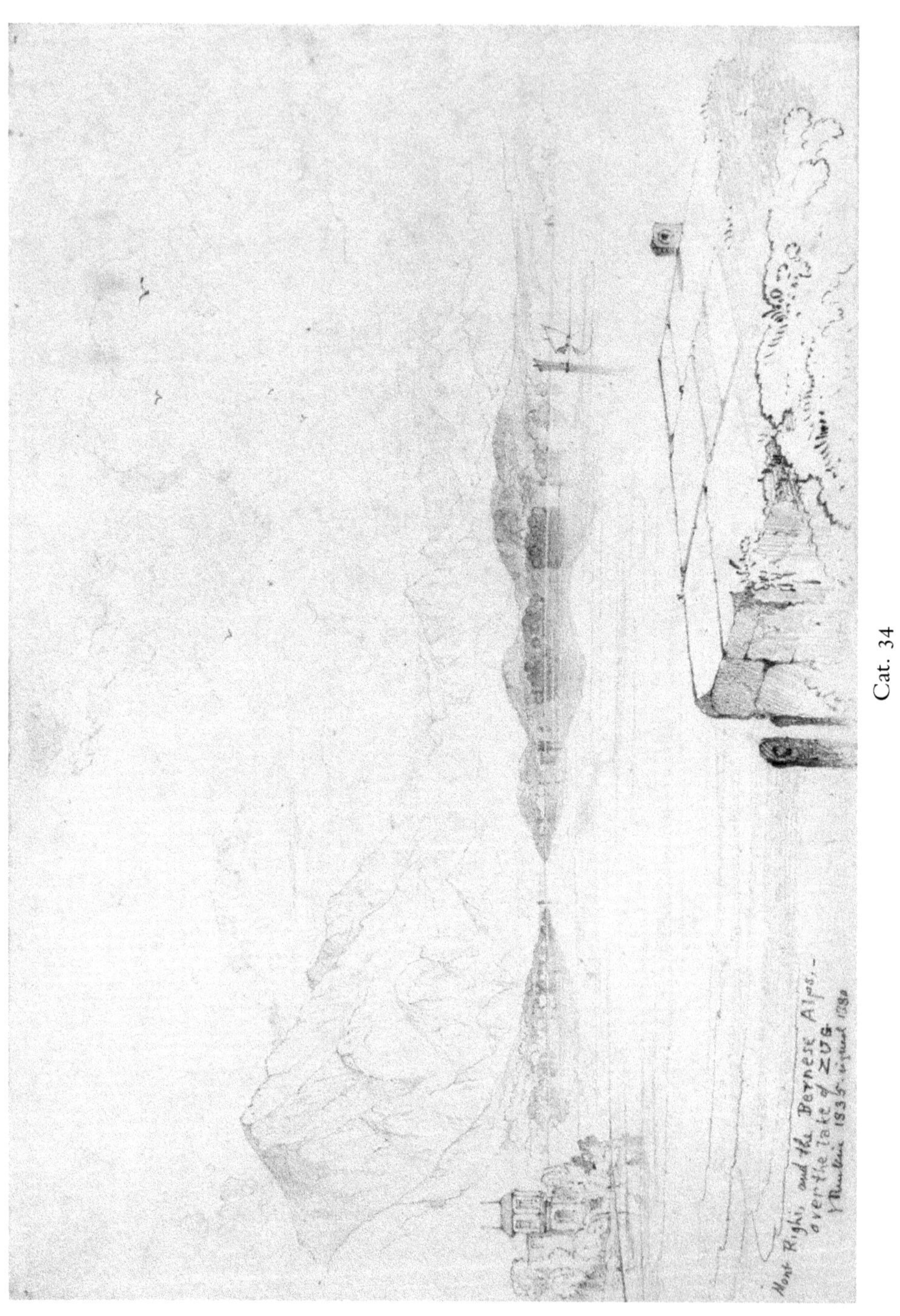

Cat. 34

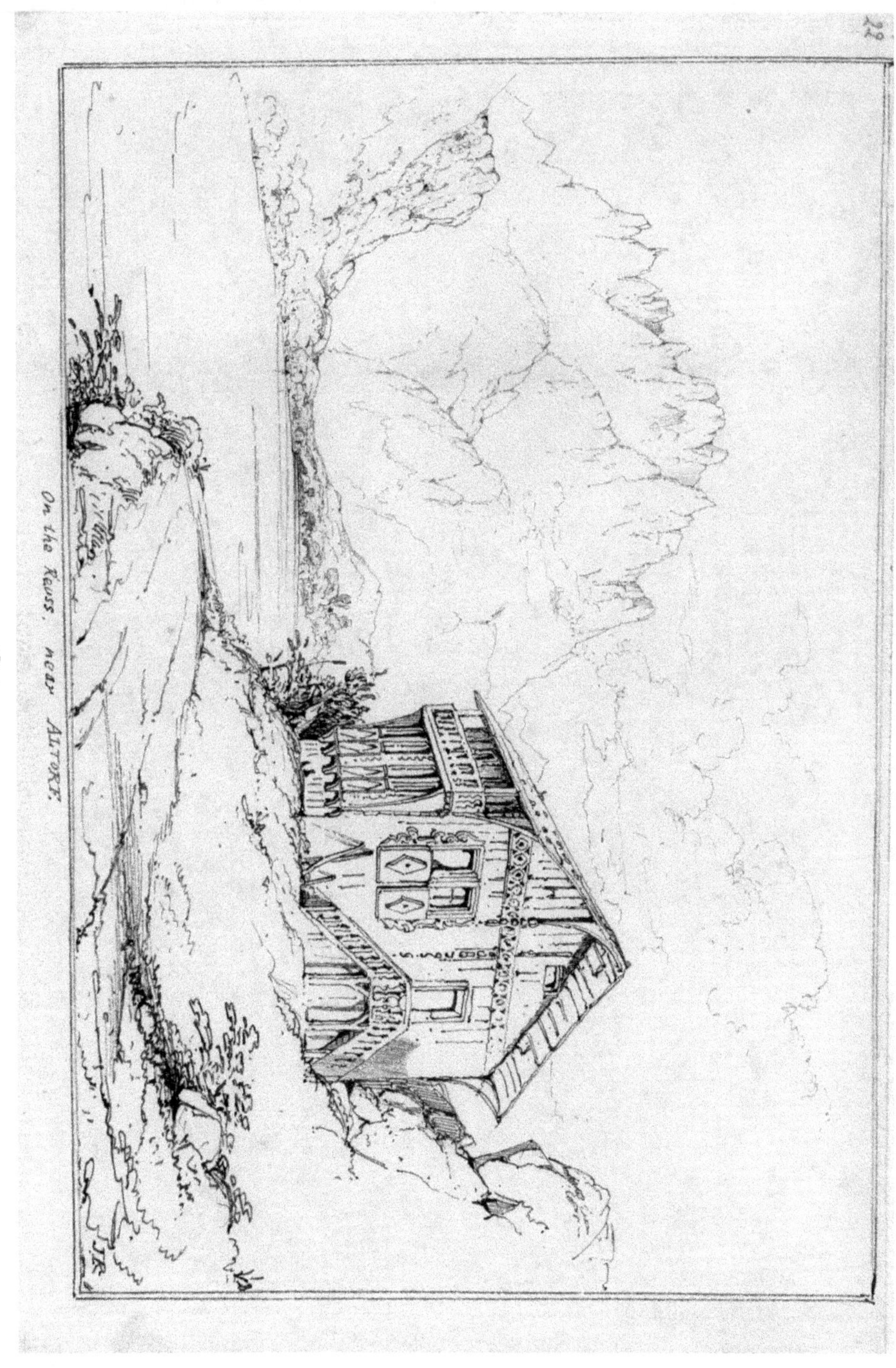

Cat. 37

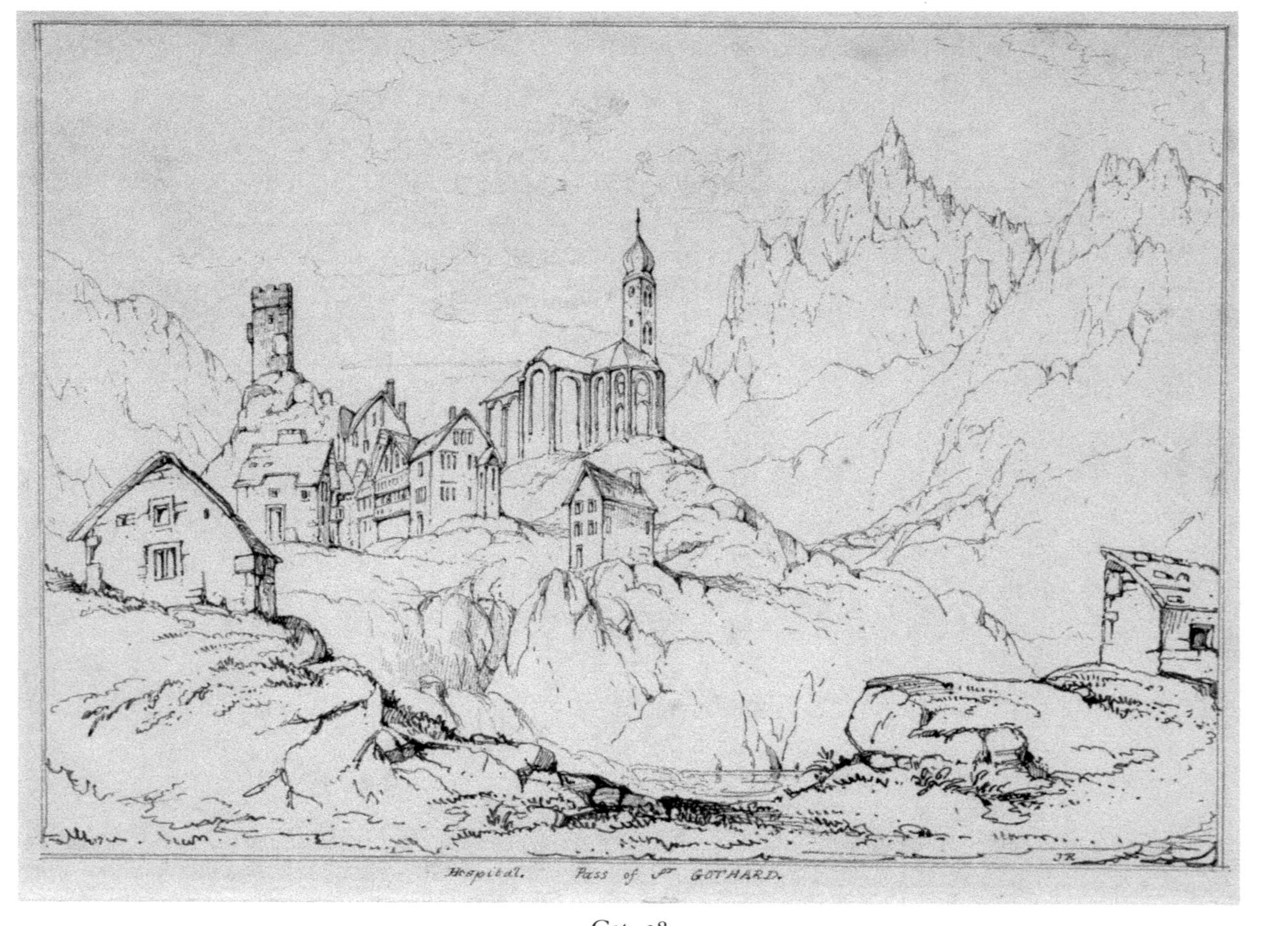

Cat. 38

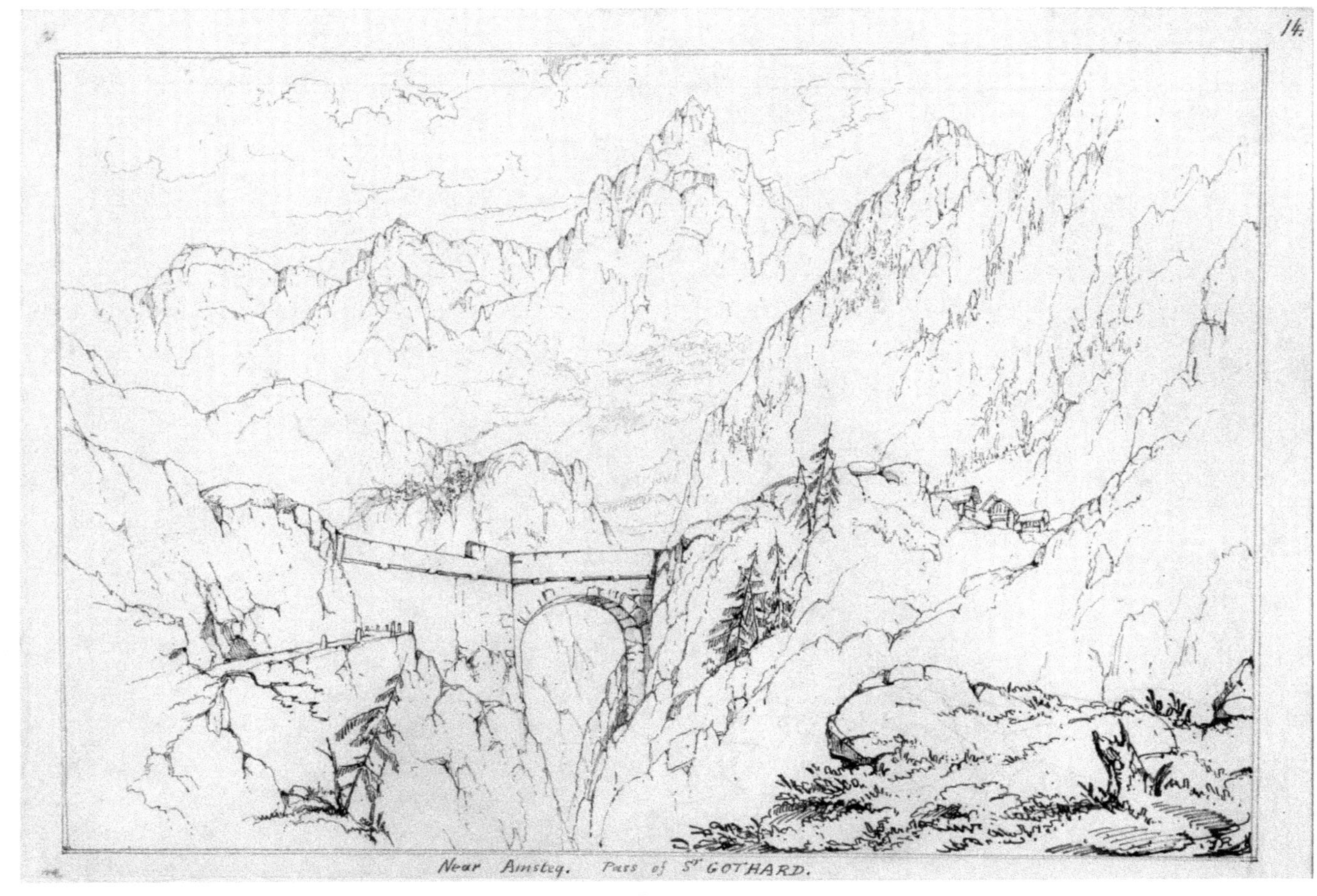

Cat. 40

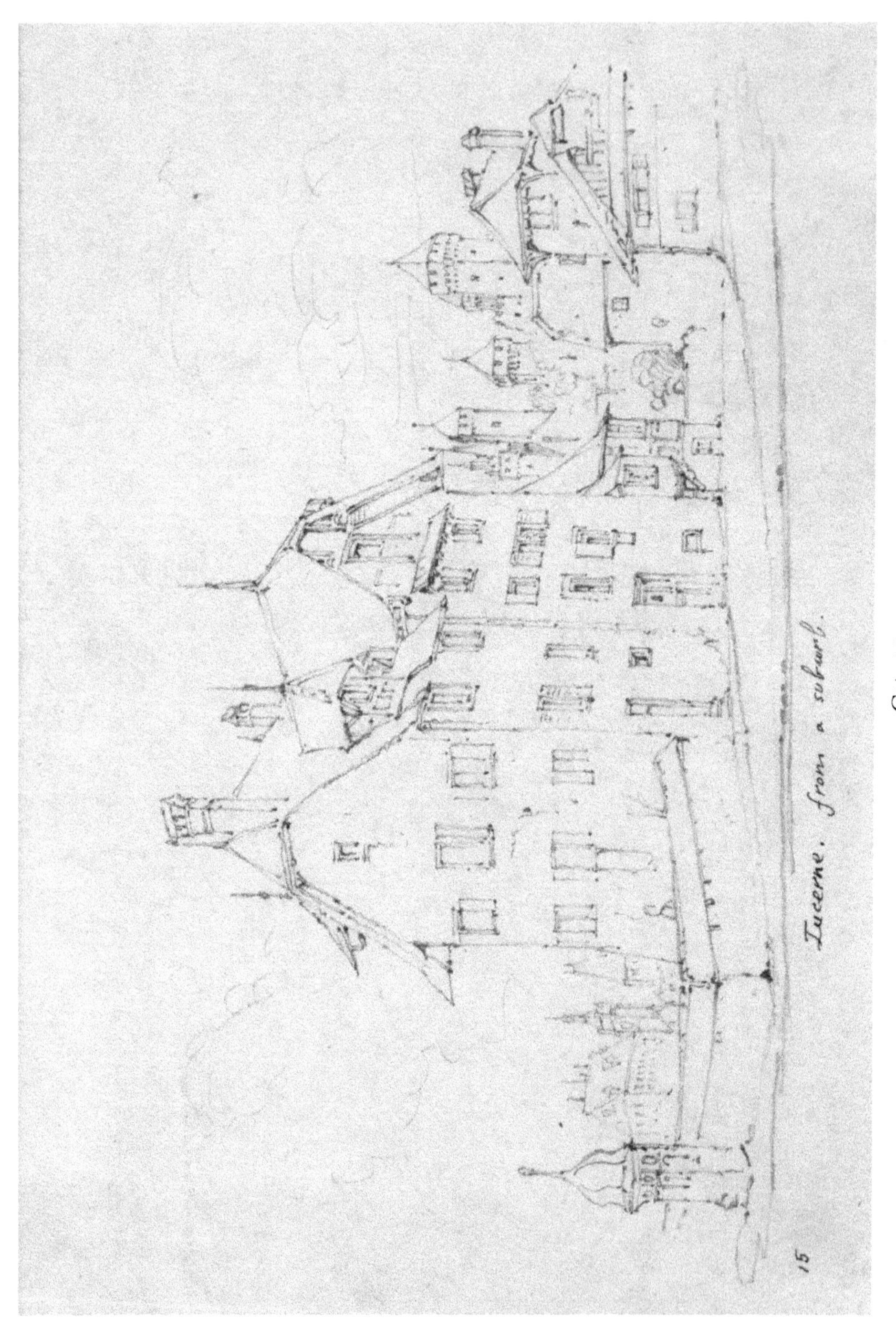

Cat. 42

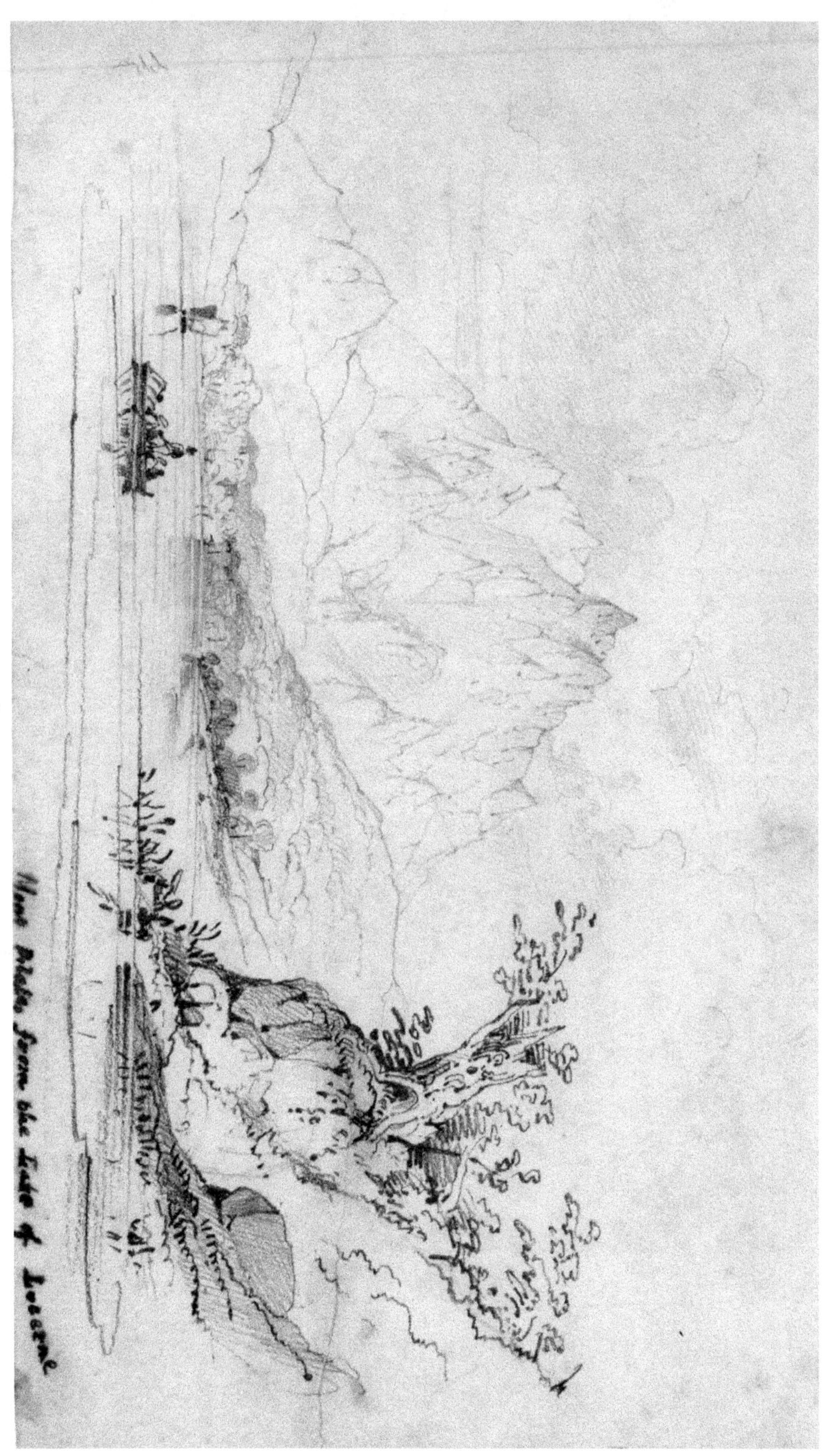

Cat. 43

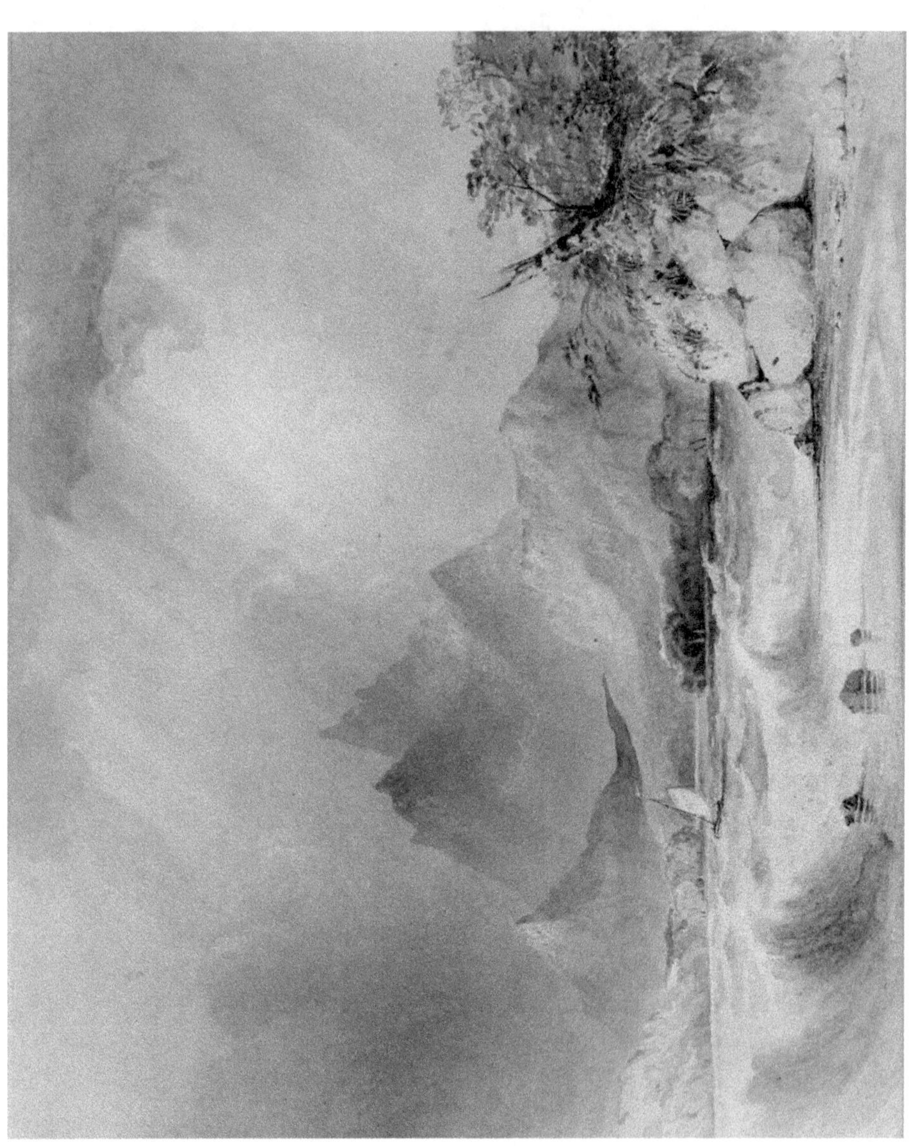

Cat. 44

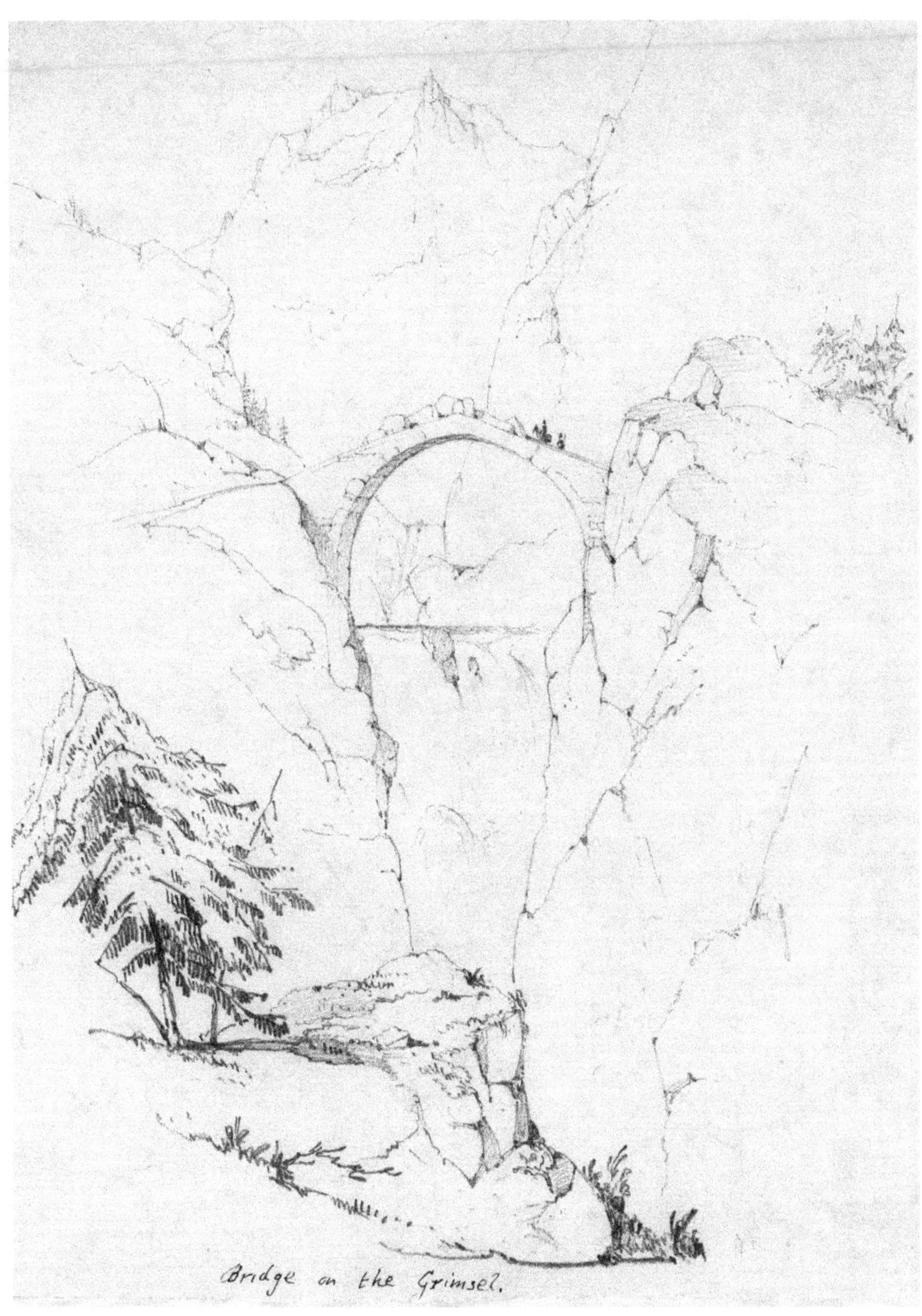

Cat. 48

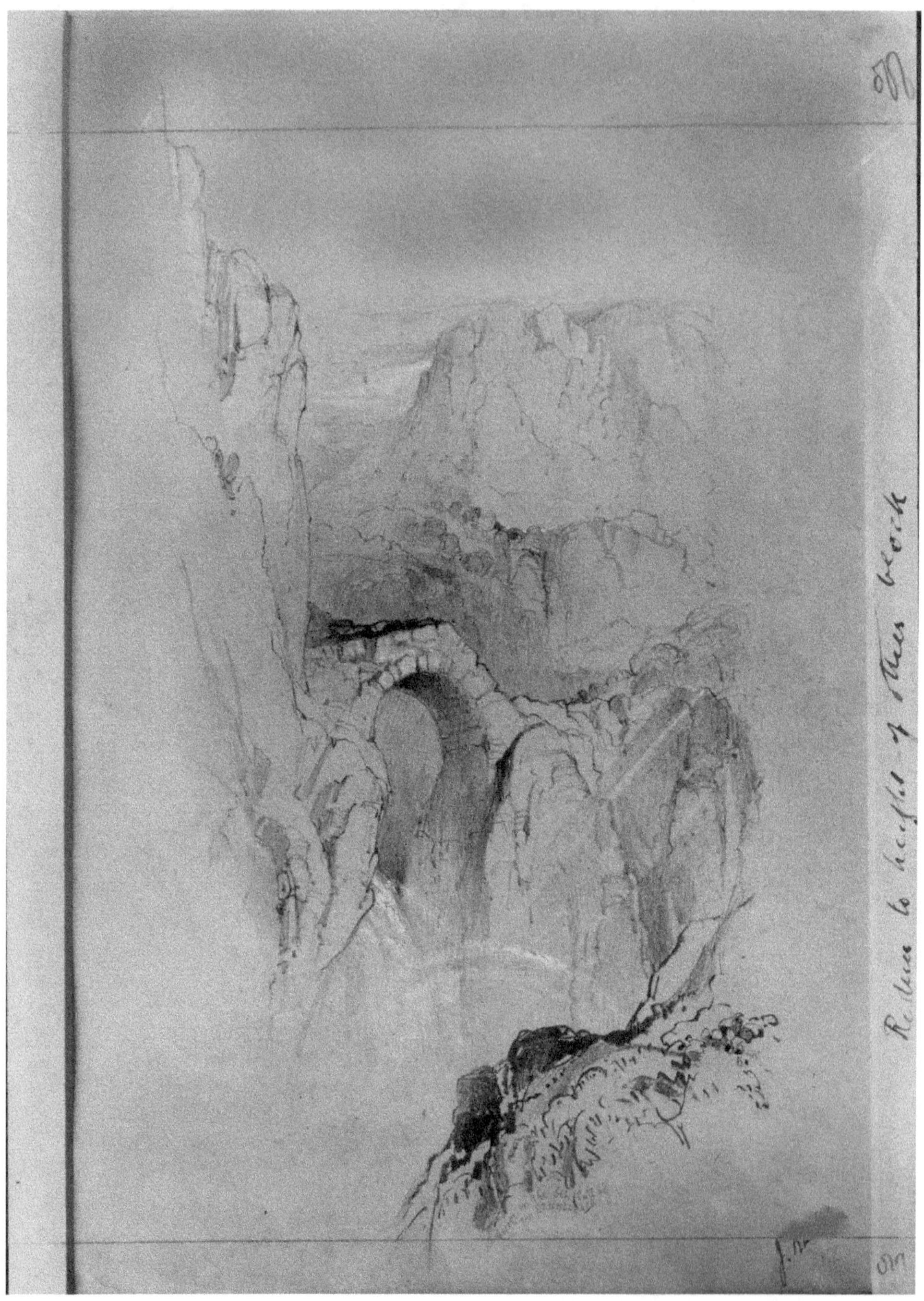

Cat. 53

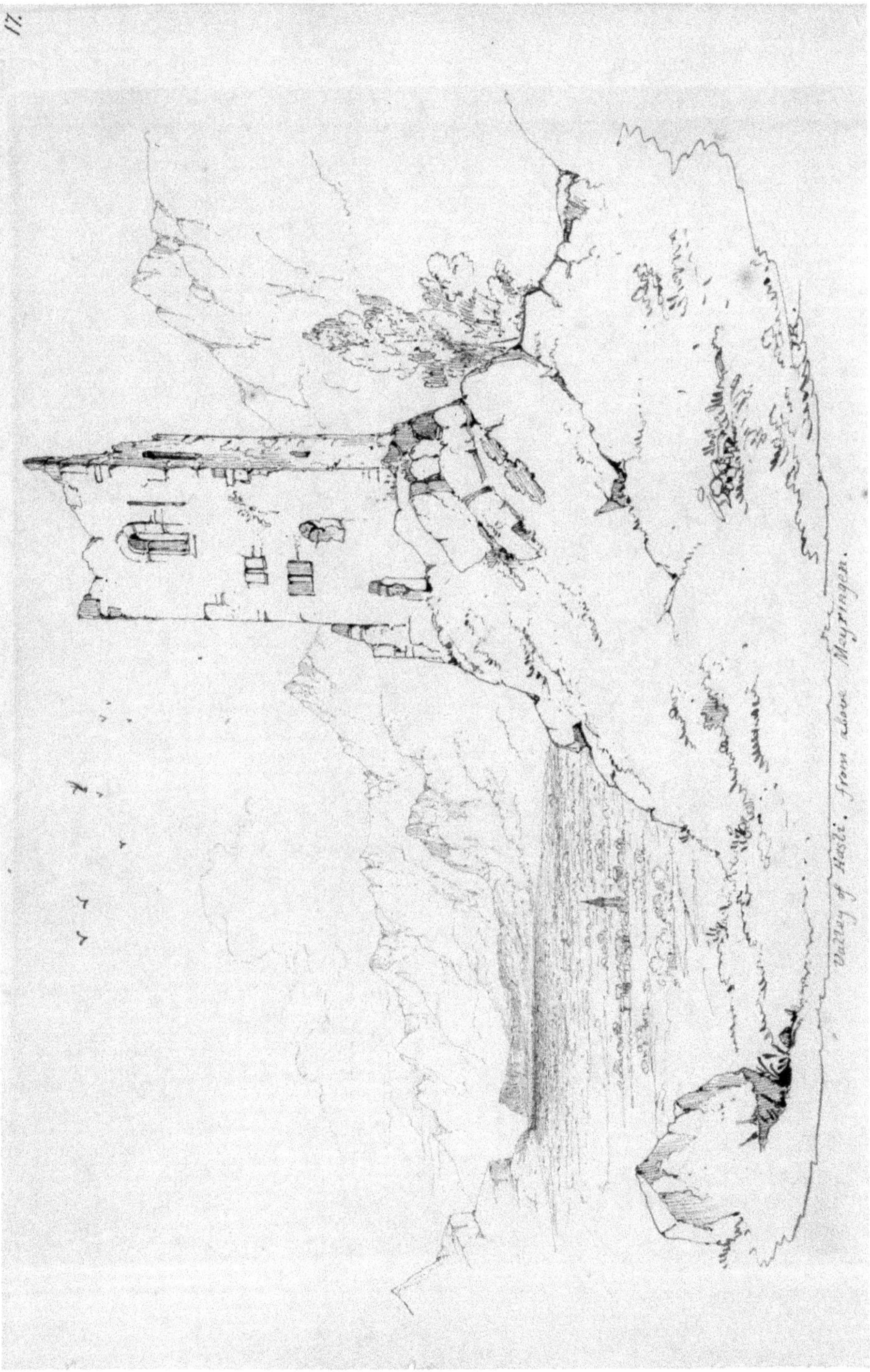

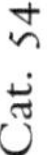

Cat. 54

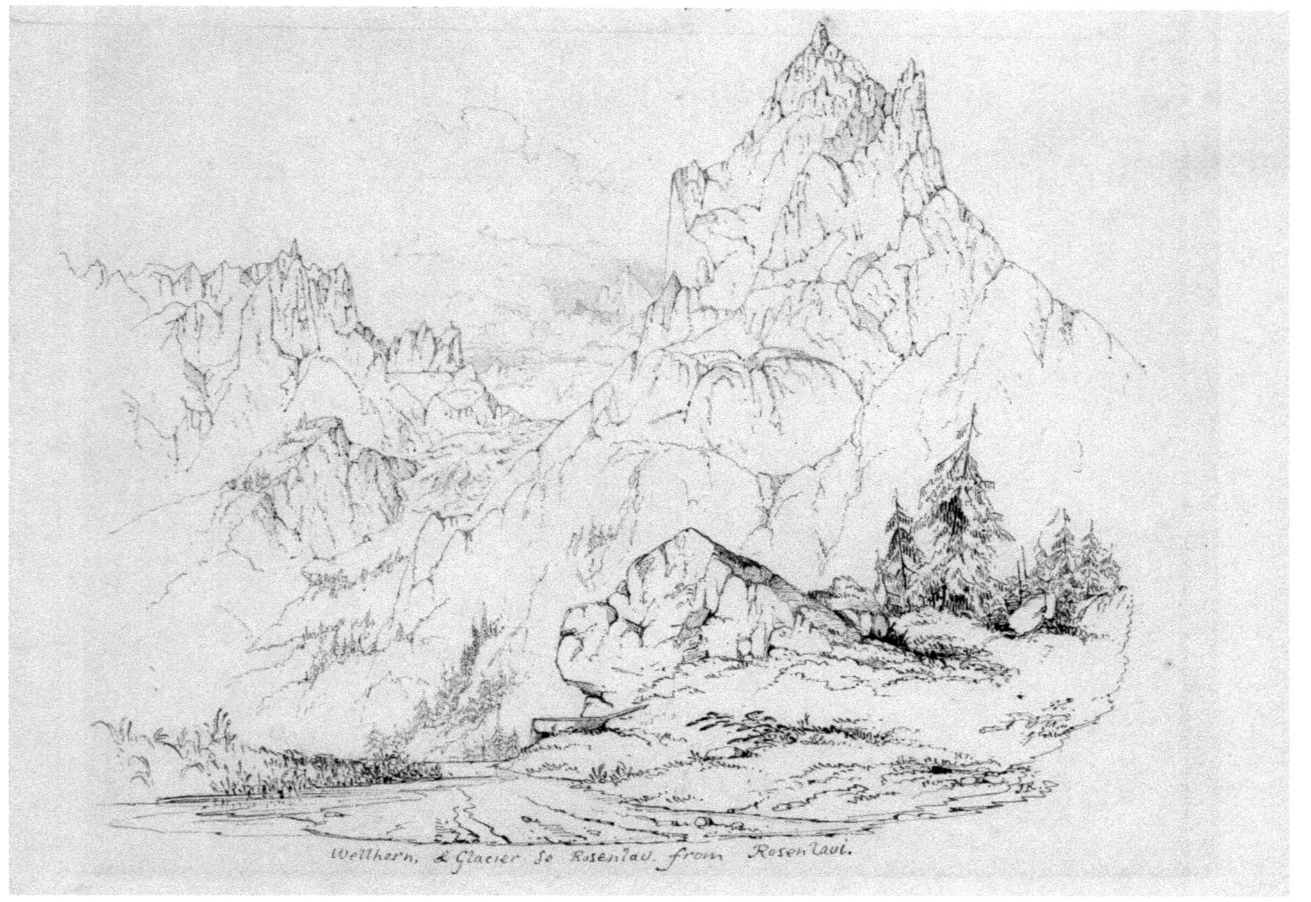

Cat. 55

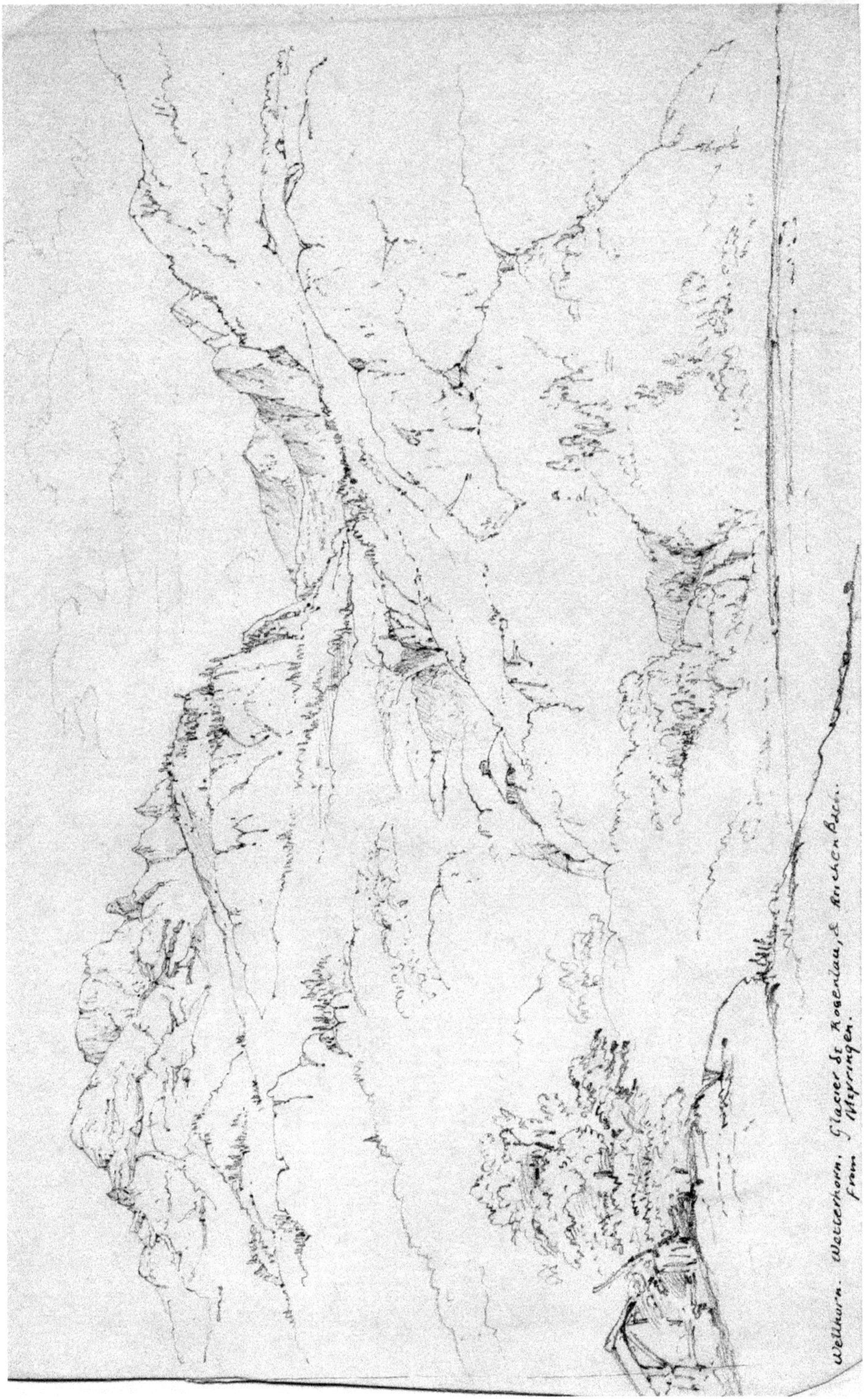

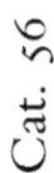

Cat. 56

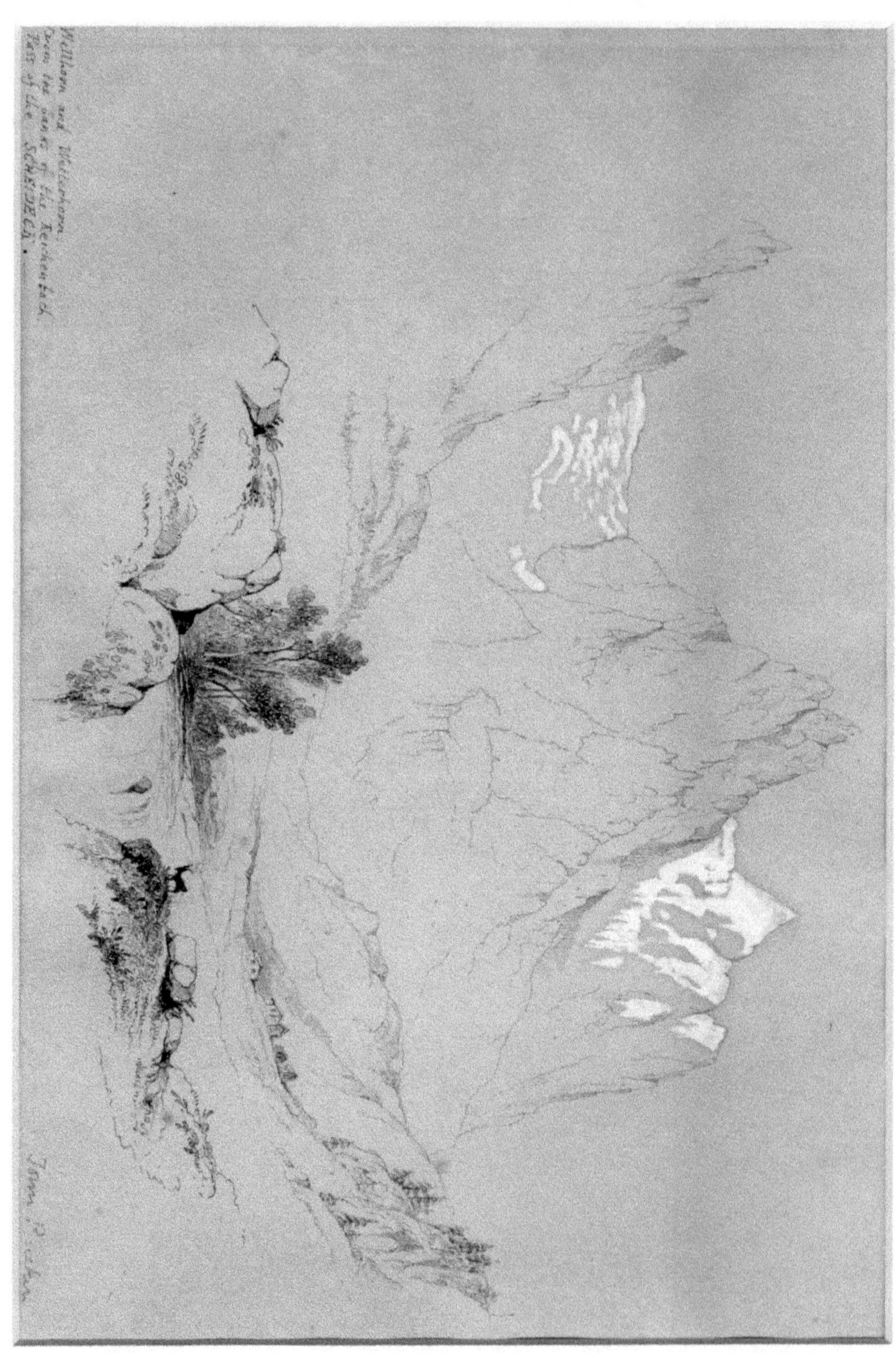

Cat. 59

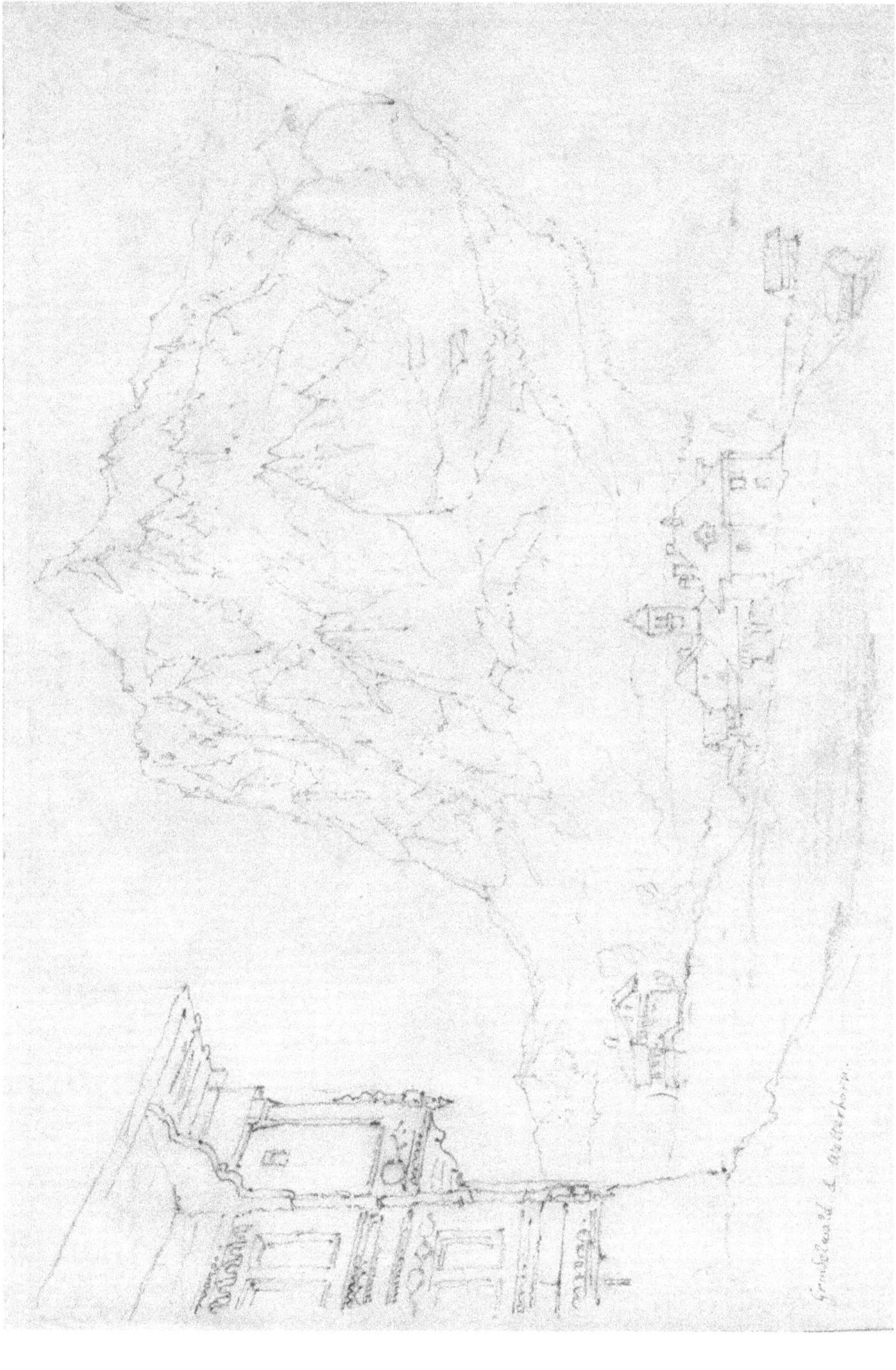

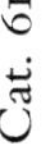

Cat. 61

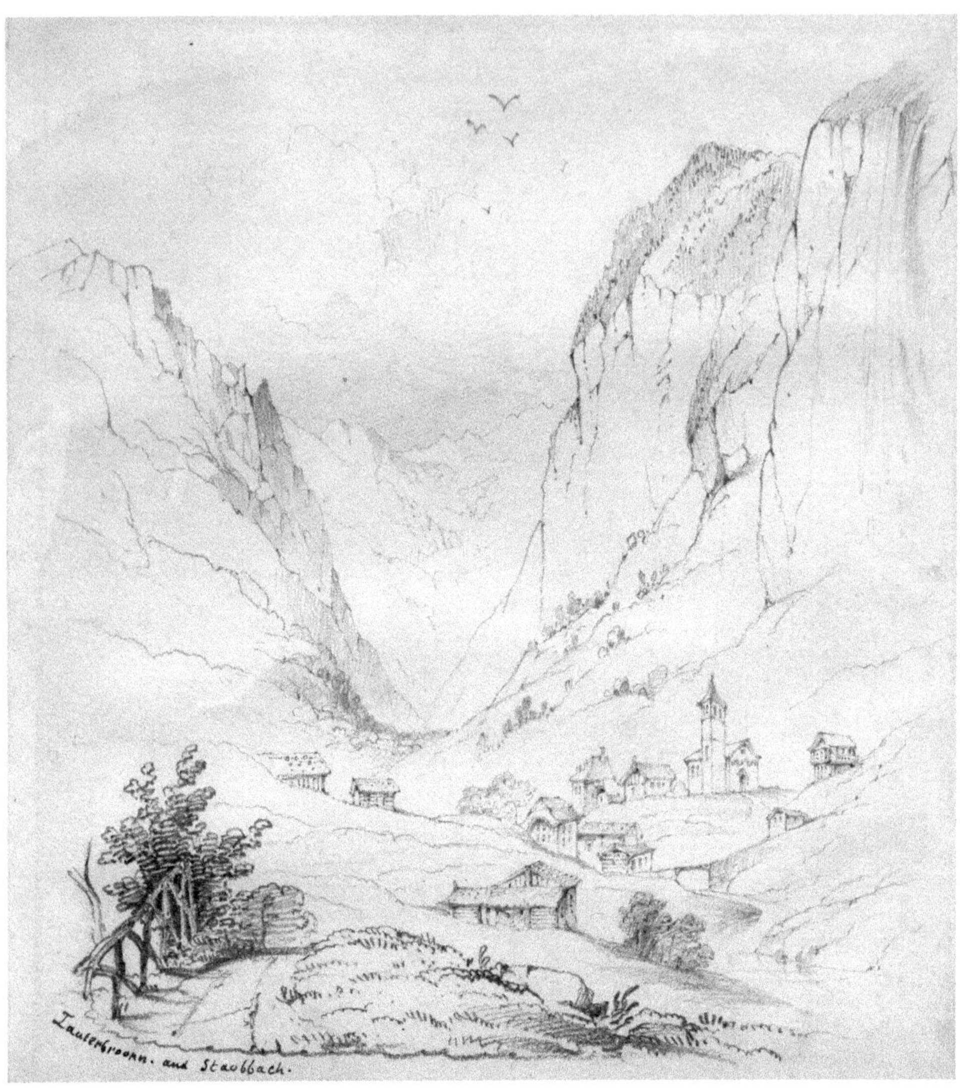

Cat. 64

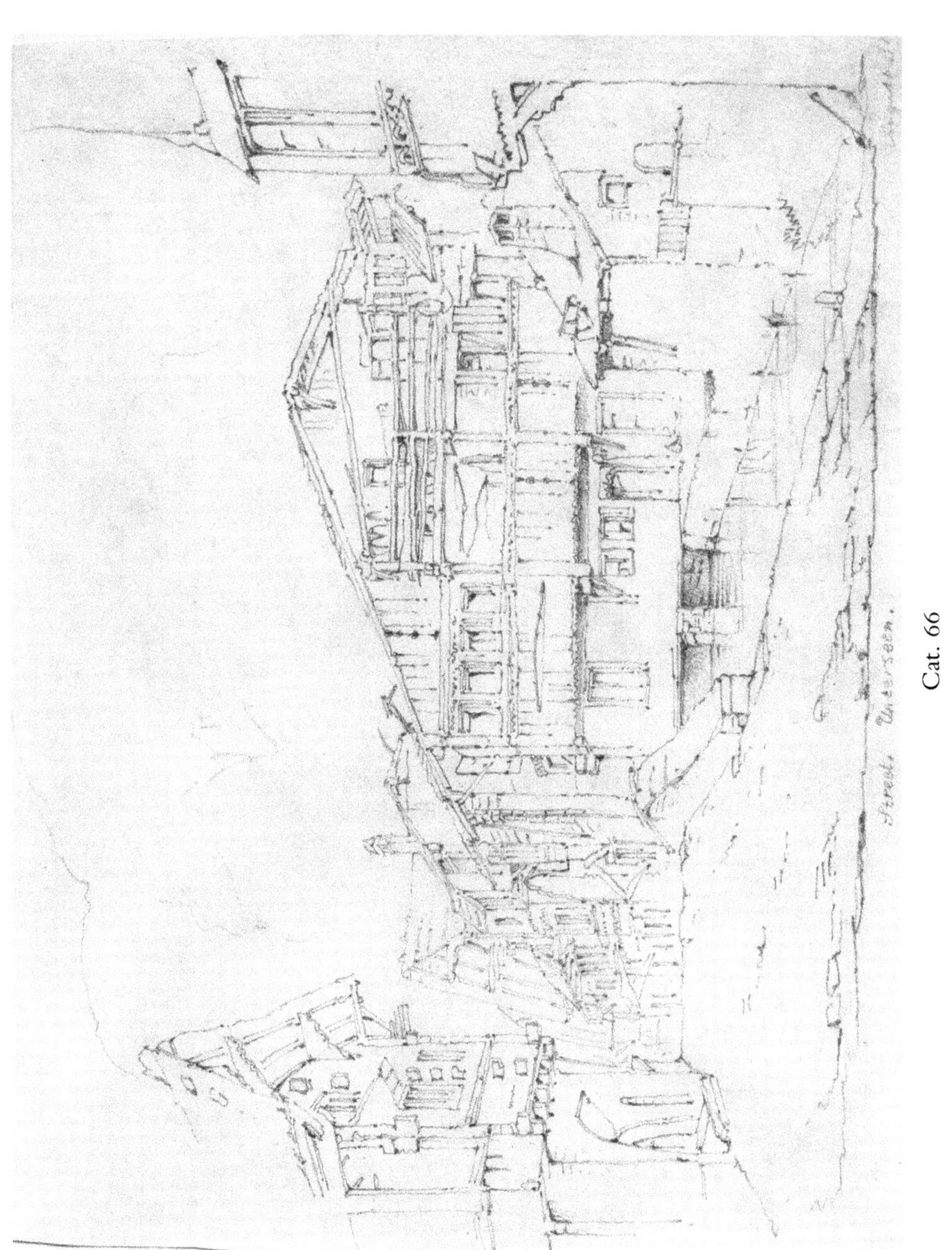

Cat. 66

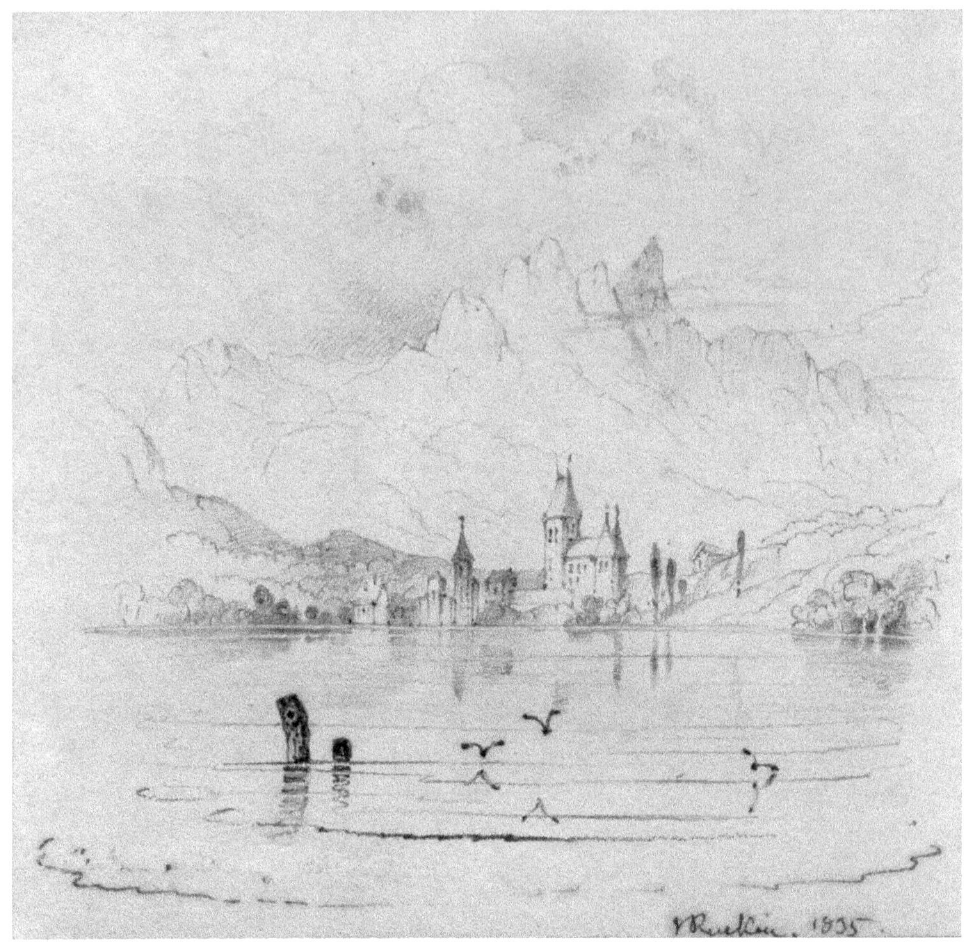

Cat. 68

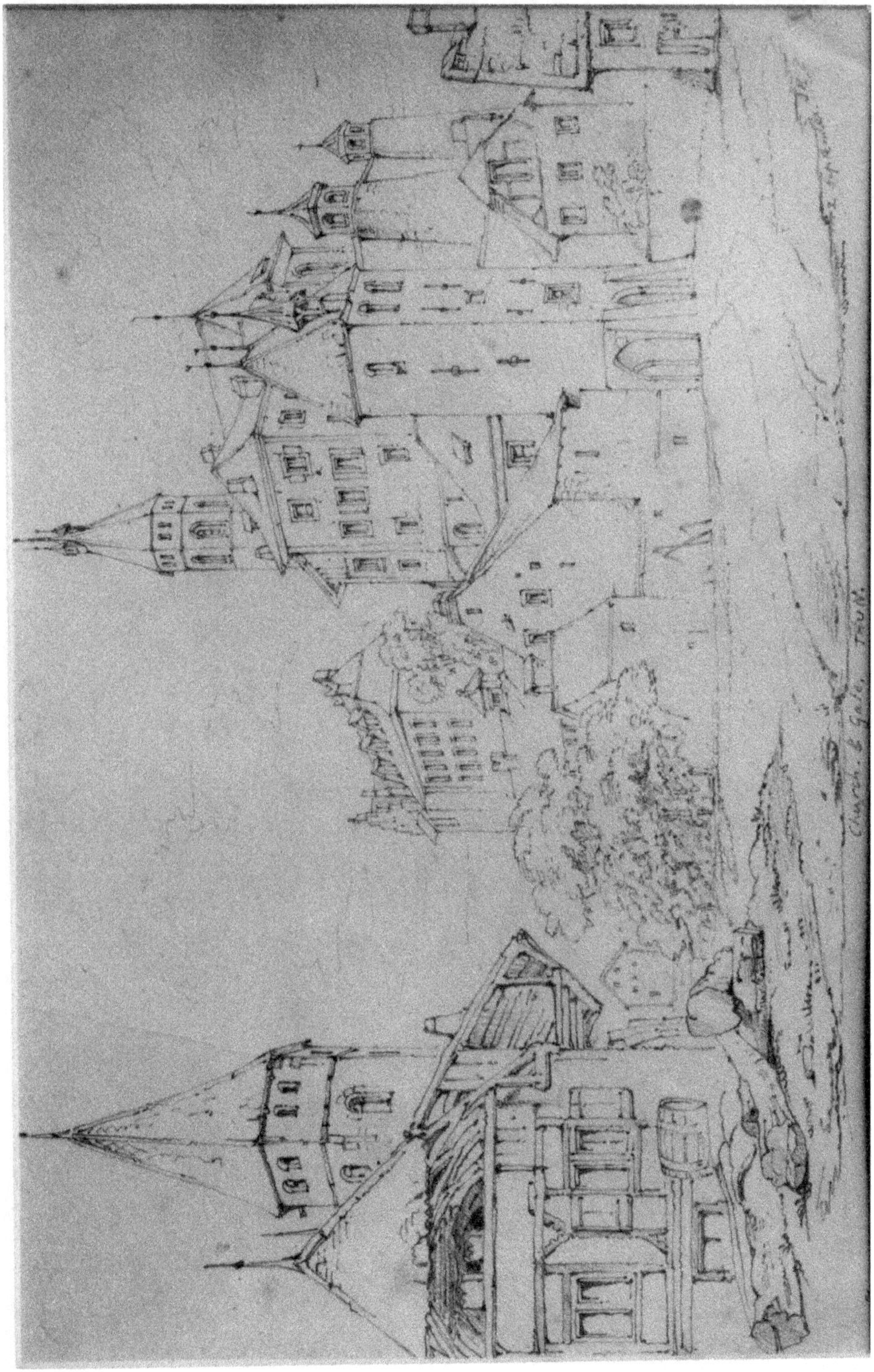

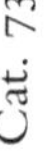

Cat. 73

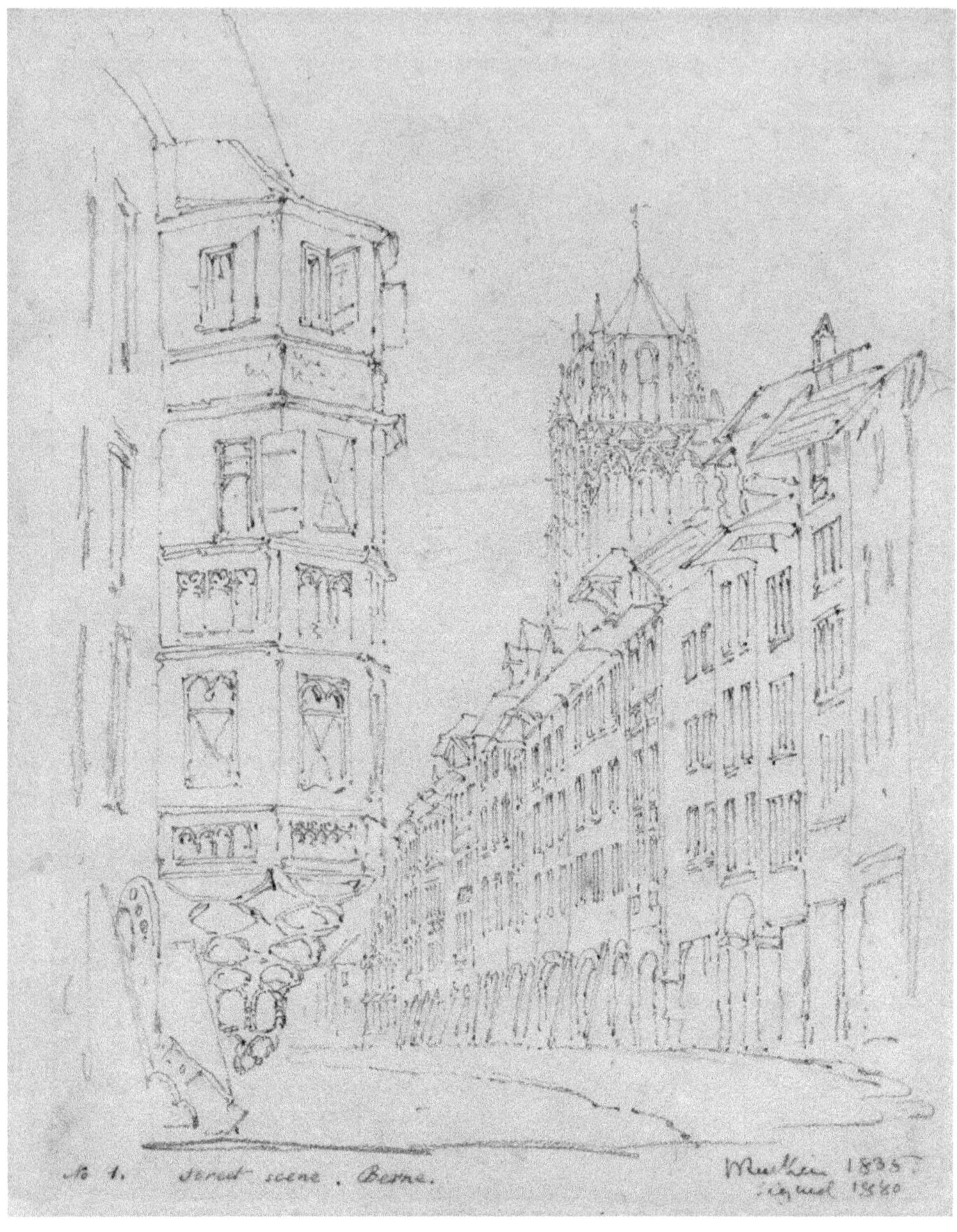

Cat. 74

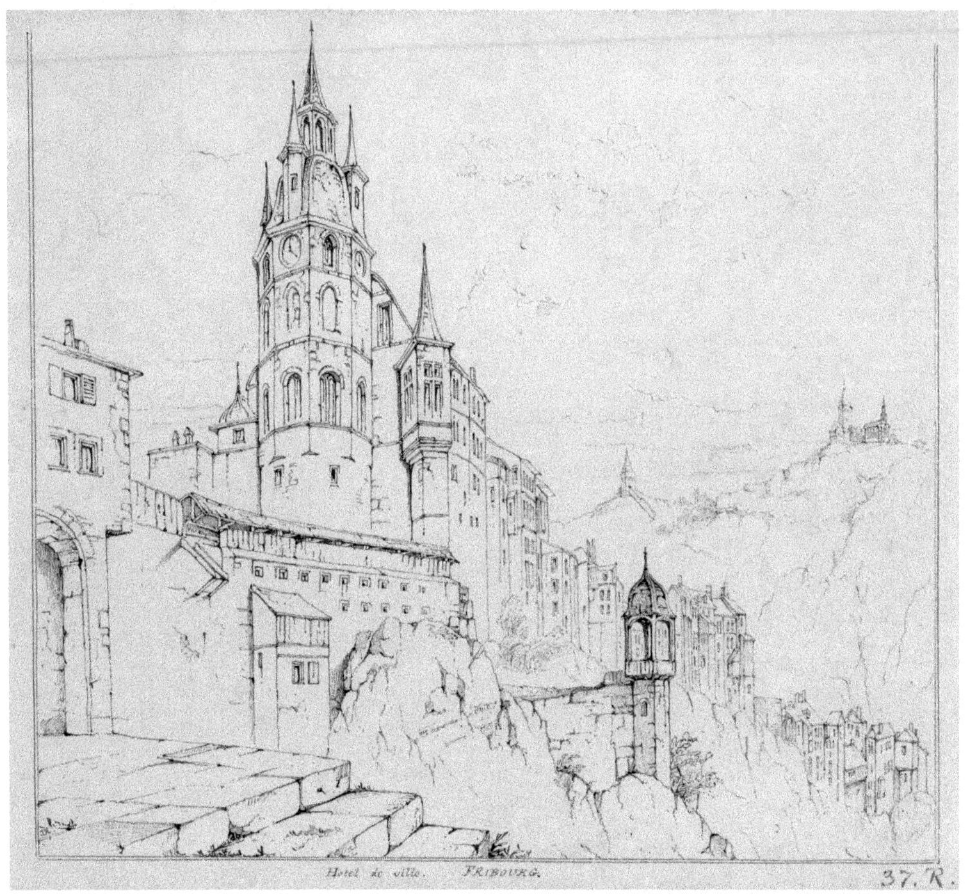

Cat. 76

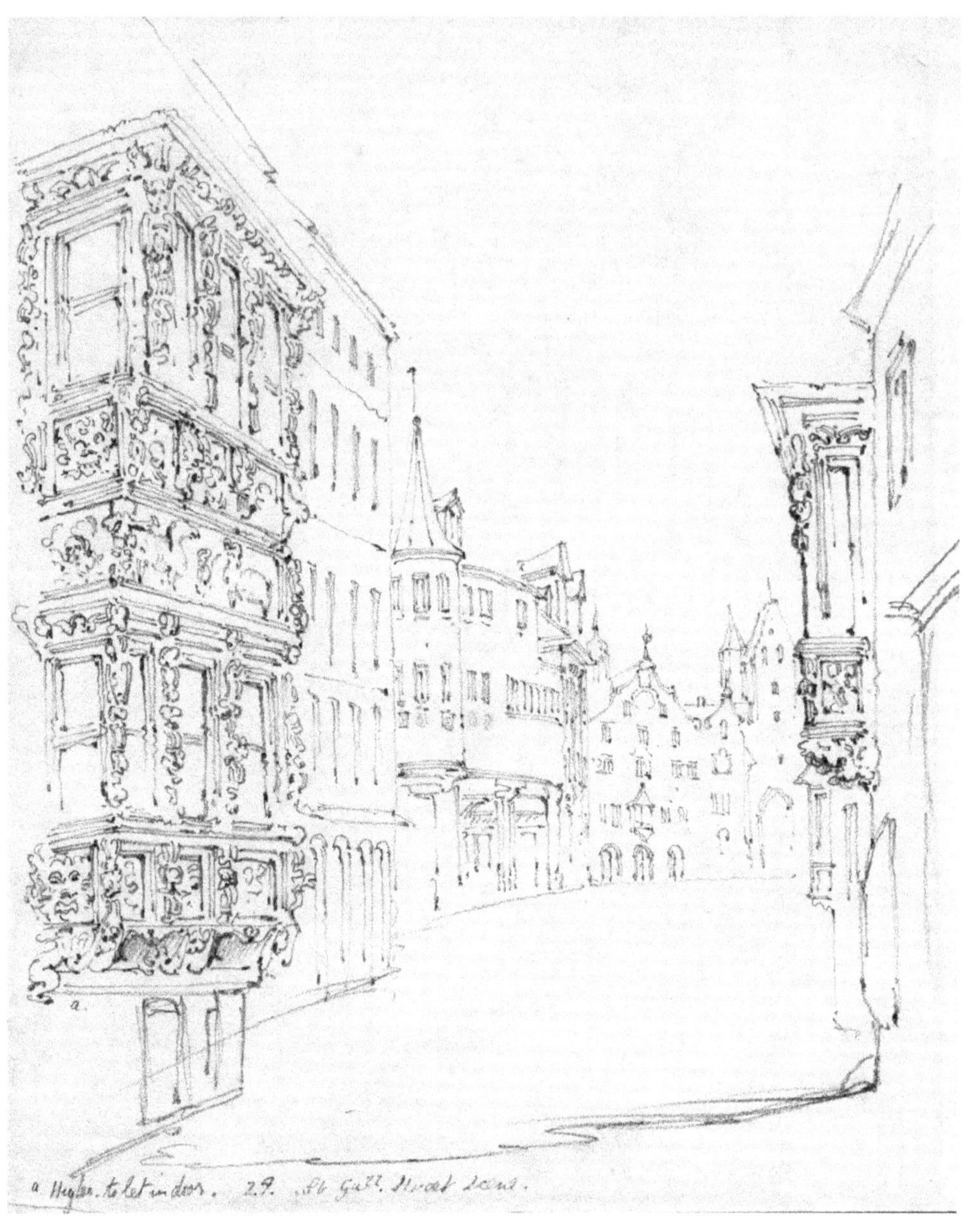

Cat. 84

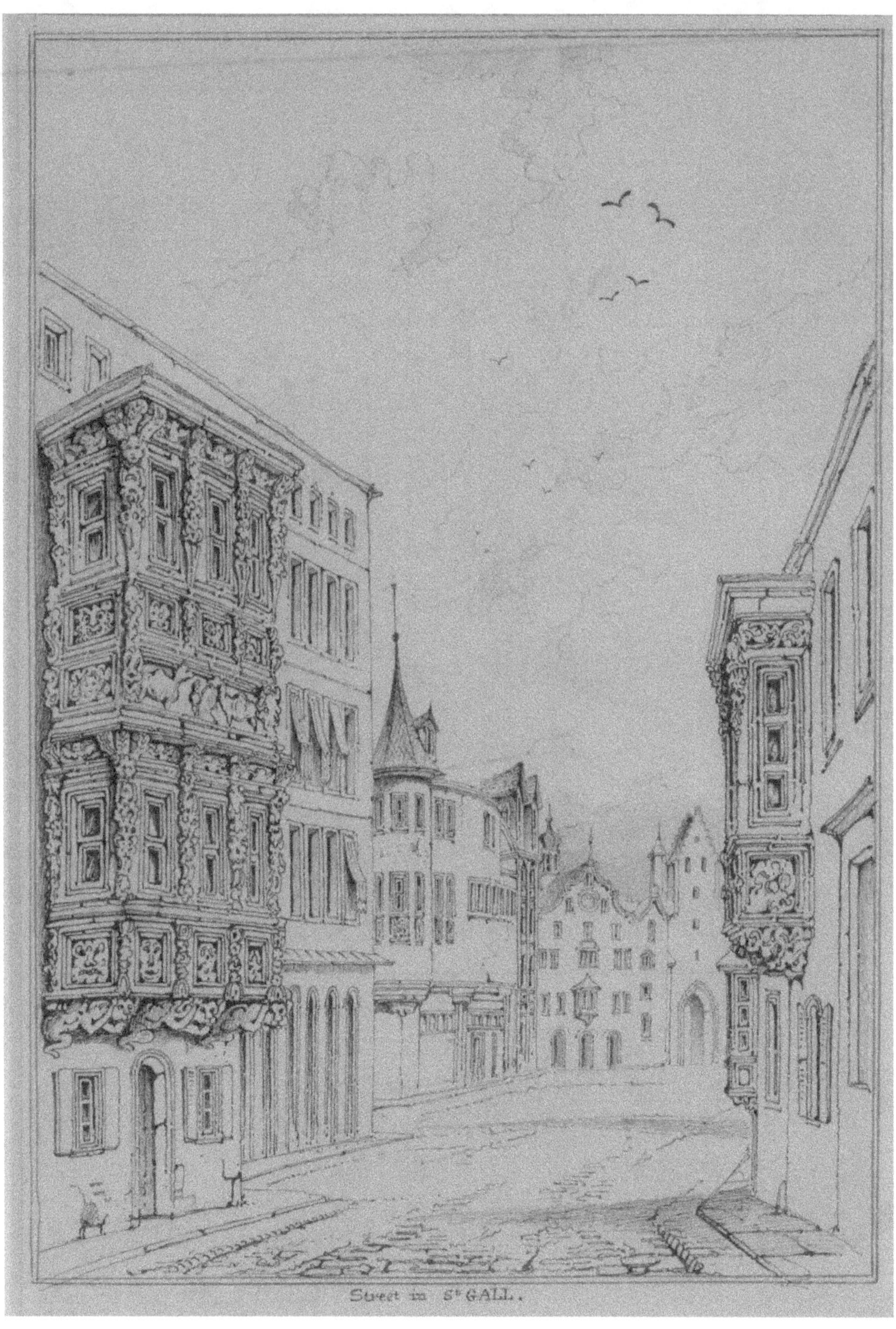

Cat. 85

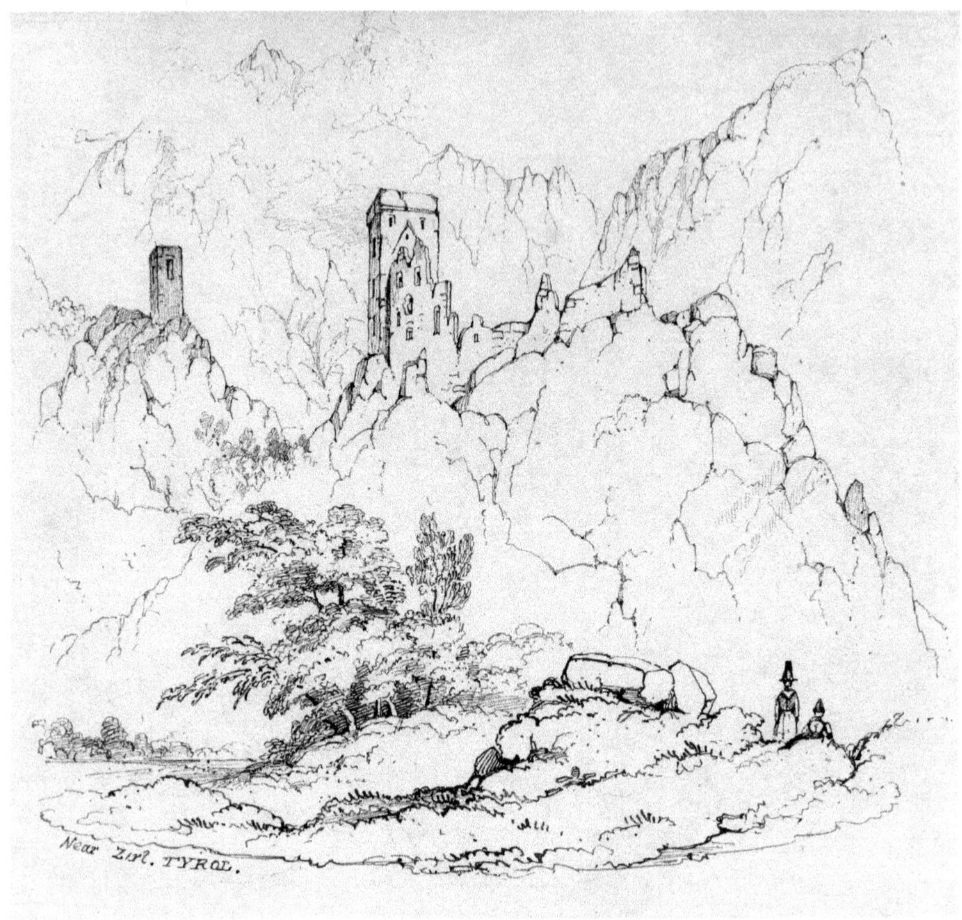

Cat. 90

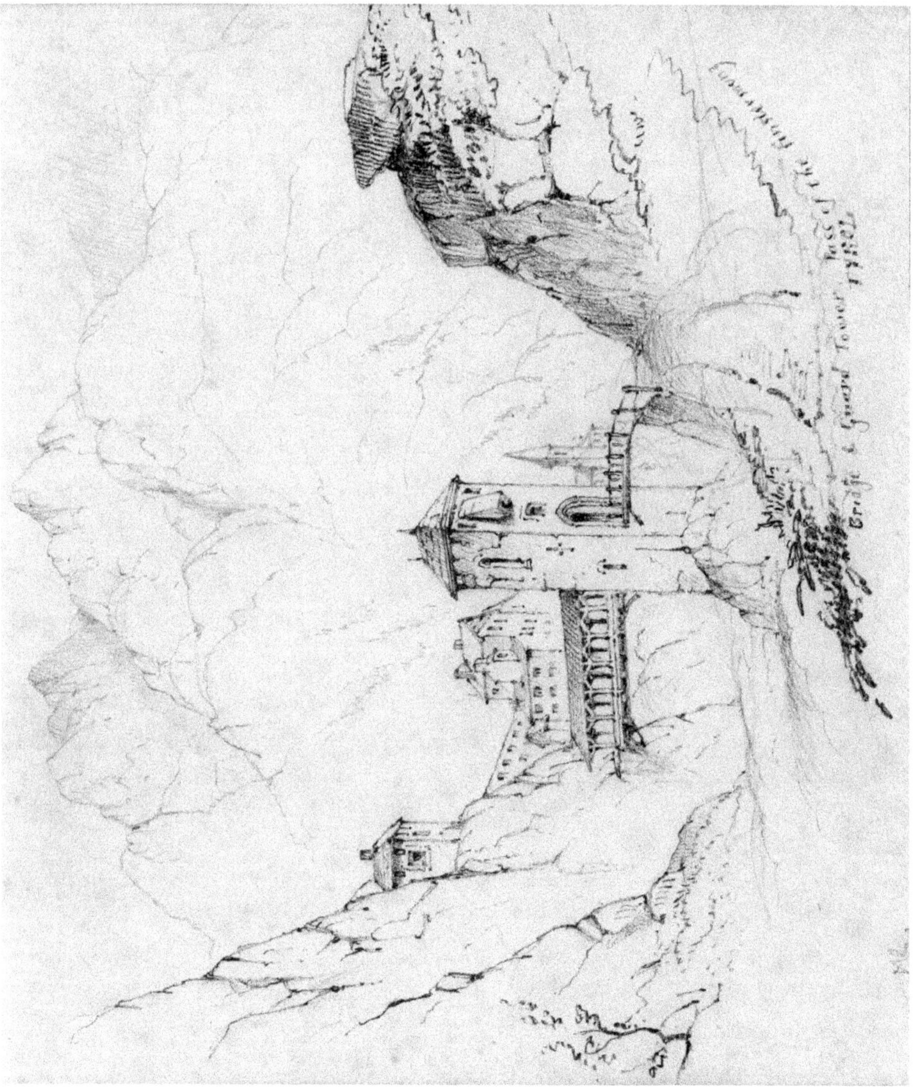

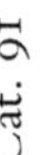

Cat. 91

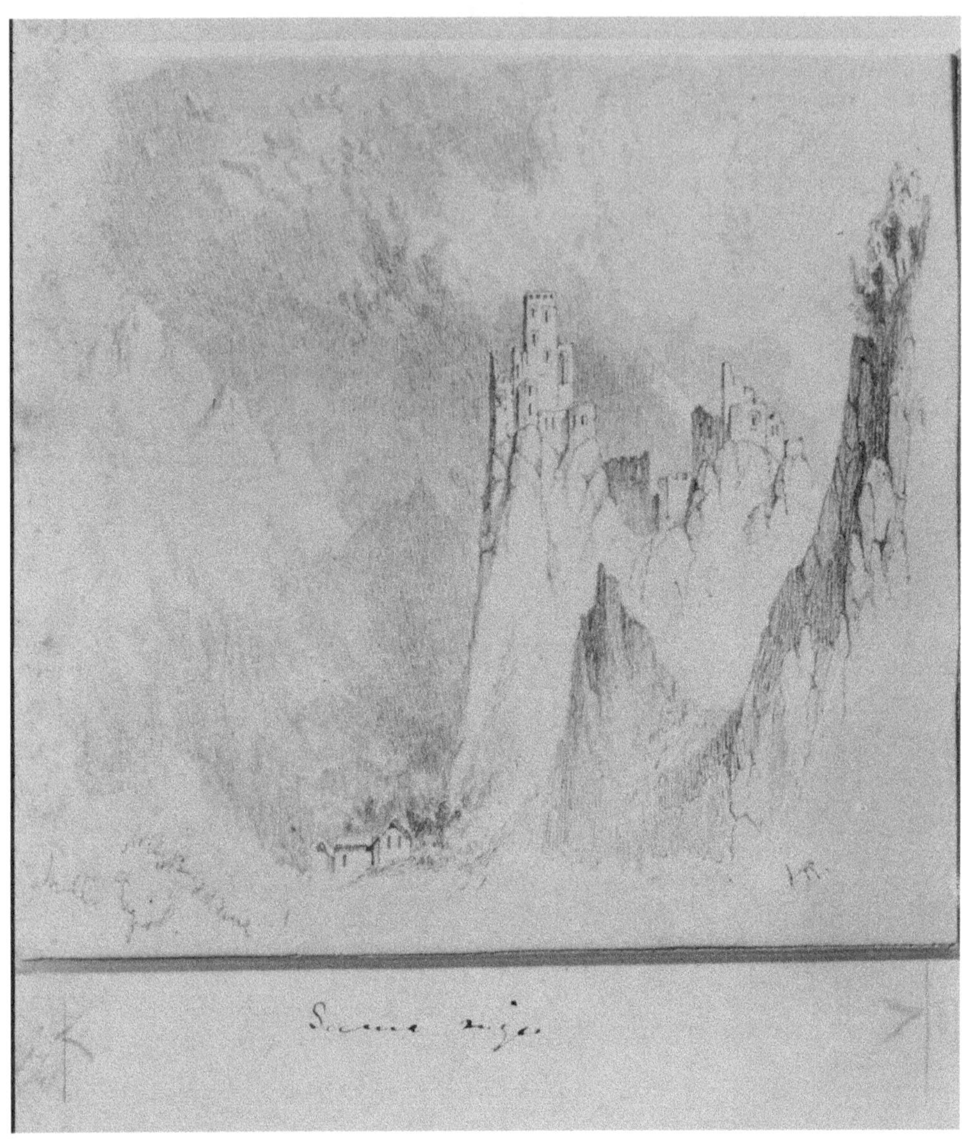

Cat. 92

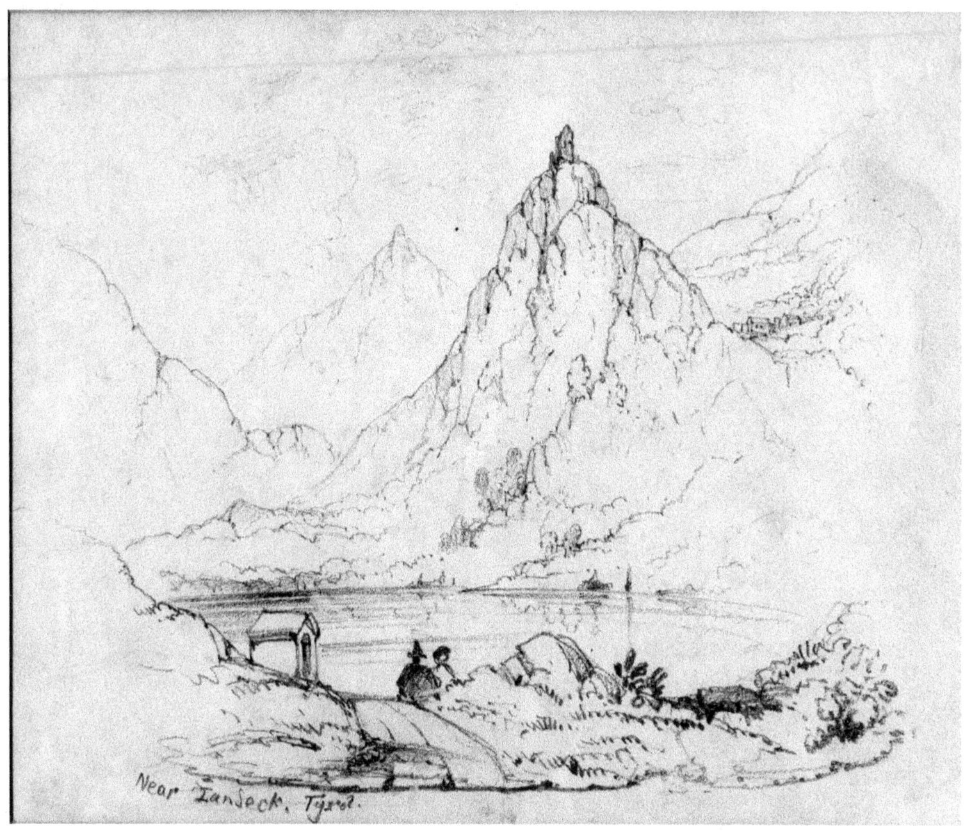

Cat. 96

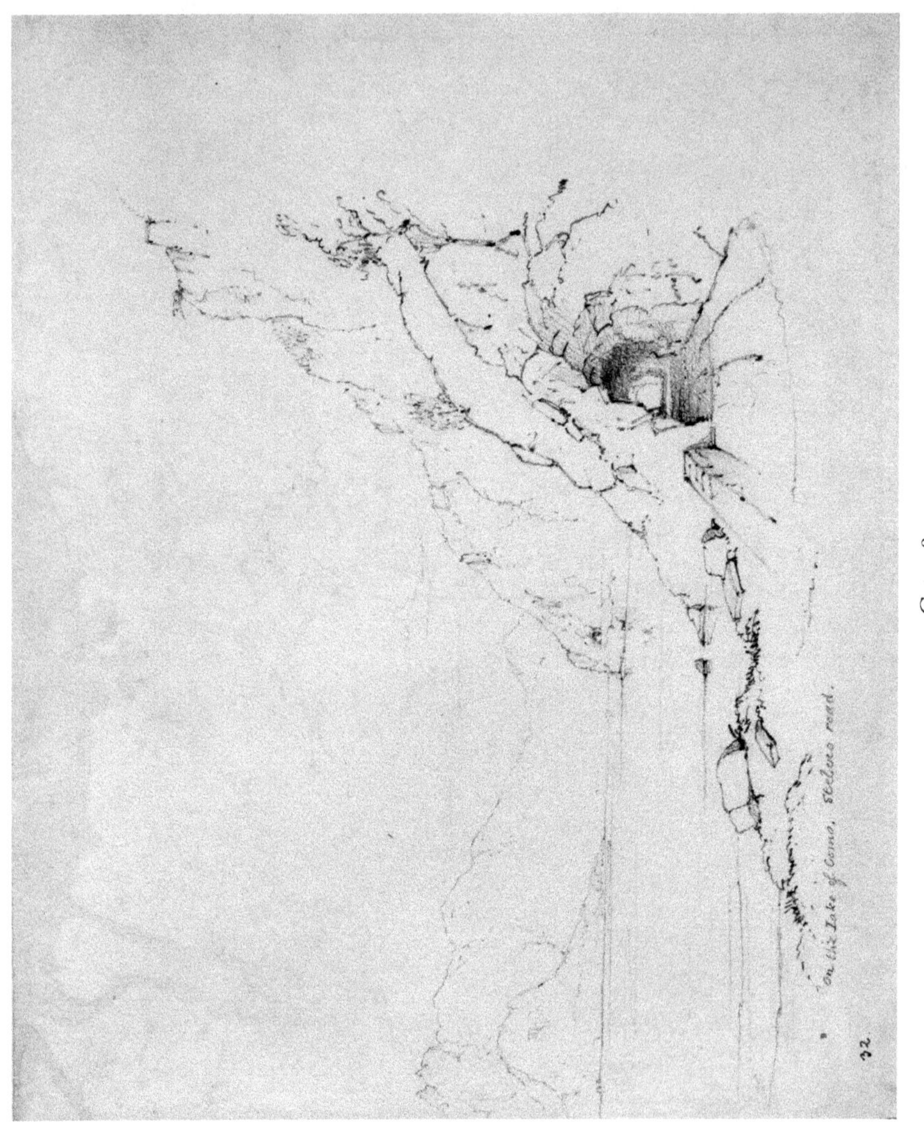

Cat. 98

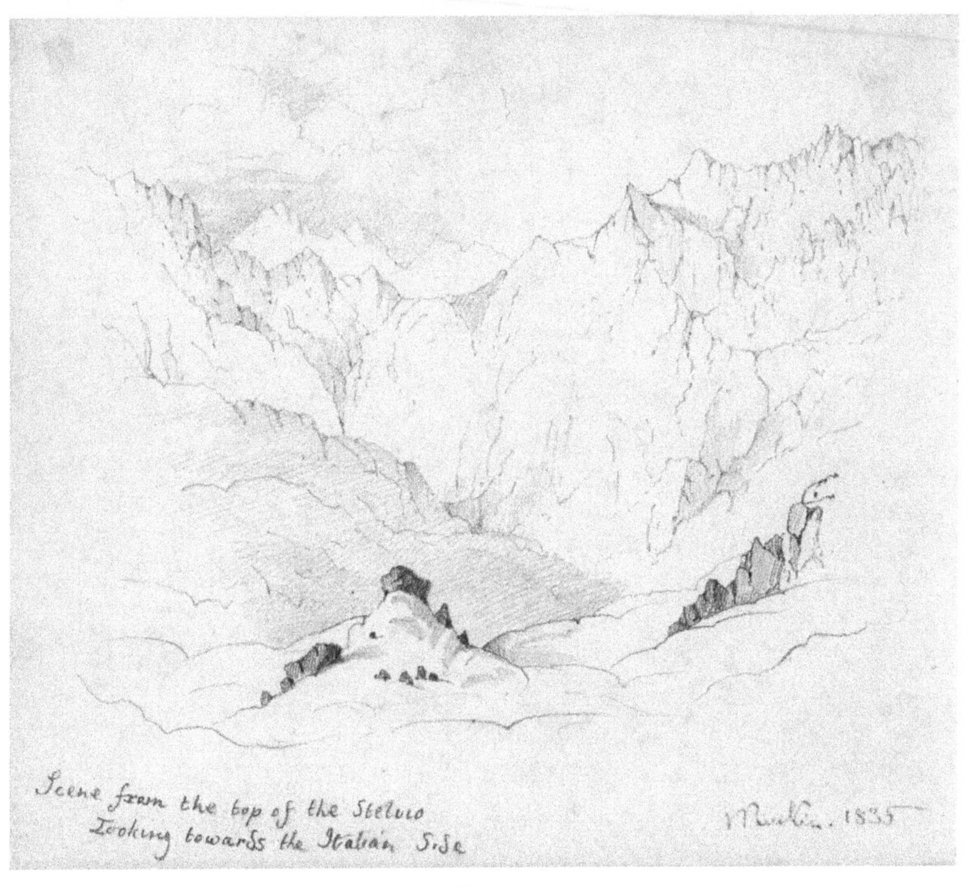
Scene from the top of the Stelvio
Looking towards the Italian Side
J Ruskin. 1835

Cat. 99

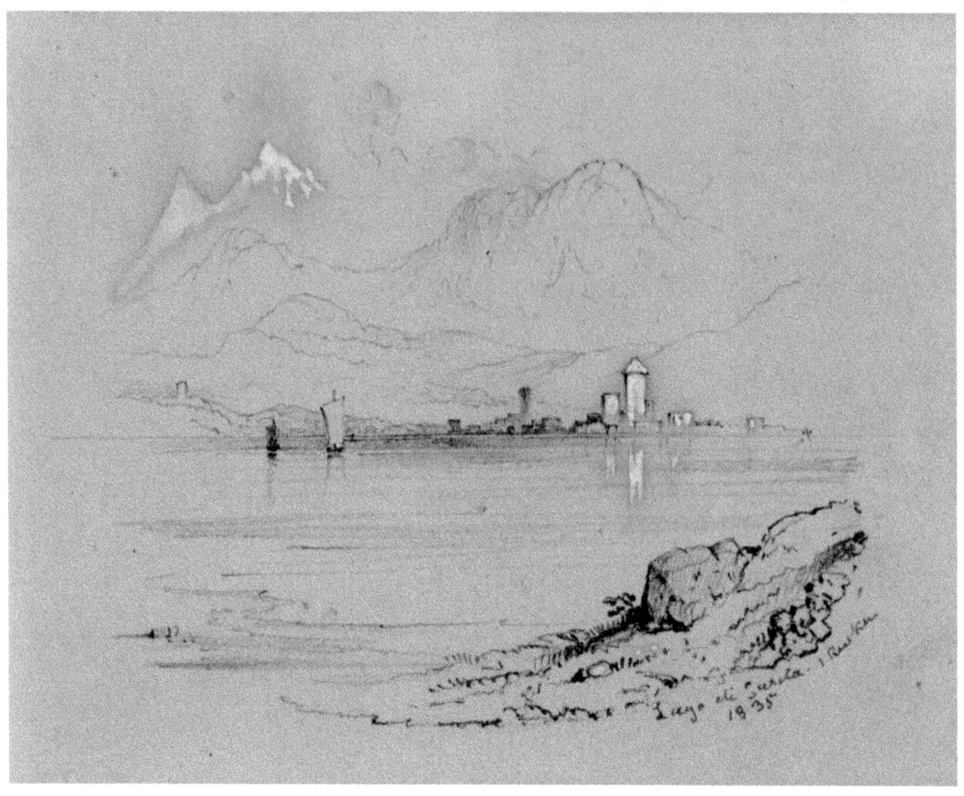

Cat. 107

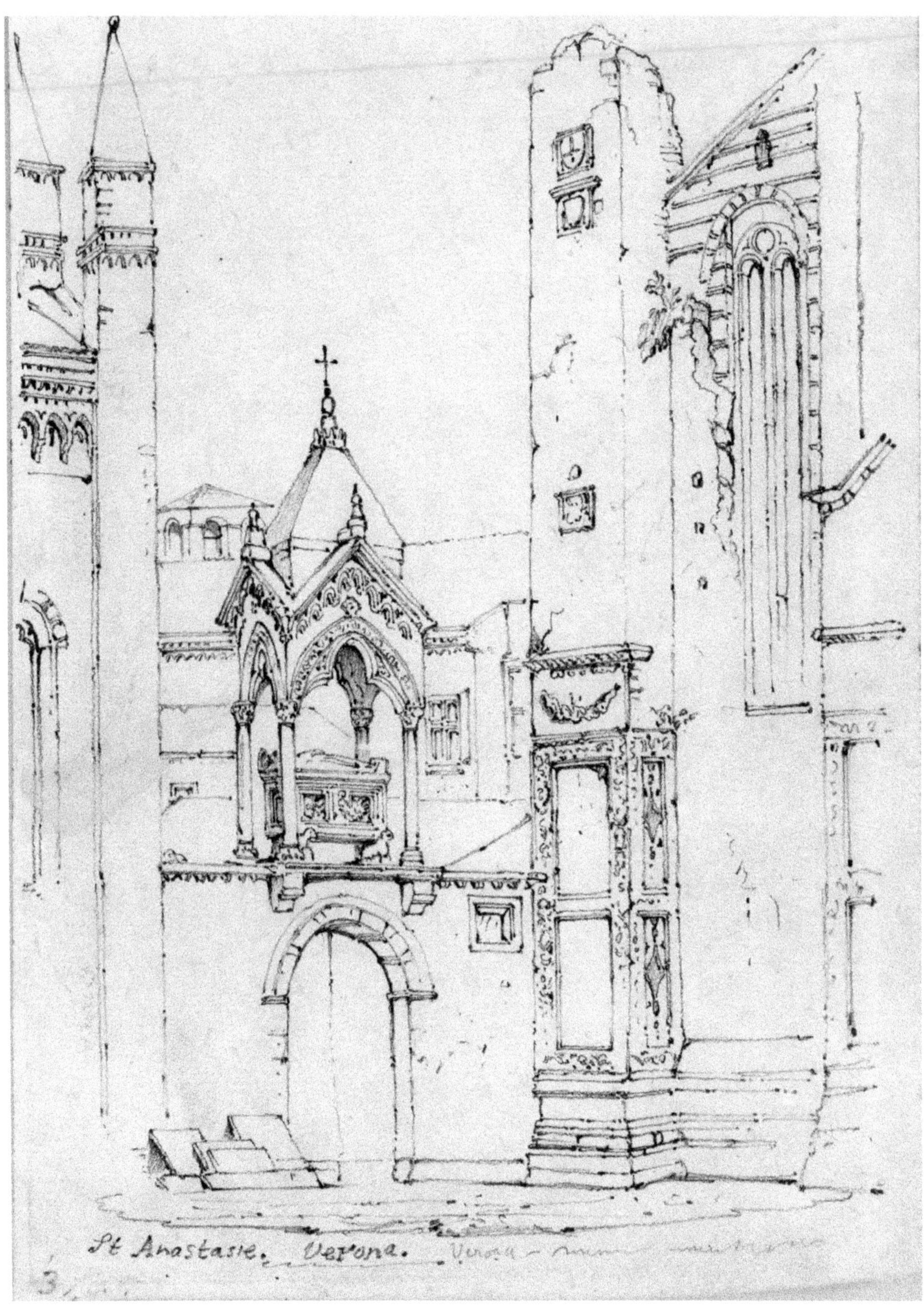

Cat. 108

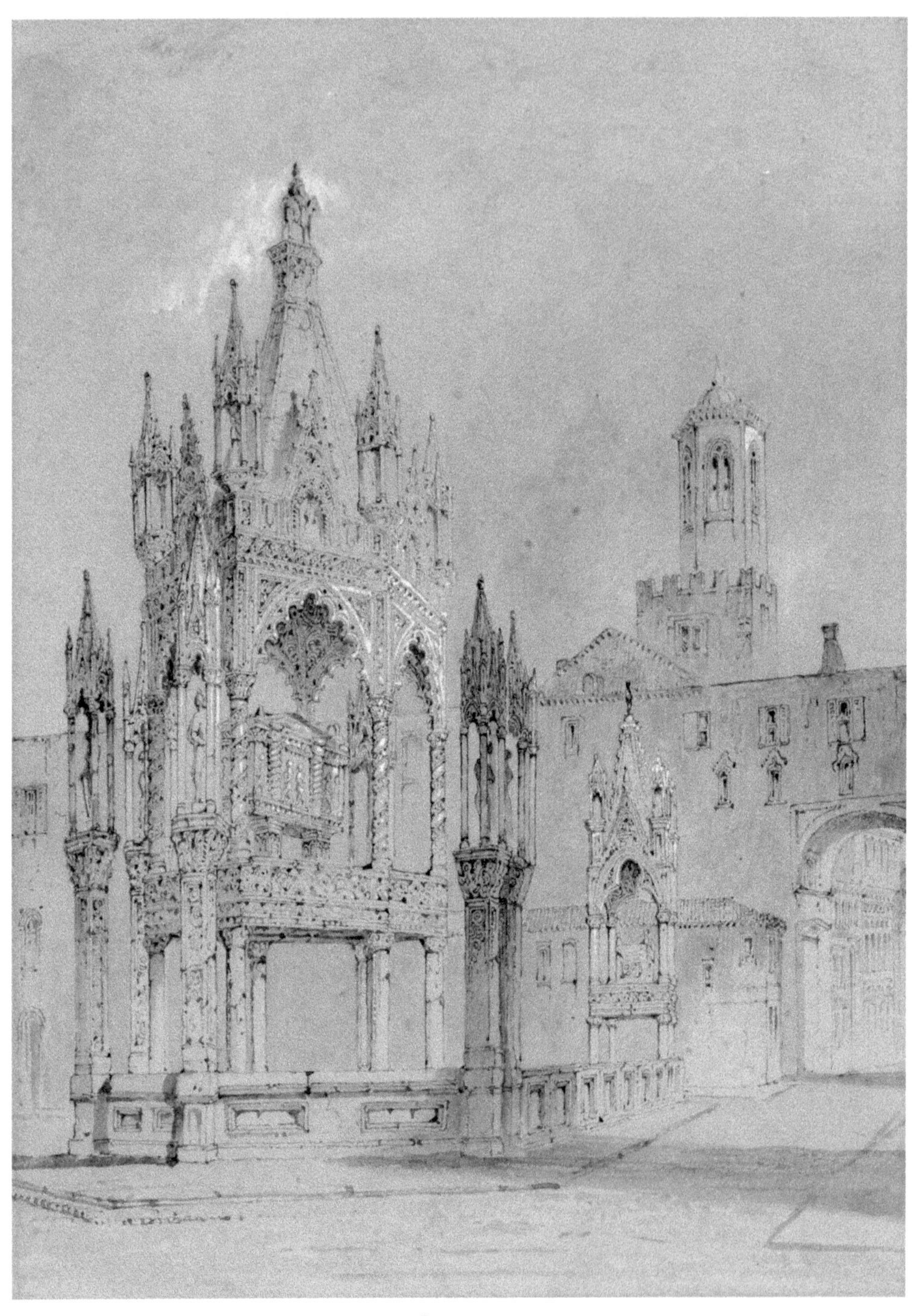

Cat. 109

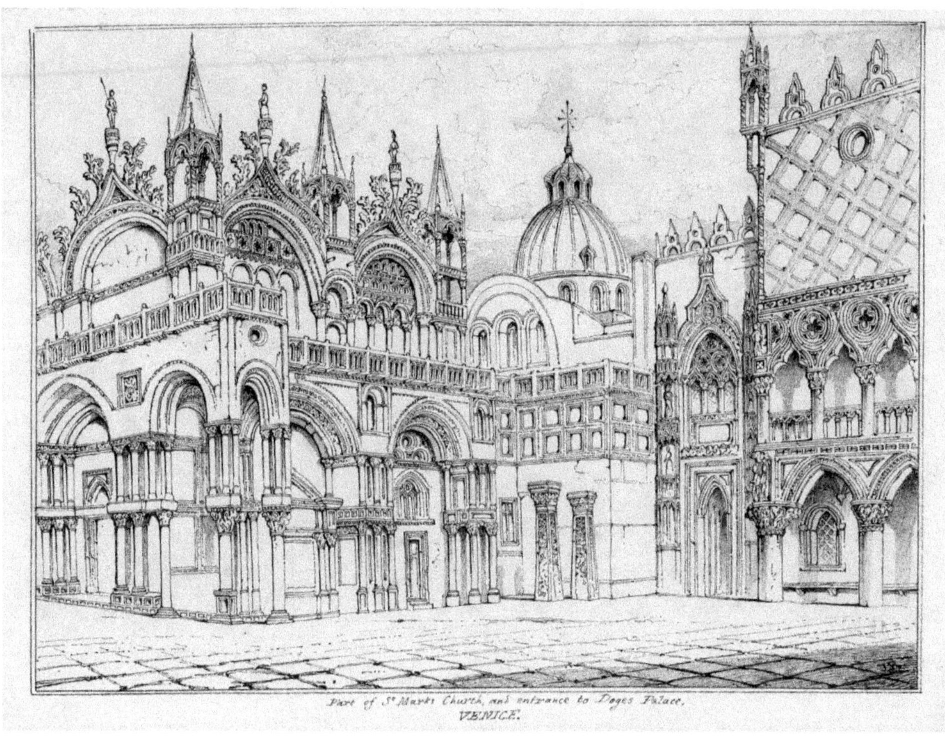

Cat. 115

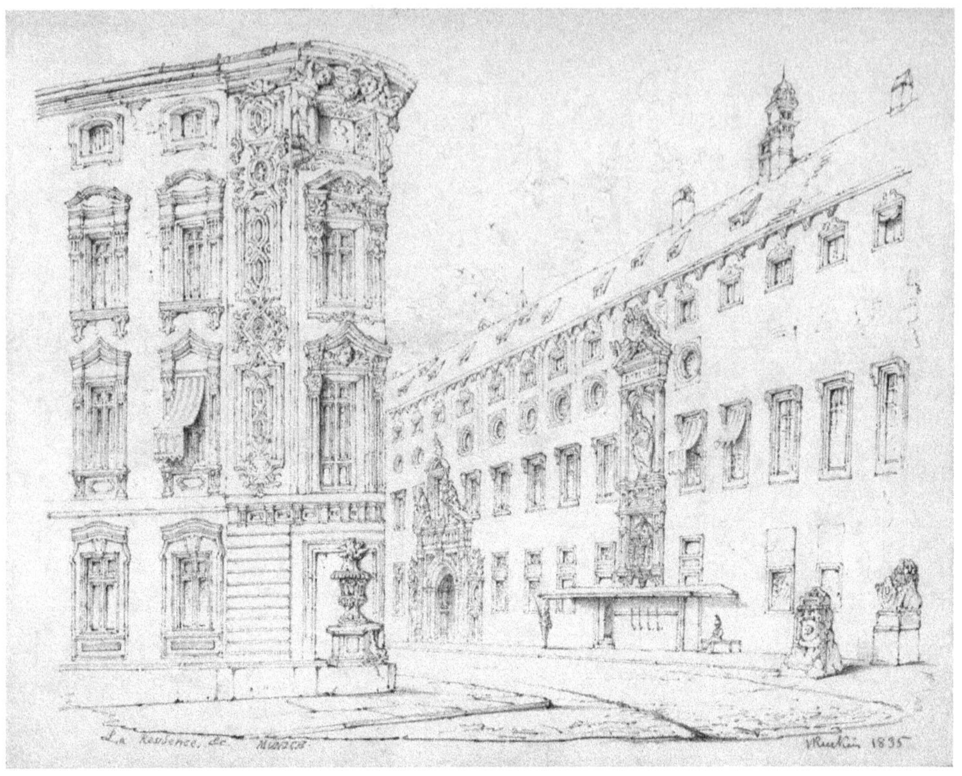

Cat. 119

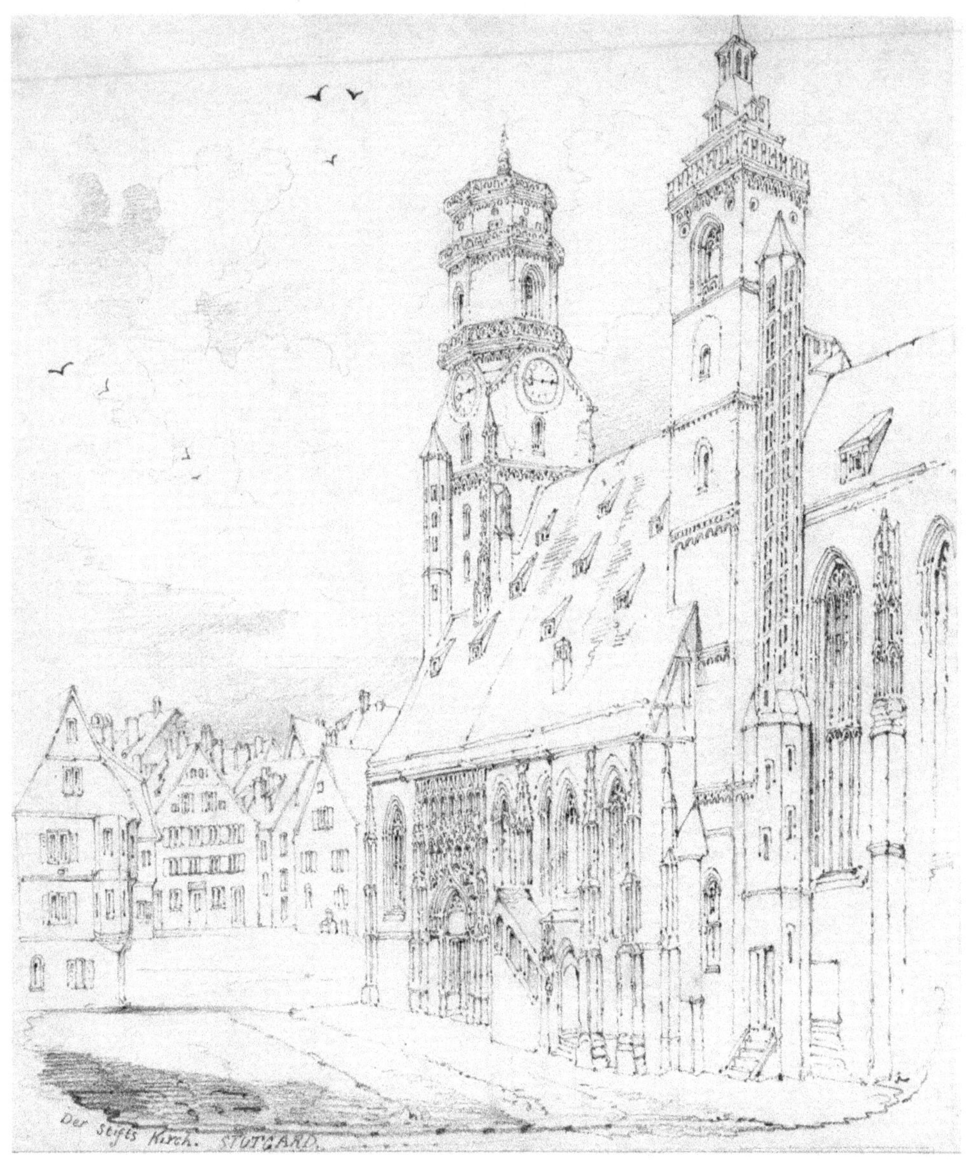

Cat. 122

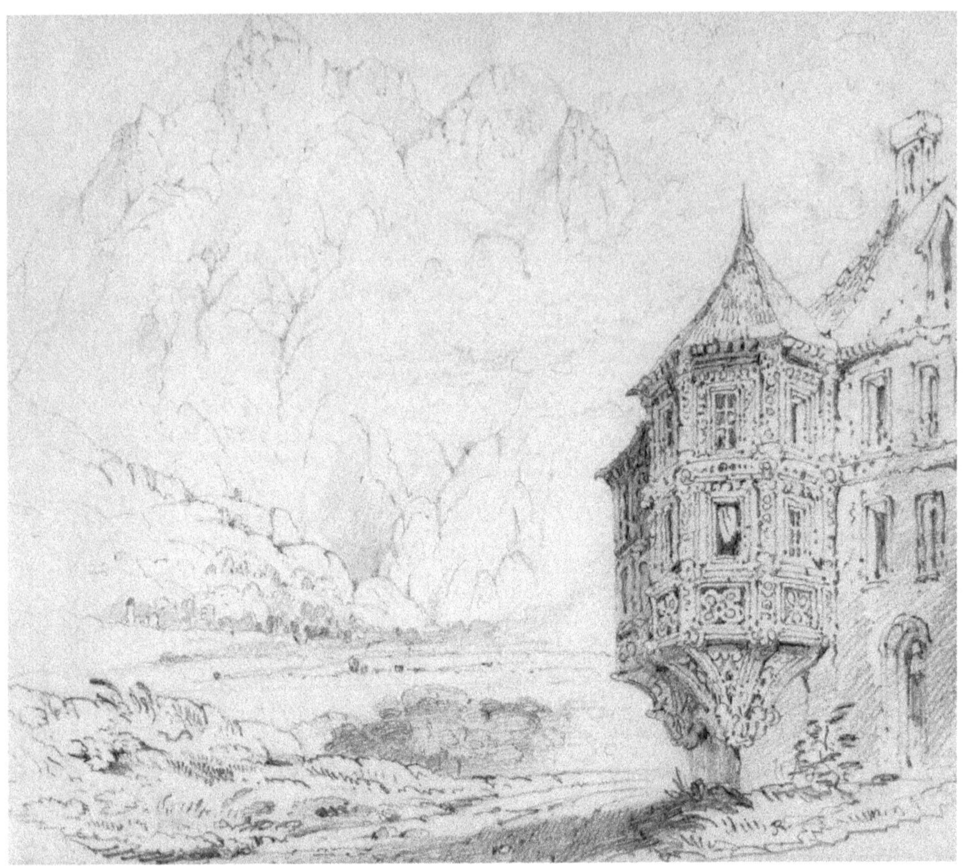

Cat. 123

CATALOGUE

LE = Library Edition (E. T. Cook and Alexander Wedderburn (eds), *The Works of John Ruskin* (Library Edition), 39 vols, 1903–12. Numbered Catalogue of Ruskin's Drawings, vol. XXXVIII, 1912, pp. 215–306.
RF = Ruskin Foundation (Ruskin Library, Lancaster University)
RF F prefix = archival photograph in Ruskin Library
Probable dates given, from John and John James Ruskin manuscript diaries.
Present locations have been included where known.

1. Dover from the Sea
(3 June or December 1835)
Pencil
Inscr. verso: Dover from the Sea 1835 Exhib Coniston 1903 No52 by J Ruskin
Ex coll. Brantwood (1912); Helen Gill Viljoen
LE 608
Morgan Library, New York (Viljoen Box 5; 1974.49:318)

2. Dover from the Sea
(3 June or December 1835)
Pencil
Inscr. in ink: Dover. from the sea. JR
LE 608; RF F630
Ex coll. Brantwood (1912); Sir Michael Sadler
University College, Oxford

3. Calais, Church Spire
(4 June or December 1835)
LE 311 (from reference in letter; medium unknown)
Present location unknown

4. Calais from the Sea
(4 June or December 1835)
Ink
Inscr. in ink: Calais from the Sea, J R.[uskin]; 2. (upper left)
Ex coll. Brantwood (1912); J. H. Whitehouse (by 1938)
LE 312
Ruskin Library, Lancaster (RF 1184)

5. Belfry, Calais
(4 June or December 1835)
Pencil, ink and bodycolour; image within double ink lines

Inscr. : Le Clocher. Calais.; JR; 3 (upper left); (partial) 2 (upper right)
Ex coll. Brantwood (1912); J. H. Whitehouse
LE 309
Ruskin Library, Lancaster (RF 1183)

6. Montreuil, View from Calais Road
(5 June 1835)
Pencil
Inscr.: Montreuil from the / Calais road. JR
Ex coll. Brantwood (1912)
LE 1147; RF F39
Present location unknown

7. Abbeville
(5 June 1835)
Pencil
Inscr. verso: Abbeville 1835? By J Ruskin
Ex coll. Helen Gill Viljoen
Morgan Library, New York (Viljoen Box 5; 1974.49)

8. Tower and Old Houses, Rouen
(9–10 June 1835)
Pencil
Inscr. in ink: Rouen
Ex coll. H. T. Butler (1912); J. H. Whitehouse, acquired 1937
LE 1431; LE vol. II, plate 20
Ruskin Library, Lancaster (RF 988)

9. Tour de Beurre and Old House, Rouen
(9–10 June 1835)
Pencil
Inscr: JR
LE 1432; LE vol. II, plate 18 (as The Cathedral Spire, Rouen)
Present location unknown

10. Street Scene, Rouen
(9–10 June 1835)
Ink and bodycolour on grey-green paper
Inscr.: JR; Street Scene. ROUEN.
Ex coll. J. R. Holliday (1912), bequeathed 1927
LE 1438
Fitzwilliam Museum, Cambridge (1451)

11. Arc de l'Horloge and Street Scene, Rouen
(9–10 June 1835)
Ink and wash
Inscr. recto: JR (lower left), Arc de l'Horloge & street scene Rouen; verso: JR 1835 by J Ruskin 1835
Ex coll. Helen Gill Viljoen
Morgan Library, New York (Viljoen Box 5:1974.49:339)

12. Church, Chalons sur Marne
(19 June 1835)
Pencil
Inscr.: Church at Chalons s. Marne and in ink: J Ruskin 1835
Ex coll. B. B. Macgeorge (1912); J. H. Whitehouse (by 1938)
LE 363; RF F36
John Ruskin College, Croydon (on loan from the Whitehouse Collection).

13. Bedchamber, Hotel du Palais, Chalons sur Marne
(19 June 1835)
Pencil
Inscr. in ink: Interior of a bed chamber. Hotel du Palais. Chalons s. Marne.
Ex coll. Haddon C. Adams, bequeathed 1971
Ruskin Library, Lancaster (RF 2019)

14. Gate of Ancient Palace, Nancy
(23–24 June)
Pencil
Inscr. in ink: Gate of the ancient Palace. NANCY; 25
Ex coll. Brantwood (1912)
LE 1170; LE vol. II, plate 19
Ruskin Museum, Coniston (ConRM1989.541)

15. Gate of Ancient Palace, Nancy
(23–24 June)
Ink and bodycolour
Inscr.: JR
Ex coll. Joan Severn, presented to British Museum, 1901
LE 1171
British Museum, London (1901,0506.2)

16. Chillon from Meillerie
Same sheet as no. 26, Rhone Valley and Bernese Alps
(1 July 1835)
Ink
Inscr.: Near Meillerie. Chillon in the distance.
Ex coll. Joan Severn, presented to British Museum 1901
LE 479
British Museum, London (1901,0506.3)

17. View near Bonneville
(5 July 1835)
Ink
Inscr.: JR; Scene near Bonneville. Savoy.
Ex coll. Brantwood (1912)
LE 245; RF F627
Present location unknown

18. Hotel de la Poste, Martigny
(14 or 22 July 1835)
Ink
Ex coll. Brantwood (1912)
LE 1108
Present location unknown

19. Tête Noire, Martigny
(14 or 22 July 1835)
Pencil
Ex coll. Brantwood (1912)
LE 1636
Present location unknown

20. Valais, from the Tête Noire Road
(14 or 22 July 1835)
Ink
Ex coll. Brantwood (1912)
LE 1776
Present location unknown

21. Mont Velan from the Hospice of the Great St Bernard
(15 July 1835)
Pencil, ink and bodycolour on toned paper; image within double ink lines
Inscr.: JR; Mont Velan. From the windows of Hospice of the GREAT ST BERNARD.; 15 (in ink, upper right)
Ex coll. Brantwood (1912); Haddon C. Adams, bequeathed 1971
LE 1780
Ruskin Library, Lancaster (RF 2036)

22. Cottage near La Cité, Val d'Aosta
(16 or 20 July 1835)
Ink
LE 103 (as 1838); LE vol. I, plate 3
Present location unknown

23. Aosta
(16 or 20 July 1835)
Ink
Ex coll. Brantwood (1912)
LE 104
Present location unknown

24. Fortress in the Val d'Aosta: Chateau St. Pierre
(16 or 20 July 1835)
Ink and bodycolour; image within double ink lines
Inscr.: JR; Fortress in the VAL D'AOSTA
Ex coll. Brantwood (1912); Christie's, 29 October 1985, lot 153 (ill)

LE 1775
Private collection

25. Pays de Valais, near Bex
(23 July 1835)
Ink, image within double ink lines
Inscr.: JR; Near Bex. PAYS DE VAUD.; 19 (upper left); 10 (upper right); [ ]3 (lower left)
Ex coll. J. H. Whitehouse (by 1938)
Ruskin Library, Lancaster (RF 1431)

26. Rhone Valley and Bernese Alps from the ascent of the Tête Noire
Same sheet as no. 16, Chillon from Meillerie
(23 July 1835)
Ink
Inscr.: JR; The Valley of the Rhone & Bernese Alps. From the ascent of the Tete Noire
Ex coll. Joan Severn, presented to British Museum, 1901
LE 1381
British Museum, London (1901,0506.3)

27. Mont Blanc and Lake of Geneva
(23 July 1835)
Ink and bodycolour; image within double ink lines
Inscr.: JR; Mont Blanc and the lake of Geneva, from the Jura
Ex coll. Sotheby's, 11 July 1990, lot 21 (ill)
Private collection

28. Mont Blanc from St Martin
(23 July 1835)
Ink and watercolour; image within double ink lines
Inscr.: recto: 12 (upper right), 15 (lower right), MONT BLANC from St Martin
Ex coll. Helen Gill Viljoen
Morgan Library, New York (Viljoen Box 4; 1974.49:256)

29. La Halle, Neuchâtel
(29 July 1835)
Pencil
Ex coll. Brantwood (1912)
LE 1194
Present location unknown

30. La Halle, Neuchâtel
(29 July 1835)
Ink
Ex coll. Brantwood (1912)
LE 1195
Present location unknown

31. Great Square, Bienne
(30 July 1835)
Pencil
Inscr.: Great Square. BIENNE; in brown ink: J Ruskin 1835; 20 (lower left)
Ex colls B. B. Macgeorge (1912); J. H. Whitehouse (by 1929)
LE 206
Ruskin Library, Lancaster (RF 1152)

32. Stein am Rhein, near Basle
(3 August 1835)
Pencil
Verso, pencil: Two studies of mountain peaks; inscr.: Done
Inscr. in brown ink: 10. on the Rhine; 23 (lower left)
Ex coll. Haddon C. Adams, bequeathed 1971
Ruskin Library, Lancaster (RF 2043)

33. Zurich
(8 August 1835)
Pencil
Inscr. recto: Zurich; verso: By J Ruskin 1835 Zurich
Ex coll. Brantwood (1912); Helen Gill Viljoen
LE 2145
Morgan Library, New York (Viljoen Box 2, 1974.49:149)

34. Mont Righi and the Bernese Alps
(10 August 1835)
Pencil
Inscr.: Mont Righi, and the Bernese Alps, — / over the lake of ZUG; in brown ink J Ruskin 1835. signed 1880
Ex coll. B. B. Macgeorge; J. H. Whitehouse (by 1938)
LE 1386
Ruskin Library, Lancaster (RF 980)

35. Old Houses, Zug
(10–11 August 1835)
Pencil
Ex coll. Brantwood (1912)
LE 2142; LE vol. I, plate 5
Ruskin Museum, Coniston (ConRM1989.542)

36. Zug
(10–11 August 1835)
Ink and bodycolour
Ex coll. Whitworth Wallis (1912)
LE 2143 (as Zug, View)
Present location unknown

37. On the Reuss, near Altdorf
(12 August 1835)
Pencil and ink; image within double inked lines

Inscr.: JR; On the Reuss, near ALTORF; 22 (upper left, in pencil)
Ex coll. T. F. Taylor (1912); J. H. Whitehouse (by 1938)
LE 1368 (possibly the same as LE 1620 Cottage, near Altdorf, location Brantwood); LE vol. I, fig. 5 (detail)
Ruskin Library, Lancaster (RF 1453)

38. Hospital, Pass of St Gothard
(13 August 1835)
Pencil and ink; image within double inked lines
Inscr.: JR; Hospital. Pass of St GOTHARD.
Ex coll. Brantwood (1912); Haddon C. Adams, bequeathed 1971
LE 1450; LE vol. II, plate 23
Ruskin Library, Lancaster (RF 2044)

39. Hospenthal, Pass of St Gothard
(13 August 1835)
Ink
Ex coll. Brantwood (1912)
LE 1451
Present location unknown

40. Near Amsteg, Pass of St Gothard
(13–14 August 1835)
Pencil and ink; image within double inked lines
Inscr. in ink: JR; Near Amsteg. Pass of St GOTHARD; 21 (upper left, in ink); 14 (upper right, in ink); 22 (lower left, in ink)
Ex coll. Brantwood (1912); J. H. Whitehouse (by 1938)
LE 79 (as Little Devil's Bridge, near Amsteg)
Ruskin Library, Lancaster (RF 998)

41. Pass of St Gothard, near Amsteg
(13–14 August 1835)
Ink
Inscr.: Near Amsteg Pass of St GOTHARD / J Ruskin 1835 / Signed & ludicrous figures scratched out 1880
LE 80 (no location given)
Brooklyn Museum of Art, New York (33.300)

42. Lucerne from a suburb
(17–18 August 1835)
Pencil
Inscr.: Lucerne. from a suburb; 15 (lower left, in brown ink)
Ex coll. Haddon C. Adams, bequeathed 1971
Ruskin Library, Lancaster (RF 2033)

43. Mount Pilatus, Lucerne
(17–18 August 1835)
Pencil
Inscr. in brown ink: Mont Pilate, from the Lake of Lucerne
Ex coll. A. E. Cropper (1912); J. H. Whitehouse

LE 1299
Ruskin Library, Lancaster (RF 1435)

44. Mount Pilatus, Lucerne
(1835 or after)
Watercolour
Inscr. on mount: This drawing was done by Professor Ruskin, and given to me. F Crawley
Ex coll. Frederick Crawley; J. H. Whitehouse (acquired 1942)
Ruskin Library, Lancaster (RF 1437)

45. 'Ancienne Maison', Lucerne
(17–18 August 1835)
Pencil
Ex coll. T. F. Taylor (1912)
LE 1057
Present location unknown

46. 'Ancienne Maison', Lucerne
(17–18 August 1835)
Ink and bodycolour
Inscr.: JR, Ancienne Maison LUCERNE; verso: by John Ruskin / given by him to me / Joan Ruskin Severn
Ex coll. Joan Severn; T. F. Taylor (1912); Claude Rogers (1968)
LE 1057A; LE vol. II, plate 22
Collection of the Guild of St George, Museums Sheffield (CGSG00540)

47. Rigi
(19 August 1835)
Pencil
Ex coll. B. B. Macgeorge (1912)
LE 1386
Present location unknown

48. Bridge on the Grimsel
(24–26 August 1835)
Pencil
Inscr. in ink: JR (lower right); Bridge on the Grimsel
Ex coll. A. E. Cropper (1912); J. H. Whitehouse
LE 822
Ruskin Library, Lancaster (RF 1310)

49. Guttanen, Sketch I (Pass of St Gothard)
(24–26 August 1835)
Pencil
Inscr.: Gutannen. Pass of St. Gothard. 1835. Signed 1885.
Ex coll. 'America' (1912); Violet Hunt
LE 824
The New York Public Library, New York (The Henry W. and Albert A. Berg Collection of English and American Literature)

50. Guttanen, Sketch II (Passage of Grimsel; verso, Valley of Grindelwald)
(24–26 August 1835)
Ink
Ex coll. G. Allen (1912)
LE 825 (and possibly 821 for verso, Valley of Grindelwald)
Private Collection

51. Guttanen, Sketch III (Valley of Grimsel; verso Passage of Grimsel)
(24–26 August 1835)
Ink
Ex coll. G. Allen (1912)
LE 826
Private Collection

52. Tower and Vale of Meiringen
(27–28 August 1835)
Verso: no. 98, On the Lake of Como, Stelvio road
Pencil
Inscr. in brown ink: Tower and vale of Meyringen.
Ex coll. Brantwood (1912); Haddon C. Adams, bequeathed 1971
LE 1126 (possibly, as Meiringen)
Ruskin Library, Lancaster (RF 2021)

53. Bridge on the 6th Fall, Reichenbach
(27–28 August 1835)
Pencil, ink and bodycolour
Inscr.: Bridge on the 6th Fall of / the REICHENBACH; in ink: J Ru[skin] (lower right, in later hand)
Ex coll. A. E. Cropper (1912)
LE 1365; LE vol. XXXVIII, plate XIV; RF F 551
Present location unknown

54. Valley of Hasli, above Meyringen
(27–28 August 1835)
On same sheet as no. 55, Wellhorn and Glacier of Rosenlaui
Pencil and ink
Inscr. in ink: JR; Valley of Hasli. from above Meyringen; 17 (upper right of sheet)
Ex coll. Brantwood (1912); J. H. Whitehouse (by 1938)
LE 836
Ruskin Library, Lancaster (RF 925)

55. Wellhorn and Glacier of Rosenlaui
(27–28 August 1835)
On same sheet as no. 54, Valley of Hasli, above Meyringen
Pencil and ink
Inscr. in ink: JR; Wellhorn, & Glacier de Rosenlau. from Rosenlaui.
Ex coll. Brantwood (1912); J. H. Whitehouse (by 1938)
LE 2126
Ruskin Library, Lancaster (RF 1086)

56. Wellhorn, Wetterhorn from Meiringen
(27–28 August 1835)
Pencil
Inscr. in ink: Wellhorn. Wetterhorn. Glacier de Rosenlau, & Reichen Bach from Meyringen
Ex coll. Haddon C. Adams, bequeathed 1971
Ruskin Library, Lancaster (RF 2055)

57. Rosenlaui
(27–28 August 1835)
Pencil
Ex coll. Brantwood (1912)
LE 1416
Present location unknown

58. Wellhorn and Wetterhorn, from the Scheideck
(27–28 August 1835)
Ink and bodycolour
Ex coll. Miss Schuster (1912)
LE 2124
Present location unknown

59. Wellhorn and Wetterhorn, from the Scheideck
(27–28 August 1835)
Ink and bodycolour on blue-grey paper
Verso, in pencil: Mountain peaks
Inscr. in ink: Wellhorn and Wetterhorn. from the banks of the Reichenbach. / Pass of the SCHEIDECK.; JR (lower right, in pencil, in later hand)
Ex coll. Miss Harrison (1912); J. H. Whitehouse (by 1938)
LE 2125
Ruskin Library, Lancaster (RF 1087)

60. Wellhorn and Glacier of Rosenlaui
(27–28 August 1835)
Ink
Inscr. in ink: JR; Wellhorn. & Glacier de Rosenlau. from Rosenlaui
Ex coll. Brantwood (1912)
LE 2126; RF F 623
Present location unknown

61. Grindelwald and Wetterhorn
(29–30 August 1835)
Pencil
Inscr. in ink: Grindelwald & Wetterhorn.
Ex coll. Haddon C. Adams, bequeathed 1971
Ruskin Library, Lancaster (RF 2027)

62. The Great Eiger, Church, and Glacier of Grindelwald
(29–30 August 1835)

Pencil
Inscr.: The great Eiger, Church & glacier of Grindelwald; verso (of mount): Drawn by J Ruskin 1835 Exhibited Manchester 1904 No 22
Ex coll. Brantwood (1912); Helen Gill Viljoen
LE 819
Morgan Library, New York (Viljoen Box 5; 1974.49:334)

63. Eiger, Church and Glacier
(29–30 August 1835)
Pencil and bodycolour
Inscr.: Breven 1836 [?] Eglise de Chamouny
Musée Alpin, Chamonix (as Eglise de Chamouny)

64. Lauterbrunnen and Staubbach
(30 August 1835)
Pencil
Inscr. in ink: Lauterbroonn. and Staubbach.
Ex coll. Haddon C. Adams, bequeathed 1971
Ruskin Library, Lancaster (RF 2031)

65. Jungfrau, Wengern Alp and Lauterbrunnen
(30 August 1835)
Ink
Inscr. (John James Ruskin): Lauterbrounn, J.J.R.; (John Ruskin): Jungfrau & Wengern Alp, Lauterbrounn J.R.
Ex coll. Ruskin Drawing School, University of Oxford
LE 916
Ashmolean Museum, Oxford (WA.RS.ED.119)

66. Old Houses, Unterseen
31 August 1835
Pencil
Inscr.: Street, Unterseen August 31; 16 (lower left, in brown ink)
Ex coll. Brantwood (1912); J. H. Whitehouse
LE 1768; LE vol. I, plate 7
Ruskin Library, Lancaster (RF 1575)

67. Old Houses, Unterseen
(31 August 1835)
Pencil
Inscr.: JR; Old houses, Unterseen; 17 (in ink)
Ex coll. T. F. Taylor (1912)
LE 1769
Art Institute, Chicago (RXI 18296/41)

68. Village on Lake Thun
(1–2 September 1835)
Pencil and brown ink (later addition?)
Inscr. in brown ink: J Ruskin 1835

Ex coll. J. H. Whitehouse
LE 1651; LE vol. I, fig. 27
Ruskin Library, Lancaster (RF 1550)

69. Lake Thun
(1835 or after)
Pencil and watercolour
Private collection

70. Thun, Town and Lake
(1–2 September 1835)
Pencil
Ex coll. B. B. Macgeorge (1912)
LE 1647
Present location unknown

71. Thun, Castle
(1–2 September 1835)
Pencil
Inscr.: September
Ex coll. Ruskin Drawing School (University of Oxford)
LE 1648
Ashmolean Museum, Oxford (WA.RS.WS.II.34; missing since 1906)

72. View of Thun
(1–2 September 1835)
Pencil and bodycolour
Ex coll. Ruskin Drawing School (University of Oxford)
LE 1649 (as 'early drawing')
Ashmolean Museum, Oxford (WA.RS.WS.II.46; missing since 1906)

73. Thun, Church and Gate
2 September 1835
Pencil
Inscr.: 2 September JR; Church & Gate, THUN
Ex coll. Brantwood (1912)
LE 1650; RF F609
Present location unknown

74. Street Scene, Berne
(3 or 10 September 1835)
Pencil
Inscr. in brown ink: No 1. Street scene. Berne; J Ruskin 1835 / signed 1880
Ex coll. B. B. Macgeorge (1912); J. H. Whitehouse (by 1938)
LE 203
Ruskin Library, Lancaster (RF 1151)

75. Street Scene, Berne
(3 or 10 September 1835)
Pencil

Inscr.: No 2 Berne; verso: 1835 M 13 (erased) by J Ruskin 1835
Ex coll. Brantwood (1912); Helen Gill Viljoen
LE 202
Morgan Library, New York (Viljoen Bequest, Box 2, V6)

76. Hotel de Ville, Fribourg
(4 or 9 September 1835)
Pencil and ink; image within double ink lines (missing from top)
Inscr.: JR; Hotel de ville. FRIBOURG.; 37.R.
Ex coll. B. B. Macgeorge (1912); J. H. Whitehouse (by 1938)
LE 733
Ruskin Library (RF 1283)

77. Fribourg
(4 or 9 September 1835)
Pencil
Inscr. recto: 27 Fribourg; verso: By J Ruskin 1835
Ex coll. Helen Gill Viljoen
Morgan Library, New York (Viljoen Box 2; 1974.49)

78. Fribourg from the River
(4 or 9 September 1835)
Pencil
Inscr. recto: Fribourg from the River; verso: 1835, M, By J Ruskin 1835, Exhibited Manchester 1904 No24
Ex coll. Brantwood (1912)
LE 730
Ex coll. Helen Gill Viljoen
Morgan Library, New York (Viljoen Box 2; 1974.49:153)

79. Fribourg from the River
(4 or 9 September 1835)
Ink
Inscr.: signed and dated 1835
Ex coll. M. Tomkinson (1912); Sotheby's, 18 March 1982, lot 153 (ill)
LE 731; LE vol. II, plate 24
Private collection

80. Chateau of Lausanne
(5–7 September 1835)
Pencil
Inscr. recto: 6 (lower left), 28. chateau. Lausanne (centre); verso: By J Ruskin 1835
Ex coll. Brantwood (1912); Helen Gill Viljoen
LE 965
Morgan Library, New York (Viljoen Box 2; 1974.49:154)

81. Tower and Fortress, Lenzburg
12 September 1835
Pencil
Verso: no. 117, Fortresses in Tyrol, near Mals

Inscr.: Lenzburg. 12 Sep
Ex coll. Charles Deering McCormick, Brooks McCormick and the Estate of Roger McCormick
Art Institute, Chicago (1970.1268R)

82. Tower and Fortress, Lenzburg
(12 September 1835)
Pencil
Inscr. verso: 1835 Manchester Exhibition No 17 by J Ruskin
Ex coll. Brantwood (1912); Helen Gill Viljoen
LE 1002
Morgan Library, New York (Viljoen Box 5; 1974.49)

83. View of Baden
(12–13 September 1835)
Ink
Inscr. in brown ink: J Ruskin 1835 / signed 1879
LE 156
South London Art Gallery (GA0429)

84. Street in St Gall[en]
(15 September 1835)
Pencil
Inscr.: a. higher to let door in; 29. St Gall street scene
LE 1448
Ex coll. W. G. Collingwood; Sotheby's, February 1966, lot 6; J. H. Whitehouse
Ruskin Library, Lancaster (RF 1477)

85. Street in St Gall[en]
(15 September 1835)
Ink; image within double ink lines
Inscr. verso: Street in St Gall, 1835
Ex coll. Brantwood (1912); J. H. Whitehouse (by 1938)
Ruskin Library, Lancaster (RF 1476)

86. Entrance to Feldkirch, Tyrol
(16 September 1835)
Pencil
Inscr.: Entrance to / FELDKIRCH / TYROL
Ex coll. Miss Susan Dwight Bliss
Bowdoin College Museum of Art, Brunswick, Maine (1956.24.261)

87. Innsbruck
(19–20 September 1835)
Pencil
Ex coll. Brantwood (1912)
LE 881
Present location unknown

88. Innsbruck
(19–20 September 1835)
Ink
Ex coll. Mrs Mackay (1912)
LE 882
Present location unknown

89. Innsbruck, Main Street
(19–20 September 1835)
Ex coll. Dr. Pocock (1912)
LE 883 (no medium or date given, but no other visit to Innsbruck is known)
Present location unknown

90. Near Zirl, Tyrol
(19–20 September 1835)
Pencil and ink
Inscr. in ink: Near Zirl. TYROL.
Ex coll. J. H. Whitehouse (by 1938)
Ruskin Library, Lancaster (RF 1020)

91. Bridge and Guard Tower, Pass of Finstermunz, Tyrol
(September 1835)
Verso: no. 95, Between Landeck and St Antoine (with figures and carriages)
Pencil
Inscr.: Bridge & Guard Tower. Pass of the Finstermunz / TYROL; JR (doubtful)
Ex coll. A. E. Cropper (1912); J. H. Whitehouse
LE 1763 (as Bridge and Guard Tower, Tyrol)
Ruskin Library, Lancaster (RF 1574)

92. In the Tyrol in the Old Time
(September 1835)
Ink
Inscr.: In the Tyrol [in the old time ?]; JR (doubtful)
LE 1764; LE vol. XXXVIII, plate 14; RF F 477
Present location unknown

93. Fortress near Trent, Tyrol
(September 1835)
Pencil and bodycolour
Ex coll. Miss Harrison (1912)
LE 1690
Present location unknown

94. Bludens
(September 1835)
Pencil
Inscr.: Pludens, TYROL and in ink J Ruskin 1835 / signed 1880
Ex coll. Robert E. Cunliffe; Mrs Cunliffe (1912); Guy C. Barton, presented 1963
LE 230
Abbot Hall Art Gallery, Lakelands Arts Trust, Kendal, Cumbria (00282/63)

95. Between Landeck and St Antoine (with figures and carriages)
(September 1835)
Verso of no. 91, Bridge and guard tower, Pass of Finstermunz, Tyrol
Pencil
Inscr.: [Betwee]n Landeck and St Antoine
Ex coll. A. E. Cropper (1912); J. H. Whitehouse
Ruskin Library, Lancaster (RF 1574)

96. Near Landeck, Tyrol
(21 September 1835)
Pencil
Inscr.: Near Landeck. Tyrol.
Ex coll. Robert E. Cunliffe; Mrs Cunliffe (1912); Hodgkinson-Smith; Haddon C. Adams, bequeathed 1971
LE 939 (as 1833, in error)
Ruskin Library, Lancaster (RF 2030)

97. Near Landeck, Tyrol
(1835 or after; paper watermarked 1835)
Watercolour
Inscr.: Near LANDECK. TYROL
Private Collection

98. On the Lake of Como, Stelvio road
(23 September 1835)
Verso of no. 52, Tower and Vale of Meiringen
Pencil
Inscr.: On the Lake of Como, Stelvio road.; 32 (lower left, in ink)
Ex coll. Haddon C. Adams, bequeathed 1971
Ruskin Library, Lancaster (RF 2021)

99. Scene from the top of Stelvio
(23 September 1835)
Pencil
Inscr.: Scene from the top of the Stelvio / Looking towards the Italian side; in brown ink: J Ruskin. 1835
Ex coll. B. B. Macgeorge (1912); J. H. Whitehouse (by 1938)
LE 1585
Ruskin Library, Lancaster (RF 1001)

100. Valtelline Mountains, from the Stelvio Pass
(23 September 1835)
Ink and bodycolour
Ex coll. Mrs Walter Druce (1912)
LE 1772
Present location unknown

101. Stelvio Road from above Trefoi
(1835 or after)

Watercolour
Ex coll. Frederick Crawley; Prof William Hume-Rothery; Sotheby's, 26 March 2004, lot 124 (ill); Sotheby's, 25 November 2004, lot 177 (ill)
Private collection

102. Bellagio, Lake Como
(25 September 1835)
Ink
Inscr. in ink: Bellagio. Lago di Como
Ex coll. T. F. Taylor (1912); J. O. Woodward, presented 1949
LE 542
Ashmolean Museum, Oxford (WA.1949.252)

103. End of the Lake of Lecco
(September 1835)
Ink
Inscr. in ink: End of the lake of Lecco
Ex coll. T. F. Taylor (1912); J. O. Woodward, presented 1949
LE 543
Ashmolean Museum, Oxford (WA.1949.253)

104. Bergamo, and the Alps, from the Road to Brescia
(September 1835)
Ink
Inscr. in ink: Bergamo and the Alps from the road to Brescia
Ex coll. T. F. Taylor (1912); J. O. Woodward, presented 1949
LE 544
Ashmolean Museum, Oxford (WA.1949.254)

105. Near Bassano
(September 1835)
Ink
Inscr. in ink: Near Bassano. Brenner
Ex coll. T. F. Taylor (1912); J. O. Woodward, presented 1949
LE 545
Ashmolean Museum, Oxford (WA.1949.255)

106. Bellagio, Lake Como
(1836)
Watercolour
Ex coll. Brantwood (1912)
LE 183 (as 'from a sketch of the previous year')
Present location unknown

107. Lake Garda
(September 1835)
Pencil and bodycolour on grey-green paper
Inscr. in brown ink: Lago di Garda. J Ruskin / 1835
Ex coll. J. H. Whitehouse (by 1938)

LE 753
Ruskin Library, Lancaster (RF 1331)

108. Castelbarco tomb, Verona
1 October 1835
Pencil
Inscr.: St Anastasie. Verona; Verona; 3 (pencil; lower left); 1st Octr (in brown ink, lower left)
Ex coll. Brantwood (1912); Brantwood sale, 1931; J. H. Whitehouse (acquired 1933)
LE 2004
Ruskin Library, Lancaster (RF 1647)

109. Tombs of the Scaligers, Verona
(1–5 October 1835)
Ink, ink wash and bodycolour on blue-grey paper
Ex coll. Brantwood (1912); J. H. Whitehouse
LE 2005; LE vol. IX, Plate D
Ruskin Library, Lancaster (RF 1662)

110. Tombs of the Scaligers, Verona
(1–5 October 1835)
Pencil
Ex coll. Mrs Cunliffe (1912)
LE 2045 (as Tombs of the Scaligers, Verona, general view, sketch on the spot)
Present location unknown

111. The Tombs of the Scaligers, Verona
(1–5 October 1835 or after)
Ink and bodycolour
Inscr.: La Scala Monument, VERONA / J.R.
Ex coll. Robert E. Cunliffe; Mrs Cunliffe (1912); Guy C. Barton, presented 1963
LE 2046 (as The Tombs of the Scaligers, Verona, general view, the same redrawn); LE vol. XXXVI, plate II
Abbot Hall Art Gallery, Lakelands Arts Trust, Kendal, Cumbria (00279/63)

112. Ducal Palace and the Salute, Venice
(6–12 October 1835)
Ink; image within double ink lines
No inscription on drawing; Doge's Palace & Chiesa della Salute, Venice 1835 (verso of photo RF F 629) probably records former inscr.
Ex coll. F. Manson (1912)
LE 1868; LE vol. XXXV, plate VIII; RF F 629
Present location unknown

113. The Giant's Staircase, Ducal Palace, Venice
(6–12 October 1835)
Pencil
Ex coll. E. B. Knobel (1912)
LE 1873
Present location unknown

114. Piazzetta and St. Mark's, Venice
(6–12 October 1835)
Pencil
Inscr.: St Marks. Venice. No 1.; 2 (lower left)
Ex coll. Brantwood (1912); Charles E. Goodspeed
LE 1918
Smith College Museum of Art, Northampton, MA. Gift of Charles E. Goodspeed (SC 1950:20–3)

115. Part of St Mark's Church and Entrance to Doge's Palace, Venice
(6–12 October 1835)
Pencil and ink
Inscr.: Part of St Mark's Church and entrance to Doges Palace, VENICE; JR (pencil); JR (ink)
Ex coll. J. H. Whitehouse
Ruskin Library, Lancaster (RF 1055)

116. St Mark's Place, Venice
(6–12 October 1835)
Pencil
Ex coll. E. B. Knobel (1912)
LE 1973
Present location unknown

117. Fortresses in Tyrol, near Mals
(October 1835)
Pencil
Verso of no. 81, Tower and Fortress, Lenzburg
Inscr.: Fortresses Near Mals. TYROL J.R.
Ex coll. T. F. Taylor (1912); Charles Deering McCormick, Brooks McCormick and the Estate of Roger McCormick
LE 1092
Art Institute, Chicago (1970.1268R)

118. Church of St Rupert, Salzburg
(October 1835)
Pencil and bodycolour
Inscr: St Rupert's Church & Fountain, SALTZBURG
Ex coll. Robert E. Cunliffe; Mrs Cunliffe (1912); Guy C. Barton, presented 1963
LE 1477
Abbot Hall Art Gallery, Lakelands Arts Trust, Kendal, Cumbria (01136/73)

119. La Residence, Munich
(October/November 1835)
Pencil
Inscr.: La Residence, &c MUNICH; in brown ink: J Ruskin 1835
Ex coll. B. B. Macgeorge; J. H. Whitehouse (by 1929)
LE 1160
Ruskin Library, Lancaster (RF 960)

120. Pulpit at Munich
(October/November 1835)
Pencil
Inscr. recto: At Munich; verso: 1835
Ex coll. Brantwood (1912); Helen Gill Viljoen
LE 1161
Morgan Library, New York (Viljoen Box 2; 1974.49:148)

121. Houses and Cathedral Spire, Ulm
(October/November 1835)
Pencil and ink
Inscr. in ink: Old Houses and Cathedral Spire. / ULM ; From the a window of the Hotel de la Poste ; (in Joan Severn's hand) by John Ruskin
Ex coll. Brantwood (1912); Ina T. Campbell
LE 1767; LE vol. I, plate 1
Santa Barbara Museum of Art, California (Gift of the Estate of Ina T. Campbell, 1953.35.43)

122. Stiftskircke, Stuttgart
(October/November 1835)
Pencil
Inscr.: Der Stifts Kirch. STUTGARD.
Ex coll. T. F. Taylor (1912); J. H. Whitehouse (by 1938)
Probably LE 1604, as Stuttgart Cathedral
Ruskin Library, Lancaster (RF 1534)

Unidentified scenes

123. Alpine Scene with building
Pencil (paper watermarked 1833)
Inscr.: JR; verso (in Joan Severn's hand) Di Pa
Ex coll. Haddon C. Adams, bequeathed 1971
Ruskin Library, Lancaster (RF 2038)

124. Mountain Scene
Pencil
Inscr.: J Ruskin 1835 / signed 1880
Ex coll. Mrs M. Sanders
Kirklees Collection, Huddersfield Art Gallery (KLMUS 1985.23)

APPENDIX I

Poems[1]

[Verona][2]

THE moon is up, the heaven is bright
With righteous light, exceeding pure;
Verona's towers are dark or light,
With lustre insecure.
The Roman ruin[3] stands supreme,
And round about it walks the gleam,
And through the arches tall;
Half-bewildered, half afraid
To rescue from the solemn shade
The sculpture on the columns laid,
Or olive on the wall.

. . . .

The arches echo now no more
With the low groans of victim dying;
Or prisoned lion's famished roar
His human prey espying;
Or shout of those who came to see
With dryer[4] thirst of blood than he—
Or gladiator's cry,
Who struggles still with fitful tread.
Oh, blessed is the vanquishèd,
And honoured in his bloody bed
Whose fortune is—to die.

[*October.*]

1 These poems were all based on actual experience during the tour. David C. Hanson has pointed out that the poem first published *c.* October or November 1834 in *Friendship's Offering and Winter's Wreath for 1835* as 'Saltzburg' (opposite an engraving by E. Goodall, based on a drawing by W. Purser) was prompted solely by the drawing, as Ruskin had not then visited this city.

2 First printed in the Library Edition, where it is noted it was written on the back of a drawing of Guttanen (cat. 49) made on the 1835 tour. It is also noted: 'Ruskin was [at Guttanen] on August 24 [...] In the Visitors' Book of the Due Torri [Hotel] at Verona there is the following entry: "Oct. 2, 1835, Mr. and Mrs. Ruskin and family" (in the father's handwriting), and then in the mother's, "bien satisfaits."'

3 The Verona Arena, an amphitheatre built in AD 30.

4 'Fiercer' is erased.

Venice[5]

THE moon looks down with her benignant eyes
On the blue Apennine's exulting steep;
Many a large star is trembling in the skies,
Lifting its glory from the distant deep.
  How high the marble carved rocks arise,
Like to a lovely thought in dreamy sleep!
Along the weedy step and washen door
  The green and drowsy surges, moving slow,
Dash on the ancient, tesselated floor;
Or still, and deep, and clear, and coldly flow
Beside their columned banks and sculptured shore;
Or waken a low wailing, as in woe,
Where sleeps beneath the unbetraying water
The victim, unrevenged, of secret midnight slaughter.
  The palaces shine paly through the dark,
Venice is like a monument, a tomb.
  Dead voices sound along the sea; and hark,
Methinks, the distant battle's fitful boom!
Along the moonlit pavement of St. Mark
The restless dead seem flitting through the gloom.
  There, melancholy, walks,—the Doge's crown
High on his gleaming hair,—the warrior grey.
How passionless a chill has settled down
Upon the senator's brow! A fiery ray
Gleams underneath the bravo's stormy frown!
Who long ago have vanished, awake,
Now start together from the various grave,—
Live in the silent night, and walk the conscious wave.

[*October.*]

5 First published in *Poems* (1891) from MS. Book viii with the note: 'Intended for the "Journal of a Tour," and possibly written at Venice, October 16–17, 1835, or at any rate soon after.' Collingwood prints as a two-stanza poem, though a line divides them in the MS. This present text is based on that corrected in the Library Edition.

[The Invasion of the Alps][6]

THE forest boughs and leaves are still;
No sound disturbs the drowsy air;
Save upon yon crag-buttressed hill;—
A motley crowd is gathered there,
The young, the fearless, and the fair;
And the old man with gleaming hair.
And there is lifting of hands in prayer:
For the foe down their valley his army hath led,
Village and hamlet in ruin are[7] red:
Like a plague, through the night they passed o'er, leaving only
The desolate hearth, and the hall very lonely.

[*About December.*]

6 First published in *Poems* (1891), from MS. Book viii. The title is Collingwood's. The present text is from that corrected in the Library Edition.

7 Corrected in *Poems* (1891) from 'is' in the MS.

APPENDIX II

Other Literary Outcomes

(a) The Ascent of the St. Bernard, A Dramatic Sketch
(b) Chronicles of St. Bernard

Note: The Great St Bernard Pass is the third highest road pass in Switzerland. Connecting Martigny in the Swiss Canton of Valais to Aosta in Italy it is located on the ridge between the two highest summits of the Alps, Mont Blanc and Monte Rosa. The Hospice for travellers was founded in 1049 by Saint Bernard of Menthon and in 1835 occupied a building dating from 1560. It was inhabited and managed by Augustinian monks, the Congregation of Canons of the Great Saint Bernard, and was famous for the breed of dogs which helped in the rescue of endangered travellers. In May 1800, Napoleon Bonaparte led the greater part of his army and artillery, 40,000 men, through the pass during the Italian Campaign, on his way to defeat the Austrians at the Battles of Montebello and Marengo.

The Ruskins had visited the pass on their previous continental tour of 1833. In 1835 they travelled from and then back to Martigny from the 14 to 22 July. Ruskin would have read Rogers's poem, 'The Great St. Bernard' in *Italy*, where it is illustrated by two Turner vignettes. He himself made a drawing in 1835 of 'Mont Velan from the Hospice of St. Bernard' (Catalogue 22). He addressed a brief description from there in his rhyming letter To Richard Fall (see above) and described it later as 'a perfectly easy and accessible pass for horse and foot, through all the summer; not dangerous even in winter, except in storm; and from the earliest ages, down to Napoleon's, the pass chosen by the greatest kings, and wisest missionaries' (35.509).

(a) The Ascent of the St. Bernard[1]

A DRAMATIC SKETCH

DRAMATIS PERSONAE

MR. R. [the Author's Father].
MRS. R. [his Mother].
MISS R[ICHARDSON, his Cousin and Adopted Sister, Mary].[2]
MASTER R. [the Author].
SALVADOR [the Courier].[3]
ANN [the Nurse].[4]
MICHEL [a Mountaineer].
A Monk of the St. Bernard Augustinian monastery.
Guide, Drivers, Travellers, and Waiters.

SCENE I

The principal parlour of La G[rande Maison Poste] at Martigny. The window commands a view of Mont Velan.

MR. R.; MRS. R.; MISS R.; MASTER R.

MR. R. *walking up and down the room with the air of an Alexander about to conquer the world.* MRS. R. *leaning passively against a table, somewhat awed by the expectation of future dangers and difficulties.* MISS R. *fully occupied in reducing the contents of a small, black, knapsack-looking bundle to the smallest possible compass.* MASTER R. *Just about nothing at all.*

MASTER R. (*looking out of the window*).
The shadows on the mountain flanks
Are grey with morning haziness.

MR. R. *(impatiently).*
What can keep the char-a-banes?
Hang the fellow's laziness!

1 There are two manuscript copies on which Cook's text is based: a fair copy in MS I[A], as described by Cook in 2.530, which extends to the beginning of Scene 5 and is entitled 'A Visit to the Hospice of St. Bernard', supplemented by sections drawn from a draft in MS viii which are not included in the fair copy. The Library Edition notes: 'The scene is laid at La Grande Maison Poste, Martigny (Sc.1 and 2); on the St Bernard Road in the Gorge of the Drance, close to the Galerie de la Monaire (Sc.3); the inn at Liddes (Sc.4); the Plan de Proz (Sc.5); and the Hospice of St. Bernard (Sc.6). The time of the journey occupied one day.' The details of the Ruskins' ascent are given in the 1835 *Diary*, pp. 66–69.

2 Mary Richardson was Ruskin's cousin who came to live with his family at Herne Hill in 1828 when she was fourteen, on the death of her Perth mother, Aunt Jessie, and who remained with the family until her marriage in 1848.

3 Salvador: See Introduction, p. 3.

4 Ann: Anne Strachan, John's nurse, who accompanied Ruskin's parents from their marriage in Scotland, travelled with the family, and stayed with the family all her life.

MISS R. *(speculatively).*
They say it's cold, and wet enough to soak one;
I wonder if I'll need to put my cloak on.
MRS. R. *(peaceably).*
We'll see, my dear, in time; you'd better take it.
MISS R. I think it's very dusty.
MRS. R. Well, then, shake it.

[MISS R. *by some circular agitations of the article of dress, fills the room full of dust, and concludes the tying up of her bundle.*
Voices below the window.

SALVADOR *(angrily).*
Bringen sie den Pferden hier !
Kommen sie, ich sage!
Wollen sie uns bleiben hier
Alle diesem Tage?[5]
MASTER R. *(still looking out of the window).*
With many a range of mountain white
The Valais meets the morn ;
Through the still air on every height
Rings clear the goatherd's horn.
The Drance is deep, the Drance is bright;
With thousand foam-globes driving white
Fast and well his billows roll—
SALVADOR *(below the window).*
Sind sie schnell ! ja, das geht wohl.[6]

The rattling of one or more vehicles is heard. It ceases. MR. R. *puts his head out of the window: His eyebrows first rise and then sink ominously low.*

MR. R. *(angrily).*
SALVADOR, how can you bring
Such a shabby sort of thing?
MISS R. *(amazed).*
I declare,
How those dirty leathers swing
Here and there!
MR. R. *(much inflamed).*
And the mule, too
I'm no fool, to
Let myself be fleeced like that.
MISS R. *(astounded).*
Did you ever?

5 'Fetch the horse! Come on I say. Do you want us to stay here all day?'
6 'Be quick! Yes, that's good.'

MR. R. *(decidedly).*
I will never
Pay for such a beast as that.
MASTER R. *(expostulatively).*
Never mind! Let us go, for the day's getting brighter;
The Hospice is high on the mountain afar—
SALVADOR *(deprecating).*
I assure you Martigny can't show us a tighter
Or easier char.
MR. R. I say, Margaret, look here!
MRS. R. How can I tell, my dear?
MR. R. And that nuisance, that rattling,
I can't bear at all.
Could you ride in that thing?
MRS. R. *(putting up her glass).*
It looks very small.
SALVADOR *(pleadingly).*
Indeed, sir, you'll find it quite open and breezy;
Your feet are not crowded, the motion is easy.
Just try, sir; you'll know then;
You'll sit at your ease.
MR. R. *(relaxing).*
I suppose we must go, then?
MRS. R. *(Submissively).*
Oh, just as you please!
MR. R. *(conclusively; going).*
Come away, then; the day's very pleasant and sunny.
MASTER R. *(as they go out).*
Of all hitherto tried ways
I like to sit sideways—
Miss R. *(as she exit).*
I think one feels funny.

SCENE 2

The outside of the Inn at Martigny, a white, Italian-looking house. On one side, a Swiss covered bridge; on the other, the defile of the Drance, through which are seen the peaks of the higher Alps. Two chars-a-bancs waiting at the door.

ANN; SALVADOR; two char-a-banc DRIVERS.

ANN *(puffing).*
SALVADOR, pop in this parcel, pray.
(Oh dear! my lame leg!)
SALVADOR *(looking about him).*
We have got a fine day.

ANN *(looking at the vehicles).*

Why, SALVADOR, how do you think we shall go?
Those cherry-banks[7] will not take four in 'em.

SALVADOR No!
This for us; the young master perhaps will go in it:
We shall soon settle that; they'll be down in a minute.

[A sound is heard, somewhat resembling that which may be obtained by the discharge of a series of crackers. It increases,

SALVADOR *(to the char-driver).*
La diligence?
CHAR-DRIVER. Ce le soit.
SALVADOR. De Lyon?
CHAR-DRIVER. Je le crois.

[A heavily loaded diligence appears under the covered bridge. A petit morceau *of a French tailor stoops his head as he passes under the immense arch. The horses turn beautifully. They slide up to the door almost on their haunches. The progressiue motion of the mountain behind at last ceases.*

ANN *(admiringly).*
Well, to be sure, how handy
They go!
A VOICE FROM THE DILIGENCE-TOP.
I say! bring me some brandy
Et d'eau,

[This summons, being not immediately understood, is not immediately obeyed.

SECOND VOICE. Superbe ! quelles montagnes !
THIRD VOICE. Sie sind lieblicher, ich mein?[8]
SECOND VOICE. Je descendrai; bien,—oui, donnez la main.
ANN (yawning).
I wish they would come!
SALVADOR (stretching). I wish they would go!
DILIGENCE-DRIVER (to his horses).
Êtes-vous fatigués? avez-vous faim ?
Vous déjeunerez bientôt.

[Exit, into the inn.

FIRST VOICE (on the top).
That one can't get one's wittles,
It is such a bore:—
I won't go travelling
Never no more.

7 char-a-bancs. The first of Ann's continual malapropisms.
8 'They are lovelier, aren't they?'

Enter from the door of the inn, MISS R. *and* MASTER R.

MISS R. (*with uplifted hands*).
What a high diligence!
MASTER R. *(theoretically)*.
Wonder it don't dispense
—As might prophesy prudent fears—
Passengers by the ears.

[*Enter from the stables the diligence-driver. He has an immense brown loaf, of the shape, size, density, and digestibility of a millstone, hanging round his left arm; his right hand grasping a* couteau *of proportionate dimensions. He insinuates himself dextrously among the legs of the four horses, administering a slice to each in its turn.*

DILIGENCE-DRIVER. Ah mes chers chevaux!

[*Observing one to have finished his slice before the proper period for so doing.*

Ne mangez-vous de trop !
Pourquoi, dites-moi, prenez-vous tant,—
Plus que les autres? Vous êtes un gourmand.
MISS R. How kind! well, it puts our postillions to shame.
DILIGENCE-DRIVER (*kissing them all round*).
Bons chevaux! beaux chevaux!
VOICE FROM THE TOP.
Comment il les aime !

Enter from the hotel, MR. R. and MRS. R.

SALVADOR. This way, ma'am,
I pray, ma'am ;
Take care of that puddle.
Not wet, ma'am ?
Now step, ma'am,
MRS. R. (*antipathetically*).
'Twill be such a huddle! .
Indeed I can't go, dear;
I'll be squeezed so !
MR. R. Oh, no fear!
Indeed, you won't find it
Uneasy; don't mind it.
My dear, it looks strange to be standing so long so;
Pray get in.
MRS. R. Very well. Let me see, where will John go?
MR. R. With them, in the other. What, cannot you trust
Him there?
MRS. R. I would rather he would not.
MR. R. Indeed, dear, he must.

MRS. R. (*getting in*).
Take care!
MR. R. Now, quick, Mary; jump in!

[MISS R. *does so, actively; thereby nearly upsetting* the char.

MRS. R. (*much squeezed*).
My dear, what a thump in—
MR. R. Now, how does the door close?
MISS R. See here, sir, it shuts on
This bit of a brass thing.
MR. R. (*getting in*). Well, fasten the button.
SALVADOR. Vous voila. C' est charmant !
Tout est pret: en avant !

[*They drive off*: MASTER R, SALVADOR, *and* ANN *jump into the other* char, *and it follows.*

SCENE 3

A rough, stony, steep and narrow Alpine road, in the defile of the Drance, bordered on one side by a tremendous precipice, beneath which is seen the Drance; on the other by tall rocks, through which runs a long gallery. A fountain springing from them flows over the road, which is seen lower down winding among the hills. The tower of Martigny in the distance; on the other side, Mont Velan.

Enter MICHEL.

MICHEL. The path on the mountain
Is toilsome and steep;
White gurgles the fountain,
Cold, pleasant and deep;
Where, forth from the dark stone,
The clear waters leap:
And many a bright spark thrown
Gems the flowerets beside,
And the moss you may mark, shown
Far 'near the deep tide.
Where green as Egyptia's gem[9]
Grass groweth wide—
Fit couch for my tired limb—
And high crags hang o'er me,
Will I sit, and see, like a dream
Beauty before me. [*Sitting down.*
How the high sun hath lent
To Mont Velan his glory!
And bright hues are blent

9 The emerald, first mined in Egypt and associated with Cleopatra.

Like the tall tempest-bow,
Whose broad iris is bent
Over worlds far below;—
So rich colours rest on
The surface of snow,
That lies the hill-crest on
For ever and aye;
That his ribbed crags are pressed on
And shut from the dav,
By garment most beautiful
Brilliant and gay.
And the Drance' bed is full
As when, just at his height,
By thick snow from the hill
He was checked in his might.
Well must be remembered
That terrible night,
When first was dismembered
The ice in an hour,
And, shattering, surrendered
Free path for the power
Of the river to flow by.
I stood by the tower
That was built long ago by
The armies of Rome;
And well might I know, by
The light through the gloom
That the floating ice gave,
That a merciless doom
Had descended on all I had died but to save,—
And I cursed the cold waters, and envied their grave.

[Two char-a-bancs *appear, winding along the mountain-road in the distance, coming up from Martigny. They disappear at intervals, finally entering from the gallery.* MR. R., MRS. R., MISS R., MASTER R., *and* SALVADOR *walking up the hill before them;* ANN *riding.*

MISS R. Dear me, what a place is this!

ANN (*in horror*)

Gracious, what a precipice!

MRS. R. (*pityingly*).

How the poor mules can climb here
I cannot divine, dear!

MR. R. (*enraptured*).

What a view!

SALVADOR We can stop here, sir,

If you desire it;
'Tis a sweet little spot here, sir,
Whence to admire it.

[*They all arrest their progress; some sitting, some standing, in admiration; except* MRS. R., *who exit, marching steadily round the rock,* en avant.

MASTER R. What a bit in the distance! Oh, SALVADOR, fetch here
My things from the carriage; I'd so like a sketch here.
MR. R. What nonsense! Be quiet; you can't have your book,—
Disturbing the luggage! Sit still here and look.
MASTER R. (*much subdued*).
Oh, I only wished, just—in a—sort of a way—
'Twould be such a picture!
MR R. It would not; you could not
Express these fine mountains; besides, sir, you should not
Be thinking of nothing but drawing all day!
MASTER R. (*giving up the point*).
How the far-spreading forest most gloomily fills
The vales at the base of these iron-bound hills!
MISS R. (*complainingly*).
I must take off my shoe! I have let stones and dust in,
And they do hurt my foot so!
SALVADOR (*looking round*). Why, where's Mrs. Ruskin?
MR. R. One never knows where she goes: where can she be?
SALVADOR. I think she's gone on, sir.
MR. R. We'll go then, and see.

[*They all exeunt in a hurry*].

MICHEL (*alone*). There they go!
Day after day these loungers through the world,
Mounted on mules, and muffled up in cloaks,
Mince through the patches of the summer snow,—
Crowd round the fire, or shiver to the lake,—
Eat up the provend of the Augustines,
And crawling down, declare they've dared the dangers
And storms of the St. Bernard.
And these youths
Come with their pencils, stumbling up our paths,
Scratching down semblances of mountain-tops—
Of our own mountains! Would the hills had souls,
That they might crush these emmets, who pass by
Tracing these most ignoble portraitures
Of our free Ice-bergs![10]

10 Compare Wordsworth's 'The Brothers, a Pastoral Poem':

These Tourists, Heaven preserve us! needs must live

But the toppling sun
Hath past the kulm[11] of heaven. I will go.

[*Exit.*

SCENE 4

A passage in the small Swiss inn at Liddes, from which open two doors, one into a parlour, the other into a table-d'hote. *In the parlour,* MR. R., MRS. R., MISS R., MASTER R., *seated round a table, on which smoke boiled mutton, veal chops, fried potatoes, etc., etc., busily employed, with mountainous appetites, in discussing the same. In the* table-d'hôte, *two English gentlemen, and a lady : Swiss, Frenchmen, Germans, and people from all parts of the world, sitting, eating, reading, lounging, waiting. At the end of the passage appears the kitchen, containing various instruments of cookery, and issuing many savoury smells. A fine blazing fire on the hearth, before which lies a large St. Bernard dog. Voices behind the scenes.*

ANN *(in a hesitating tone).*
What! through the kitchen?
SALVADOR. Yes, just by there.

Enter ANN *through the kitchen, stumbling over the dog.*

ANN *(much amazed).*
Bless the beast! what makes him lie there?

[BERNADO *gets up, sleepily and after a long yawn, and and longer stretch, goes up, shaking his ears, to* SALVADOR, *as an old acquaintance.*

ANN. There's a monster! What an ear!
Send the fum dy chamber[12] here. *(To the cook.)*

[Exit into another room.

ENGLISH LADY (*in* table-d'hôte).
How shall I be best able
To get myself seated?
MRS. R. (*to* MR. R.).
My dear, that's detestable!
How can you eat it?
These unwholesome made dishes

A profitable life: some glance along
Rapid and gay, as if the earth were air.
And they were butterflies to wheel about
Long as their summer lasted; some, as wise,
Upon the forehead of a jutting crag
Sit perch'd with book and pencil on their knee,
And look and scribble, scribble on and look,
Until a man might travel twelve stout miles,
Or reap an acre of his neighbour's corn. (1–10)

11 hill: a German toponym.
12 femme-de-chambre: chamber maid.

Are the worst things for you.
MR. R. These chops are delicious;
Just try one,-pray do.
MRS. R. *(warming).*
That sheep's been a tough thing,
And not fit to boil.
Potatoes! they're nothing
But ashes and oil.
MR. R. My dear, it's odd so to say.
AN ENGLISH SHAM CHAMOIS-HUNTER *(stumping out of the* table-d'hôte *with crook, pike, etc.,* a la Suisse).
Où est mes côtelets?
ENGLISH LADY. There's a party just mounting, see!
Oh, I'm so frighted
Lest on the mountain we
Should be benighted!
FIRST ENGLISH GENTLEMAN (*to waiter*).
Portez dîner
WAITER (*all alive, exit-ing*).
Oh oui, monsieur, oui, oui, oh oui !
FIRST VOICE (*louder*). Et notre.
SECOND VOICE (*louder*). Et notre.
THIRD VOICE (*roaring*). Et notre, aussi.

[*Waiter stands stilt in an* embarras.

SECOND ENGLISH GENTLEMAN. There, don't shilly-shally ;
Go! get along! ally!

[*Exit waiter, and enter* SALVADOR, *in a hurry.*

SALVADOR. Now, ma'am, may I order
The mules?
MRS. R. Of what sort are
Those beasts, SALVADOR? for
I never can bear to
Permit Master John there to
Ride a broken-kneed mule. You
Know he makes it a rule to
Look everywhere,—anywhere,—
Never take any care.
I hope that the guide'll
Lead his horse by the bridle.
SALVADOR. The mules are so steady, ma'am !
Now are you ready, ma'am ? [*Exit.*
MASTER R. *(enthusiastically).*
I love, as the sun sets,

Mid snow-wreaths to wend up
The hill.

MISS R. (*yawning*).
Dear, *how* sleepy one gets!

MR. R. (*calling down the passage*).
And, SALVADOR, send up
The bill.

[*Enter from the kitchen, a moving cumulus, composed of hats, bonnets, great-coats, cloaks, tippets, furs, muffs, snow-shoes, and other habiliments. It approaches. Under it appears* ANN.

MASTER R. I think I'll make a sonnet on
The scenery around.

ANN. Ma'am, will you put your bonnet on?
The mules are coming round.

[*She deposits the greater part of her load on a side table.*

MISS R. (*subtracting her bonnet from the bundle*).
How you've crushed it! Where's the glass?

ANN (*investigating*).
There, in the corner.

MRS. R. (*advancing to the angle of reflection*).
Let me pass.

MISS R. My face is quite flat, look!
What a bad glass! They've cracked it.

MR. R. (*abstracting another portion from the mass*).
And you've squeezed up my hat, look!
How badly you've packed it.

[*A pause during which the operations of wrapping up continue and the heap of habiliments gradually decreases. Enter regiments of dishes, supported by regiments of waiters. They proceed into the* table-d'hôte. *The tables are occupied, and the company actively so.* BERNARDO *has followed the waiters, and approaches the first table.*

FIRST ENGLISH GENTLEMAN. A guest is come to share our feast.
ENGLISH LADY. Oh la! I cannot bear the beast.

[*As* BERNARDO *approaches, she jumps off her chair. The dog turns indignantly away from the quarter where he perceives his company is not requested, and makes the round of the tables, now and then receiving, with much dignity, the donation of a spare bit fat.*

ENGLISH LADY (*over the table*).
Now, have done with those chops,
For these long forenoon stops
Keep us always so late.
I am sure, if we wait
Get to the place there, we
Shall be all overtaken
By night. Leave that bad bacon!

ENGLISH GENTLEMAN. Don't get in a foment!
I'm coming this moment.
There, put on your things.
These same chops are fine things.
MISS R. Now, where's my tippet? 'I'is below such
A heap.
That thing you cannot ride in.

Enter SALVADOR, *accoutred. for the journey.*

SALVADOR. I've brought the bill, sir.
MR. R. Dinner,—so much,—
I'm glad they've put the mules and guide in.
Why, Ann, you've pushed my bows aside in
Your hurry. Look! they're out of shape.
There, smooth my collar; dust my cape.

[MISS R. *occupies herself in setting to rights the crooked bows, by certain peculiar dextrous twirls of the finger and thumb, whereby edges are pulled out, and rotundities pushed in.*

MASTER R. Oh, dont be ill at ease about
The little rout that Ann makes;
They'll blown be by the breeze about
Till they're as flat as pancakes.
ENGLISH GENTLEMAN (*finishing the last cutlet, and jumping up*).
Waiter, waiter! Kitchen-wench!
ENGLISH LADY. Dear, why don't you call in French ?
They'll never understand you thus.
ENGLISH GENTLEMAN. Garcon, veny !
Ain't there any
Body to attend to us? [*Enter waiter*
ENGLISH GENTLEMAN. Portez ici notre compte, et
Les chevaux; nous voulons monter.
MR. R. (*to* SALVADOR).
You'll pay the waiters. That will do.
I'm ready: Margaret, are you?
MRS. R. Yes. Mary is not: she is apt enough
To take some time.
(*To* MISS R.) You are not wrapped enough.
MISS R. Me ! ! ma'am, I'm sure I never keep you waiting.
Just wait a minute ;—oh, we shan't be late in—
ENGLISH GENTLEMAN (*to waiter who enters with the bill*).
Nommez vous ce
Diner? Tout ce
Que nous venons
Manger n' est qu' un
Cotelet seul, et
C' etait tout brulé.

Vous essayez
Me faire payer
Pour ce vin de table—
Qui est miserable—
eux francs! deux francs!
Et je ne peux d'en
Boire.

WAITER. Tous les Anglais, quand ils l'ont
Goutés, ont dits qu'il est bon.

GENTLEMAN. Bon! Ce nest que du vinaigre !
Et comment ce so pe si maigre
Est-il chargé la si haut ?
Ce n'est, je vous dis, que de I'eau ?

MISS R. Oh, here come the horses! Did ever *you* see
Such old dirty saddles?

MRS. R. That can't be for me.

ANN. And here is some more, ma'am.

SALVADOR. They're all at the door, ma'am. *[Clock strikes three.*

MISS R. There's three o'clock, I do declare.

MRS. R. It cannot be so much already.
Now, John, in mounting do take care.

MR. R. *(preparing to go).*
Don't slip your foot ; this wooden stair
Is broken, rotten, and unsteady.
Don't be in a hurry, for
If you——

MRS. R. Mary, aren't you ready?

MARY *(scampering down the passage, with her half-tied bonnet flying in the rear).*

What is all the scurry for? [*Exeunt.*

SCENE 5

A wide, stony, and desolate plain among the mountains, surrounded by dark and bare peaks, haf-covered with cloud. The Drance, now diminished to a mere torrent foams among the rocks which lie scattered in the foreground. A slight vestige of a path among the stones and turf, which zigzags to the summit of a huge rock on the left, turns sharply round its overhanging top, and disappears. Immense sweeps of snow on the flanks of the mountains, which descend into the plain, crossing the mule-path in some places; in others forming precarious bridges over the torrent of the Drance, whose dark waters have worn away beneath them. In front, the plain is compressed into a dark and silent gorge, running up among the mountains, and hidden in mist and cloud.

Enter ANN, *on mule, with* GUIDE *leading.*

ANN. Well, after this! Oh, dear, I'm so vexed!
I'm sure, I wonder where we'll go next.

This rain and mist 'ull wet us through;
This is such an uneasy seat.
I say, man, whippy le chivell, do! (*to the guide*).
It don't alley veat.

[*Enter the cavalcade.* MASTER R. *with straw hat peculiarly turned up, a* la *parson; Looking curiously at every stone that his mule kicks.* MRS. R. *looking wondrous blue.* MR. R. *spurring up, fast and fearless. On the remaining mule, a cloak and bonnet, recognisable for* MISS R.'s, *out of which at top peeps a little red nose.*

MR. R. Well, this is very fine.
ANN (*aside*). I han't
An idea what they'll show us up here.
VOICE FROM THE NOSE. It's late: I'm half afraid we shan't
Have any sort of tea or supper.
MASTER R. It darkens on us fast to-night,
I think we'll have to race for it.

[*Mule stumbles: he looks down.*

There! there is some chiastolite ;
I thought this looked the place for it.
Guide, donnez-moi ce gros pierre.
MRS. R. There are some Alpine roses there,
Just by the snow; if 'tis not wet,
I really wish the guide could get
A bunch or two. I'd like to pack
Them in my pocket-almanack.
I think if they were stuck with some
Cement or other, glue or gum,
If I could make a small collection,
They'd be a pleasant recollection. [*Looking about her.*
Where are the people going to take us?
My dear, they can't intend to make us
Climb up those rocks! Do stop the guide:
We've lost our way. John cannot ride —
MR. R. (*as his mule scrambles up the rocks*).
We haven't time to walk; we must
Get safely in before it's dusk.
MASTER R. (*as* MRS. R.'s *and his own mules follow*).
Long-eared brutes although they be,
When you climb the cliffy scar,
Mules they are the best by far—
A most sagacious sort of brute,
Quick of eye and firm of foot.
Well the beast that I'm astride on
Knows to nose his way, nor slide on

Polished rock or faithless snow.
This is pleasant sort of riding;
Better knows he where to go
Than the guide can guide him.
Lay the reins upon his neck;
Where he chooses let him step;
He will take you safely so.

GUIDE *(to* ANN).
Voulez-vous des fleurs?

ANN *(indignant).*
Leave off your gibberish; I was near off!
This beast will have me quite and clear off.

GUIDE. N'ayez pas peur;
Si vous ne craignez rien
Vous irez bien.

MASTER R. Did you look up the valley where
There was a little light then
Shone through the dark and misty air?
I think I saw the Hospice there.

MR. R. *(laconically).*
You saw things out of sight, then.

MASTER R. This mica all is brown and murky;
There is some as black as ink. [*They come towards the snow.*
There! There's pink snow! I've heard it said
That on this pass 'twas often red.

MRS. R. Why's John making all that stir? I
Hope the mules won't sink.

MR. R. Why, the snow's a little dirty,
And he calls it pink.

MASTER R. Bluely bends the snowy bridge
O'er the Drance's sullen sweep,—

ANN *(to* GUIDE). Are you allying on the nige?
La! I wonder if it's deep. [*Soliloquizing.*]
Where can we be going to sleep?
I am sure there cannot be here
Any sort of town or inn!
What can master want to see here?
Oh, that I were down agin!

[*They leave the snow and wind up the rock.*

MR. R. (*appearing on the turn at the summit*).
This is ugly. Mind you, all,
Here there is no sort of wall.
Margaret—that's well: now, John, you:—
Mary—gently ; —that will do.

SALVADOR. Now, sir, one more stretch of snow
Then we have not far to go.

[*Exeunt.*

SCENE 6

The great dining-mom of the St. Bernard ; at one end a hearth with a fire equal to those which used to be kindled by old English squires when an ox was to be roasted whole on Christmas Day. At the other end, barred and double-barred shutters exclude the tempest which is heard whistling without. A long table runs through the whole length of the hall, round which appear seated two St. Bernard MONKS, *busily occupied in carving for the multitude,* MR R., MRS. R., MISS R., MASTER R., ENGLISH LADY *and* GENTLEMAN, *he of the pike, a vivacious French old* LADY *of quality, her young daughter, and other miscellaneous characters to the number of eighteen.*

MR. R. Here is all one can desire:
After riding such a way,
In such a place, on such a day,
One is glad to feel the fire.
ENGLISH GENTLEMAN. May I trouble you to pass this?
'Tis a very fine ragout.
MR. R. *(to the* MONK).
Pray, sir, is such weather as this
Quite a common thing with you?
MONK. Sir, we seldom have, if ever,
Pleasanter or milder weather.
We have a sunny day and clear
About a dozen times a year.[13]
Sometimes, ere his race is run,
We in the morning see the sun;
But what of that? Our peaks so proud
Are rendezvous for rain and cloud.
The vapour comes ;—our mountain-wall
Within its chasm doth bind it here;
So, if there is a cloud in all
The aether, you will find it here.
And beautiful it is to us,—

13 The Library Edition notes: 'In the MS. the following fragment of prose description immediately precedes this dramatic sketch: There were sweet sounds mingled with my dreaming, and a thousand airy orbs of moving coloured light floated around me, and a bright shower of silvery light fell upon me, and I started and looked up. It was cold, very cold, and the crisp ice of the July morning shot its long fleecy crystals over the narrow window. Break the veil away, and look out. There was no sunshine — the Augustines have not a perfectly clear day twelve times in the year — yet the landscape was dazzling white with broad sheets of pure summer snow that clung to the rugged crags as if it loved them, and grew broader and deeper and whiter as it climbed up into the clouds through which it shone like a flood of sunlight, while the tall steep crags that rose forth of it past away into the grey mist.'

As beautiful as rare,—
When all the clouds that pass us by
Melt into beautiful blue sky
And crystal mountain-air.
And every flower and every herb,
That now lie shivering and low
Upon their beds of driven snow,
Spread forth their leaflets wide,
Lift up their heads, their blossoms show,
And deck the mountain-side
With hues like sunset red.

FRENCH LADY. Superbe !

MISS R. John, you've splashed me!

MASTER R. Well, don't frown so.

MISS R. I wish you would not spoil my gown so.
Look, what a mess! I'll have to call up
Ann: you've made such a splutch[14] of it.
I wish you'd sup your gravy all up,
And not give me so much of it.

ENGLISH GENTLEMAN. When the Alps were crossed by Bownapartey,
Pray, sir, wa'rnt it at this part he
Took his army over?

MONK. Here along the mountain wild
Half his army fast defiled.
Night sank before the half had crossed,
And from the fortress of Aoste
Up through the gloom the firing came
In lambent sheets of lurid flame.
The fitful flame extended, and the wide expanse
Reddened the sky between the stars, and smote
Upon each soldier's wearied countenance,
Where many wild and strange emotions float;
With some, along the mountains many a league,
Enthusiasm battled with fatigue;
Some on the cold and lifeless snow were lying,
Some dreaming in their sleep, some dead or dying,
Or ceased their weary step with languid eye,
And laid them down to sleep, and slept to die.

14 A large mess.

(b) Chronicles of St. Bernard[15]

I

INTRODUCTORY

A NIGHT AT LE HOSPICE

IT was a delicious day in the beginning of July, when after a laborious climb I gained the highest ridge of the pass of the Great St. Bernard, and stood beside the celebrated Hospice. The outside of this building is remarkable for little except its ponderous strength; and frequent descriptions of it have made it familiar to every reader. As I ascended the high steps which afford access to the elevated door, I was received and welcomed by one of the good monks, with whom I had become acquainted on a previous expedition;[16] and who will be remembered with gratitude, affection, and respect, by everyone who has had an opportunity of intercourse with him, however short, or who has afforded an opportunity to him of exercising his overflowing benevolence.

Two of the dogs, the oldest, were as usual beside him. They appear to consider it incumbent upon them to do the honours of the house to every traveller, and express their welcome with look and gesture in the true spirit of hospitality. The dogs of St. Bernard are perhaps the most efficient humane society in the world. I patted the enormous head of the largest, and he lifted up his dark eye, with a singular expression—marvellous sad, I thought; it was not exactly philosophical, it was not a reasoning light, but a kind of calm melancholy—as if the animal was in the habit of feeling deeply. — It might be fancy. "That dog has saved eight human beings," said the monk. I looked at him again, but reverentially, poor fellow; his very walk was noble, grave—I would that I had done as much, thought I.

When the monk had shown me my room, he offered to walk round the lake with me to the site of the ancient Temple. He led me through some low vaulted passages, and opened a back door towards the lake. How glorious was the burst of landscape, the narrow green water lay as on the bosom of the hills, still, so still, looking up to the bright clear heaven with its steadfast eye, and the eternal snows that glittered on its borders sloped down underneath the pure green waves. High on the left rose from its borders the crags of Mont Mort, looking black among the fields of silver which were scattered among them, and beyond in enormous peaks and jagged precipices rose a chain of red and bare Alps, so precipitous that the snow could not cling to them, though It lay between them and at their base in brilliant and dazzling sheets, and here and there on some more bulky summit lifted itself up against the infinite blue of the heaven that arched over all without a single cloud,

15 Cook's text is based on the MS, *Early Prose Writings*, held in the Rare Books Manuscript Collection, Princeton University Library. The framework may have been influenced by Sir Walter Scott's *Chronicles of the Canongate*, First Series, 1827 (short stories); Second Series, 1828 (novel: *St. Valentine's Day, or, The Fair Maid of Perth*).

16 The tour of 1833.

looking like the unfathomable depth of a transparent ocean. Far down the valley glittered the snowy crests of the mountains of Cormayeur.

The monk stood beside me; he did not speak: long as he had resided here, often as his eyes had gazed upon this very view, aye, even until the solitude lay wearily upon his soul, he still felt how glorious was that landscape, how beautiful was the silence of its loveliness.

At length we past on, and drew near a French party who were standing on the edge of the water. As we approached we heard an old lady very voluble in her admiration. "Que cela est superbe, quel air pure et frais, que! ciel bleu, quel séjour delicieux." "Ah," said the monk. I understood the volume expressed in the word, for I had been at the Hospice, if not in another season, It least in different weather. We walked on. "The French," said my companion, "speak always from the impulse of the moment. Had this summer wind been the least cold, she would have said (quel temps vilain, quel séjour horrible."

The rocks on the shore of the small lake seem full of a life in death; over the cold grey stone, beside the lifeless beds of the pale snow, that clasps it in its chilly arms for ever, grew the wild bright beautiful flowers, the laughing blossoms looking silently up from their desert couch to the cold air, lightening in the darkness of the fearful solitude like pleasant dreams in a life of misery, like the gentle smile on the lips of the dead. They will only live here ; they must be kissed by the keen wind, rooted on the bare rock, bedewed by the evening cloud, as it rolls along their valley, and buried under the deep snow, or they will die; they reminded me of the strange gladnesses, the tearful joys, that are known only to the broken heart and the desolate spirit.

Off scampered the dogs to the snow, four of them at least, the fifth following with his stately step, and joining in the gambols of the younger, much with the air of a philosopher, who though engaged in meditations on the vanity of life, is not above contributing to the amusement of those whose years are not yet top heavy, who are less wise, and more merry. Two frolicsome puppies pulled his ears unmercifully, and rolled him over and over on the snow, which is to the St. Bernard's dog what the soft hearthrug is to a ladies' lap-dog: the scene of all its enjoyment.

When you have reached the site of the Roman temple, the distant though narrow prospect is suddenly opened; you surmount the ridge which confines the waters of the little lake and look down a sweep of bare but turfy valley, with immense slopes of mountain rising sheer up on either side, around which winds the mule-path to Aosta, looking much like a whip lash of enormous length, whirled out by the arm of a giant; far down the green vista the pines begin to appear jagged and stunted, struggling against the coldness of the air, and among them the glittering roofs of the chalets of St. Remy. To avoid the immense circuit made by the mule-path road in descending, there is a steep foot-path up the almost perpendicular crags of Mont Mort, which takes you straight up to the level of the lake, but which had much better be avoided by all travellers whose feet are not thoroughly accustomed to mountain climbing. The monk's practised eye soon discerned a gentleman on the path apparently in the act of illustrating the proverb that the farthest way about is the nearest way home. It was pretty evident that he had got into that very disagreeable state of fixture from which nervousness prevents your advance, and impossibility your return, and in which, however beautiful the prospect, however agreeable. your situation, or however elegant your attitude, a person becomes peculiarly sensible of the delights of change. A pause ensued of some ten minutes of no small interest to us, and apparently of no small inconvenience to him, at the end of which the monk was about to hurry to his assistance, since, had he slipped his foot through fear or accident, he might have had a disagreeable slide, roll, or tumble of about a thousand feet into the valley; but before the good monk had advanced far the object of his solicitude seemed to take heart of grace, and disengaged himself from his disagreeable position, dislodging at the same time a mass of stone of considerable size, which, as it crashed, thundered, and bounded down the mountain side, fifty feet at a leap, dashing showers of fragments off the stones which it encountered in its descent, showed clearly how very inconvenient it would be for any thing or person of softer material to descend in the same manner. Our friend, once unfixed, was now rapidly approaching us, a young Englishman, as we soon discerned by step, air, and countenance; he was equipped as pedestrian travellers in Switzerland usually are, in the loose dress of thin Holland, which, confined only by a leathern belt at the waist, allows the arms and legs a delightful freedom of movement; the knap-sack at his back and the strong but light pole, terminated at one end by a strong polished chamois horn, and at the other by that iron spike whose inestimable utility can only be known to Swiss travellers, completed his equipment; with the exception of a kind of pannier, dependent from the belt at the waist, and something like a barber's apron, whose ponderous and rattling swing at once explained the gentleman's choice of the precipitous short cut, as it proclaimed itself full of those worthless and ugly bits of chucky stains, which, dignified with the name of "specimens," become in the eyes of a certain class of people of such inestimable value. He also bore a hammer in his right hand, which might, in the hands of a giant of the olden time, have become the terror of all the adventurous knights who ventured within reach of its swing.

"That appears a difficult path, sir," said I, as he came up.

"Horrid, sir, horrid. Loose shale—partial state of decomposition—rocks defoliating in the direction of the cleavage."

"You seemed to have got into a difficult situation at one point."

"Awkward, sir, awkward—very awkward."

"What a thunderbolt you sent into the valley. How it dashed the rocks to pieces, like a single hero overwhelming an army. How the roar of the fall rose along the mountains."

"Quartzose rock imperfectly crystallized—very hard—good specimen— sorry I lost it."

"Rather too large for carriage though, except on its own legs," said I. (It was a mass about four feet square.)

"Ah—yes—inconvenient," replied my companion, as we regained the mule-path.

"Much better road this," said I; "'tis pleasant to get on it again."

"Ah — yes—very solid—all gneiss."

"Very nice," said I, not clearly understanding him.

"'Gnn-eiss,' I said, sir" responded the knight of the hammer rather gruffly, "primitive rock,—all hard."

"Oh! I beg your pardon—yes," and a pause ensued.

As we gained the highest point of the ridge the monk turned and bade us look back to the mountains of Cormayeur. A few rosy clouds were scattered on the heaven, or wrapped about their bases, but their summit rose pure and glorious, just beginning to get rosy in the afternoon sun, and here and there a red peak of bare rock rose up into the blue out of the snowy mantle. "How beautiful," said I to my companion; "those peaks of rock rise into the heaven like promontories running out into the deep, deep blue of some transparent ocean."

"Ah—yes—brown, limestone—strata vertical, or nearly so, dip eighty-five and a half," replied the geologist.

"And those clouds," continued I, "look how they pass over the infinite heaven, like pleasant thoughts rising out of the serenity of a beautiful mind. Now, they are congregating in that chasm on the mountain; see, they seem to clasp the rugged rocks lovingly—"

"Singular fault in the beds there—saw it yesterday," remarked my companion, "much distortion—ripe vein—iron pyrites and zinc — that's the reason it attracts the clouds."

"Probably," said I.

"Certainly, sir," said he.

"Yes," said the Father; "there is a storm gathering; we had better walk on towards the Hospice."

As we passed the site of the temple I pointed the pale pink starry flowers out to my companion. "Look," said I, "how they smile upon the green and yellow melancholy of that cold heartless stone."

"O—ah, quartz in veins and nests—half crystallized—cavities inside, probably — let's see."

Crash, went the merciless hammer, and down went, overwhelmed in the ruin, a lovely cluster of my poor flowers. I have them yet, their corpses at least, for their soul is gone.

Another awkward pause ensued; it was broken by the monk. "At the foot of the short cut which you took, sir," he said, "is the spot where some years ago a brother of St. Bernard and a domestic perished by an avalanche, while assisting some travellers; their bodies were swept down to the valley below and were not found till the ensuing summer."

"Oh, horrid, horrid, whereabouts?" replied the man of stone.

"Just at the foot of the path, there is a small cross—there under a large projecting rock."

"Oh—ah I remember—zigzag crystallization—black scharl, and brown mica,—chlorite, inside—hey—very fine specimen—knocked a bit off," Another long pause, until the monk, finding that nothing else would do, took him on his own ground, and they entered into a mineralogical discussion on the St. Bernard, which lasted till we arrived at L'Hospice.

When we reached the ridge of the pass, and looked down on the Swiss side, we beheld the heaven below us, for the horizon was far below us, charged with heavy masses of thundercloud; they strode up the valley, paused a minute beneath Mont Velan, then wreathed him in their dense masses in an instant, like volumes of smoke coming up from some vast conflagration, and then burst down upon us, filling the ravine with fire at every flash, and chastising the waves of the quiet lake with billows of mingled wind and water. I watched it some time from the window of my room; and on its abatement, descended to the public room, just in time to witness the arrival of a French lady and gentleman, who had ascended, a little too late in the day, from Martigny.

The monk was escorting the couple to their room, quite in silence—they could not speak from terror, vexation, and fatigue; you might as well have expected articulation from a half-drowned cat. I stood aside on the landing- place to let them pass; as they walked upstairs the water ran down from them downstairs in two streams, as if they had been two walking umbrellas that had been up all day in a south rain, and the lady's dress hung on her like the rags on a mop just dipped into the bucket. I longed to give her a circumgyration. I thought they might have shaken themselves a little before they came upstairs. The good monk would certainly have to bucket the water out of their room. I slipped downstairs as I would have passed two Newfoundland dogs, just emerging from the water, before they have given themselves the dextrous disencumbering shake, and, finding nobody in the public room, sauntered into the chapel; like an ass, the mineralogist was there before me. I found him standing before the monument of Desaix.[17]

"Beautiful monument that," said I, determining to endeavour to draw him into something like conversation.

"Oh—ah—yes—Carrara, I think, isn't it?"

"I don't know the sculptor's name—not Canova, I think," said I hesitatingly.

"Carrara marble—I say, sir, carbonate of lime, cream white, inclining to snow white—lustre slight, waxy, glimmering—owing to imperfect crystallization—takes a good polish—hey?"

"Oh yes, Carrara or Parian marble, I suppose." "Parian's fine granular — 'tisn't Parian."

"Very likely—"

"It's softer than Parian, feels waxy—greasy—don't it?" said he, drawing his fingers down the limbs and draperies, which he could reach, and rapping with the end of his stick the top of the monument, "it sounds dead—you hear — very soft."

" I see you're not fit to be trusted here by yourself," thought I, and in pity to the monuments I accompanied him round for a full hour, listening to remarks on the different marbles of the columns and mosaics of the altar; and by seasonable drawings back, or well-introduced questions, the answers to which would, I knew, set him thinking for ten minutes at least, I was instrumental in preserving many

17 Louis Charles Antoine Desaix, 1768 –1800, a French general who was killed by a musket ball at the moment of victory in the Battle of Marengo. His monumental tomb with sculptures by Jean Guillaume Moitte is located at the Great St Bernard Hospice, where it was moved in 1805.

fine pieces of sculpture from the fatal rap of his stick or the inquisitive stroke of his greasy paw.

At length, at six o'clock, the usual hour for the meal which is dinner to the company, supper to the monks, we entered the public room. The company were just arranging themselves at the table. They consisted of the French lady and gentleman aforesaid; the old French lady whom we first encountered on the edge of the lake; a young lady, a daughter; a delightful young Oxonian, on a pedestrian tour; a raw Scotchman, very proud of his climbing achievements; three stupid brutes of German scholars; another German, remarkable for his immense moustachios; an English artist, very gentlemanly, but rather particular in his conversation, like the geologist; a fat Englishman, a regular John Bull, and his lady; the geologist, myself, and two other somebodies whom I did not notice, at the head of the table, making up the number to seventeen. Two monks presided at the feast, and my seat happened to be exceedingly fortunate for conversation;—one monk on the opposite side of the table, a little to my right, and opposite to him, beside me, the old French lady and her daughter; the other monk was near me on my left; and opposite to him the lady and gentleman who had been so drenched in their ascent; the geologist was, fortunately, high up the table; the artist near; the Germans within sight; and the young Oxonian between me and the monk on my left.

The cuisine of St. Bernard is most excellent, and we hungry travellers would have done justice to far worse cheer; the consequence was that there was very little conversation for the first half-hour, excepting a few remarks from my Oxford friend on the appearance of the French couple opposite, who had exchanged their saturated dress, having no change of their own, for clothing given them by the monks, which, being made to fit all corners, hung on them as it would on two pegs; and their dolorous countenances were, as my companion averred, of 'the complexion of' pickled onions, and much of the expression of an ill-cut door-knocker, which he said he well remembered having once nearly thrown him, when a child, into a fit.

They were nevertheless the first to break silence.

"Quel climat vilain—quel séjour horrible," said the lady.

"Ah," said the monk, with peculiar emphasis, looking at me. "But you have been very unfortunate in your day," he continued.

"We are always unfortunate," replied the lady, in a low, dolorous whine. "Have you had little fine weather on your journey, then?"

"There's no fine weather out of Paris," muttered the old gentleman, between two immense spoonfuls of vermicelli soup.

"What route did you take to Switzerland?" inquired the Oxonian. "By Dijon, over the Jura, to Geneva."

"Splendid pass that," he replied; "you must have enjoyed that, at least, very much."

"*It rained all the way.* We didn't see it, sir," replied the lady; "et j'avais grand peur."

"Of what, ma'am?"

"Of being upset—or robbed, sir—such dreadful precipices, such lonely roads—mon Dieu !"

"You went to Chamouni, I suppose," said the monk. "Oui, monsieur."

"Beautiful valley," said the Oxonian.

"I've seen nothing beautiful out of Paris," grunted the old gentleman. "Did you ascend the Montanvert?"

"Non, monsieur."

"Great pity; it is a noble view."

"So they told me, mais j'avais peur," said the lady. "Or to the source of de I' Arveron."

"Mon Dieu, non, monsieur—j'avais tant peur." "You saw Mont Blanc, at any rate?"

"Non, monsieur—il pleuvait toujours."

"Will you take some more soup, sir?" said the monk to the elder German.

"Ya," putting out his plate. The monk filled it, he drew it back without a word, and began swallowing the soup in immense ifp-ing[18] spoonfuls—a great portion of which ran back into his plate in two streams from the ends of his now drooping moustachios.

"Some more soup, sir?" to the fat English gentleman.

"Thank you," he replied politely, but muttered to himself as he drew back his plate — "Soup! Such soup! O Lord!—worms and water."

The dialogue continued between the monk and the opposite couple. "So I suppose you came by the steamboat to Vevay?"

"Non, monsieur,—j'avais peur," replied the lady.

"Which side of the lake did you take?"

"By Meillerie, monsieur, mais il pleuvait—mon Dieu! nous étions si mouillés—nous n'avons rien vu."

"You went to Chillon, I suppose?"

"Mon Dieu, non, monsieur—il y a un magazin de poudre—et j'avais peur."

"You have indeed been singularly unfortunate, and encountering this storm here, after all."

"Mon Dieu — j'avais tant peur," said the lady; "les éclairs et la pluie, et le vent, et les mulets."

"But I can answer for your having a fine day to-morrow," said the monk; "this storm will clear the air entirely."

"J'ai peur," said the lady, with a low sigh, and she settled herself in solemn silence to her plate.

"Some venison, sir?" said the monk to the English gentleman, having before him a delicious dish of chamois with red sauce, beautifully cooked.

"Thank you"—then, to himself, "Venison! Such venison! O Lord!" "There's a good deal of imagination in that man's stomach," said the Oxonian. "I can read at this moment the thoughts of his inside: there is a light of other days illuminating his interior; and beautiful dreams, yet not all dreams, are passing over the mirror of his—mind—I was going to say,— stomach, I mean, and it's a good large one. First comes a vision of a plateful of turtle—the fair fat, transparent as a chrysophrase, beautifully green, lustrous as an opal, floating swanlike on the richness of the exquisite brown. See what fancy will do: he opens his lips expecting to feel them

18 Sic: Ruskin's coinage.

cemented together with the delicious congelation of liquid. Now the vision is changed: in imagination he is about to cut into the sirloin of beef. All over the beautiful brown, with soft and gentle distillation flowing like spontaneous pourings forth of the spirit of poetry from some mighty mind, descend the streams of crystal gravy, melted ruby, in soft, soft silence descending, the voiceless flow of meadow waters by night not more soothingly sublime. In goes the imaginary knife with a sweet, rich sound, as it buries itself in the pure marrow, and the delicate slice is lifted, and lo! the exquisite shading from the outward brown to the interior rose, that rises over the white bone like the blush of the dawn of the morning upon some snowy Alp. Alas! the dream is too beautiful to continue, his eyes descend to his plate, his mouth, watering for the feast of fancy, feels the impoverishment of the reality; all is vanity and vexation of spirit."

"Nay," said I, "if you will condescend to leave your poetical roast beef, and taste what is now getting cold upon your plate, you will find the old fellow not so badly off."

"By Jove, that's capital," said the Oxonian, after the trial, "better than any venison the old gentleman ever eat at a Lord Mayor's dinner."

After another eating pause, he addressed the artist, who was on the

opposite side of the table: "You seem to have a valuable portfolio with you," he said; "I suppose you find this beautiful country rich in subjects?"

"In extraordinary subjects, sir, but not good ones; the objects are out of proportion, there is a want of good keeping in the landscape."

"I find a want of good keeping in the rascally hotels," replied the Oxonian, "for they keep nothing but your money, and I don't call that good keeping."

"I mean, sir," said the artist, raising his voice a little, "that the mountains are always too large to keep their distance."

"And the men too impudent," replied the Oxonian. "My landlord the other day—"

"Landlords—such landlords—O Lord," interrupted the old gentleman, lifting up his eyes. "There was a chap last week, at some of their confounded out o' the way crack-jaw places—I always asks for a private room—that's genteel and respectable—so, after dinner, says I, have you got a bottle of good wine, says I — so—says he, you shall have a good un—and while I leant back in my chair, thinking of nothing at all, in he comes with the bottle. La, I says, says I, that'll do, says I—so—says he, I'll keep you company, says he—and down he squats—in the armchair, like a lord—and finished my bottle o' port, and be d-d to him."

"What sort of port was it?" inquired the Oxonian; "for on that point, in my opinion, depends the heinousness of the offence."

"Port! Such port! O Lord!" replied the old gentleman, with a kind of gasp, and then, as if overcome at the recollection, and unable to give utterance to his feelings, he sank again into silence.

"Well, sir," continued I to the artist, who appeared to have been following the track of his own thoughts, "do not you think the climate fine?"

"Very good, sir; often fine warm ochre tints, but 'tis too clear—utter want of all aërial perspective."

"But are not the skies very beautiful?"

"Fine ultramarine, certainly, very transparent; difficult to get the clear tint; it requires a great deal of washing out, and spunging—"

Roar, came a gust of wind up the valley, its wings loaded with perfect billows of sleet, which it threw against the double windows of the room like a sea breaking over a vessel with a heavy surging dash. Everybody looked up with a start to see if the fastenings were safe, and a cold shudder passed over the French couple; it spoke to their feelings, "Oh, j'ai tant peur," said the lady.

"There's a pretty washing out for you," said the Oxonian; "I suppose that's what nature calls 'spunging her ultramarine,' hey?"

The artist rose and walked to the window, and I followed. It was a most glorious storm; the gust of wind, which had brought such a burst of rain with it, had swept away the nearer clouds with the hollow of its hand, and a strange red light was bursting through the columns of rain that were walking along the mountain peaks like armies of half seen archangels, and the peaks of the opposite hill rose against it, even the snow as black as ebony, and down the valley the red setting sun, meteor-like, was seen standing still amidst the tumultuous war of the clouds, and shook his flaming hair into the storm, like the countenance of an evil angel breathing forth a lurid pestilence, while the tempest at the instant had dashed away the mist from Mont Vel an, and the snow stood forth in red, with the conflagration-like glow—but still, so still—so noble—so majestical—it shone forth in the blackness of the scowling hurricane

like the still small voice that is heard above the roar of evil passions in a tumultuous and tormented soul.

While I was looking out I heard the artist at my elbow talking to himself.

"High clouds, indigo and light red—touch of ochre—good many coats—lights clean rubbed—sun scraped pure ochre—snow white, with a tint of carmine— hills, cobalt and pink madder,—a little blue black—I'll get the outline tomorrow—very good subject."

"Confound all artists and geologists," thought I, as I walked back to my seat at the table. The Oxonian touched my elbow. "Listen," said he. The dessert, consisting of dried fruits of different kinds, had just been set down and the other monk, whose attention had been almost exclusively occupied by carving for the multitude, was engaged in conversation with the old French lady, describing in an interesting manner the state of the Hospice in winter.

"Travellers," he said, "ascend the mountain in the summer months, when the sky is clear, the air calm, and the sun warm; they see a little snow on the ground, feel the night-wind a little cold; hear, perhaps, a roll among the hills, the sound of a distant avalanche, and descend, supposing that they have braved the dangers and experienced the difficulties of the passage of Mont St. Bernard. I assure you, they have about as much idea of them as a child wading on the sea-shore, when the ripples are licking the sand softly, has of a hurricane on the Atlantic. Imagine, if you can, this valley buried under one sheet of snow, from ten to forty feet high, and the mountains, instead of being jagged with crags, and broken with precipices, becoming immense smooth- sided mounds of snow, among which not a single rock appears to direct you; and that snow, not yielding and watery, like snow in the plains, but a fine, dry, hard-frozen dust which drifts before every swirl of the resistless wind in enormous clouds, impenetrable to the eye and choking the lungs. Suppose a temperature many degrees below zero, in which the only means of preserving the extremities unfrozen is to give them severe blows with the pole, and keep them in constant motion—and you will have some idea of a fine day in winter, at the Hospice of St. Bernard.

"Superbe," said the lady, "et les avalanches, sont-ils fréquent?"

"As long as it freezes," continued the monk, "they are small, descend slowly, and may be avoided, but—le premier coup de serac[19]—c'est le coup de mort pour les voyageurs.'[20] Fields of snow, sometimes from previous thaws and frosts, frozen into compact masses or rendered solid by their own weight and the pressure of superincumbent beds, slide down from every mountain side, with a force and velocity which I can compare to nothing but to that of a common ball of equal size, and with a roar—like ten concentrated thunders— the smoke of their shattering seen like thick white clouds on the hills."

"Superbe," again remarked the old lady.

"White smoke," soliloquized the artist; "good accident in a distance." "But a very disagreeable accident near, I should think," said the Oxonian. "I mean, sir, you misunderstand, sir—"

"I hope I shall miss standing under any such things," said my friend; "what's the old lady saying?"

I caught the last sentence of the monk, who had been going on with his description. "But, ma'am, if they fall with their heads downwards, we always find them dead."

"Superbe," replied the lady.

"'Pon my word," said the Oxonian, "she seems to travel just as the guide- books recommend—with a good-natured disposition to admire everything that comes in her way. I never heard such an epithet applied to a person being tumbled heels uppermost before."

"I believe you ascended from Aosta," continued the monk; "in that case, you passed underneath the slope of Mont Mort, which is the most dangerous spot for avalanches on the whole pass of St. Bernard; you no doubt noticed the steep, unbroken precipice to the valley, furrowed by their descent."

"Oh, sans doute-c'est vraiment superbe," replied the old lady.

"Mon Dieu—et il nous faudra descendre par la demain—oh, que j'ai peur—"

The melancholy half-suppressed whine of the one lady broke in upon the clear and cheerful accentuation of the other, like a passing bell interrupting merry music. Everybody looked up at her; she was a real spectacle—the shrivelled brown of her colourless face had become white with horror; her mouth open, its corners drawn down, the white of her eyes turned up, the whole expression aghast,—a lady of the woeful figure. Even the monk could hardly keep his countenance, while he put her out of pain by assuring her that the passage in summer was perfectly safe, and

19 Swiss French for a block or column of glacial ice.

20 See the 1835 Diary, 15 July, for this information which was given to Ruskin himself.

passed by two or three thousand individuals in the season—without the slightest accident—and that the only evidence which she would have of the occasional danger of the spot was the mass of debris in the valley, mixed with masses of snow discoloured with earth, the yet remaining vestiges of winter avalanches.

"Hem," said the geologist, "avalanches, *the* cause of alluvial deposits in elevated valleys—interesting fact—never thought of it before."

As the cloth was removed a proposal for tea originated somewhere among the ladies. The Oxonian offered to produce some of the real herb—a very difficult thing to procure in Switzerland; but the monk would not hear of such a thing, and insisted on supplying us from the stores of the convent. And he left the room to order it. "For my part," said the Oxonian, "having Plato in my pocket, I intended to endure being poisoned with a politeness worthy of his master;[21] but for the rest, confound his hospitality, say I." Nevertheless, when the tea was brought in it was found to be far superior to our expectations: the water was actually boiling, and though the English gentleman received his first cup with his usual — "Tea—such tea—O Lord!" —he returned his cup four times; even the French lady seemed to recover a little from the shock which her nerves had undergone, and as we drew close to round the wood fire, and listened to the howling tempest outside, I will venture to say that there have seldom been a merrier party in old England on a Christmas Eve, than were assembled that night in the large old shadowy hall of the hospice, bidding defiance to the Christmas climate of St. Bernard, in the month of July.

It was about six o'clock on the following morning that my dreams became musical and full of dancing light; and as the sleep fell away from the eye and ear of the mind, like a soft misty veil, and I roused myself and looked up, I found my brain in considerable confusion from a strange mingling of sights and sounds. The clear, crystalline, mistless mountain air shone in at

the small window, full of sunbeams so bright, so pure, so dazzling in their whiteness, that their light seemed to be full of cold, and the panes were all fleecy with fantastic frostwork, traced by the silent firizers of the chill morning air of July. I broke it away and looked out; the storm of the evening had swept away every atom of mist from. the air, and over the crisped lake, over the pure snow, over the desolate hills, over the boundless heaven was breathed the glory of the morning; the pulses of the pure air were full of radiance, and every crag and every snow-wreath seemed resplendent with an inward lustre of their own; and the high summits flashed forth into the dark blue like pyramids of white fire sent up from some sacred altar into the holiness of the heaven. I drew back dazzled, and believing myself to be still dreaming, for amid the stillness of the excessive solitude was heard the swelling of the solemn and beautiful melody which had mingled itself with my sleep. I rubbed my eyes, and shook myself, but it still came rolling on, now loud, now low, now dying away, accompanied by rich and well-modulated voices. At last, having thoroughly awakened myself, I remembered the morning mass. I was soon in the chapel.

21 Plato was the most famous pupil of Socrates who uncomplainingly accepted the verdict of death by poisoning himself with hemlock.

I have heard the sacred music of the mass roll and reverberate among the immeasurable twilight of the vast cathedral aisle, and the cadences of the chaunted *Te Deum* passing over the heads of thousands bowed at once. I have held my breath when, in the hush of a yet more sacred silence, the secret prayers of the population of a city rose up in their multitude, till every breath of the incensed air became holy, and the dim light around was full of supplication; but more sublime than the sacred tones that shake the dusky aisles with their tread, more holy than the hush of the bended multitude, were those few voices, whose praise rose up so strangely amid the stillness of the terrible solitude, and passed away and away, till the dead air that sleeps for ever and for ever, voicelessly, like a lifeless spirit upon the lonely mountains, was wakened from its cold silence, and that solitary voice of praise was breathed up into the still blue of the heaven rising from the high Alps as from one vast altar to the ear of the Most High, sounding along the vacancy of the illimitable wilderness, where God was, and God only.

When the mass was over, I remained alone for some time in the chapel, in that state of mind in which you do not think, in which the brain seems incapable of forming any distinct idea; you feel only it is a strange losing of the soul in a multitude of its own most sublime sensations; it is, if I may so express it, a sensual gratification of the mind.

We mustered pretty strong at breakfast, but breakfast is always a stupid, mumchance,[22] bread-and-butter sort of an affair. Everybody's intellect seemed to be frozen up or half asleep, and the silence of the old hall was little disturbed, save by the munching of toast, the swallowing of coffee, and a few words from the two ladies—the one "superbing" a little at the cloudless view of Mont Velan from the windows, and the other "peuring" away at the mules and the saddles, and the roads and the precipices and the avalanches. The guides were running up and down stairs for bundles and portmanteaux, the mules clattering about on the wet rocks before the door; everybody was occupied in preparing for their departure, and nobody seemed to relish the idea of their difficult and slow ride through the bitter cold air of the morning. Blue cheeks, purple fingers, red noses, black cloaks, and brown tippets were of frequent occurrence round the table; in short, everything looked very uncomfortable. Nevertheless, before the general break up, out we all went to see the house of the dead, a sight which it is quite as well to see by good clear morning sunlight, since a nervous person might have excessively disagreeable dreams after an evening visit.[23]

It required considerable resolution to open the outer door, and make the plunge into the thin biting air, for the thin atmosphere of these high regions, though it does not cut you in two, like a sharp east [wind], nor bite into you like a keen frost, yet insinuates its delicate substance into every pore, and fills blood, nerve, and vein with its penetrating cold. The rocks were covered with little running streamlets issuing from different crannies, the remains of the night storm, and flowing silently and almost invisibly over their polished faces, rendering them as smooth as glass; and the artist, who was just remarking to me that the landscape,

22 Silent.

23 See the description of the morgue in the 1835 diary, pp. 66–67, and 'John James Ruskin's Diary', p. 288 below.

though not exactly picturesque, was one well adapted for trying experiments of effect on, or, as he technically expressed it, "for tumbling about in," exemplified the truth of his opinion by slipping his foot and falling on hands and knees on a smooth, wet, round block of this foreground, as he called it. The geologist came up at the instant. "Good example of aqueous denudation and arrosion,[24] that," said he, as the artist rose.

"Aqueous what, sir?" replied the artist, rather gruffly, and rubbing his knees. "Denudation and arrosion, sir."

"He means, sir," interrupted the Oxonian, "that if you have skinned your knee, the cause is arrosion, and the effect denudation."

"I don't mean any such thing, sir," answered the geologist; "I was speaking of this rock—you see, sir, the beautiful effect of the water on it, takes off edges and angles, gets it all rounded off, no vestige of fracture or cleavage."

"Umph," muttered the artist, "good bit—rather heavy."

"Not above 7, or 7·50, sir," replied the geologist; "there is always a variation in the specific gravity of compound rocks."

"Nonsense;" replied the artist; "heavy in effect, I mean—massive."

"No such thing, sir—foliated; who ever heard of gneiss being massive?" "Stupid ass," muttered the artist to himself, as we reached the dead house. It is a low stone house, built against the side of Mount Mort, roofed strongly, with one small square window, cross barred, which serves the purpose both of door and window. When the monk had unlocked the grating the gentleman scrambled in, but the fat Englishman got fixed when he had insinuated himself half-way, and kept kicking his heels in the endeavour to make further progress, while the people within were bawling to him to keep out of the light.

"Are you anything of a mathematician?" whispered the Oxonian to me.

"I have solved a few problems," said I.

"Then perhaps you have tried the very difficult one of filling a square hole with a round stopper?"

"Can't say that I ever did," replied I.

"One of our professors, after a twelve days' trial, proved it, as he thought, to be impossible, but there s a Q.E.F.[25] for him," said the Oxonian pointing to our fat friend in the window.

"Is there any smell, sir?" he continued, addressing the old gentleman.

"Smell—such a smell—O Lord!" replied he, scrambling out with much difficulty, and glad of an apology for his retreat, on which the Oxonian instantly jumped in and I followed.

There were from ten to fifteen corpses in different positions round the walls, some crouching, some sitting, some standing upright, and in different states of preservation. They were all brown,—those which had been only two or three years there had both features and expression perfectly preserved; this latter, especially when indicative of agony or struggling, rendered horrible by the ghastly gleaming out of the whites of the eyes from the brown face, the irises and pupils being quite

24 A gnawing away.

25 An abbreviation for the Latin phrase 'quod erat faciendum' ('that which was to be done').

black. The flesh and clothes of those which had been longer exposed were falling from the bones like black rags; some were reduced to mere skeletons; and these again, as they fell to pieces with age, paved the floor of the charnel-house with their bleaching bones, which we crushed beneath our feet at every step.

The geologist walked up to the corpse of a mother, who had perished clasping her child: the brown arms still grasp the skeleton, and the rotting face grins down upon it, with its yellow teeth and white eyes, and there is a love still lurking about its horror.

"Very well preserved indeed," said the geologist, in the same tone in which he would have spoken of a pot of pickles. "That's a child, is it—don't its nose look bituminous, hey?" appealing to the artist.

"Humph," replied the latter, "curious group—fine single light from the little window on it—the effect is very picturesque; it's a good colour too, that tint of the flesh—vandyke brown with a little sienna."

"That's what I say, sir," replied the other; "colour of elastic asphaltum— isn't it?—or bog earth: by-the-by, bog earth is a great preserver from corruption; you know' there was a man lost in a bog, who was found twenty years afterwards in a perfect state of preservation, hair and all, and when they drew off his stockings his legs were quite white and fair."

"Real bog trotters," interrupted the Oxonian; "and didn't the fellow who found him say he was the natest jontleman alive, barring that he was dead?"

We had' a few more philosophical remarks from the geologist on the carbonate of lime in the form of bones; the old lady put her head in, looked round, and exclaimed, "Quel cadavres superbes," and then we all scrambled out, heartily glad to get out of the sick, heavy, damp, charnel-house atmosphere.

The mules were waiting on our return to the hospice. Nobody would mount however except the Oxonian and the English gentleman; the first shook me heartily by the hand, bade farewell to the kind monk, and hoping, as he said, to meet 'me again in a warmer climate, he kicked his mule into a trot, to the horror of the ladies and soon disappeared behind the promontory of the temple of Jupiter. The French lady and gentleman set off walking on the same road. I wished them good speed, and remarked that they had at last got a beautiful day. "Mais j'ai peur d'un orage," she replied, in her dolorous tone, and we parted. The English gentleman mounted, and walked his mule down on the Martigny side, muttering, "Roads—such roads—O Lord!" the French lady and her daughter took the same direction, affirming that the day was super be; the German stalked off for Aosta; and the mountain top was solitary once more.

"You will be very dull here," said the monk, to whom I had previously intimated my intention of remaining at the Hospice for a few days, in order to ramble about among the neighbouring hills.

"On the contrary," I replied, "you keep a great deal of company. I expected an austere monkish society, and I find you giving evening parties every day in the season; and in the daytime I shall be paying visits to the neighbouring mountains, whom I consider very genteel and agreeable society, although they certainly receive their visitors rather coldly."

"If you should happen to be tired of such company," replied the monk, "I believe I can find you some amusement even within the walls of our lonely hospice. For the present, however, I would recommend you to climb the hill on your right; you will find the ascent difficult, but not dangerous, and the view from its summit is noble. Stay, one of the dogs shall go with you—Sino, Sino!" Sino came bounding off the snow, the monk by a word made him understand his duty, and he attached himself to my side, and we set off together.

I found the ascent difficult, delightful, and long; the view from the summit, which commanded the Mont Blanc and the range of intermediate Alps, was most splendid, and I returned to the hospice somewhat late in the afternoon, a little tired, but much gratified (I am sorry I met with no adventures to make the expedition interesting, but such was the case: the weather was fine, and the air delicious).

I was the first of the guests, and finding the great room look rather solitary, I asked the monk to allow me to spend the hours before dinner-time in their library.

"I am afraid you will find few books there of a very amusing character," he replied; "but I will give you a manuscript which, if you can decipher it, will, I think, enable yon to pass your time agreeably."

"No black letter, I hope," said I. "I am no antiquary, and value manuscripts chiefly for what is, I believe, usually considered a great deterioration of their value, clean leaves and legible characters."

"Nay, it is not for their antiquity that I recommend our chronicles, but that I believe you will find them rather interesting. You must be aware," continued he, "that the monks of St. Bernard, being many of them of noble family, have not all devoted themselves to religion from their youth; the lives of a few have been unhappy, and of most eventful, and we consider it a profitable employment of our leisure hours to review and meditate on the events of the life we have past in the world. Many of us have written our histories, and here and there you will find the narrative of considerable interest; and sometimes we have added, when we could discover them, the histories of those persons who have been lost on the mountains, and whose bodies have been recognised. I think you will find the Chronicles of St. Bernard comprising such a variety of scenes and characters as would adorn fiction, and I do not suppose you will consider them less interesting because they are true."

I was of course much delighted with the anticipation of the perusal of this manuscript, and expressed myself so to the father.

"Perhaps," he continued, as we walked up into the library, "you observed in the floor of the chapel this morning a square slab of black marble, with a single name upon it, and no inscription."

"Velasquez, was it not?" I replied.

"True," said the monk; "you will be more interested, I think, in that slab, when you have glanced your eye over these sheets," and he took out a roll of paper from a drawer. "They were partly written by him who now reposes beneath that slab, and the parts which he left unfinished were supplied by another monk.'

I pounced upon the papers in a most ill-bred manner, hardly thanking the father, and carried them off to my own little room, that I might be secure from interruption. The manuscript was curiously written, partly in the first person, mingled with reflections and wanderings of thought, as the parts of the life of the individual had influenced his feelings; here and there the language was confused, and the writing broken, scratched, and blotted, as if written by one suffering from severe mental pain. Blanks were left at intervals, some remaining, others filled up by another hand, which had likewise concluded the narrative by relating the death of the writer, and the circumstances immediately preceding it. I found the narrative so interesting that I sketched down the outlines of it, and have afterwards filled up the tale from memory at my leisure. If I have lost some of the life and reality of the tale from relating it in a more regular manner, the disadvantage is, I think, compensated by avoiding the want of connexion and the disjointed style which pervaded the original.

II

Velasquez, the Novice[26]

CHAPTER I

"There is a noble city in the sea;
The sea is in the broad, the narrow streets,
Ebbing and flowing, and the salt sea-weed
Clings to the marble of her palaces."
—ROGERS.[27]

THE morning sun shone brightly on the little village of Mestre, and the white walls and flat roofs, which, simple as they are, impress so peculiar a character on the Italian landscape, as one touch of a master characterises a picture, were relieved against a sky of that brilliant blue which is only produced by the crystal clearness of a southern air, that clearness which is so tantalizing to the wearied traveller, by diminishing one half his apparent distance from the spires of the city of his destination. Various in colour as in form, the gay Venetian blinds hung over the glassless windows, or the luxuriant tresses of the vine, purple with their heavy clusters, furnished a greener and cooler shade. The water of the narrow canal, which runs up the middle of the street, lay basking green and clear in the heat; and lazily, yet lightly, floated the motionless gondolas upon the *sleep* of its surface. Heavier barges were scattered here and there among the smaller boats, rendering more remarkable by contrast the graceful form and fairy lightness of the surrounding gondolas; but a spirit of slumber, the attendant of the noon-day heat of Italy, lay on air, water, and land; the leaves of the vine stirred not, the waves of the dull sea heaved not, and gondolier and peasant lay wherever shade was to be obtained: the one under the awning of the barge, or the cover of the gondola, and

26 The character Velasquez seems to be unconnected directly with the Spanish painter, Diego Velasquez, 1599–1660, who did visit Venice several times and was heavily influenced by the leading Renaissance Venetian painters. This fragment is related about a novice who has left a record of his experiences as the monk promises Ruskin.

27 From 'Venice' in *Italy*, which in fact starts: 'There is a glorious City'.

the other in the corner of the street, or under the projecting roof—between sleeping and waking, dozing away the daytime with sunny dreams.

At the present day, the noon-time in Mestre, or indeed in most villages of Italy, is seldom allowed to remain so undisturbed; the quiet of the little street is broken in upon by crowds of English travellers—satin bonnets, silk gowns, and brass buttons flash everywhere among the graceful dirtiness of Italian costume; the gondolas, filled with chattering company, dart to and fro, going or returning; the disturbed waters are astonished by the sounds of cheerful volubility, which render it ridiculous to apply the epithet silent to gondolas of the present day; while the gondoliers are compelled to get rid of all their ancient prejudices in favour of lovers' hours, nocturnal glidings, and moonlight songs, and to stretch to the oar in the heat and brightness of noon.

Such, however, gentle reader, was not the case at the period we speak of,

Some two and twenty years ago, when the peace between France and England

was lately established, and the English gentleman was accustomed to remain by his Christmas fireside, instead of seeking, swallow-like, for summer skies and brighter air in more southern climates.

The presence of an English family, therefore, about to embark for Venice was a sight strange enough to make the near sleepers half open their heavy eyes and lift their drowsy heads in succession, as the party passed along the quay towards the place of embarkation. Their appearance was such as might be expected at the time when a tour on the Continent was a thing to be thought of only by persons of high rank, or at least of great wealth and respectability: they were excellent specimens of the higher order of English. The individual on whom the eyes of the wakening peasants seemed first to rest, was one who indeed seemed more like the creation of a dream than a creature of reality, although the delicate brightness of her fair complexion was far different from the dark countenances which flit before the dreaming eye of the Italian; yet, although the whiteness [of] alabaster brow which shone so brightly among its light brown tresses, and the pure red of the beautiful lip, proclaimed her English birth, the bright darkness of her hazel eye gave her countenance the fire of expression and light of thought which is seldom seen but in the maidens of a more genial climate. She leaned, although her light form and elastic step seemed little to require such support, on the arm of an elderly gentleman, whose countenance, although time had set his seal but lightly on the hale and vigorous brow, was yet marked by the peculiar shade of seriousness, inclining at some moments even to melancholy, which testifies that the life of the soul has been longer than that of the corporeal frame—the visible half sadness of thought by which Vandyke has breathed such nobility into the features of some of his portraits. This character of the countenance was perhaps still farther enhanced by the colour of the hair, which was worn rather longer than was the custom of the period, and whose singular darkness was little diminished by the presence of a few white heralds of old age.

But the remaining individual of the party was evidently a stranger. He was dressed in a dark crimson doublet, partly covered by a light black cloak, whose lengthy folds were gathered together and thrown gracefully over the left shoulder, affording a rest for the right arm, and his 'long dark hair was partly confined by a black velvet bonnet, encircled by a gold chain of delicate workmanship. His countenance, though very dark, was distinguished by the delicate transparency of complexion which is peculiar to the natives of the south; the haughty, but beautifully curved lip, the aquiline nose, the shadowy brow, and the flashing eye contributed to form a countenance extremely handsome in itself, and perhaps rendered more so by the spirit of pride that sat on the lip and flashed in the glance, which was yet softened by the same air of severe thoughtfulness, which, however naturally it may shadow the brow of age, produces a strange and impressive countenance when it is seen on the features of youth; for the individual in question could hardly be more than nineteen or twenty.

Such were the party who' became the object of attention to the idlers of Mestre as they walked down towards the place of embarkation under the shade of those long arcades so perpetual and so useful in the cities of Italy, where they are not only delightful as protections from the sun, but are rendered gay and amusing by being turned into a kind of bazaar by the lower orders of tradesmen, whose shops occupy the spaces between the pillars. They were followed by a sinister-looking Italian in the capacity of a courier, and by a grey-haired serving-man, probably a steward, whose glance was curiously cast aside on the strange objects around him, as he followed his master with measured step, with a mixture of curiosity and contempt, and, as he past the lounging peasants and dozing gondoliers, of indignation.

As he approached the quay where the black gondola was lying on the pure water, the point of junction hardly discernible, and the prow and stern curled up, as if disliking to touch the fluid, his glance testified still increasing disapprobation.

"Those must be dangerous waters indeed," he muttered, "where people go to sea in coffins."

"Thou wilt find," replied his companion, "that a Venetian gondola is like the mourning coat of an heir, sad-coloured indeed outwardly, but with much merriment within—and for the sea, its waters are smooth and calm enough; but," he continued, with a slight smile, "they have indeed been rather dangerous in their time, and if there are coffins enough above, there is that below which is some want of them."

"And no wonder," replied the steward, "such a craft as that could no more weather a breeze than a cockleshell."

"Not that there are ever any storms in the lagoon," returned the Italian, with the same ironical smile; "but people have a strange knack of sinking in it; hey, Antonio," turning to one of the gondoliers, "thou knowest something, they say, of the way the fishes used to be fattened."

Antonio's dark eye gleamed grimly, but he made no reply, and was about to assume his place in the stern of the gondola when he was arrested by a strong grasp on the shoulder. The intruder was another gondolier, who took the oar out of Antonio's hand, and whispering, as he drew him back, a word in his ear, which seemed to check the rising expostulation, he stepped into the boat.

"How now, Antonio," said the courier, somewhat surprised, "dost thou not row in thine own gondola?"

"Not when there is anyone fool enough to do it for me," replied the gondolier, in a low voice.

The man who had supplied his place differed considerably in appearance from his comrade. The darkness of his skin appeared rather a casual bronzing than a permanent complexion, and his light brown hair and bright grey eyes were yet more remarkable distinctions; while his costume, although the same as that of the other gondolier, was not quite so ragged, not half so dirty, and not a quarter so gracefully worn. It was observed, likewise, that he staggered and nearly lost his balance when he stepped upon the narrow and easily-moved stern of the gondola, a circumstance which raised an exultant laugh among Antonio and his comrades. Nevertheless, he brought the gondola well up to the quay, and when the party were seated, shot it down the canal with an ease and rapidity which showed him to be by no means an inexperienced waterman, although he was deficient in the peculiar graceful motion with which the gondolier usually bends to his oar; and there was something in the expression of his quick eye, and the attentive turn of his head, which might have put it into the head of an attentive observer that he both understood, and was interested in, the conversation of the party whom he was conveying.

There are few sensations more novel and delightful than those occasioned by your first "swim in a gondola,"[28] Swift as an arrow, but silent as death, is your motion over the path of green sea—the oars dip without a sound, and the deep water flows voicelessly from under the keel. It is like being borne in a vessel of dreams through a city of beautiful silence, when the eye wakes, but the ear sleeps; and if the cry of a gondolier, or the dash of a wave on the marble shore, breaks the stillness for a moment, it is like an echo—not a sound —like the ghost, not the being, of a voice, That person must indeed be garrulous who, when he first finds himself floating on this sea of silence, feels no spirit of conformity coming upon him; every word seems an intruder, a peace-breaker, an agitator, a poacher upon the demesnes of silence, and the conversation by which the feelings are best expressed is to be still.

Such at least seemed to be the feelings of our party, who glided down the winding canal for some time without a word being spoken by any individual. Yet there was little of interest in the scene itself, except that every turn of the canal might open upon Venice and the Adriatic; for the banks of the Brenta at this spot are only lines of straight green fortifications of considerable height, which are one of the principal defences of the city of Venice from the land, and which prevent any extended view from the canal by which they are intersected.

"What a cloud-gazer art thou, Velasquez," said the elder gentleman, at length; "is there such peculiar interest in yonder blue horizon that thou hast not an eye for the earth?"

"Can you show such 11 heaven in your cold climate?" replied Velasquez, "Not so full of light, perhaps, but equally beautiful," replied the elder' gentleman.

"You think so because its beauty is to you as a stranger—to me it is like the voice of an ancient friend," said Velasquez. "Is it strange," he continued, but speaking low and rather to himself than addressing another, "how the spirit of that heaven, the shadow and soul of the clime, is mingled with the minds of those who dwell in its

28 See Rosalind: 'or I will scarce think you have swam in a gundello' (*As You Like It*, IV. I. 37–38).

beauty—and as if the spirit of man were joined with the air that he breathes, and the hearts of the south are like its heaven, deeper in their feeling—more beautiful in the light of thought, more glorious in their mightiness, more serene in their stillness—when the storm cometh it is fiercer?"

"Velasquez," said the young lady, "I will have no soliloquies so scandalizing to the north spoken in my *presence-sotto voce,* if you please, and then you may enjoy your own thoughts without anybody's contradicting them." "Nay, Ada," said Velasquez, "it is such a heaven as this which should be the home for one so beautiful as thou; in thine own clime thou wert like a thing of light in a dwelling of darkness."

"Neither will I be complimented at the expense of my country," replied Ada playfully; "I love mine own white clouds, and morning mists, and dewy showers, and variable sky better than this perpetual burning blue,"

"O Ada,"[29] said Velasquez, "it is a clime of poetry, and its heaven is like music to the eye."

"Truly," said Ada, "I think it is one of music to the ear also. Listen."

And indeed, as she spoke, the light sea breeze came trickling over the water in the direction of Mestre, made musical, as it seemed, by clear and sweet voices, which, though low at first, and distant, became gradually more distinct, until a large gondola, impelled by three or four rowers, shot into sight round one of the bastions, and came quickly up with the smaller vessel. Its load was light, being composed chiefly of baskets of brilliant flowers, which are in request at Venice just in proportion to the difficulty of obtaining them; and while the rich blossoms left the breezes behind faint with perfume, the dark-featured and bright-eyed flower-girls, who reclined in the boat, half concealed among the luxuriant flowers, were chanting an ancient song, of the time probably when Venice was in her pride. Although there was little art in their singing, the voices were clear and beautiful, and the gondoliers kept time to the melody with the beat of their oars, while the soft and musical accents of the Italian added greatly to the sweetness of the music. The fragment of the song which was heard as they drifted by was wild and melodious, but it loses much by being translated out of its original language. It ran somewhat thus ;—

I

"The isles of the ocean are set for her seat,
There are waves at her waist—there are rocks at her feet;
Peerless and proud must the diadem be
That is meet for the brow of the queen of the sea.

2

There are jewels of price in the slumbering wave,
The pearl in the shell and the coral in cave.
And the crystal is clear and the ruby is red,
Where their brightness is but for the eyes of the dead.

29 The Library Edition notes: 'here the MS. has "Adèle" corrected to "Ada."' Ruskin met Adèle — Clotilde Domecq, with whom he fell in love, at the beginning of 1836 when she and her sisters stayed at his home.

3

But the smile of the ocean is cheerless and chill,
Its depth is all lightless, its heart lyeth still;
The rocks of its rushing are barren and hare,
And the weed, slowly waving, is all that grows there.

4

There's the morn with its gold, and the noon with its blue,
The night with its starlight[30] —the dawn with its dew,
But the light of the eye of the heaven is in vain—
Not a floweret will bud on the merciless main.

5

From the banks of the Brenta our blossoms are brought,
They are bright as the dreams of a young maiden's thought;
And the tribute of Earth shall the diadem be
That we weave for the brow of the queen of the sea.

6

They all have sweet voices, and each hath his moral,
We have bays for the bard, for the soldier his laurel,
And a crown of red roses shall wreathe the young head,
And the cypress that withers not, leave to the dead."

The boat passed rapidly on, and the words of the song became indistinguishable in the distance, although far and long over the quiet waters came a wave of dancing music, growing faint and fainter as the gondola glided rapidly away.

"It is singularly appropriate," said Velasquez, as the last notes died over the water, "that the cypress tree should be so frequent in the Italian landscape as to become almost a characteristic feature."

"And why, Velasquez," said Ada, "should the melancholy be mingled with the beautiful?"

"Thou wilt find it so generally, Ada. What is most beautiful has usually a sad light over it that hallows its loveliness; or, in the words of your own poet, what is 'most musical is usually most melancholy.'[31] But I meant that the cypress befits the landscape of Italy, because she is a land of tombs, the air is full of death—it is the past in which she lives, the past in which she is glorious—she is beautiful in death, and her people, her nation, are the dead; and the throne of her pride is the *hic jacet*.[32] The echoes of her mountains are like the voices of the departed; the blue of her heaven seems brightened with spirits; the desolation of her palaces full of a life in death. Every nation has its tree, Ada: Greece had its myrtle, Spain hath its olive,

30 The Library Edition notes: 'In the MS. the word "starbeams" is added in his mother's hand.'

31 Of the nightingale: 'Sweet bird that shunn'st the noise of folly,|Most musical, most melancholy!' (Milton, 'Il Penseroso').

32 The Library Edition notes that 'the substance of this passage was afterwards used in *The Poetry of Architecture*', where the Milton quotation is the motto for the chapter on 'The Italian Cottage'.

France hath its lily, England her rose, and Italy, whose people are the dead, hath her cypress. Oh, it is beautiful to me, the tall and melancholy trees watching over the sepulchre of her earth."

"And they are green for ever," said Ada.

"Yes," replied Velasquez; "the love of the living may change or may fade, but our love to the dead" —and he pauses for a moment, and then went on in a low and altered voice — "changeth not and perisheth not. There is a shrine in the holiness of the heart, when the light of the love of the departed burns for ever and ever. No fear, no envy, —no dark passions of man can come into the silence of the sepulchre, for there is the dwelling of love alone. Oh, blessed, blessed are the dead; should they not sleep sound in the grave, Ada, curtained with the love of the living?"

Ada's dark eye glistened like lightning among rain, and her lip quivered redly ; but the gondolier seemed to have an intention of cooling Velasquez's enthusiasm, for he splashed the water on him unmercifully with some awkward back strokes of his oar.

"And the evil of their memory is forgotten," continued Velasquez, "and their fame and their honour is remembered alone, and in the hearts of those who weep it is beautiful as the tree which keepeth watch over their tomb; it is green for ever. Oh, blessed, blessed are the dead."

As he spoke, the boat shot like an arrow round the last grassy bastion of the canal, and the gondolier, stooping forward on his oar, exclaimed in a voice of exultation, " Venezia !"

CHAPTER II

"Underneath day's azure eyes
Ocean's nursling, Venice, lies,
On the blue and beaming line
Of the waters crystalline.
Column, tower, and dome, and spire
Shine like obelisks of fire,
Pointing— with unconstant motion
From the altar of dark ocean
To the sapphire-tinted skies,
Like the flames of sacrifice."
—SHELLEY.[33]

AND, as if summoned out of the deep at the word, the city of palaces rose into their view, her towers and cupolas running far along the line of the blue sea, which was seen stretching away to the southward into the glow of the distant heaven, while here and there the line of its horizon was broken by an island of sculptured marble, or dotted with the sails of innumerable shipping. The city itself was at the distance of about two miles, but not the slightest haze diminished the clearness with which its buildings were defined upon the eye; the column of St. Mark's rose high

33 Slightly adapted from Shelley's 'Lines written among the Euganean Hills', 94–111.

and distinguished towards its centre, and the noble domes of the churches of San Giorgione and della Salute glittered in the brightness of the noonday sun, like the chief gems of the diadem which the Adriatic wears so royally.

Nevertheless, as the forest of towers and cupolas which belong to the principal parts of the city are seen, on the approach from Mestre, rising from behind a comparatively low and confused line of building, which consists chiefly of the suburbs and habitations of the lower classes, there might be perhaps a slight feeling of disappointment in the silence with which our travellers at first regarded the prospect which lay before them. But, as the swift gondola passed rapidly on its invisible path, as it advanced along the frequented thoroughfare of waters, which, distinguished only by a line of low piers from the trackless infinity of the Adriatic, leads from the last land to the gates of Venice, as they shot past that low shrine, which, washed for ever by the surrounding surges, is so appropriately named the Madonna del Aqua," and to which the gondolier breathes his low, short prayer as he darts by (a duty, by-the-bye, which the gondolier of our party most impiously forgot, or praetermitted), and when they beheld the noble city gradually extending its line, and, as it were, stretching its arms wider and wider around them, and could distinguish the entrances of her streets, paved by the sea, and the haughty lines of marble palaces by which they were bordered, all feeling of disappointment gave way to one of reverence, admiration, and delight.[34]

"Now I could wish myself a wave of the sea," said Ada, "that I might dance for ever about such shores as these.[35] Look, Velasquez, how they come beaming in from the far south, rolling and bounding in the glory of the sunbeams, and then dash into the streets in robes of sapphire and silver, and pass singing as in procession by the white columns and sculptured stones that rise up horn beneath their brightness. Do they not seem as if they saw and felt, and rejoiced in the light of their own loveliness?"

"They are deep, Ada, darkly and sadly deep," replied Velasquez; "and to my ear their dash sounds like low sobs—as of lamentation."

"They are as the Pharisees of old, my daughter," said the elder gentleman, "like unto whited sepulchres. If thou wert a wave of Venetian water thou wouldst see many a strange sight, as men say, besides the brown weed and the white marble."

"Velasquez," replied the young lady, "you always take the dark side of thinjıs, if you can; I think the darkness is your element: you are a perfect owl.

"And you, Ada," replied Velasquez, "are a bird of paradise, a being of light."

"Hem," said Ada![36] in a kind of "thank-you-for-nothing" tone.

Their gondola now entered the lower extremity of the grand canal, and the scene to which they were thus introduced was one of such rapid change and singular beauty, as to compel the eye to keep in an almost disagreeable state of activity. I have said that the crowds of travellers of different nations, who have lately inundated Italy, had not yet deprived the city of Venice of much of its

34 Ruskin's first description of the approach to Venice.

35 Compare Florizel: 'When you do dance, I wish you/A wave o' th' sea, that you might ever do/ Nothing but that' (*The Winter's Tale*, IV. 4. 140–42).

36 The Library Edition notes: 'Here again the MS. has "Adèle" corrected to "Ada."'

original character, although its change of government and withering state of prosperity had brought the shade of melancholy upon its beauty, which is rapidly increasing, and will increase, until the waves which have been the ministers of her majesty become her sepulchre. On entering the grand canal, therefore, our party found themselves in the midst of a black crowd of gondolas, which darted hither and thither over the green water in such numbers as almost to conceal it; swiftly, indeed, but in a singular and almost unbroken silence, and with such calmness and majesty of motion as entirely prevented its rapidity from giving to the scene the least appearance of what the English expressively term "bustle"; while their sombre and un varied blackness, funereal from their multitude, was singularly contrasted with the brilliant and dazzling colours of their draperies, or of the costumes of their inmates. Above, on each side of the wide canal, rose lines of high and magnificent palaces—some graced with the rich Grecian architecture of the time of Palladio; others, older, were ornamented with projecting balconies and beautifully sculptured windows, whose rich Moresco arches were usually executed in a fine red marble, relieved on the whiter marble of which their walls were composed; while the bright colours of the projecting blinds which, in almost every form, hung gracefully over them, protecting the apartments from the heat of the sun, added yet farther to the brilliancy of the piles which rose up against the darkness of the blue of the sky. Here and there a noble flight of marble steps, against which the almost invisible water rose and fell in lazy heavings, led up to the portal of some magnificent church supported by columns of the richest material, variegated with innumerable colours, and their bases ornamented with mosaics of verd-antique and lapis lazuli; while from the dim yet gorgeous obscurity within were heard the sounds of the noonday mass, chanted by the mellow and sonorous voices of the white-robed choristers. Farther on might be seen a narrow opening between the fronts of the palaces, where the deep water lay black and motionless, and some narrow and silent canal retired from the brightness of the daylight into a dim and twilight shadow, where the occasional gleam of some bewildered sunbeam was seen far through the distant darkness like a star; and the deep cry of the gondolier, as he turned the prow of his shadowy vessel into some yet more sunless chasm, came wandering along the damp, still air of the obscurity like a lamenting spirit. No effect could indeed be more striking than the universal silence, combined with such populous and cheerful motion, and the contrast of these drear and dusky recesses with the light and gaiety of the Grand Canal, whose palaces were now becoming more splendid every moment, and the gondolas, if possible, more crowded. The casual glances which were obtained of their inmates were extremely interesting: now a group of dark-haired maidens left the air musical with the half-drowsy, delicious melody of their lutes; now a lady lay sleeping under the shade of the gondola, her veil blown aside by the sea breeze, and leaving, dim discovered, the vision of beauty, the noble and elevated countenance, the lips half open and the soft heaving breath passing between them as between two half-expanded rose leaves, the delicately pencilled brow, the dark eyelashes, beautiful as the midnight of the south; now, stern and stoical, sat some young Venetian, his arms folded on his breast, and his dark, calm features full of that scarce-concealed fire which tells of secret pride unabating and passions unquenched;—and now, reclining weariedly on the cushions of the gondola, lay some old and venerable nobleman, his countenance such as we imagine in a Foscari or a Dandolo, and his noble but melancholy glance resting on the splendour of the old palaces that rose before him as the vessel glided on, at once remembering their pride, lamenting their decay, anticipating their ruin; while above, in the shade of the Moorish windows, was seen, here and there, the flash of bright eyes, or a white arm resting on the marble balcony;and in the quiet of the air there was something like the sound of sweet, low voices, which made itself sensible, without being heard, as the eye perceives a glimmering in the twilight sky of a summer evening, though it cannot distinguish a single star.

Such, then, were the general features of the scene which displayed itself to the eyes of our travellers as they glided up the principal street of Venice, and which appeared to occupy, in a most interesting manner, not only their attention, but also that of their gondolier; for that anomalous individual not only seemed much embarrassed by the task of guiding his long boat among the crowd of the other gondolas, but seemed to gaze around him on the various objects which we have endeavoured to bring before the eyes of our reader, with a very marked and, in his case, unaccountable curiosity in his eye, which differed greatly from the steady and unmoved but lynx-like glance with which the other gondoliers directed their respective vessels. Now, with uplifted eye, he appeared to be measuring the altitude of a church tower; now, with listening ear, endeavouring to catch the strain that fainted over the waves from some elevated window; and now seeking with earnest glance to penetrate the obscurity of some dark canal; while, in consequence, he was once or twice roused from these interesting reveries by his oar being nearly struck out of his hand by the beat of an advancing gondola, or by a rude encounter between the prow of his own and the projecting steps of a palace, or the stern of a heavier vessel.

The two domestics sat in the stern of the gondola; the Italian looking on the scene before him with the indifference of one to whom the sight afforded no novelty, yet with a marked pride on his lip as he observed the effect produced on the strangers by its splendour. The Englishman, on the contrary, although he gazed around him with much wonder and curiosity, was very cautious of exposing himself in the act of admiration. Peter Hayward had, indeed, while majordomo of his master's house in old England, been remarkable for his determined abhorrence, softened down, however, by a yet more inveterate contempt, of all foreign customs, usages, or persons, including all individuals who were not English under the generic name of Frenchmen; and strictly obeying Nelson's favourite precept to his midshipmen respecting that nation, which he was in the habit, moreover, of repeating to all the youngsters who happened to come in his way, enforcing and recommending its observance as one of the chief points in the code of moral duties owed to his King and country by every Englishman; on which consequential monosyllable Peter was in the habit of laying considerable emphasis, particularly when nourishing his favourite anti-Gallican principles in youngsters just breeched, by way of teaching them, as he said, to entertain a due and proper sense of their own importance as individuals of the great nation. In fact, the instillation of these loyal and English principles into the tender minds of the rising generation was one of the chief employments and amusements of the winter evenings of the majordomo, when, surrounded by a chubby-cheeked audience, his feet on the well-warmed hearth, his back supported by a venerably carved armchair, his grey hairs escaping from under a brown woollen nightcap, and his eyes lighted up with enthusiastic fire, he might be seen in his glory, paper in hand, descanting on the achievements of his beloved Nelson; exulting over the defeats of Admiral Bruise and Admiral Villain, as he was pleased to entitle the heroes of the Nile and Trafalgar;[37] his voice faltering and the light of his eye becoming dimmed with tears whenever he alluded to the event which rendered the victory lamentable; and then, spectacles on nose, he would interrupt the passages which he read aloud from those interesting periodicals, which formed his only literature, with exclamations of delight, exultation, or anathema, and intersperse his lecture with exhortations to the young fry around him, of which the purport of every sentence was a "go and do thou likewise;" and nothing ever gave him more rapturous delight than to observe from the bearing of the more forward of his auditors, from the switch being grasped firmly in the hand, from the knitted brow, the compressed lip, the firm step and sparkling eye, that he had succeeded In transfusing into their minds some of his own anti-Gallican energy.

Such being the feelings and prejudices of our steward, it was not extraordinary that, Owhen, with great reluctance after the peace was concluded, he accompanied his master on his tour, through continental countries, Peter's animosity to the inhabitants was only restrained by his contempt! and he passed on through town and country with the same fixed sneer on his countenance, carefully repressing any inclination to admire or be pleased with any thing or person, and muttering to himself, as to the only attentive auditor whom he could find, remarks of complaint, depreciation, and scorn. A slight degree of ascetic humour about the old man, which sometimes disguised to a certain degree the real benevolence of his heart, contributed still farther to this disposition; while, in conversation with persons of his own rank, he had contracted a habit (from having been long the undisputed oracle of the kitchen) of treating his own opinions with great deference, and those of others, particularly foreigners, with utter neglect or contempt; so that, although he suffered his opponent or his companion, as the case might be, to speak in his turn, he very seldom (even when it was an answer to some question proposed by himself,) paid the least attention to what he said, but followed up his own chain of thought while his antagonist was speaking, and quietly pursued it aloud, when he had concluded, thus taking very philosophical means to prevent any irritation, on his part, from argument or opposition on that of his companion. The intermixture of conversation thus occasioned was sometimes rather ludicrous, especially as a slight hesitation or impediment in his speech rendered it easy for his opponent to break in upon him with remarks or arguments which it was probable he would not hear, and certain he would not attend to.

The manner of the Italian, on the other hand, who was acting as cicerone to

37 Vice-Admiral François-Paul Brueys d'Aigalliers, Comte de Brueys, 1753–1798, was the French commander in the Battle of the Nile, and Pierre-Charles-Jean-Baptiste-Silvestre de Villeneuve, 1763–1806, the French admiral who commanded the French fleet at the Battle of Trafalgar.

his companion, was considerably varied. Now he was voluble in expatiating on the beauty of the palaces, or the wealth of their former possessors, and sometimes would plunge into a sea of vague tradition, or of real history, which would have been extremely interesting to a more attentive auditor, and then he would suddenly draw back like a snail into his shell and assume the manner of one who knew more than he was willing to disclose, throwing out vague answers and dark hints, the meaning of which our steward seldom took the trouble to fathom.

"Splendid," exclaimed Hayward involuntarily, as the boat came in front of an old Moresco-looking palace; then, recollecting himself — "paltry affair, all glitter and gingerbread."

"That palace," replied the Italian, "belonged to one of the most ancient families of Venice; the last scion was driven away by—"

"Cursed damp ground-floor, I should think," interrupted the steward, in continuation of his disparaging remarks on the building.

"The last scion of which," resumed the Italian, "was driven into banishment by the inveterate hatred of—"

"Rats and mice in the cellarage, plenty, aint there?" remarked the imperturbable steward.

"Was driven into banishment," again returned the Italian, "and remained in the—"

"Comical little attics, hey?" continued Hayward.

"While his father, agonized with grief, while wearing the ducal crown—" pursued the Italian.

"Regular queer old chap that, looking out of the gridiron there," said the pertinacious steward, "like a cat out of the dairy window. I say Mr. Gigamaree—"

"Giacomo, sir—" interrupted the Italian.

"Well, Mr. Jackomo, I say, what precious good care you Italians take of your pantry windows—all barred up like points of view in Newgate; plenty plate inside, I suppose?"

"Hum," said the Italian, with his usual sardonic smile; they had a kind of—of plate, as you say, that was very liable to tarnishing, particularly from breath."

"Ah ! " said Hayward, "I thought as much—brass candlesticks and plated snuffer-trays, I suppose?"

"And the bars," continued Giacomo, in the same tone, "were more, I fancy, to keep the plate from getting out, than the thieves from getting in." "The deuce they were," replied Hayward, in astonishment.

"Ay," replied the Italian, "the old miserly fathers had more bars and bolts drawn upon their daughters than on all the gold in their coffers; you know the thieves in the one case were not so cognizable to the police as in the other.' "Whew!" said Hayward, finishing off' with a long whistle, then muttering to himself, "that's all of a piece; in old England we set no bars on young ladies but their own discretion; and—for police-stuff—you've no police."

"Think you so?" replied the Italian; "we had formerly a pretty strict One—"

"Nonsense, don't tell me; haven't seen a constable out of England."

"I daresay not," replied Giacomo, "it was the peculiar power of our police that it was unseen; it was in the air, the water, and the earth, the noon and the night,—the palace, the canal or the lagoon."

"Don't be gammoning[38] me, Mr. Jackorno," began the steward, somewhat angrily.

"I tell you truth," answered the Italian. "In Venice, it was wont to be said, that—"

"You've no Lord Mayor," interrupted Hayward. "That her water was full of ears," continued Giacomo. "You've no magistrates," pursued Hayward.

"And her air full of tongues," returned the other. "You've no aldermen."

"And her heaven full of eyes," continued the Italian.

"You've no trial by jury!" exclaimed the steward, his voice rising as he enumerated the deficiencies of Italian government.

"Hush," said the Italian, "speak not so loudly here. See you this building on your right?"

The house to which he pointed was situated at the corner of one of the narrow canals which branch off from the principal street of Venice. It was not large, but bore evident marks of having been in its day distinguished by more than ordinary splendour, which rendered more conspicuous the too legible marks which the slow finger of decay had traced upon its ruinous magnificence. The line of exquisitely formed Gothic windows were divided from each other by columns of a deep red porphyry carved into the form of spiral shaped wreaths, and crowned by capitals of intricate and beautiful workmanship, while the corners of their arches were occupied by rich wreathed flower-work in white marble, and the door, supported on each side by the same kind of spiral column, which Raphael has used in his painting of the beautiful gate of the Temple[39] was finished by a reversed arch, charged with ornament of the richest and most varied character. Yet the house was apparently uninhabited, and fast falling to ruin; there was no door in the portal, and the unopposed water rose over the marble steps and dashed unheeded into the hall, where the green weeds had long rooted themselves in the interstices of the tesselated pavement. The termination of the hall was lost in darkness; and the low breeze whistled through its recesses, and passed moaning away, as if at a great distance; and the dark walls and glassless windows above, and the gusty music more lonely than the silence of the inhabited buildings, all spoke of darkness, and desolation, and decay.

"There are strange traditions about that palace," said Giacomo. "Wretched old crows' nest," said Hayward; "it should be pulled down for the materials—"

"It is said," continued the Italian, "that it belonged once to a young nobleman who was betrothed to a fair daughter of one of the highest families of Venice j it was the time of the last war with the Turks, and the young Giuseppe went forth in the gallies of the Doge, and returned, with his ship's prow wreathed with laurels—"

"Gallies, indeed! pretty gallies," interrupted Hayward; "why, one English frigate would have blown you all out of the water."

38 Colloquial for 'deceiving'.

39 One of the cartoons now in the Victorian & Albert Museum.

Now, it was a principle of the Italian never to notice any of the steward's interruptions, or to dispute any of his opinions, however contrary they might be to his own, since he had always found that no advantage was to be gained by so doing; he therefore quietly continued—

"Giuseppe returned in triumph; he met the mourners returning from the celebration of a funeral as he crossed the Piazza San Marco—from the funeral of a maiden. They had left his betrothed in the arms of a stern bridegroom," said the Italian, and he smiled.

"Poor fellow!" said Hayward, with a slight faulter *[sic]* in his voice.

"There was mourning in the palace of her father," continued Giacomo ; "they had buried her in the vaults of the church of San Paolo, and thither went the lover to meet his bride. Some say the maiden was only in a deep trance; the love of Giuseppe brought forth the living from among the dead; the physicians had been mistaken."

"Confound the physicians," exclaimed Hayward; "pretty physicians to bury a person in a swoon."

"Ay, but," continued the Italian musingly, "some men say she had strange dreams in that swoon. Some hinted that Giuseppe had held intercourse with the ancient tribes of the Arabians, and had learned dark secrets from the sages of the East—words of power, even to raise the dead."

"Fudge!" said Hayward.

"I know not," replied the Italian. "Men say that a change came over the maiden after that time, and she seemed influenced by thoughts and feelings different from those of this world. She had been before as gay and bright a butterfly as ever fluttered to seventeen, and they say she was never seen to smile again."

"Nonsense," said Hayward; "it was enough to make anybody a little down in the mouth to find themselves clapped up in a coffin before they were dead."

"They died both in one day," continued the Italian; "and that gave rise to more whisperings. It was thought that—"

"Stuff! I don't want to hear all your ridiculous tittle-tattle," interrupted the steward. "In England the women only are gossips, here the men seem to have nothing else to do-idle rascals."

"Well, but," said the Italian, "they left one son." "I daresay they did," said Hayward.

"And he," continued Giacomo, in a lower voice, "it is said, yet lives." "Well," said the steward, "what of that; he's had nothing to do with your rascallv doctors, that's all."

"Few have seen him, and those love not to speak of him," continued Giacomo; "but they say he dwells in this building."

"Then he must be confoundedly rheumatic," replied the steward. "Pretty damp hole for an old gentleman to warm his gouty toes in."

"You see it is higher than the rest of the houses," said Giacorno, "What I he lives in the garret, I suppose?" said Hayward.

"The gondolier, when benighted in the distant lagoon," said the Italian, "has frequently seen a light burning within those high Gothic windows, which vanished if they approach near it by the canals."

"Well," said the steward, "I suppose he puts out his candle when he goes to bed, lest he should set the house on fire; and no great damage done if he did."

"They say he learned dark secrets from his mother, and can read the countenances of the stars," replied the Italian. "Those who have seen him say that his features bear marks of unnatural old age, and are remarkable for their excessive calmness; yet with the peculiar light in his glance which is peculiar to those who have the evil eye—"

"Gammon!" said the incredulous Hayward.

"And those whom he has looked on are changed; there is a fear cast like a mantle upon them, and a horror comes upon their spirit, as if they had spoken with the dead," continued Giacomo, but in the low muttering tone which showed that he was rather musing to himself than addressing his incredulous auditor. "If ever man had a heavy account of crime upon his head, it is that man. Before he was twenty he became one of the ten;[40] and they bowed before him in fear; all hated him; but those who breathed a word against him, were not; and he moved through the world with an immoveable smile upon his lips, and his glance was death; they say it was by his order that the young Francesco was murdered at the bridge foot."

"Murdered!" interrupted the steward, "where were your famous police then, hey, Mr. Jackomo?"

"Unseen, all seeing—and permitting," said a voice, seemingly close beside him.

"The devil!" exclaimed Hayward, springing up in the gondola. The voice was clear and distinct, and musical, though very low. There were no gondolas near them, and no persons within sight. The Italian started, but instantly recovered his composure, and if he did not actually smile, there was a very visible inclination so to do, traceable upon his features.

"What is the matter, Hayward?" said the elder gentleman; "you will upset us all if you jump up in that manner."

"Why, sir," said Hayward, stuttering between astonishment and indignation, "it's—it's some cursed juggling trick, sir."

"What is?" inquired his master.

"Why, sir, didn't you hear, sir? some one spoke just now, sir."

"You must be dreaming, Hayward; I heard no one speak," replied the gentleman.

"Sit down and be quiet," whispered the Italian; "it's only a trick of the old trade. I was telling you something of it just now, but you would not listen to me."

"I'll tell you what, sir," began the steward; "don't you be playing off your jokes on me, sir—rascally deception, sir."

"Nay, I had nothing to do with it, I assure you; I suppose the author of the voice wished to convince your incredulity a little, that's all."

The circumstance, however, seemed to have made some impression on the steward, for the rest of his conversation was addressed to the Italian in a much lower and more subdued tone; while, during Giacomo's replies, he was heard muttering to himself, "All nonsense—must be"—then in a kind of reaction of feeling — "cursed

40 The Council of Ten, from 1310 to 1797, was one of the major governing bodies of the Republic of Venice which notoriously acted in secrecy.

queer, though—must have overheard what I said— pooh !—stuff—legerdemain—don't understand it, though—very odd—and yet —no—all a cheat—he's a knave—and I'm an ass."

But though he came to this very philosophical conclusion after so many pros and cons, he spoke not again so boldly during the rest of their voyage; and cast around him, every now and then, certain peculiar, uncomfortable— looking glances which made it evident that he had disagreeable doubts respecting the kind of, and number of, the company he was in.

CHAPTER III

> "What am I, sir? nay, what are you, sir ?—O immortal gods! O fine villain! A silken doublet! a velvet hose! a scarlet cloak! and a copatain[41] hat!" —*Taming of the Shrew.*[42]

[*End*]

41 With a high crown or peak.

42 Act v. Sc. 1.

APPENDIX III

John James Ruskin's Diary, 1835[1]

Scabeus[2] My Father's account of journey of 1835. Beginning at Poligny[3]

30 June Left Poligny at 8 oClock & never passed a more delightful day — The Sky unclouded the air cool. the Road one of Napoleons rising thro a grand opening between Rocks & Trees of unequalled beauty, passing over fields of grain & vines & grass studded with pretty Cottages & farm Houses. varied again by Woods & grounds covered with Bushwood Briars & Thorns or towering Heights of most magnificent Pines till you glide down the fine road into Morez sunk between very high Hills on a small Rivulet deep but romantic & with spots of green sward & gardens & fruit Trees on every side There is one bad turn into Morez the Road descending very rapidly & turning too suddenly. Arrived at 4 oClock after some walking & great I would say the most continuous Enjoyment I have known any Long days Journey to yield.

1 July Left Morez for Geneva the Road ascending long Hills on Sides of Ravines without Parapets & then among Firs but winding openly again & on a level magnificent Shelf round the sides of Hills near their Top, from which you look

[end of page]

down a thousand feet into the long wide Valley separating two parallel Ranges of the Jura — When you are high on the Jura & 17 miles from Geneva the whole Range of Montblanc the Lake & the fine Pays de Vaud & part of Savoy open at once upon you a pass of the Mountain thro which the Road is carried bringing you at once from the French Side to the Swiss open Country for as to Swiss Scenery the Road all the way from Morez or perhaps Le Rousse is romantic & Alpine — we walked 7 miles down to Gex — John took a Sketch & we reached Hotel des Etrangers at 3 oClock.

1 to 6 July Geneva very hot. Roads deep in Dust. Lake most lovely. Mont Blanc visible all the time. the middling & lower Classes all find occupation & the Sick are provided for. No Beggars seen or allowed but Want of Equipages & of Great

1 There are no separations between the entries for the different dates in the MS.

2 This flower is the first of a series, the names of which are written at the top left of the diary pages. Depressions in the sheets of the MS indicate that plant specimens, presumably as named, were at one time pressed between the pages of the notebook.

3 Inscribed by John Ruskin on the end paper.

People make these Swiss Towns very dull or monotonous — part of Geneva upper Town very triste & Sombre.

6 July to St Martin over a Road super excellent & thro a country possessing every possible feature of Beauty. Hotel de Mont Blanc

7 July Chamouni in 5 hours by Chara Banc to Union[4] — 8 July up to Col de Balme 12 miles

[end of page]

Geranium

all on Mules 4 mules 2 Guides Road bad & steep Wild spot but splendid View of Mont Blanc & the Alps on Martigny side –

9 July John & I to Montanvert up & down on Mules 1 Guide

10 July to Glacier Bossons clear pure splendid. Went 3 miles for 6 francs in carriage holding 4 & walked up. 11 July to St Martin by Baths of St Gervais finely situated near a Cascade, all private Baths — also drinking Waters Iron like Tunbridge Sulphur like Harrowgate[5] an Earthquake lately made the Waters so generally clear; quite turbed. Lovely Country down to St Martin, the view from Gallery of Montblanc Hotel in every direction wonderful the River Arve the Vale rich in Grass Wheat Barley Oats. Grass Hemp. Gardens Orchards Woods ascending Hills — Fruits Walnuts Pears Apples Cherries, Nuts Cranberries Barberry Bushes Sweet Briar sloes

Pasturage rich & green crowning heights & Woods of Beech Oak, pine The best & hardest Melezes– The prodigious Mountains & fine Rocks whose sides

[end of page]

only can be said to be raked where very precipitous their tops bearing Grass or Corn & Chalets here & there appearing & pines. The contrast in this country betwixt exceeding natural Richness of Soil & extreme personal poverty of appearance in all the Inhabitants is inexplicable — on

13 July We went from St Martin 6 oClock going 20 miles to Bonville to Breakfast thence with one set of Horses 30 miles or 35 to Thoron only stopping 75 minutes to bait — on to St Gingoulfe 20 miles making 70 to 75 miles first thro the fine County about 25 miles on Geneva Road & thro [...?] Country down to Borders of Lake along Napoleons beautiful Road & a Country combining all that is lovely in Creation disposed with a Taste as to Wood & Pasture etc that would make us believe in some fairy help or that the arrangement of Wood & division of ground to produce the finest effect was best known to the most Ignorant in fact to Naturals for strange & most melancholy is it to find this Paradise possessed by Creatures the Victims of Disease of Goitre of Idiotism. Looking Senseless & poor & miserable in the midst of Beauty & Abundance

4 The Union Hotel at Chamonix.
5 Harrogate is a spa town in North Yorkshire.

[end of page]

Heartsease panseys

There is something very mysterious in all this I would pronounce the Ride of 75 miles from St Martin to St Gingoulfe by Thuron to be taking every yard of the Road to be perhaps the finest in the World. Yet not a Chateau appears or Country House of any Consequence. no great farm Steading: no persons of respectable or Substantial appearance — Everything Human appears to groan in Wretchedness in proportion as the Country smiles. & yet they say that they are well off & pay few taxes — a Poll Tax of 6/ or 7/[6] a Man & about £2 on 100 acres Land Neither does the Church seem to take much from them

14 July to Martigny. Road changes to middling & thro low Lands — The Goitres & Cretins swarming Filth & Wretchedness mark the Valois & indeed every Catholic part of this Country.

15 July Left Martigny at 6 oClock in chara Bancs. For Laddes[7] there got 6 mules & 1 for Hay & 1 for Luggage. 8 in all got to Hospice St Bernard at 5. dined 1/2 past 6. Pere Barras very kind. 6 dogs only as keep is very costly. Breed Danish & Spanish — They change if removed Castor a fine large Dog. Saw them sporting

[end of page]

in the snow — The dogs make their way thro the snow like a man swimming keeping the <head — More> follow them & hallow loudly every day at some distance from the Hospice. The thaws are most dangerous as old snow being formed into Ice — later Snow falls but the air gets between & in a Thaw it expands & the whole sheet of last snow slides down in a moment — Sliding Avalanches in Winter strike in a moment Rolling snow in Spring & Summer may be avoided. Three Gui Domestics of St Bernard & a Traveller coming up the Station Side in 1825 were carried down by an Avalanche sliding from the precipice to the Road & down to the River at a great Depth below. It was here that Buonaparte slid down — Mass at St Bernard 6 oClock. Music very fine — The Dead House very Impressive — The figures of persons perished remain long in this air entire — the Hair perfect. The attitude striking — a woman clasping an Infant to her Breast — Men pressing their hands together as in resignation, others in a sort of Despair. Countenances expressing Cold — The Lake not frozen — Sky clear — air very

[end of page]

Dewberry

agreeable. No Grouse in Switzerland

16 July to Aosta 24 miles Crown Hotel — finest pink Champagne. Fine Remains Octavius Augustus Cæsars Triumphal Arch Victory over Salussians A.U.[8] 724.[9]

6 6 or 7 shillings.
7 Sic, for 'Ladies'?
8 That is, A[nno] U[rbis], 'from the founding of the city [of Rome]', usually dated at 753 BC.
9 The triumphal Arch of Augustus lies outside the town of Aosta, built in 35 BC in honour of

built Aosta in 3 years called after himself. Roman Bricks covered with Cement, like stone — Old walls 12 feet Thick Vale of Aosta lovely Vines all trellised the Heat being too great to let them be on the Ground — The People in this Vale are almost without exception — Idiots, Goitres & Jaundiced in colour & ugly & filthy to a disgusting degree — This said to be the low enclosed hot country here & in the Vallais where the very high Hills prevent a proper Circulation of Air. That influences the Health of Residents few persons of middle Station in this Country All Lawyers Clergy Doctors Employees & Peasants Harvest this year most abundant but as one days Wages will keep people all the Week they will not work. The Water is very bad & full of Granite Dust which may form Goitres also the practice of carrying Burthens on the Head may make throats bad– The continued propagation of a Race so defective & unmixed must tend always to

[end of page]

degenerate

17 July Cormayeur by a good tho narrow Road thro the Vale of Aosta ascending gradually — fine Castles — Vines beautiful — The Vale of Cormayeur rich in Grass, Corn — Vines & Fruit Trees. People filthy & poor & miserable. Houses most deplorable collections of huge Beams & Stones dark dismal. Savagely clumsy. Cloathing of Men coarse. Women frightfully ugly. Church Catholic dismally dirty.

18 July to Allee Blanche over a high Hill owing to a Bridge being washed away. The back of Mont Blanc rising before us in awful Majesty. Precipitous pointed Rocks.

20 July to St Didier Baths like Bath Water but not so warm. The Waters Cormayeur pungent or like Soda purgative. also strong Sulphurous Water worse than Harrowgate. To Aosta –

21 July to St Bernard clear & warm for that height — fine weather. two hours after our arrival or say 6 oClock persons arrived drenched with rain & forced to strip & put on Hospital Cloaths — Slept upstairs N° 14 good Room

22 July to Martigny

[end of page]

Crowsfoot like Coronilla

23 July Tete Noir John & I on mules. Steep ascent & steeper descent — Stony road by River Side — Trees & stones thrown down torn up by storms in a way not elsewhere to be seen. The Winds must act in the Pass with extraordinary Violence.

24 July to Bex & Vevay — The Valais presents an aspect betwixt the Soft & the Savage The Sad & the beautiful It is a place that Summer touches but Winter prevails & leaves a track of Desolation — so perpetually coming upon this devoted Valley

Augustus, to celebrate the victory of consul Varro Murena over the Salassi.

that it will probably never be but a Ruin & a wreck of Nature to the end of time. It is a portion of the world destroyed before the end of all things Cross the Bridge at St Maurice to enter Canton of Vaud. It is quite refreshing to leave a Catholic to enter a Protestant Country. So neat so orderly so healthy, so rich & thriving in all appearance are the Protestants so active & animated & lively The Catholics are on the contrary so poor & lazy & filthy & melancholy. Their Houses Cottages Fields & Gardens alike neglected or only tended in the most slovenly manner. The Road proceeds by Castle of Chillon — good & thro a fine Vine country. The stone walls & entire vine growth

[end of page]

near the Lake makes it monotonous but you have glimpses of the high Country in rich & varied Cultivation & Splendid Lake forever before you

25.26 July Vevay a most agreeable Town the Three Crowns a very supr[10] Inn if they keep their Cook. The Lake is very accessible here. the Country above the Vines very lovely. The Lake appeared here one forenoon about 10 oClock roughened by a fresh Breeze in greater beauty than I had ever seen it– deep Blue but varying its hue & shades & touched with white foam. A single large Boat with its picturesque Sails was scudding across from Vevay to the far off shore.

27 July Vevay 28 July Lausanne making a new Road near Lake a lovely Ride on a lovely morning & the Living figures of a fine Peasantry improve the scene. Lausanne improves on a second visit — fine Houses & Walks. Its suburbs & surrounding Country superior

28 July to Iverdun a beautiful Country in high Cultivation Road hilly but good Iverdun a fine old Town The Maison Rouge very Comfortable. The Ride from

29 July this Town before Breakfast from Iverdun situated at extremity of Lake along side of Lake of Neuchatel thro Grandson to Concise to Breakfast at that early

[end of page]

Potentilla

hour was most lovely. The Lake opens out in great Breadth. the fine country gently sloping towards its opposite shore & the magnificent chain of Alps in the distance the Vineyards & pretty Buildings around you & good road all render this the most enchanting Ride possible. Neuchatel always looks an elegant & princely Town & the Rooms at Falcon very fine. a chair cover dark brown ground large yellow Flowers good effect. The Town noisy at night. Wood choppers, Watchmen, etc. Curious mode of using Hatchet reversed

30 July to Bienne by a good Road thro a highly cultivated Country great part Canton of Berne — coming in sight of Lake only at Bienne end — St Pierre Island at a distance: after Dinner to Soleure — the change of entring this Catholic Canton greatly to the worse filth & misery & bad Road but not as in the Valais There

10 Superior.

seems a struggle here betwixt the benumbing Influence of Catholicism & the Swiss habits of Cleanliness & Industry. Soleure a beautiful altho Catholic Town — almost magnificent, noble Greek arch Church. The Bridges River Ramparts large Houses & fine Suburbs very picturesque.

31 July Early to Balstall a most lovely ride with

[end of page]

Alps in sight. Rich Country noble Road fine Cliffs on left of bright limestone bearded with shrubs & pines but partaking of the Beauty of Derbyshire Rocks & woods It is Range of Jura Mountains which at Balstall after passing two Feudal Castles on pointed Rocks you ascend & cross by the gentlest ascent & most gradual Descent of the most elegant Road I ever saw. A perfect Model of a way to glide over a Hill with pleasure & safety. The Road continues level passing thro a rich Country thro Liechstall till near Basle you see the Rhine winding down this fine Vale to wash over the City of Basle the picture of Cleanliness in all its parts. The Gates & Walls & the few Country Houses in the Lichstall side very fine. Town Hall very Swiss — the Cathedral German Protestant very curious. of Red Sand Stone fine Carving: The Cloisters entire & very solid. The Tombs numerous but ponderous & suited to the Stile of Church. Tomb of Erasmus in Church. Old Council Hall. Crypt below. Intelligent man to show Church. Great Merchts in Ribbons sent by

[end of page]

Campanula Harebell

Havre to So'[11] America. Many Jews. Great printers formerly.

3 Augt to Stein by Banks of Rhine good Road & rich & beautiful Country. 4 Augt a Rhine Fog on to Schaffhausen the Country still very fine but not such good land as you approach Shaffhausen. This Town improves kept in great order very clean. pretty Swiss Houses in every Street.

5 Augt Crossed Rhine with Carriage in Boats the Bridge being under Repair — The falls appear more striking on a second Visit They excel all others — Alps clouded Rainbow at falls at 11 oClock.

6 Augt to Constance part of Road very good — part bad in Lands belonging to Ensiedlen. This Convent has £20,000 a year St Augustine Convent near Constance £6000 a year St Bernard £4000. From Basle Vignes appear all the way, but a great many near Schaffhausen. also towards Constance but a great deal of Hemp grows in the low Constance side & you see Women at this Season beating it in every Town. Constance a dull decaying Town with very few Houses so good as Schaffhausen. Half Catholic half Protestant The Aug's Convent half a mile from Constance

[end of page]

on the Ragatz Road is worth seeing for the beautiful church in one altar Chapel of which are the Life & suffering of our Saviour in Figures from 12 to 15 Inches of

11 South.

Box Wood executed in the most striking & beautiful manner possible. It occupied one man 40 years but what a conception & Imagination must he have had & what execution. There is painted Wood like Rock opening in Shelves & Recesses & the various figures are placed high & low & all around. This far finer than than[12] the cut Ivory at Certosa because so free & speaking the Expression of all the Characters. The Convent is very large & very rich in Vineyards Houses etc only 15 Monks. the outhouses appear immense. They receive Strangers.

7 Augt to Winterthur by a middling Road fine Country but still Hemp. more vines & pasture than Corn. The Savage[?] a most comfortable & cheap Inn & obliging people. Winterthur an apparently wealthy manufacturing place. fine people healthy Children very clean. to Zurich

8 Augt a long 12 miles woody & hilly Country — The Houses round Zurich for many miles very numerous white & green & smiling with pretty Gardens. many Weavers but no appearance of poverty nor even dependence no Squalid misery & filth alternating with Splendour

[end of page]

Nettles

& yet no boisterous assertion of Independence as appears I think in the air & manner of every American & the Servants are in Switzerland in as perfect subordination as in England a moral & educated Race high & low a natural charm never heard of. Mr Kerez of Sword an Imposing <Swiss> Greed & selfishness enter into Swiss Character. unkind to Relations. Zurich people fond of Music — habits hereditary. Climate & light Taxes unfavourable to Exertion.

10 Augt to Zug along West side of Lake thro the most lovely Vicinity or suburbs a Town ever had for 4 miles till you ascend Mont Albis too bad & steep a road for any Carriage fine view of Lake of Zurich & Zug & Alps from signal post. Road down worse & worse. Carriage two Drays & fixed in a hole, so many Cross Roads going round Zug no post or some & people silent, very difficult to find right Road. Cerf Inn Zug excellent Land lady Mrs Suter played piano cerentola[13] admirably. Mr S played 3 Jews Harps & Guitar & sung German saw an old Swiss House of Louis 14th time Many Roman remains in Switd. Cæsar hated Helvetians & beat them but the Roman Governors were mild & humanized them till

[end of page]

they in their turn invaded other States. The Germanni & then the Allemanni a fiercer race & the Burgundians fell on Switzerland & on Italy & on Gaul. The Franks originally German came after the Ostrogoths Huns had entered Switzerland & drove them out & introduced Christianity. There were kings of the Burgundians & Allemanni the Austrians under whom the Swiss continued but Charlemagne King of the Franks improved their state. The priests then effected some good in

12 Sic.

13 Possibly tunes from Rossini's opera in two acts, *La Cenerentola*, 1817.

civilizing & preserving Records & began to labour in Convents till priests again became Princes & Princes Tyrants & Tell rebelled. There is freedom now it is true but a perpetual Jarring of Interests & quarrelling Zug Nunnery very clean. rich in Lands the Swiss Gov't will not permit them to buy more Land with them accumulating wealth, because it would deprive others of Land. Fine Churchyard Gilt Crosses & tablets. An American Gentn said the Episcopal Church of America supported by th'm contribution was flourishing very much.

12 Augt Zug to Art 8 miles fine Road Lovely Road towards Schwytz as in all Catholic Cantons it gets very bad Zug an exception. melancholy Sight of Ruins of Goldau[14] & sombre Lake of Lowertz. Road from Schwytz

[end of page][15]

Guelder Rose

to Brunnen very bad — Left Carriage & rowed to Fluellen past Tells chapel — grand scenery on sides of Lake. proceed 2 miles to Altorf where Tell Shot at the Apple &c

13 Augt from Altorf very hot place & dull up to St Gothard by new Road to Amstegg a place with clean new Inns Town often in great part washed away by River Kerstlen or Reuss. The country near Altorf abounding in Fruits The Pass of St Gothard magnificent all the way to Devils Bridge remarkable by the height of Rock cut the elegance of the new Bridge. the terrific old one the Noisy & awful tumbling of Waters the Rainbows on the Fall It alarms & delights at once. The Road slopes only <8pos> as usual with best Roads. Bridges numerous light & elegant. The Rocks on upper part of St Gothard grand the lower parts of surprising Beauty & Grandeur Pasture soft. Trees beautiful high peaks precipices jagged & various — tremendous often but nothing of the desolate & ruinous appearance of the Valais. Scenery all finished perfect Rock & tree & Turf. Zig Zags of Road very beautiful but it constantly wants repairs. Hospital in a pretty Valley of great length & nearly as good as Chamouni more of a home smiling the quiet[?] Look — over

14 Augt to Airolo on Italian side steep descent by Zig Zag See the Valley far towards Bellinzona beautiful

15 Augt After sleeping at Hospital down to Fluellen poor Inn Robber taken there

17 Augt In rain to Brunnen a most dirty Inn & place.to Art & Lucerne last part of Road very fine pasture & Fruit Trees. Lucerne lovely romantic appearance with its white walls forming an Angle behind it & its Old Towers; one of the most beautiful of Swiss Towns from the Lake

19 Augt to Righi by Weggis first Water 2 hours from Lucerne & then a very easy ascent. arrived in clouds at Rigi Calm. improved Inn. Storm of Rain, Forked Lightening Loud Thunder Crackling high Wind after. Clear Starlight at 2 morning Last <Qr> moon beautiful at 3. Light just breaking over mountain at 4 at back of

14 See the Diary 1835, n.16.

15 A page is torn from the MS here, but the text is continuous.

House. 1/2 past 4 Wooden Trumpet blown at 5 Sun Rose most sublime The Snowy Alps Titles Young Frau The Lakes the immense Range of Hill & Dale. Zug lies so at your feet like a mirror & all the Vallies bursting into light a few white clouds lying over a near Valley. about 70 people assembled in ten minutes from Culm & Staffell & gazed for ten minutes half hurried down, some got round a pedlar bargaining for

[end of page][16]

Elderblossom

Wooden Spoons & Nut Crackers.x

21 Augt to Alpnach 2 1/2 hours by water good inn

22 Augt Beautiful Ride to Lungera near Lake in the Basin of Hills round & gradually sloping on Horses to Meyringen over Brunig very stony but thro Woods of Oak Beech Walnuts & Rocks

23 — Sunday Meyringen picturesque Costume Black Red & white Sleeves. Reichenbach Cascade Six falls very striking

24 Augt trip to Grimsel. 9 miles Gutannen 6 more to Handek 6 more to Hospice two fine Valleys & grand passes Road Stony & along dangerous Precipices over Blocks of Granite. Handek seen from above the most impressive & grand Waterfall we had yet seen. confined much & then spreading out & falling over 270 feet

25–26 Augt confined at Hospice with 22 persons in a Snow Storm. Horses short of food. Cattle all brought in from the Hills. Hay refused to Horses

27 Augt Down to Meyringen. Horses go without slipping or stumbling over Granite slightly cut for Horses feet

28 Augt Meyringen dull. 29 rose at 4 Rode over the Sheideck starting at 1/4 past 5. Steep ascent

[end of page]

but the pass you enter at Top after an hours riding opens to you the Wetterhorn & Wellhorn in all their grandeur & Limestone Rocks of surprising Beauty Alps & Pines & Rushing Streams. The situation of Rosenlaui where we breakfasted a scene of most Wild magnificence imaginable & mixed with a Softness that made it enchanting. Proceed through the Woods to top of Scheideck. The great Eiger shows his top isolated over the Col of the green Scheideck like an Iceberg on a green Ocean. Pass close under Wetterhorn & Wellhorn descend on a Black Slaty Ground to Grindelwald Close to Glaciers supr & inferior Black Eagle Inn fine situation near Glaciers & Wellhorn & Eigers & the Valley truly beautiful & yet in the midst of this Scene where every Cot & chalet & House is a picture — you see that with every Inmate it is a Life of Privation & of constant Struggle. Buried half the year in the Snow the Summer is scarce long enough to let them lay in their Fuel

16 A page is torn from the MS here, but the text is continuous.

& Provision for the Winter.

31 Augt Early by Valley in a Caleche[17] to Lautenbrunn. this closed Valley at the foot of the Wengern Alp very lovely. the Jung frau at the top of it. The Cascade Staubach Singular from its Gauzy form. Came

[end of page][18]

Salvia

down a good Road 9 miles to Interlacken —

1 Sepr Left Unterseen 8 oClock by Steam Boat & in an hour & a quarter to Thun <15fr.> Iron Boat made in Pieces and sent from Paris cost £4000.

2 Sepr at Thun charming Views & walks. The alps very Plain & near. 3 Sepr to Bern 18 miles good Road but Country not so striking the second time as the first

4 Sepr Bern not so clean — not swept by Women as before. Peasantry not so striking. Democracy has not mended Bern. Charges very high for Lodgings to Fribourg very catholic in appearance. Friars Monks etc. Suspension Bridge extremely high & long — Organist playing at all hours & begging:

5 Sepr to Lausanne fine Road first Part hilly: the country very beautiful

6 Sepr French Service Cathedral very crowded — Clerk sat with his hat on —

8 Sepr to Vevay Road on this side of Lake very narrow & bad: why are the roads on Lake thro Vineyards so very narrow & the Roads in other parts of Switzd so broad & good at least in Protestant Cantons like Vaud.

9 Sepr: Excessive Rain: to Bull up the longest Hill we have travelled: but the Country most Romantic in Wood & Hill & Rock & Stream. Bull a fine old Town

[end of page][19]

but we could not walk — on to Fribourg all the way a Country of infinite Beauty & all human Comforts the Houses & Gardens elegant. the Fields highly cultivated the Soil productive every thing flourishing. The approach to Fribourg beautiful all the Environs of this Town & the Town itself seem to escape the withering & Loathsome effects of their Catholic Religion.

10 Sepr to Bern 11th to Morgenthal wet ride but Country admirable wonderful Cattle. beautiful situation of Inn near the Aar.

12 Sepr To Baden. Passed Aarburg a high castellated Town & about 17 miles from Morgenthal the pretty Town & fine castle of Lenzburg. John went back to draw it. The fine Vales rich Land — Views of the Bernese Alps. excellent Road render this a charming Ride

17 Or calash: a light carriage with small wheels seating four passengers.
18 A page is torn from the MS here, but the text is continuous.
19 Page torn out?

13 Sepr very wet. 14th Sepr to Winterthur — to Zurich wood & cultivated & so to Winterthur. Tobacco common round Frybourg & Berne. Autumn Crocus s towards Baden & towards Winterthur & St Gall

15 Sepr to St Gall. Country cultivated in every Spot. Turnips Potatoes Hemp etc Character not so striking by Swiss. Houses towards St Gall good & painted — with Dutch neatness — appearance of Wealth. St Gall remarkable for clean white Houses & seeming

[end of page][20]

Pinks N Strawberry

Wealth & comfort. Stirring Lovely aspect of Town [...?] Beautiful antiquity of shops & Houses — church most beautiful in Fresco's & Paintings & carving & marbles & yellow & Gilt Figures. three Organs. Square round church full of ordnance — Road out of St Gall very lively with Peasants Cattle Carts etc good Houses & Gardens & Merchts coming along in Gigs. The High Land above St Gall laid out in uninclosed Patches like Scotland very Poor. Road to Rosbach full of orchards & Corn Hemp

16 Sept <&> this a very pretty Town indeed. rising from the Lake clean & wealthy in appearance; the Country on to Rheineck the same — soon after cross the Rhine in large Boat go by its side & then along an immense plain of Peat moss & wet grass perhaps worse from recent rains — At the last Town of this plain in which I believe Werdenberg also is, we observed the Hebrew character on Buildings — here too we first saw the Austrian soldiers in White Jackets <Sights light> blue pantaloons Hungarians all in light Blue small shabby men. Feldkirk a dull Town — except for two large Factories & Mills — The Situation lovely in going from it towards Pludens-Rock & River — the Vineyards also rise above Town.

[end of page][21]

17 Sepr the Road to Pludens most magnificent in Scenery — the fine pasturage — the Gardens — the rich Soil for its elevation — The fine short Grass & [...?] the chalets low in comparative height — the swelling undulating Hill, so inhabitable & having so much of a cheerful English Look to what Swiss Hills have make the Tyrol very striking but the People seem Catholic & filthy & some cottages are poor & mean The Road proceeds up on the fine Pass of the Vorarlberg zig zagged like Alpine pass. Slept at a poor Inn St Anton 18 miles up the Hill before coming to Landeck

18 Sepr to Landeck splendid Road joins there the Great Road from Italy proceed towards Inspruck thro Valley of the Inn 56 miles of finest Road & finest scenery imaginable slept at Obermeiminge

19 Sepr to Inspruck — this City is truly beautiful Rich Spanish stile of Architecture — in a lovely plain with magnificent Rocks & Mountains touched now with snow

20 Several pages are cut from the MS here, but the text is continuous.

21 Page missing?

surrounding the City & Environs in a way that cannot be described, so grand & open so high & yet so soft so reposing — no Scene can be finer: Fine Music at Cathedral & in the High Church the beautiful Bronze Figures

[end of page][22]

Orchis

ranged down both sides of church round Monument of Maximilian[23]

20 Sepr 1/2 past 10 Grand Military Mass — Austrians & Hungarians marched out of Church to full Band playing in Gallery — Procession of Host very numerous of Town & Country People in consequence of a sudden Death said to be Cholera. People clean & Women & children handsome — Men constantly smoking country People & Houses dirty enough, more signs of lasting Catholicism in the Tyrol than in any Country. Crosses Crucifixes figures, painted Walls. Saints Relics offerings — The Religion seems loved & followed

21 Sepr To Landeck a lovely day

22 — To Mals 40 miles towards Stelvio thro Vales by Hills & Rocks of unequalled Beauty — the Road good every yard & Kept up in a way not elsewhere imagined.

23 — Pure bright Sky on 9 miles of Road to Brad where new Stelvio Road begins & goes up easily to Trafoi then 18 miles of precipitous Zig Zag about 5 Turns, the upper part on the Steep Side of one Hill covered in a great part with Wood & propped every where — The Snow in many

[end of page]

parts 7 feet deep in detached Heaps. Coverings pouring Wet down from Snow lying on Top. The View of Rocks & of Glaciers of the Ostler Spitz very wonderful you rise 9000 feet high & seem so near the masses of Snow on the Hills around you that it seems like ascending Mont Blanc — When at the top the Basin of Rock & curiously figured Rocks in front very striking. after a long run almost level in a valley come Zig Zags to let you down to the Side of an immense Ravine, down which you run on the same fine Road through Seven Galleries cut in the Rock — the jutting Rocks fringed with various underwood & Trees — shewing themselves one behind the other the Range of Mountains before you give a noble Scene. reached Bormio at 1/2 past 5 a most wretched Town & dirty Inn of horrid aspect but Beds as usual in Italy large & good — German gradually changing To Italian Language — Faces dark & handsome The Stone on very top of Stelvio divides Tyrol from States of Lombardy.

24 Sepr To Montagno a gradual descent from Bormio by the Adda some fine Scenery the Vines on all spots of Rocks & trellisses in low grounds but Houses &

22 A page is cut out of the MS here, but the text is continuous.

23 The Imperial Church (Hofkirch) in Innsbruck contains the carved marble tomb of Emperor Maximilian the First. Twin rows of 28 larger than life-size statues flank the empty sarcophagus representing important contemporaries and his heroes.

Buildings of every Kind the most

[end of page][24]

Unknown

fine in their fronts the chief feature observable by [...?] is the exact proportions & the pillars being only placed where they seem useful & also the ornament increasing ascending to elevation Ionic to Corinthian or composite- Doric or Rustic to Ionic. The Walk up to Madonna del Monte very fine Views beautiful — Olympic Theatre beautiful Model of Greek Theatres by Palladio

5 Octr to Padua a large dull Town with arched pavements & narrow streets dull & dreary St Antonio Church large Vast fine monuments fine Bronze Statue outside — Church of St Augustine regular & beautiful. The finest sculpture of our Saviour taken from Cross I ever saw. Noble space & amphitheatre round — Statues of Professors

The Hotel de Ville old & vast with Livys Monument: 300 feet is the length of Hall

6 Octr Left for Venice. the same rich lovely Country bursting like buds in Spring with overproduction & overhung with Grapes. at Dolo you have passed down by Banks of Brenta, lined the whole way with palaces, pleasant magnificent & gardens superb though stiff[?]

24 A page is missing from the MS here on which there was text now missing. There is a torn remnant of 4"x 1/2" on which '2 Oct' remains on the facing side and the word 'lakes' on the back. This final page is crossed through from the four corners.

GENERAL INDEX

Aglionby, William, *Painting Illustrated in Three Dialogues* 6
The Amaranth 17
Aquinas, St Thomas 24

Barbauld, Anna Letitia 16
The Book of Beauty 17
Bossuet, Jacques-Bénigne 21
Brockedon, William, *Passes of the Alps* 27
Byron, George Gordon, Lord 4, 16, 17, 21, 32, 162, 164
  Childe Harold's Pilgrimage 7, 26
  Don Juan 7, 26
  'The Prisoner of Chillon' 162 n. 10
  The Two Foscari 164 n. 15

Caesar, Augustus 154, 288
Cervantes 160 n. 6
Charlemagne 292
Charles the Bold 155 n. 18, 162
Charles Felix of Sardinia 50 n. 8, 142 n. 65
Combe, William, *The Tour of Dr Syntax in Search of the Picturesque* 22
Comte de Brueys, François-Paul Brueys d'Aigalliers 280
Cook, Thomas 8
Cruikshank, George 3, 17, 30, 167
cultural tourism 6–8
  the Grand Tour 6–7
  the Romantic Tour 7

Dale, Thomas 160
Dessaix, Louis Charles Antoine 259 n. 17
Domecq, Adèle 32, 274 n. 29, 277 n. 36

Ebel, Johan Gottfried, *Manuel du Voyageur en Suisse* 4, 47 n. 4
Edgeworth, Maria, *Harry and Lucy Concluded* 16, 17
ekphrasis 25
empiricism 24
Erasmus 291
Eustace, John Chetwode, *A Classical Tour Through Italy* 7
evangelicalism 21–23

Fall, Richard Whiteman 151, 237
Fielding, Anthony Vandyke Copley 18–19, 28, 31, 167–68
  Between King's House and Inveroran, Argyllshire 18
  Friendship's Offering 3, 17, 28, 233 n. 1

geology 14–15, 21, 25–26, 27, 78, 108, 128–29
Gessler, Albrecht 156, 162
Gilpin, William 18
The Brothers Grimm, *German Popular Stories* 17

Hannibal 163
Hanson, David 15, 233 n. 1
Heath, Charles 20
Helsinger, Elizabeth 23–24
Hilton, Tim 3, 24 n. 42, 27, 167
Homer 16, 17
Horace 162
Hunt, John Dixon 125

illustration 24

Jameson, Robert, *A System of Mineralogy* 15, 21, 27
Jones, Willoughby 160
Joyce, Jeremiah, *Scientific Dialogues* 14, 16

The Keepsake 17

Loudon, J. C. 41, 167
  The Architectural Magazine 41
  Loudon's Magazine of Natural History (1834) 3, 15, 27, 41 n.1
Livy 16
Lucian 16

Maximilian I 297
Milton, John 17
  'Il Penseroso' 275 n. 31
Murray's Hand-book for Travellers in Holland, Belgium and North Germany 8
Murray's Handbook for Northern Italy 11

Napoleon Bonaparte 161, 237, 287–88
natural theology 21, 24
Nelson, Horatio 279–80
Norton, Charles Eliot 2
Nugent, Thomas, *The Grand Tour* 6

organicism 26

Parsons, Nicholas T. 6 n. 14, 7 n. 18, 8 n. 20
the Picturesque 17–18, 26
Piggott, Jan 31 n. 51, 151–52, 160–61
Plato 265 n. 21

Pliny 164
Pope, Alexander 17, 26, 152
Pringle, Thomas 17
Prout, Samuel 20, 26, 28–32, 167– 68, 152
  Sketches in Flanders and Germany, 28, 31
  'Tournai', 29

Raphael 282
Richardson, Jonathan, *A Discourse on [...] The Science of the Connoisseur* 6
Richardson, Mary 1, 3 n. 8, 13, 14, 17
Roberts, David 20, 28–29, 168
Rogers, Samuel:
  'The Great St. Bernard' 237
  Italy 2, 7, 12, 20, 26, 28, 32, 113 n. 20, 167
  Poems 28
  'Venice' 270
Rossini, Gioachino Antonio, *La Cenerentola* 292
Rousseau, Jean-Jacques 162
  La Nouvelle Héloïse 162
Rowlandson, Thomas, 'Dr Syntax Tumbling into the Water' 22–23
Runciman, Charles 17
Ruskin, John:
  tours:
  in Britain 1–2
  on the Continent 2–6
  works:
    'Andernacht' 17
    The Ascent of St. Bernard 11, 27, 28
    'The Battle of Waterloo' 16
    Chronicles of St. Bernard 27, 32
    The 1835 Diary 27
    Deucalion 15, 16, 22
    Dilecta 28
    'Enquiries on the Causes of the Colour of the Water of the Rhine 15
    Ethics of the Dust 15
    'Eudosia; or a Poem on the Universe' 16, 17
    'Facts and Considerations on the Strata of Mont Blanc, and on ... Twisted Strata' 15
    Fors Clavigera 13
    'Fortress in the Val d'Aosta' 30
    'Fragments from a Metrical Journal' 17
    'Glen of Glenfarg' 16
    'Harry and Lucy Concluded [...] PRINTED and composed by a little boy and also drawn' 16
    Iteriad; or Three Weeks Among the Lakes 14
    'The Jungfrau from Interlaken' 20
    'A Letter from Abroad' 27
    'Letter to Willoughby Jones' 27
    'Lines Written at the Lakes in Cumberland' 17
    'Loch Achray and Ben Venue' 18
    Marcolini 32
    Modern Painters 5, 11, 12, 15, 21, 25, 157 n. 24
    'Mount Pilatus' 21
    'A Night at Le Hospice' 22, 27
    'Observations on the Causes which occasion the Variations of Temperature between Spring and River water' 41 n. 1
    'On Skiddaw and Derwent Water' 17
    'On the Old Road' 23
    The Poetry of Architecture 5, 19, 41 n. 1, 168, 275 n. 32
    Praeterita 2, 5, 9, 10, 16, 20, 23, 25, 122 n. 13, 123 n. 16, 134 n. 42
    Proserpina 16
    'The Puppet Show; or, Amusing Characters for Children' 16
    'Reply to Blackwood' 5, 21
    'Salzburg' 17
    'St Goar' 17
    The Stones of Venice 11
    Valasquez, the Novice 27
    Verse Journal, A Tour Through France to Chamouni 9, 26, 50 n. 8, 52
    'View of Oxford' 30 n. 49
    'Watch-Tower at Andernach' 30
Ruskin, John James 1, 2, 3 n. 8, 15–18, 21–22, 28, 41, 71, 286–98
Ruskin, Margaret 1, 2, 15, 21–22

de Saussure, Horace Bénédict, *Voyages dans les Alpes* 4, 15, 27, 41 n. 2, 48 n. 6, 72, 140
Scott, Sir Walter 16
  Anne of Geierstein 155 n. 18
  Chronicles of the Canongate 255
  The Monastery 16
Shakespeare, William 164
  As You Like It 273 n. 28
  King Lear 140–41
  The Taming of the Shrew 285
  The Winter's Tale 277 n. 35
Shelley, P. B., 'Lines written among the Euganean Hills' 276
Sheridan, Richard Brinsley 27
the Society of Dilettanti 6
Southey, Robert 17
  The Spiritual Times 17
Starke, Mariana:
  Information and Direction for Travellers on the Continent 8
  Letters from Italy 8
  Travels on the Continent 8
Sterne, Laurence 2
Strachan, Anne 1

Tell, William 156, 162, 293,
Thucydides 162
Tintoretto 8
Transactions of The Geological Society 26
transportation 8–14, 144–47, 163–64
Turner, J. M. W. 20, 28, 31, 32, 167–68
  The Alps at Daybreak 28 n. 48
  Como 113 n. 20

Goldau 78 n. 16
Hannibal Crossing the Alps 18
The Pass of St. Gothard, near Faido 13
St Maurice 12

Urry, John 7

Vasari, Georgio, *Lives of the Artists* 6

de Villeneuve, Pierre-Charles-Jean-Baptiste-Silvestre 280 n. 37

Walton, Paul 30–31, 167 n. 2
Wordsworth, William 26, 28
'The Brothers' 245 n. 10
Guide to the Lakes 26

INDEX OF PLACES

❖

Aarburg 295
Abbeville 28, 119
  Saint Ouen 120
  Saint-Vulfran 119
Airolo 82–84, 293
Altorf 293
Aosta 162, 264, 288–89

Baden 295
Basle 291
Bellinzona 293
Bern 295
Bienne 290
Bonneville 287
Boulogne 161

Calais 118–19, 151–52, 160
Chalons 123
Chamonix 148–50, 160–61, 287
Chillon 155
Lake Como 164
Constance 291
Cormayeur 154–55, 289

Dijon 160
The Dôle 130–31
Dover 117, 151, 160

Fribourg 295

Geneva 136–38, 161–62, 286–87
  Lake Geneva 134–38, 155, 160–61, 163
Granson 155, 162, 290
Grimsel 294
Grindelwald 163

Hospice of St. Bernard 47, 66–70, 152–53, 160, 237–54, 255–70, 288
Hospice of the Grimsel 156–59, 294

Innsbruck 160, 163, 296–97
Interlaken 295

The Jura 44, 47, 72, 75, 105, 125–35, 152–53, 161, 286, 291
The Jungfrau 74, 76, 96, 99–102

Landeck 297
Lausanne 290, 295
Lauterbrunnen 163, 295
Lucerne 293

Martigny 237–45, 287, 289
Meillerie 162
Meiringen 163, 294
The Mole 139
Mont Albis 292
Mont Blanc 47–48, 52–55, 57–60, 71–73, 75–76, 93, 95, 100–02, 134–35, 137, 147–49, 154, 161, 237, 269, 286–87, 289
Mont Breven 55, 67, 72
Mont Eiger 76, 99, 103, 106, 294
Mont Mort 66–67, 69, 256, 264
Mont Niesen 102
Mont Pilate 84–85, 105, 158
Mont Rigi 77–78, 84, 86, 104
Monte Rosa 53, 237
Mont Rossberg 77–78, 86
Mont St. Gothard 81, 156–57, 293
Mont Titlis 85
Mont Velan 67, 75, 153, 238, 243
Mont Wellhorn 95–96, 294
Mont Wetterhorn 76, 86, 95–100, 103, 294
Montanvert 287
Montreuil 161
Morez 286
Morgenthal 295
Munich 160,

Nancy 124–25, 160
Neuchâtel 290
  Lake of Neuchâtel 290

Oxford 21

Padua 298
Paris 122
Plombières 126,
Poligny 286

Reichenbach Falls 94, 294
Rheims 123–24, 160–61
The Righi 155–57, 293
Rome 160, 164
Rouen 28, 120–22, 152, 160–61

Falls of Schaffhausen 76–77, 153–54, 291
Soleure 290–91
Stelvio 297
St Gall 296
St Martin 287–88

Thun 159, 295
Tyrol 163

Lake of Uri 156, 162

Venice 27, 28, 163–64, 234, 270–85
Verona 163–64, 233
Vevay 163, 289

Wales 53
Winterthur 292, 296

Zug 292–94
Zurich 155, 292, 296

www.ingramcontent.com/pod-product-compliance
Lightning Source LLC
LaVergne TN
LVHW081257100826
845148LV00005B/901